EXPLORING BUSINESS

A GLOBAL PERSPECTIVE

MICHAEL E. LIEPNER

Business Studies Director
Thornlea Secondary School
Thornhill, Ontario

JANE G.N. MAGNAN

Business Studies Director
Thornhill Secondary School
Thornhill, Ontario

MCGRAW-HILL RYERSON LIMITED

Toronto Montreal New York Auckland Bogotá Caracas
Lisbon London Madrid Mexico Milan New Delhi
Paris San Juan Singapore Sydney Tokyo

EXPLORING BUSINESS: A GLOBAL PERSPECTIVE

ISBN 0-07-551422-2

2345678910 F 32109

Printed and bound in Canada

Canadian Cataloguing in Publication Data
Liepner, Michael, date
    Exploring business : a global perspective

Includes index.
ISBN 0-07-551422-2

1. Business. 2. Canada – Economic conditions – 1991 –
        I. Magnan, Jane G. N. II. Title.

HF5351.L54 1993   330   C93–094460–7

PUBLISHER: Andrea Crozier
SENIOR SUPERVISING EDITOR: Marilyn Nice
DEVELOPMENTAL EDITOR: Mia London
COPY EDITOR: Wendy Thomas
PHOTO RESEARCHER/PERMISSIONS EDITOR: Mary Beth Leatherdale
COVER AND INTERIOR DESIGN: Matthews Communications Design
COVER AND PART-OPENER ILLUSTRATIONS: Russ Willms

REVIEWERS

CONTENTS

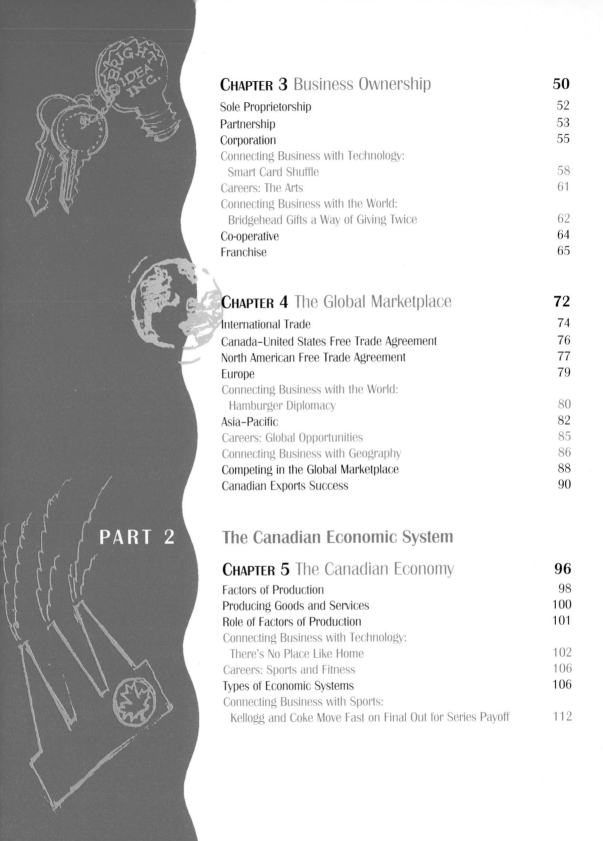

PART 3 Government, Labour, and Business

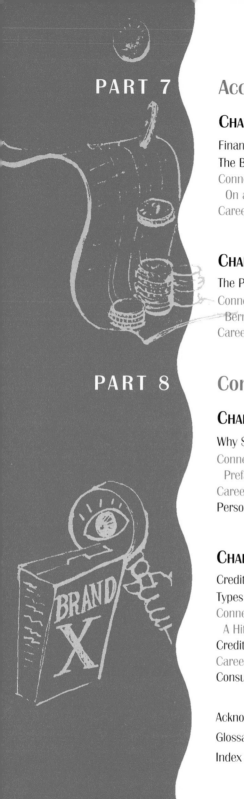

INTRODUCTION

XPLORING BUSINESS: A GLOBAL Perspective explores our rapidly changing world of new technologies, careers, globalization, and the increasing fragility of the environment. Throughout the text you will learn about the connection between these changes and the world of business.

You will learn how business is connected to various aspects of your day-to-day personal experiences in life, in your community, and in the global community. You will also learn that business is linked to other subject areas, such as geography, mathematics, technology, law, the arts, history, language, and sports.

The features of *Exploring Business: A Global Perspective* are designed to engage you actively in exploring business and making connections to real situations.

Chapter Focus

Each chapter begins with a list of points that outline the focus of the chapter. This outline will assist you in understanding what you should know, should be able to do, and should value once you have completed the chapter.

Cross-Curricular Connections

In each chapter, you will find one or two sections under the heading Connecting Business With... In these sections, you will discover relevant connections between business and the environment, community, globalization, technology, and a variety of subject areas. These sections profile innovative Canadians from coast to coast.

Business in Action

Business-in-action features appear throughout the text to maintain a high level of interest and reinforce concepts discussed in the text with real-life examples.

Careers

Career exploration is integrated into the text. In each chapter, you can explore things you do well, things you like to do, career options, and skills and attitudes you will need.

The career activities are cross-curricular in nature. You will explore careers in business and other subject areas, such as math, law, health, science, technology, the arts, entrepreneurship, media, and sports. By exploring careers in different subject areas, you will understand the connection between business and other careers.

Focusing on Business

These questions and activities are designed to help you understand the chapter.

Exploring Business

These activities provide you with opportunities to interact with your classmates and your community through surveying, interviewing, debating, and role-playing. Keeping informed of new events is important, so you will also be reading newspapers, magazines, accessing electronic information sources like CD-ROMs, watching television news programs, and listening to radio news broadcasts.

Questions and activities that lend themselves to computer applications include specific instructions or are identified as ideal computer activities by a computer icon in the margin. You are encouraged to use the computer wherever possible, such as in creating your organizers and bulletin board displays, writing reports, editorials, résumés, letters, and creating data bases and spreadsheets.

Working with Math

These activities provide you with an opporunity to apply your math skills using real-life information and data. In many cases, you will be using a computer to complete these activities.

Points to Remember

A brief list of key concepts covered in the chapter will help you in reviewing what you have learned.

Key Terms

Each chapter ends with a list of key terms. These terms appear in bold type in the chapter and will help you to expand your vocabulary.

Colour Insert

The colour insert brings marketing to life and enhances the study of the different types of advertising media and packaging.

Glossary

The glossary of key terms at the end of the book helps you to look up and reinforce business terms easily.

EXPLORING

BUSINESS

A

GLOBAL

PERSPECTIVE

PART 1

Introduction
to
Business

CHAPTER FOCUS

After studying this
chapter you will
be able to:

define the role of
business in our society

•

distinguish between
goods and services

•

distinguish between
needs and wants

•

recognize that all the
participants in the
business environment
are interdependent

•

identify the key issues
affecting today's
business environment

The Business Environment

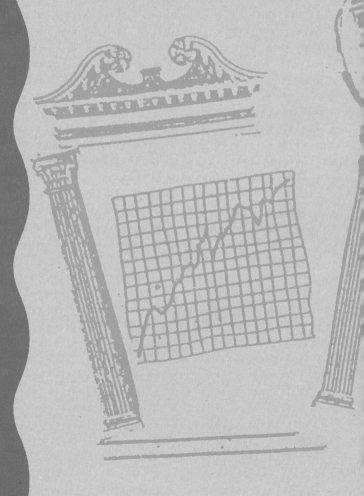

ANY YOUNG PEOPLE ENTER THE
business world at the age of 11 or 12
without even realizing the important
role they play in it. Your first paper
route, baby-sitting job, snow-shovel-
ling job, or lawn-cutting job involved you in a business.
Why did you take on some of these tasks? Why were you
asked to do these jobs? What role does business play in
our lives? In this chapter, we will examine the difference
between goods and services and how consumers and
businesses depend on each other. A brief examination of
the growth of Canadian business will help you understand the Canadian business environment as it exists
today and what businesses will have to do to be successful in the future.

What Is Business?

What is business? The short answer is that **business** is the production and sale of goods or services. Businesses can be as small as the vendor selling jewellery on the corner of a busy intersection and as large as Toyota or IBM.

Business is a major and influential part of Canadian society. Everyone is involved in the business world to some extent because we all make, buy, sell, or exchange goods and services. We need and want what business provides. Sometimes we resent the prices we pay or the hours we work but, usually, the relationship between business and the individual is good.

The business world has always revolved around two interest groups: producers and consumers. **Producers** make goods or provide services and **consumers** buy them and use them. Any item or product that you can purchase, possess, and use is a **good**. Your binder, a computer, a roll of steel, and a potato are all goods. **Services**, on the other hand, are not physical objects. They are acts — helpful acts — in exchange for pay. A haircut, a plumber's work, and a consultation with your doctor are examples of services.

Some businesses provide both goods and services; for example, a computer store that sells computers and repairs them is providing a good (the computer) and a service (the repair).

Producers of goods are divided into two groups, manufacturers and suppliers. A **manufacturer** is the company or business that produces the goods. A **supplier** provides the consumer with the good or service. For example, a furniture manufacturer produces couches and a furniture store supplies them to consumers to be purchased. A dry cleaner supplies a service: dry cleaning.

Producers supply goods or services to consumers like yourself and to businesses. Goods, such as food and clothing, that consumers purchase directly to satisfy their needs and wants are called **consumer goods**. The consumer who purchases a good for his or her personal use is called an **ultimate consumer**. Goods that businesses purchase from producers are called **industrial goods**, and the consumer, which in this case is a business, is called an **industrial consumer**. For example, if you bought a loaf of bread to eat from a bakery, you would be the ultimate consumer. However, if a restaurant bought bread from the same bakery to make sandwiches to sell to its customers, the restaurant

Pars Bakery in North Vancouver produces goods for both industrial and ultimate consumers.

would be the industrial consumer. As you can see, producers (manufacturers and suppliers) and consumers together make up the business environment.

Needs and Wants

The consumer plays a critical role in the business environment. Business exists to serve the needs and wants of consumers, to manufacture products and provide services that the consumer needs or wants.

Needs are essential things that people lack, and must be fulfilled in order for people to live. Shelter, clothing, and food are all needs. However, needs are not restricted to physical necessities. We all have a need to feel safe and secure, to be loved, and to explore and understand our world. **Wants** are things that we would enjoy having but that are not essential for our survival. Buying a second winter jacket, for example, fulfils a want rather than a need.

At the age of 11 or 12, when you accepted the baby-sitting job or delivered the newspapers, most of the money you earned was probably to satisfy wants. Consider all your possessions: clothes, books, sports equipment, compact discs, and so on. Do these fulfil needs or wants?

The needs and wants of consumers will vary significantly according to age, marital status, income level, and so on. Teenagers might spend their money on clothes, school supplies, music, and other forms of

································· NEEDS AND WANTS ·································

entertainment. Seniors might spend their money on travel, health products, and personal safety or security. Businesses try to be aware of these differences and will try to produce goods or provide services to meet the needs and wants of a particular group. They will also advertise their products accordingly.

As society and its values change, so do consumers' needs and wants; for example, many business opportunities have been created as a result of consumers' concerns for a healthier environment (such as the demand for recycling facilities). Also, the amount of money Canadians have had available to spend on their wants has increased over the years, and they have demanded new goods (such as VCRs) and new services (such as unlimited access to cable channels). The relationship between business and consumers is obviously an important one. Businesses must constantly stay in touch with the marketplace and monitor the demands of the consumers. This interdependence can mean the difference between success and failure for a business.

FUNCTIONS OF BUSINESS

We come into contact with business regularly but often do not think about what goes on behind the scenes. Consider Nadia and Oren, who are deciding whether to start their own lawn-cutting service. There is a lot more to think about than initially seems apparent. They will have to be aware of any competition and the prices that the competition is charging. They will have to promote the business — otherwise, how will anybody know the business exists? Nadia and Oren might have to obtain financing in order to purchase the necessary equipment, and this would involve a certain amount of risk. They will also have to decide which tasks each of them will perform. Will they be equal partners?

·························· FUNCTIONS OF BUSINESS ··························

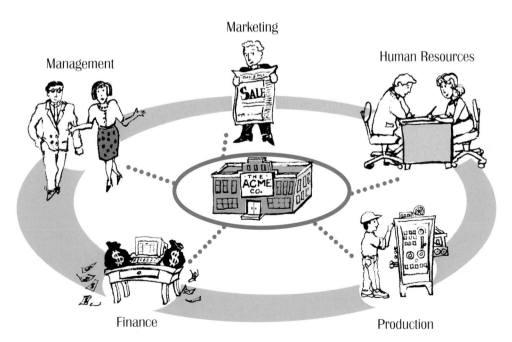

Management

Marketing

Human Resources

Finance

Production

CONNECTING BUSINESS WITH THE COMMUNITY

BREAKFAST FOR HUNGRY STUDENTS

If Carol Gabriel has learned anything as president of the Uniacke Square Tenants' Association, it is "Don't wait to raise money before you start doing what needs to be done."

Three years ago, the energetic single mother of three put that lesson into practice, launching a volunteer-run breakfast program for youngsters who were going to school on empty stomachs.

Before starting the program, Gabriel says she knocked on every door in her Halifax public-housing project to ask neighbours what their community needed most. The answer: educated young people who could break the poverty cycle. So when parents said children were missing breakfast, either because of poverty or because they came from single-parent families where there wasn't time

for proper meals, Gabriel moved fast. "If kids go to school hungry," she explains simply, "they can't learn."

Halifax schoolchildren participate in Carol Gabriel's community-run breakfast program.

For the first two years, Gabriel and four volunteers collected all the food — hot and cold cereals, milk, bread, jam, juices — from among their neighbours, many of whom were on social assistance. They also prepared the meals and supervised the 20 to 30 children who showed up each morning at the tenants' association community centre.

Gabriel didn't even try for outside funds in the beginning. "Money's tight, no matter what you want to do," she says.

"You start out by doing it yourself and then you work out where to get the money to keep it going."

During the last school year, with the program firmly established, Gabriel was able to line up some corporate sponsors, with Kraft and Quaker Oats joining a local bakery, a dairy, and a food wholesaler to donate supplies. She also talked Ottawa into paying for three unemployed local people to serve the breakfasts.

An important part of the program, Gabriel says, is the sense of responsibility it evokes in the community at large. "Our whole push is to motivate people to make changes in their own lives and in their own neighbourhood."

1. In your opinion, is Carol Gabriel satisfying the community's needs and wants? Explain.

2. What did Carol Gabriel mean when she said, "Don't wait to raise money before you start doing what needs to be done"? Explain why you agree or disagree with her.

3. Is there something you or a group of your friends can do for your community? Share your ideas with the class.

How much money would they like to make? In addition to these questions, there are many external factors that are beyond the control of the owners of a business and that can have an effect; for example, what will Nadia and Oren do if it is a rainy summer? These are just some of the many questions that have to be considered and answered when operating a business. All of these considerations are functions of business and can be organized into five categories: production, marketing, finance, human resources, and management.

Production

One of the basic functions of any business is the production of goods and services. **Production** is the process of converting a business's resources into goods and services. In the case of the lawn-cutting business, Nadia and Oren will take their labour, tools, equipment, and money, and convert them into the service of lawn care. Naturally, this process varies with different types of businesses. A bicycle manufacturer requires larger amounts of money, more specialized machinery and equipment, and much larger premises than a dry-cleaning service.

If we take a closer look at the production process, we can see that it involves a number of factors, or elements. These factors are commonly called the **factors of production** and include land, capital, labour, technology, and entrepreneurship.

······················   THE FIVE FACTORS OF PRODUCTION   ······················

When **land** is defined in economics — that is, as a factor of production — it refers to the natural resources used to produce goods and services (for example, the wood for a furniture company or the aluminum for the bicycle-manufacturing company). **Capital** includes all the machinery and equipment required to produce goods and services.

Labour is the human element of production and includes all mental and physical work that people put into the production of goods and services. **Technology** is the application of scientific research and knowledge to improve the production and distribution of goods and services. For example, the Ford Motor Company invented the assembly line that helped the company produce more cars. This allowed Ford to sell its cars at a lower price, which made it possible for the workers to afford the cars they helped produce. The fifth factor of production is **entrepreneurship**, the activity of entrepreneurs, and is discussed in more detail in Chapter 2. The entrepreneur is the person who brings together all the factors of production and starts the business. In this sense, the entrepreneur is the person who usually provides the money and takes the risk in starting the business. The factors of production will be discussed in more detail in Chapter 5.

Marketing

When we hear the term marketing, we tend to think of advertising, but marketing actually includes a lot more than just advertising. **Marketing** can be defined as all the business activities to plan, price, promote, and distribute goods or services to satisfy consumer needs and wants. This may involve making contact with the consumer to find out what goods or services may be required, and this process is referred to as market research. For example, Nadia and Oren may discover that their customers want the service of lawn watering while they are on holiday.

Market research assists businesses in determining the needs and wants of the consumer and reduces the risk of providing goods or services that the consumer does not require. The marketing function of a business can be extremely costly and requires careful planning to obtain the best results. Marketing is discussed in detail in Chapters 15 and 16.

Finance

All businesses need to keep accurate records of the money that is coming into and going out of the business. They must keep track of who owes the business money, to whom money is owed, how money is spent, and whether there is enough money in the bank to pay the bills. This managing of money is referred to as **finance**.

Large businesses usually have accounting departments, which are responsible for managing the funds of the business. In small businesses, the owner of the business usually takes on the financial responsibilities.

Regardless of their size, all businesses must keep accurate financial records in order to know whether they are making a profit.

Human Resources

Human resources are the "people aspect" of a business — in other words, the owners, managers, and employees. Businesses depend on their employees and must recognize the importance of hiring and keeping good employees. Large businesses provide a wide range of benefits in order to attract and keep enthusiastic and committed employees; for example, many businesses provide dental plans, life insurance, and pension plans. Some businesses offer free trips to their salespeople if they meet certain sales quotas or provide memberships to recreational clubs to maintain high morale among the employees.

A large business usually has a human resources department that is responsible for hiring employees. Depending on the type and size of business, the human resources department may be involved in negotiating wage agreements and maintaining employee records.

Management

Management can be defined as the planning and organizing of all the business activities. Managers have to set the short- and long-term goals

Calvin and Hobbes © Watterson. Distributed by Universal Press Syndicate. Reprinted with permission. All rights reserved.

for the business and organize the employees and other resources so that the goals can be achieved. Managers must have the ability to communicate clearly and effectively because their job requires a great deal of interaction with many different types of people. Managers have to possess leadership qualities and be able to motivate their employees. The effective management of a business can often mean the difference between its success and failure.

INTERDEPENDENCE

In the Canadian business environment, consumers and producers need and rely on each other. This mutual reliance and need is called **interdependence**. Consumers need producers to manufacture and supply the goods and services they use every day. Producers need consumers to buy the goods and services they manufacture and supply.

Businesses must pay attention to the needs and wants of consumers. The North American automobile industry learned this lesson the hard way. It did not change the size or fuel efficiency of its cars in the 1970s, a time when oil prices were rising steeply, so consumers bought smaller and cheaper-to-run foreign cars.

On the other hand, businesses that have recognized consumer demand for products that do not harm the environment have benefited. Within a week of Loblaw's introduction of its "Green" line, the store had sold $5 million worth of phosphate-free laundry detergents, biodegradable diapers, bathroom tissue made from recycled paper, and unbleached coffee filters.

The interdependence between consumers and producers enables businesses to run efficiently, but it can be a disadvantage for consumers, because when the supply of a product is very low, the price rises.

Many businesses are both producers and consumers; for example, a jeans manufacturer makes clothes but must buy, or consume, the materials that go into making the clothes: denim, zippers, thread — and the equipment necessary to run an office: telephones, photocopiers, desks, and so on. Such businesses wear two hats: as consumers, they understand their customers' desire for the cheapest prices; as producers, they know they need to be profitable to stay in business.

FACTORS AFFECTING BUSINESS SUCCESS

- **Competition** When several businesses produce similar goods or services to satisfy consumer needs and wants, they are considered to be in competition. Businesses compete against one another to attract consumers to buy their goods or services instead of the goods and services of other businesses. To compete for the consumers, businesses use different strategies, such as advertising, providing prices lower than the competition, and providing better service.

- **Service** As business becomes more competitive, providing better service to the customer is more important than ever. If two businesses offer consumers essentially the same goods or services, the business more likely to succeed is the one that provides superior service. This might include extended store hours or delivery service. A pizza store that is open until two in the morning and provides free delivery will likely be more successful than a pizza store that is open only until eleven o'clock at night and provides no delivery service.

- **Satisfaction** Customer satisfaction is essential to succeeding in business. A satisfied customer is far more likely to return to the business at a later date than is a dissatisfied customer, especially in today's competitive marketplace.

- **Investment** means spending money on something that is expected to produce a profit. In order to purchase the machinery, equipment, and buildings that are usually necessary to operate a business, the business owners invest in the business, often by using some of their own money and borrowing money from a bank.

- **Profit** is the amount of money a business has left after all the expenses have been paid. Profit is one of the main reasons for going into business, but there are other important reasons. These may include the desire to be one's own boss, or the desire to pursue an idea. Other than providing an incentive to go into business, profit is important because it can be reinvested into the business to expand and create new goods or services, and thus provide more jobs.

- **Risk** is the chance of loss of money or reputation that businesspeople take when starting or operating a business. No business is without risk and only with careful planning can the risk be minimized. It can rarely be eliminated. The successful businessperson is one who takes a calculated risk.

FOCUSING ON BUSINESS

1. List five items that you purchased over the past two days. Were they needs or wants?

2. Define *goods* and *services*. Give an example of each.

3. Name two businesses that manufacture products.

4. Distinguish between needs and wants. Give examples of two of your needs and two of your wants.

5. Name two businesses in your community that provide consumers with both goods and services. State the goods and services provided.

6. List and explain the five functions of business.

7. List and explain the five factors of production.

EXPLORING BUSINESS

8. Using your resource centre and local newspaper, select two articles, one that describes a successful company and another that describes a company that is having financial difficulties or is close to going out of business. Prepare a brief summary of each article and outline the reasons for the company's success or failure.

9. With a partner, interview someone in one of the businesses below. Report your findings to the class.

   • A member of a service profession, such as an accountant or a lawyer

   • A retail store manager

   • A manufacturer

   • An employee in a leisure-related service industry (for example, an employee in a gym, a theatre manager, the manager of a video rental store)

   • A real estate agent or broker

   • A car salesperson

   • A restaurant owner

   Before you conduct the interview, prepare a questionnaire and include the following questions:

   • How has the business environment changed over the last five years?

   • What were the causes of these changes?

- How did the changes affect the business?
- What did each person do to address these changes?
- What are each person's predictions for the business environment over the next two years?

10. Write a brief newspaper article explaining how the following situations might affect business.

    a. Consumers find they have more money to spend.

    b. Manufacturers are having difficulty obtaining the materials necessary to produce a particular product.

11. As a class, brainstorm different business opportunities that have been created out of concern for a healthier environment.

12. Create a three-column organizer. In the left-hand column, list the purchases you or your family have made in the last month. In the middle column, state whether it was a good or a service. In the right-hand column, state whether it was purchased from a manufacturer or a supplier.

13. View at least eight television commercials. Record the goods or services being advertised. How many of the goods and services advertised do you or your family use or have in the house? Do you think you were influenced by advertising to buy these items? Explain.

14. Explain why the following goods may be classified as both a consumer and an industrial good: tomatoes, wood, flour, paper. Discuss the reasons with a partner.

15. In a small group, brainstorm the activities of a student painting business that would be involved in the five functions of business: production, marketing, finance, human resources, and management.

WHAT THINGS DO I DO WELL?

Employers say that they look for these basic skills in hiring employees. See how you rate!

1. Using the chart, identify five skills you possess and five skills you would like to acquire or develop further.

2. Form small groups and create a list of all the skills that group members would like to acquire or develop further. Brainstorm ways to develop these skills.

3. Choose one of the skills you want to develop further and draw up a plan outlining the steps you would take to develop the skill. Over the next month, implement the plan.

PERSONAL SKILLS	ACADEMIC SKILLS	TEAMWORK SKILLS
For a good attitude and a sense of responsibility, do I ... • have self-confidence? • have the energy and desire to get the job done? • manage my time well? • take changes well? • have creativity? • have initiative?	To communicate, think, and learn, do I ... • understand, speak, and write correctly? • know how to listen? • read and understand written materials? • know how to solve problems? • know how to use technology? • like to learn new things?	Being part of a team, do I ... • get along with others? • listen to others? • respect the opinions and ideas of others? • know how to lead others?

How Business Has Changed

The business environment is always changing. One hundred and fifty years ago, the main method of doing business was in the form of bartering. This meant that people would trade their goods and services for other goods and services. The way of doing business has changed dramatically since then. To survive such changes, people in business must constantly examine the changes and be prepared to take advantage of them. Let us look at some of these changes and the business opportunities that these changes have created.

Growth of Small Business

In all sectors other than manufacturing, a small business is defined as one that has fewer than 50 employees; in the manufacturing sector, a small business is one that has fewer than 100 employees. Over the last decade, small business has steadily increased its contribution to the economy. In fact, over 95 percent of all businesses registered in Canada are small businesses. Almost half of all Canadians are either self-employed or work for companies with fewer than 100 employees. With every passing year, another record is set in the number of new small businesses that are registered in Canada.

Today's successful small businesses focus on the customer. Their main goal is to attract and retain clients by satisfying existing needs and anticipating new ones. They develop a close relationship with their customers, find out what they want, and are thus able to serve them better than their competitors. Faced with an increasingly challenging environment, Canada's small businesses will have to stay in tune with the changing business environment and take advantage of some of the current trends and opportunities.

Growth of the Service Sector

The most significant growth of small businesses has been in the service sector. Over 27 percent of new businesses are in the business and personal service sectors of the economy.

Service businesses do not provide a physical product for their customers. Instead, as the name suggests, they provide a service. Services cover a wide range of jobs — some examples are travel agents, consultants, editors, store clerks, garbage collectors, lawyers, doctors, and other professionals.

The service sector has grown because Canadians have more money and less time for personal matters than they had 50 years ago. People are willing to pay others to clean their houses, prepare and serve their food, do their accounts, or wrap presents for them.

Services that may be even more important in the future are computer programming, communications and telecommunications, financial planning, and, because Canada has an aging population, any services that are critical to the elderly, such as health care.

Globalization

Canadian businesses are no longer limited to operating only in Canada. They now do business all over the world, from Asia to South America, and businesses based in many other countries operate in Canada. This process of internationalization is called **globalization**.

Globalization gives businesses in Canada and in other countries the chance to expand their markets and increase profits by selling around the world. Because more businesses are competing for the same customers, businesses become more efficient, and customers get the benefit of lower prices. The changes in eastern Europe over the last few years have created markets for many businesses to provide products and services demanded by local consumers. Following McDonald's move into Russia in 1990, many other companies have realized the potential of this part of the world.

Countries around the world are forming themselves into trading blocs to encourage trade across national borders. These free-trade blocs are discussed in detail later, in Chapter 4.

The Environment

Worldwide concern for the environment has had a significant impact on business. The depletion of the ozone layer, global warming, and the huge amounts of garbage that industrialized countries produce from disposable products and overpackaging have forced businesses and consumers to become more conscious of the environment. As well, as is true of most societal changes, concern for the environment has provided entrepreneurs with business opportunities.

As the world is encouraged to reduce, reuse, and recycle, many businesses are rethinking how to dispose of their garbage and how to reduce the amount of garbage they produce. For example, service stations, trucking companies, and car dealerships pay significant fees to dispose

The Daughter of Invention

When inventor Robert Dickie caught his nine-month-old daughter fiddling with an electrical plug, he realized how hazardous it could be if she

ever worked the plug out of the socket. That worry led him to devise a plug that curious little hands couldn't grasp. Dickie's plug is the first modification of the North American wall-plug in 75 years. The Flatplug is 6 cm thick and lies flush against the wall. Its tapered edges make it difficult for small hands to manoeuvre, but adults can easily remove the plug by pulling on a folding brass ring.

To market the Flatplug, Dickie formed Paige Manufacturing Inc. in September 1989 and raised more than $1.5 million from private investors. Since last December, when the first Flatplug extension cords hit Canadian Tire stores, Paige has received orders for more than 100 000 plugs.

The firm has also made inroads into the United States, signing Chicago-based Ace Hardware Corporation to sell an initial 30 000 Flatplugs last April.

Winning an award last November from *Popular Science* magazine as one of the best new products of 1991 threw the plug into the global limelight. Now, with worldwide patents in place, Paige plans to plug into markets in Europe and Japan in the near future.

CONNECTING BUSINESS WITH ENTREPRENEURSHIP

1. Why could you consider the Flatplug innovative?
2. How is Robert Dickie an entrepreneur?

of used motor oil. One Canadian company is offering these businesses a recycling solution by installing a specially equipped furnace that burns used motor oil as the sole source of fuel. It is a legal and safe way to heat the premises.

Business Ethics

Ethics are standards of conduct that society believes people should follow. Businesses, like individuals, must also follow ethical standards. At one end of the scale, there are businesses that knowingly break the law, for instance, by dumping garbage illegally. Many businesses obey the letter of the law but do not move beyond. At the other end of the scale are the businesses that try to make their communities better places in which to live. For example, they may voluntarily reduce the amount of pollution they create.

A company's values are part of its corporate culture, its code of behaviour. The corporate culture will have an impact on the company's goals and policies and how it implements them. It will help determine how the company treats its employees and customers. Consumers today have more power than they had in the past; as a result, they are demanding that companies behave ethically towards the environment. Many companies will have to rethink the way they do business.

Technology

Technology is scientific knowledge applied to practical uses. Whether businesses are selling technology or using technology to provide a good or service, technology is one way of gaining a competitive edge in business. Many small businesses have come to rely on technology but are having difficulty finding people who can use the new equipment. One communications satellite company in British Columbia feels that it is so important to keep up with the latest developments that it has hired an engineer who has the sole responsibility of looking at new technology.

The most "basic" new technology is the computer. Computers allow businesses to produce sophisticated products and maintain accurate records. Even a small business can invest in such technology these days because it is so much less expensive than it was even four or five years ago. Other new technologies include facsimile (fax) machines, answering machines, and voice mail. And who knows what the future will bring?

BUSINESS *in action*

BOWLING FOR DOLLARS

The experts are calling bowling the game of the '90s: non-strenuous and highly social, a sport young and old alike can enjoy. The trouble is, bowling doesn't offer the variety of experiences — running, catching, backhanding or slam-dunking — that most sports do. Throwing a ball down a lane is kind of one-dimensional for kids growing up with Nintendo.

Developer Karl Fay knew all that last summer when he opened Classic Bowl, a $10-million bowling centre, as anchor tenant of his new sports-oriented shopping plaza. To attract the masses he needed to make his Leisure Centre a success, he invested close to $500 000 to install a computer-controlled system that turns bowling into a real-life computer game.

BowlerVision, the system Fay chose for his 10-pin bowling centre, is a combination scorekeeper, pinsetter, instant replay, video coaching system, and computer game. Serious bowlers can analyze their form on a computer screen by replaying any shot to reveal the path the ball travelled, how fast it went, and at what angle it struck the pins. Rookies can call up instructional videos that tell them where to place their feet or how to make a 7–10 split.

Fay thinks BowlerVision is the future of bowling. The 60-lane bowling centre features bright, airy surroundings, bar service, and day care. But it's BowlerVision, he says, that encourages bowlers to stay longer and come back more often. "It's not just throwing the ball down the lane."

POINTS TO REMEMBER

- Business revolves around producers and consumers.

- Business exists to serve the needs and wants of consumers. Needs are essentials, such as shelter and food, whereas wants are things that consumers enjoy having, but are not essential for survival, such as a holiday.

- Functions of business are production, marketing, finance, human resources, and management.

- Factors of production include land, capital, labour, technology, and entrepreneurship.

- The business environment is constantly changing. Important changes include the growth of small business, growth of the service sector, globalization, concern for the environment, business ethics, and technology.

FOCUSING ON BUSINESS

16. Briefly explain the role of small business in today's business environment.

17. In a small group, discuss why ethics are important in business.

18. Why is it important for businesses to pay careful attention to the desires of consumers?

19. What is meant by "All participants in the business environment are interdependent"?

EXPLORING BUSINESS

20. With a partner, visit a business in your community and find out how it uses the products or services of other businesses. Share your findings with the class.

21. Prepare to debate the following statement: "Small business is becoming increasingly important to the health of the economy." Use your resource centre and conduct interviews with members of the business community to prepare your position.

22. Prepare a list of all the video rental stores, record stores, and clothing stores in your neighbourhood or community. For each of the three types of stores, select the one you visit the most. Why do you use one store more than the others?

23. People will often give many reasons for not wanting to start a business. Below are some of the most common objections. With a partner, role-play to show how a person might express these objections and how the other person might respond and attempt to overcome them.

   • I do not know where to obtain the financing.

   • I do not have a good idea.

   • Somebody is already doing that.

   • It's too risky.

   • I'm not good at anything.

   • How do I know it will work?

24. Using your resource centre, select a specific industry and research the impact of new technology on that industry. Be specific and provide examples wherever possible. Write a two-page report outlining your findings.

25. Form small groups and answer the ethical dilemma posed by the following case. As a class, compare answers. Did most groups come to the same conclusions?

   You are a sales manager for a family-owned manufacturing company. Your boss is the owner's niece. While she's away, a customer who usually deals with her calls in an order. When she finishes, the customer says she hopes the order will be processed in "the usual way." While filling it, you discover that your boss has been keeping two sets of invoices. The copy sent to customers is inflated by 2 percent, while the one going through your company's books charges the right amount.

   Presumably, your boss and her helpers at the other companies are sharing the difference. Since your company is getting paid the proper amount, it is unaffected by the double-invoice system.

   Your boss will certainly deny your allegations, making it your word against hers, unless the owner decides to investigate further. You fear the owner would side with her niece. Even worse, she could agree with you, but not fire the niece, which would make your situation untenable. You could leave the company, but the job market is sluggish and you have no immediate prospects.

   Do you

   a. tell the owner and let the chips fall where they may?

   b. leak the information to some of your suppliers and let them bring the situation to the attention of your company's owner, a move likely to damage your company's reputation?

c. confront your boss, knowing that this may end your career?

d. start looking for a new job?

e. say nothing? If you know what the boss is doing, other people may find out, too. Let *them* handle the problem.

f. Other.

WORKING WITH MATH

26. Refer to the table Canadian Minimum Wages, below.

a. Select the minimum wage for your province and one other province. Create a bar graph comparing the rate in each province in 1975 with that of 1992. Which province increased the most?

b. Calculate the percentage increase in your province from 1980 to 1992.

c. Calculate which province had the greatest increase between 1975 and 1992.

d. Calculate the difference between the highest and lowest minimum wage in 1992. Calculate the increase as a percentage.

CANADIAN MINIMUM WAGES
(hourly rate for experienced adult workers)

Jurisdiction	1965	1970	1975	1980	1985	1990	1991	1992
Federal	$1.25	$1.65	$2.60	$3.25	$3.50	$4.00	$4.00	$4.00
Nfld.	.70(m)	1.25(m)	2.20	3.15	4.00	4.25	4.75	4.75
	.50(f)	1.00(f)						
PEI	1.00	1.25(m)	2.30	3.00	4.00	4.50	4.75	4.75
		.95(f)						
NS	1.05(m)	1.25(m)	2.25	3.00	4.00	4.50	4.50	5.00
	.80(f)	1.00(f)						
NB	.80	1.15	2.30	3.35	3.80	4.50	5.00	5.00
Que.	.85	1.40	2.80	3.65	4.00	5.30	5.30	5.70
Ont.	1.00	1.50	2.40	3.00	4.00	5.40	6.00	6.35
Man.	.85	1.50	2.60	3.15	4.30	4.70	5.00	5.00
Sask.	$38/wk	1.25	2.50	3.65	4.50	5.00	5.00	5.00
Alta.	1.00	1.55	2.50	3.50	3.80	4.50	4.50	5.00
BC	1.00	1.50	2.75	3.65	3.65	5.00	5.00	5.50
Yukon	1.25	1.50	2.70	3.35	4.25	5.97	5.97	6.24
NWT	1.25	1.50	2.50	3.50	4.25	5.00	5.00	6.50

n.a.= not available;   m = male;   f = female
Source: Labour Canada

KEY TERMS

business	industrial goods	technology
producer	industrial consumer	entrepreneurship
consumer	needs	marketing
good	wants	finance
service	production	human resources
manufacturer	factors of production	management
supplier	land	interdependence
consumer goods	capital	globalization
ultimate consumer	labour	ethics

CHAPTER 2

Entrepreneurship

CHAPTER FOCUS

After studying this chapter you will be able to:

define entrepreneurship

•

identify the characteristics of an entrepreneur

•

assess your aptitudes

•

apply the techniques of brainstorming and problem solving

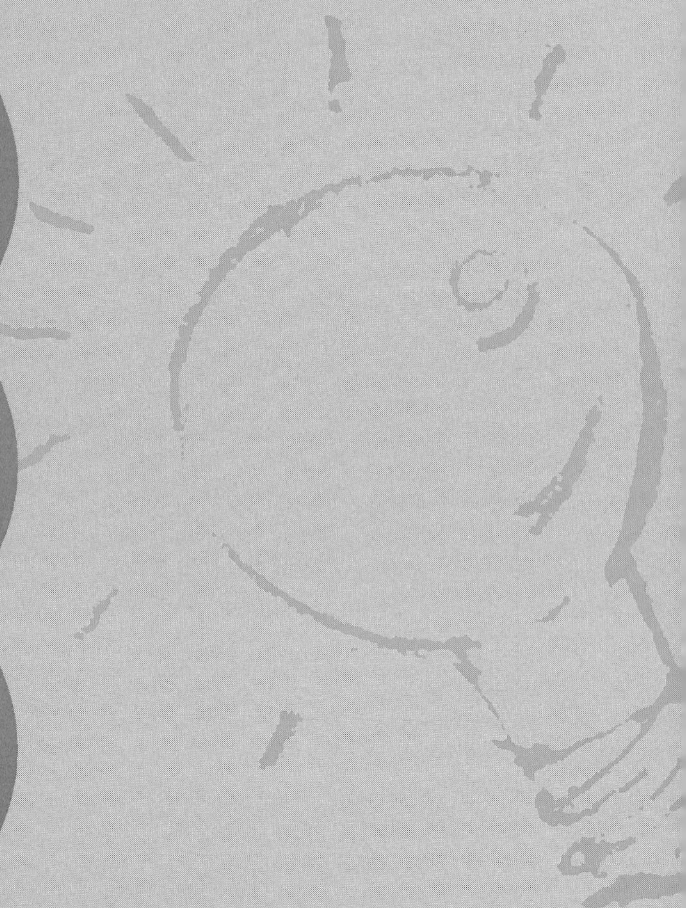

SMALL BUSINESSES IN CANADA WERE responsible for creating over half the jobs in the country between 1986 and 1989. This trend has continued in the years since then.

Many of these businesses were started by entrepreneurs, but what is an entrepreneur? Can *you* be an entrepreneur?

In this chapter, we will examine the characteristics of an entrepreneur, and you will be able to examine your own characteristics and determine your interest in entrepreneurship. We will evaluate the role of hobbies and aptitudes in an entrepreneurial venture. Entrepreneurs use problem-solving techniques and brainstorming to generate ideas; you can practise these skills throughout the chapter.

WHAT IS ENTREPRENEURSHIP?

The word **entrepreneurship** comes from the French word *entreprendre*, which means to undertake or pursue opportunities. An **entrepreneur** is a person who recognizes an opportunity, organizes the money and other resources to undertake the venture, and assumes most of the risk associated with the venture. It is important to note that the definition is not restricted only to a business. Raising funds for a school project or putting on a rummage sale are ventures that involve entrepreneurship.

Entrepreneurship is not restricted to people of a particular age, colour, sex, or race. Anybody can be an entrepreneur — all you have to do is decide what you would like to do!

WHAT DOES IT TAKE TO BE AN ENTREPRENEUR?

Research has shown that entrepreneurs have common characteristics. These characteristics include commitment and determination, initiative, ability to set goals, persistence, self-confidence, ability to take risks, ability to deal with failure, honesty and reliability, and creativity and innovation.

Commitment and Determination

Making a **commitment** is like making a pledge or promise, either to yourself or to others. **Determination** is the drive or firmness of mind with which that commitment is carried out.

Think of anyone you know who does well at something, and the chances are that person has commitment and determination. The immigrant from Central America who learns English in the evenings, or students in a band who practise at least an hour a day are showing commitment and determination. Such people frequently excel at what they do.

Initiative

Initiative is the ability to take action without being prompted by others. Entrepreneurs are willing to take responsibility for starting a venture. They are prepared to take a leadership role and work hard at organizing the venture.

Ability to Set Goals

It is very important for an entrepreneur starting a new venture to set goals and stay focused until those goals have been achieved. Goals help in making plans. You need short-term and long-term goals in order to accomplish any task. Think of your hobbies, your part-time job, or your studies. You are most successful in them when you have clear goals about what you want to do and when. Without setting goals, a great deal of time can be wasted.

Persistence

Enterprising entrepreneurs must realize that their venture may run into difficulties that will need to be overcome. Entrepreneurs do not allow these difficulties to interfere with their goals. They must demonstrate **persistence**, or perseverance, in order to survive the tough times and continue to work toward their goals.

Self-Confidence

A person who is fully assured of herself or himself has **self-confidence**. It is important that you believe in yourself. If you do not believe in yourself, how can you ask someone else to believe in you? Entrepreneurs are able to sell an idea or themselves because they have confidence in their abilities. People who are self-confident are also usually optimistic — they see the glass half-full rather than half-empty.

Reprinted by permission of United Features Syndicate

Ability to Take Risks

When you expose yourself or are exposed to the chance of loss or bad consequences, you are taking a **risk**. You take risks every day. Every time you raise your hand in class to answer a question that you are not

PRESERVE OUR TREES, NO FLYERS PLEASE

"I don't think of myself as an environmentalist," says 37-year-old Lorane Poersch, "but an everyday sort of person. I'm always on the lookout for good ideas." Two years ago, Poersch decided to do something about the annoying avalanche of junk mail at her door. "I hand-lettered a sign that said, 'PRESERVE OUR TREES, NO FLYERS PLEASE.' And it worked!" Soon, friends were asking her to make signs for them, and Poersch realized she had a viable item for her Winnipeg-based Desert Rose Productions Inc., a company she founded in 1984 to develop environmental products.

Next year she expects to distribute 30 000 of the $10 green-and-white signs (made from non-returnable pop bottles) to stores in Winnipeg, Toronto, and Los Angeles and through Global ReLeaf, a national forest-establishment program. "I like the idea of using garbage to create something useful."

Before working on the sign, Poersch produced and marketed natural-fibre travel cases carried by such stores as Holt Renfrew and Brettons. Now she's developing a line of

Lorane Poersch manufacturers signs from non-returnable pop bottles.

recycled plastic products, like rulers and binders, for children who she says are her best supporters.

Every summer, Poersch spends several weeks on a windswept arm of Great Bear Lake, NWT, where she helps operate one of Canada's last fly- in fishing lodges. Her office there is a long way from a road or hydro line, let alone a landfill site. "Most of this country is so clean and beautiful," Poersch says. "We owe it to the next generation to keep it that way."

1. What contributions are you making to protect the environment you live in?

2. List the ways in which your family recycles. List the ways in which your class recycles. What do you throw away that could be reused?

3. With a partner, think of some entrepreneurial ventures to solve environmental problems.

sure about, you are taking a risk. The saying "Nothing ventured, nothing gained" is an easy way to sum up the thinking of many entrepreneurs. Entrepreneurs are always taking risks, but this does not mean they are gamblers. They are calculated risk-takers; they examine all the risks to reduce the possibility of failure.

Ability to Deal with Failure

Success involves trial and error. This means that some endeavours may result in failure. Does this mean you stop trying? Not if you are an entrepreneur! Everyone learns from mistakes. If you try something and it does not succeed, don't quit, but take the time to reflect on what went wrong and learn from the experience.

Honesty and Reliability

Business is very competitive and consumers are increasingly demanding better service. Entrepreneurs must be honest and reliable if they hope to retain the confidence of the consumer. Any venture embarked upon today requires a high commitment to honesty and reliability. If these characteristics are not evident, the business is not likely to succeed.

Creativity and Innovation

An important aspect of entrepreneurship is the ability to find creative and innovative ways of solving problems. Some people are both entrepreneurs and inventors. **Inventors** discover new products and services. Canadian inventors include Armand Bombardier, who invented the snowmobile, and Olivia Poole, inventor of the Jolly Jumper.

When we eat McIntosh apples, Pablum, frozen fish or instant mashed potatoes, we are eating foods that originated in Canada. Canadian inventors have also provided us with basketball, five-pin bowling, table hockey, the Laser sailboard, and Trivial Pursuit.

Innovators create new or improved ways of doing something. For example, opening a new grocery store is not innovative, but offering a service that allows customers to shop for groceries by phone and to have the merchandise delivered is enterprising, innovative, and creative.

Vicki Kerr came up with the idea of using the potatoes on her family's farm to make healthier potato chips. The rest is Canadian entrepreneurial history.

FOCUSING ON BUSINESS

1. In your own words, define *entrepreneurship*.

2. List two things that you have done recently that display entrepreneurial characteristics. What are these characteristics?

3. Why are commitment and determination important characteristics of an entrepreneur?

4. Explain the importance of setting goals.

5. Why is it important to have self-confidence?

6. Explain the meaning of the expression "Nothing ventured, nothing gained."

7. How can we learn from failure?

8. Explain the difference between *invention* and *innovation*.

9. How can reliability and honesty be related to the success of a venture?

EXPLORING BUSINESS

10. Create an organizer, listing the common characteristics of an entrepreneur in the left-hand column. In the right-hand column, state which of the characteristics you feel you have. Give examples to support your answers. Then compare your answers with a partner. What are the similarities? What are the differences?

11. Find two newspaper or magazine articles that relate to entrepreneurship. Using these articles, discuss the definition of an entrepreneur with your friends or family. Develop your own definition and present it to the class.

12. With a partner, interview three people involved in business. Ask each person to provide you with a definition of entrepreneurship. Outline the similarities and differences among their definitions. What conclusions can you reach? Share your findings with the class.

13. Create an organizer listing five circumstances in which you took a risk. For each circumstance, state the outcome of your risk taking. Explain the worst thing that could have happened. What was the best thing that could have happened?

14. Write a short story describing an occasion when you wished you had taken a risk but did not. Be prepared to present your story to the class.

15. With a partner, role-play a situation that illustrates risk. This can involve any aspect of risk, but should provide the audience with a clear understanding of the situation that involved risk.

16. In a small group, read and then discuss the following quotations. Briefly record what each quotation means and how it relates to an entrepreneur.

"The ability to learn faster than your competition may be the only sustainable competitive advantage."
   Arie De Gues, Royal Dutch/Shell

"You're only here once. This is the real play, not a dress rehearsal. Are you going to wake up at 60 and say you wish you had? If that is the case, you better 'had' right now."
   John Wiggins, owner of Ontario's Creemore Springs Brewery

"I can conceive and create, but I cannot carry on a routine job."
   Lord Beaverbrook

"It is a very funny thing about life. If you refuse to accept anything but the best — you very often get it."
   W. Somerset Maugham

"Remember always that you have not only the right to be an individual, you have an obligation to be one. You cannot make any useful contribution in life unless you do this."

Eleanor Roosevelt

17. With a partner, select a Canadian entrepreneur who interests you. Use your resource centre, newspapers, and current business magazines to research his or her background. Present your findings to the class in the form of an interview.

18. Interview an entrepreneur in your community to find out what entrepreneurial characteristics the individual feels he or she possesses and why. Ask if you can videotape the interview. Share your findings with the class.

19. With a partner, create a bulletin-board display that illustrates the following entrepreneurial characteristics:

- commitment and determination ✓
- ability to set goals
- honesty and reliability
- initiative
- persistence
- creativity and innovation ✓

CAREERS

WHAT DO I LIKE TO DO?

The best job for you is the one you do well and enjoy doing. Here is a short quiz to help you get started. There are no right or wrong answers — but your answers will point you toward the kinds of jobs that may be right for you.

1. Record the activities from the following list that you would like to do.

WORKING WITH PEOPLE	WORKING WITH THINGS	WORKING WITH IDEAS AND INFORMATION
• caring for, helping, or serving people	• using tools, machines, or computers	• solving puzzles or problems
• working as part of a team	• maintaining or fixing things	• studying and/or reading
• leading or supervising people	• finding out how things work	• doing experiments or researching a topic
• convincing people or negotiating	• making things with my hands	• writing, playing music, or drawing

2. Take a look at how you answered the "What Do I Like to Do?" quiz. Which areas have the most activities that interest you? Now match your interests with the categories of jobs below.

WORKING WITH PEOPLE	WORKING WITH THINGS	WORKING WITH IDEAS AND INFORMATION
• social worker • hotel manager • flying instructor • physical trainer • security guard • educational counsellor • day-care helper • teacher's aide • customer service representative • addiction counsellor • police officer • teacher	• welder • millwright • carpenter • residential energy technician • veterinary attendant • radio technician • pollution control technician • audio-video service technician • electrician • crime detection lab analyst • telecommunications specialist • computer programmer • software designer	• aerospace engineer • advertising director • public relations agent • pollution control inspector • pilot • manager, food and beverage • buyer assistant • photographic technician

3. List the three jobs that interest you the most and explain why.

HOBBIES

It is not uncommon for entrepreneurs to turn their hobbies into business ventures. Often people develop a hobby until they become experts in a particular field. Combined with other skills required to be an entrepreneur, this expertise can lead to a successful venture. Examples of how hobbies could lead to businesses are the coin or stamp collector who decides to open a store, or the jogger who decides to start a runner's clinic.

APTITUDES

Entrepreneurs often draw on their natural talents and apply them to their ventures. These natural talents are referred to as **aptitudes**. Some are listed below.

• Some people have a natural ability to use written and spoken words to convey their ideas and emotions or to describe events effectively. We can all learn to be more effective communicators, but some people seem

BUSINESS *in action*

CLIMBING THE WALLS

Bob and Brian Bergman, brothers and fellow climbers, have turned their passion for rock climbing into a successful business, one where climbing enthusiasts hang out — literally.

As members of the Canadian National Climbing Team, "as professional as you can get in Canada," they needed somewhere to train in the winter. And, as successful entrepreneurs around the world know, if it doesn't exist, build it. Besides, according to Brian, "getting into a business that was a hobby would be a great job!" So the Bergmans, together with Bob's wife, Sharon, did. With $50 000 in savings and a $7500 grant, Bob, Brian, and Sharon launched Joe Rockhead's Climbing Gym in August 1990.

Named after a character in "The Flintstones," the gym allows climbers to fine-tune their skills on walls twelve metres high, of texturized panels bolted with fibreglass-and-sand handholds.

Joe Rockhead's offers beginner and advanced lessons and "walk-in" climbing facilities. Customers can even rent the whole gym, complete with climbing instructions, for parties that veer away from the usual.

The business has grown steadily since its beginnings. Originally, Bob and Brian were the only two employees, but since then two other staff members have been hired. Membership is solid: there are 350 yearly members and 30 to 70 rock-climbing enthusiasts pass through the doors every day. According to Brian Bergman, thousands of customers have gone through the door since Joe Rockhead's was founded. But this business is about more than just making money. For Brian, it's enhanced his quality of life: "It runs itself and gives me enough money and time to climb. I don't need a day job." According to his brother, the business only has one way to go: straight up.

Can't You Hear the Whistle Blowing?

CONNECTING BUSINESS WITH SPORTS

The score was tied with nine seconds to go at a pre-Olympic basketball game in Brazil in 1984 when referee Ron Foxcroft, a trucking executive from Hamilton, Ontario, spotted a foul by the visiting team. He blew his whistle, but nothing happened. The cork pea had jammed. "There was mayhem," Foxcroft says. "I vowed that if I lived, I was going to make a whistle that didn't jam."

Foxcroft spent $150 000 and three years designing a better whistle. Then he took two months off from running Fluke Transport Group (motto: "If it's on time, it's a Fluke") to sell his innovation across Canada. When sports teams and retailers yawned, he targeted his fellow refs as a last resort.

The breakthrough came one night in Indianapolis during the 1987 Pan-American Games. Foxcroft took one of his two prototype whistles into a dormitory housing 400 sleeping referees. Two 115-decibel blasts later, the wide-eyed refs were hounding him to buy their own ear-piercing whistles. Foxcroft boldly said they could be ordered with full payment — $6 apiece — up front. He left Indianapolis with orders for 20 000 whistles and

The NBA, NFL, and CFL all use whistles supplied by Ron Foxcroft's company, Fortron International Inc.

$120 000, enough to begin manufacturing.

Today, Ron Foxcroft's Fortron International Inc. sells $4 million of whistles a year to distributors in 81 countries. Customers include sports leagues such as the NBA, NFL, and CFL, as well as the police and military, hunters and joggers. In fact, Foxcroft says Fortron's profits are five times higher than those of Fluke, his $15-million-a-year trucking and warehousing company.

Foxcroft also saves some energy for his home town. After trying unsuccessfully for an NHL franchise, he led a team of 54 investors that brought a World Basketball League team to Hamilton last May. When head-office problems killed the league in August, Foxcroft spearheaded a group hoping to turn the five Canadian teams into an all-new Canadian league.

And in his spare time? Foxcroft still referees 60 U.S. college basketball games a year.

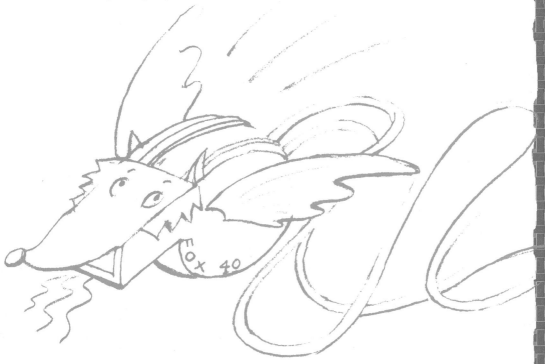

1. Briefly explain how Ron Foxcroft turned his part-time refereeing job into a successful business.

2. What are some other business possibilities for the whistles?

to have a natural talent to explain their thoughts in a very effective manner. This ability is important when you are trying to explain your venture to others.

- People who are perceptive are usually good listeners. They have the ability to understand the intentions, ideas, or emotions that other people express. This ability will help entrepreneurs in reacting to suggestions or ideas that might affect the venture.

- Some people are artistically inclined and can paint, draw, or write music or poetry. This aptitude can be used to provide an enterprising person with an opportunity to create a venture.

- We all know people who are mechanically inclined. These people enjoy taking things apart and finding out how they work. Some people are always tinkering with their bicycle, car, lawn mower, and so on, and they can turn these spare-time activities into profitable businesses.

- You probably know many schoolmates whom you would consider as talented athletes. In part, this is often due to the fact that they have natural strength, endurance, or co-ordination that makes them athletic. If such people pursue their talents, they often excel to the point that they can use their talent to embark on a venture. For example, a hockey player could operate a hockey camp.

- Some people have extraordinary organizational skills. They have the ability to carry out their tasks extremely well, and they can evaluate and prioritize their ideas effectively. This skill can often be seen in the way some of your fellow students organize their notebooks or plan projects. Some people are able to organize their tasks much more easily than others.

There is no guarantee, however, that a person who has one or more of these aptitudes will be any more successful at entrepreneurship than anyone else.

PROBLEM SOLVING

Entrepreneurs frequently encounter problems when starting up and operating a business venture. In business terms, a **problem** can be defined as the difference between the present situation and the desired one. **Problem solving** is finding the answer to a problem. It is important to deal with problems immediately by trying to seek out the best possible solution. To effectively solve problems, entrepreneurs often use a problem-solving model similar to the one at the top of page 45.

HOW TO SOLVE A PROBLEM

1. Identify the problem and determine the desired situation.

2. Once the desired situation has been identified, generate as many ideas as possible to solve the problem. One effective way of generating ideas is by brainstorming (which is defined below).

3. All possible solutions should be carefully evaluated.

4. The best solution should be selected and implemented.

5. Changes to the present situation should be evaluated to determine whether the chosen solution has solved the problem.

BRAINSTORMING

Entrepreneurs are constantly looking for new or innovative ideas. One method often used to generate ideas is brainstorming. **Brainstorming**, which is usually done in groups, means the participants discuss sudden ideas to solve a problem; even bizarre ideas are offered, since they sometimes lead to a practical and innovative solution. Entrepreneurs frequently use brainstorming. To be most effective, a few simple rules as outlined below should be followed.

• Make certain that everyone is involved and that all the participants understand the problem that needs solving.

• Write down every idea that is suggested. The brainstorming process encourages quantity of ideas, not quality of ideas. Do not pass judgement on any of the ideas suggested at this stage.

• Try to have fun and keep the ideas flowing.

POINTS TO REMEMBER

• The word entrepreneur comes from the French word *entreprendre*, which means to undertake or pursue opportunities.

• Characteristics common among entrepreneurs include commitment and determination, initiative, ability to set goals, persistence, self-confidence, ability to take risks, ability to deal with failure, honesty and reliability, and creativity and innovation.

• Risk is an important consideration when embarking on a venture. The idea is to obtain as much information as possible about the venture so that the risk is minimized.

- Many entrepreneurs turn their hobbies into business ventures.
- Brainstorming is a method of generating ideas to solve a problem.
- Using a problem-solving model is an effective way of finding the best solution to a problem.

FOCUSING ON BUSINESS

20. Define aptitude.
21. Why is the ability to communicate effectively important to an entrepreneur?
22. How can being perceptive benefit an entrepreneur?
23. List at least two reasons why brainstorming could be an important technique for anyone to learn.
24. List some ventures that could result from your hobbies.

EXPLORING BUSINESS

25. Review some of the aptitudes of entrepreneurs in the following areas: communications, perceptiveness, arts, mechanics, athletics, and organization. Choose three that you possess. Give an example of how you have used each aptitude in the past. How could you use each aptitude to become an entrepreneur?

26. Using your resource centre, find an article from the local newspaper that describes an entrepreneur. Summarize the article and indicate the entrepreneurial characteristics referred to in the article. In a small group, share your articles with each other. List the common characteristics shared by the entrepreneurs.
27. In groups of three or four, brainstorm a solution to the problem described below.

    Your business has just received 10 000 lead pencils. You ordered only 1000, but unfortunately, you cannot return the pencils. Since your company uses only 1000 pencils per year, this leaves you with 9000 pencils you do not need. Your task is to think up ways to use the extra pencils. Be as outlandish as possible. When you brainstorm, no idea is too far-fetched.
28. Form groups of three or four. Each member of the group should examine the business-opportunities section of the newspaper or a business magazine, and bring at least one idea for a business to the next class.

Discuss the advantages and disadvantages of all the ideas brought to the group and select one that you all agree has the most potential. Record the reasons for your decision and share your findings with the class.

29. Imagine that you are an entrepreneur. Write a newspaper article describing yourself and your business venture.

30. Watch a film or television show about an entrepreneur. In a short report, explain what you learned about the entrepreneur.

31. With a partner, select a newspaper or magazine article describing a business venture experiencing a problem. Brainstorm a solution to the problem. Share your idea with the class.

32. **What Is Risk?**

To laugh is to risk appearing the fool,
To weep is to risk appearing sentimental,
To reach out for another is to risk involvement,
To expose feeling is to risk exposing your true self,
To place your ideas, your dreams before the crowd is to risk their
   loss,
To love is to risk not being loved in return,
To live is to risk dying,
To hope is to risk despair,
To try is to risk failure.
But risks must be taken, because the greatest
hazard in life is to risk nothing. The person
who risks nothing does nothing, has nothing
and is nothing.
One may avoid suffering and sorrow, but simply
cannot learn, feel, change, grow, love — live.
Chained by the certitudes,
The individual is a slave
And has forfeited freedom.
Only a person who risks is free.

Write a short essay outlining what this poem means to you.

33. With a partner, debate the expression "If you are not making mistakes, you are not doing anything worthwhile."

WORK ATTACK FOR A BIG MAC

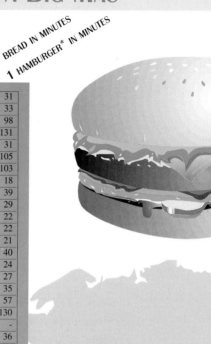

CITY	1 KG OF BREAD IN MINUTES	1 HAMBURGER* IN MINUTES
Amsterdam	9	31
Athens	9	33
Bogotá	23	98
Bombay	27	131
Brussels	12	31
Buenos Aires	26	105
Caracas	75	103
Chicago	18	18
Copenhagen	4	39
Dublin	12	29
Düsseldorf	12	22
Frankfurt	13	22
Geneva	10	21
Helsinki	27	40
Hong Kong	14	24
Houston	10	27
Johannesburg	7	35
Kuala Lumpur	40	57
Lagos	216	130
Lisbon	23	-
London	11	36
Los Angeles	15	20
Luxembourg	9	20
Madrid	10	54
Manila	86	165
Mexico City	37	235
Milan	17	33
Montreal	10	21
Nairobi	31	82
New York	22	26
Nicosia	8	40
Oslo	12	43
Panama	50	66
Paris	18	39
Rio de Janeiro	30	79
São Paulo	32	106
Seoul	18	30
Singapore	39	70
Stockholm	40	61
Sydney	12	18
Taipei	16	34
Tel Aviv	9	33
Tokyo	14	21
Toronto	10	20
Vienna	12	30
Zurich	9	20

* A "Big Mac" and a large portion of fries. The price of the product cited is divided by the weighted net hourly earnings in 12 occupatio

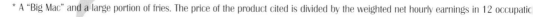

Reproduced with permission of *The Globe and Mail.* © 1991.
Source: Union Bank of Switzerland

WORKING WITH MATH

34. A Toronto resident needs to work only 20 minutes on average to buy a Big Mac and a large portion of French fries at a local McDonald's, while the average wage-earner living in Mexico City requires 235 minutes of labour.

    The accompanying chart on page 48, based on statistics gathered by the Union Bank of Switzerland, shows the minutes of work required to satisfy a Big Mac attack in cities around the world. Also listed are the number of minutes of labour needed to buy one kilogram of bread. In each case, the price of the product was divided by the weighted net hourly earnings in 12 occupations.

    With only 20 minutes of work necessary for a Big Mac and fries, Toronto tied Los Angeles among North American cities and beat out Montreal at 21 minutes, New York at 26, and Houston at 27.

    a. Assuming a person works eight hours a day, calculate the percentage of a day's work that would contribute to purchasing a Big Mac and a large portion of fries in six cities of your choice. Compare your findings with those of a partner.

    b. What conclusions can you make with regard to the amount of work required to purchase a Big Mac and fries in the cities you examine in a?

    c. Assume that in each city a person works seven hours a day. Calculate the percentage of the day that he or she would have to work to purchase 1 kg of bread.

KEY TERMS

entrepreneurship	risk
entrpreneur	inventor
commitment	innovator
determination	aptitude
initiative	problem
persistence	problem solving
self-confidence	brainstorming

Business Ownership

CHAPTER FOCUS

After studying this
chapter you will
be able to:

distinguish between
the different forms of
business ownership

•

understand the
advantages and
disadvantages of each
form of business
ownership

•

outline the
requirements of
opening a business

NCE A PERSON HAS DECIDED TO GO INTO business, he or she must decide what type of business ownership to establish. Should it be a sole proprietorship? A partnership? A corporation? A co-operative? Or perhaps a franchise? All these examples are forms of business ownership.

The form of business ownership is important not only to the person starting the business but also to those who interact with the business — in particular, the suppliers. Suppliers are interested because the responsibility for paying them varies depending on the form of business ownership.

Over time, the form of business ownership can change. As a business grows, the owner might find it necessary to change from one form of ownership to another. A business that begins as a sole proprietorship may become a partnership. The owner might need more funds for expansion or the new partner might offer the business a particular and important skill.

In this chapter, we will discuss the different forms of business ownership and examine the advantages and disadvantages of each.

SOLE PROPRIETORSHIP

A **sole proprietorship** is a business that is owned and operated by one person. The owner is responsible for all operations of the business and assumes all the risks. Most small businesses are sole proprietorships or partnerships.

Advantages of a Sole Proprietorship

This chef owns and operates his restaurant.

A sole proprietorship is easy to organize and has minimal start-up costs. If it is operated under the owner's name, it does not have to be registered. But if the business uses a name other than the owner's or adds "and company" or other words, the business must be registered with the proper government agency. Registering a company costs less than $100.

Another advantage of a sole proprietorship is that the owner, the sole proprietor, keeps all the profits from the business and can make all the decisions. Any conflicts of opinion in operating the business are eliminated. And being one's own boss is very important to many people.

In a sole proprietorship, all financial information can be kept confidential. Keeping some aspects of the business confidential can be important for its success.

Disadvantages of a Sole Proprietorship

In a sole proprietorship, the owner and the business are legally one. This means that the owner assumes responsibility for paying the debts, or **liabilities**, of the business. This responsibility is called **unlimited liability**. If the debts of the business are greater than the profits, the owner will have to pay the debts from his or her personal income or assets.

Furthermore, it can be difficult for the sole proprietor to obtain funding to expand or for everyday expenses. Banks often require collateral when lending money. **Collateral** is security that the borrower offers against a loan, such as property pledged as guarantee for repayment. If a sole proprietor cannot meet the lending requirements of the bank, he or she might not be able to obtain additional funding.

Sole proprietors are responsible for all aspects of operating the business: sales, marketing, accounting, and so on. However, the owner might not have the expertise needed to make the best business decisions in each area. As we discussed in Chapter 1, a business involves a number of different functions, and few people have expertise in all.

PARTNERSHIP

A **partnership** is a form of business organization in which two or more people jointly share in the ownership and operation of the business.

Partnerships are similar to sole proprietorships but are a bit more complex to organize. Since more than one person is involved in the business, the partnership must be created by either a verbal or written agreement. It is in the best interest of the partners to draft a written agreement, called the **articles of partnership**, or partnership agreement. If there are any disputes in the future, the terms of the partnership agreement will be upheld in court. Whenever two or more people form a business, they should consider the issues of financing, ability of the partners to contribute equally, decision making, management, profit sharing, and termination of the relationship. A partnership agreement must be signed by all the partners and will usually include the following information:

- name and location of the business
- purpose of the business
- names of the partners

- amount of the partners' investment
- how the profits and losses are to be divided
- duties and responsibilities of each partner
- procedures for handling a partner's share of the partnership upon termination, retirement, or death of a partner
- procedures for dissolving the partnership

Advantages of a Partnership

As with sole proprietorships, partnerships are inexpensive and easy to organize. The start-up costs often involve only a registration fee.

All the partners in a partnership provide capital to start the business. If additional financing is needed, partnerships can often borrow more money than sole proprietorships since the partners can combine their personal assets as collateral.

Between them, partners can bring more expertise into a business because each one will often have a different area of knowledge. Together, they can provide better management and operation and reduce the risk of business failure. If the business is not doing well, the partners share the debt according to their partnership agreement.

Disadvantages of a Partnership

Partners who take an active role in operating the business have unlimited liability for the debts of the business. Even if two partners are sharing profits 50-50, each is 100 percent liable for any debts of the business. As with a sole proprietorship, each partner's personal assets can be used to pay off the debts if necessary. This is of concern, particularly if one of the partners has few or no assets. In such a case, the other partner(s) will have to assume responsibility for the debts.

If the business is successful, the partners share the profits of the business according to the terms of their partnership agreement. This is the case even if one partner feels that he or she is making a greater contribution than the other partner(s).

Probably the most common problem faced by a partnership is the disagreements that arise between or among partners. Many partnerships are dissolved because partners find they are unable to resolve their differences. These differences can involve money, management of the business, or simply an unequal division of time spent or interest taken in the business.

CORPORATION

A **corporation** is a legal entity that exists independently of its owners: the shareholders. Corporations are complex in nature and can be classified as private corporations, public corporations, Crown corporations, or non-profit corporations. A **private corporation** can have a maximum of 50 shareholders; its shares are not offered to the public. A **public corporation** has no restrictions attached to its shares, which can be sold to the general public. The shares of public corporations are purchased or traded on stock exchanges, such as the Toronto Stock Exchange and the Vancouver Stock Exchange. The stock market will be discussed in more detail in Chapter 11.

Crown corporations are owned by federal, provincial, or municipal governments and their function is usually to provide some form of special service to the public. Some examples of Crown corporations are the Royal Canadian Mint, B.C. Hydro, Canada Post, and the Alberta Heritage Savings Trust Fund.

Non-profit corporations are corporations that are not organized for the purpose of making a profit. They are most commonly organized to undertake fundraising, to do research, or to lobby for a particular cause. The United Way is an example of a non-profit organization.

A corporation is brought into existence by drawing up and filing with the proper government agency a document called the **articles of incorporation**. This is usually done with the aid of a lawyer. The articles of incorporation document usually includes the following information:

- name of the corporation
- location of the registered head office
- number of directors of the corporation
- name, address, and signature of each incorporator
- any restrictions on the type of business activity in which the corporation may engage

Advantages of a Corporation

Unlike sole proprietors and partners, shareholders are liable for the debts of a corporation only to the extent of their financial involvement in that corporation. This obligation is called **limited liability**. To illustrate: if a shareholder invests $5000 in a company and the company

THE TOP 20 CANADIAN CORPORATIONS
RANKED BY SALES

1. BCE Inc.
2. General Motors of Canada Ltd.
3. Ford Motor Co. of Canada Ltd.
4. George Weston Ltd.
5. Canadian Pacific Ltd.
6. Brascan Ltd.
7. Imperial Oil Ltd.
8. Alcan Aluminium Ltd.
9. Noranda Inc.
10. Chrysler Canada Ltd.
11. Seagram Co. Ltd.
12. Ontario Hydro
13. Provigo Inc.
14. Thomson Corp.
15. Hydro-Québec
16. IBM Canada Ltd.
17. Imasco Ltd.
18. John Labatt Ltd.
19. Hudson's Bay Co.
20. Petro-Canada Inc.

Source: *Canadian Business*, June 1992

fails, he or she will lose the $5000 but no other money or possessions.

Limited liability is probably the greatest advantage to the shareholders of a corporation and can be identified by one of the following words in its name: Limited (Ltd./Ltée), Incorporated (Inc.), or Corporation (Corp.).

A corporation often involves many people who have a financial interest in the business. This provides the business with easier access to financial resources. In addition, if the corporation requires a loan, the amount of security available tends to make loans easier to acquire.

A corporation has a life apart from its founders. The death or retirement of a shareholder does not mean the end of the corporation. Ownership is easily transferable, unlike a sole proprietorship or a partnership. Shareholders can sell their shares or buy more by finding a buyer or seller.

Disadvantages of a Corporation

A corporation is a complicated structure and usually requires the services of a lawyer to set it up. Because the corporation must be registered in every province in which it intends to do business, the process can be time-consuming and expensive.

In sole proprietorships and partnerships, the owners usually run the company and work for it. In a small corporation, the shareholders may also work in the business, but in a large corporation, the business is managed by employees. They may not have the same level of commitment to the business as the owners of a sole proprietorship or a partnership.

Public corporations are legally required to publish an annual report outlining the financial position of the organization. This information could benefit competing businesses.

BUSINESS *in action*

VERY SPECIAL EFFECTS

A former graphic designer with the National Film Board, Daniel Langlois began creating his own software when he couldn't get the effects he wanted with existing products. After raising $350 000 from private investors, Langlois formed Softimage Inc. in 1986. More than six years later, the firm has tied up a large chunk of the $50-million global market for 3-D graphics software. Images generated using Softimage software are now seen everywhere from Sugar Crisp TV ads to Steven Spielberg's dinosaur epic, *Jurassic Park*.

© 1993 Universal Studios/Amblin Productions.
Photo courtesy of Industrial Light & Magic.

SMART CARD SHUFFLE

CONNECTING BUSINESS WITH TECHNOLOGY

Last May, I.D. Clark, secretary of the Treasury Board, made a speech to Uni-Forum Canada, a group of presidents of major Canadian information-technology companies. In it, he outlined Ottawa's vision of how its services will be delivered in the future, a vision that he hopes will be under way by the end of the decade.

"Electronic service will be the norm," he said. "Government services will be available seven days a week, 24 hours a day, through automated-teller machines or conveniently located service booths. They may also be accessed from home computers."

Of such visions are fortunes made in the software industry. Among those hoping to cash in is a tiny Ottawa company called T-Base Research & Development Inc. T-Base consists of seven people.

T-Base president Sharlyn Ayotte and her team are making no boasts about becoming another Microsoft. Instead, they are quietly concentrating on one specialized niche [small market segment] — ways of controlling access to computer systems using smart cards and other devices — and pursuing

Sharyln Ayotte, president of T-Base Research & Development Inc.

growth through alliances with major multinational corporations.

Ayotte knows that Clark's vision can't happen without smart cards, which she defines as "a computer on a card." These contain more information, and are, therefore, much more fraud-proof than an ordinary card with a magnetic strip....

But the smart card's day is coming and T-Base is working toward it with two multinationals — Canon Canada Inc. and Digital Equipment of Canada Ltd....

With Digital, T-Base is working on a joint proposal for a federal pilot project to create a system of automated service booths to dispense Unemployment Insurance Commission (UIC) benefits. The rationale here is cost-cutting. With postage and processing UI claims costing Ottawa about $100 million a year, the smart card could replace mail delivery of benefits cheques. Instead, recipients would head to the nearest service booth and punch in a personal identification number (PIN). Once the computer accepted your PIN and walked you through the regular set of UI questions (e.g., "Are you ready and able to work?"), it would dispense your money in cash, or as an electronic transfer to a bank account, or directly credit it to your smart card.

But to make such a system financially feasible, Ottawa would have to put other services on it and persuade other levels of government to join in. It's conceivable, for example, that via a smart card, you could one day automatically transfer a portion of a federal pension cheque to pay off a parking fine.

Ayotte worked in sales and as a computer programmer before she and two partners bought T-Base in 1990. She has a computer science degree from the University of Manitoba that she took in Braille (she is legally blind).

T-Base is an example of the current trend in the industry toward very specialized niches and partnerships with major players. "Small research and development organizations usually have a hard time dealing directly with governments," Ayotte says, "because governments aren't sure if a small firm will be there tomorrow.... The only way small firms can survive is to partner with major ones and get them interested in new niche markets."

This strategy also allows a company like T-Base to concentrate on what it knows — technology — and let someone else worry about the rest. "Digital and Canon already have distribution channels," Ayotte says. "So why reinvent the wheel?"

1. In your own words, define the *smart card*.
2. With a partner, brainstorm other applications for the smart card.

FOCUSING ON BUSINESS

1. Define *sole proprietorship*.
2. Review the advantages of a sole proprietorship. Which advantage do you think is the most important? Why?
3. How might a large amount of debt affect a sole proprietorship?
4. Review the disadvantages of a partnership. Which disadvantage is the most serious? Why?
5. Define *corporation*.
6. Explain the major difference between a private and a public corporation.
7. In your opinion, what is the main advantage of a corporation as a form of business organization? Why?
8. What is a *Crown corporation*?

EXPLORING BUSINESS

9. Examine the business section of a newspaper. Select one article that relates to a sole proprietorship, a partnership, or a corporation. Write a brief report describing the business and any other interesting findings.
10. With a partner, list the names of two businesses in your community that are sole proprietorships, two that are partnerships, and two that are corporations. Explain how you decided which names represent which form of business ownership. Why do you think each owner chose that particular form of ownership? Present your findings to the class.
11. In small groups, create a poster to display examples of sole proprietorships, partnerships, and corporations.
12. Darach McGee meets Andrea Retteghy, a university classmate. After discussing old times, Darach and Andrea discover that they are both interested in opening a business that would provide a disc jockey service. They are both prepared to invest $4000 in this new venture.
    a. Would it be to their advantage to form a partnership or to each form a sole proprietorship offering the same service? Explain.
    b. What are the factors they should consider before they decide?
    c. How would you advise them?
13. With a partner, interview a sole proprietor, a partner in a partnership, or a president of a corporation. Find out what goods or services the business provides and why the person selected this type of business

ownership. Also find out their opinion of the advantages and disadvantages of this type of business ownership. Write a newspaper article to report your findings.

14. In small groups, contact a Canadian corporation and obtain a copy of its most recent annual report. Each group should select a different corporation and then prepare a brief report to present to your class outlining the most relevant data from the report. Your report should include the following: name of the corporation, location of the head office, type of industry, number of employees, total profit or loss, and any other interesting information.

CAREERS

THE ARTS

1. As a class, choose six careers that involve the arts. The arts comprise such things as music, drama, dance, museums, and visual arts. Possible careers in the arts are artist, promoter, producer, performer, director, writer, curator, tour guide.

2. In home groups, each group member should select one of the six careers to research.

3. Form an expert group of students from other groups who have the same career as you to conduct research with them. Focus on the formal education needed, what the job is like, and how business relates to the arts.

4. Return to your home group and describe what you learned in your expert group. Prepare a group report on the six careers. The report can be written, presented as a video, illustrated on a poster, or displayed in any other appropriate form.

BRIDGEHEAD GIFTS A WAY OF GIVING TWICE

CONNECTING BUSINESS
WITH
THE WORLD

There are no sale signs, no discounts, and no flashy displays.

And in a year when most store owners are complaining about shoppers' reluctance to part with their cash, there's also no whining.

Welcome to Bridgehead, a sort of United Nations General Assembly in a broom closet.

Here 500 items from 60 co-operatives in 25 developing countries are selling like ice cream in a heat wave.

Just 14 months out of a Toronto church basement, the Bridgehead store has seen a 10 percent increase in sales this Christmas over last year, when $150 000 worth of merchandise was snapped up in November and December, said Pina Gianneschi, marketing manager, retail stores and national accounts, with Bridgehead Inc.

And with those two months accounting for over half the store's annual sales, Gianneschi admitted she's pleased.

But shoppers crowding into the tiny 26m² said it's neither the selection nor the prices that lure them in and keep them coming back.

"People who come here are looking for a way to share what they have with others who have so little," said Varda Burstyn, who spent about $180 on everything from red leather boxes made in

St. Mary's training centre in Ahmebad, India, supplies embroidered goods to Bridgehead.

India to Christmas decorations from Bangladesh.

"It's overwhelming how bad things are (in the economy) this year," she said. "Things here are modest, pretty and bright. They're not glamorous, and this year that's very appropriate."

Owned by Oxfam Canada, which supports community-based, sustainable development projects around the world, Bridgehead Inc. sells wares from groups in some of the poorest countries on earth.

"People who shop here know that the people who made the products benefit directly from the money that is spent," Gianneschi said.

Named after an engineering term for the part of a bridge that sits on land and is "the first block to building a link," Bridgehead operates another store in Ottawa.

It pays an average of one third of the final selling price of a product to its manufacturers, who include weavers in Thailand, scarf-makers in India, and brass-rimmed-basket crafters in Bangladesh.

The money pays craftspeople for their work and helps them develop their own community programs.

The remaining two thirds of the money from store sales pays for operating costs and charitable donations for Oxfam Canada, Gianneschi said.

Bridgehead began ten years ago, when four people pooled $30 000 of their savings and began selling coffees and teas they purchased from developing co-operatives.

In 1985, it was bought for $1 by Oxfam Canada, who launched a mail-order catalogue two years later.

Marian MacGregor, a regular shopper at the store, called the concept "politically correct. They're the type of gifts that give twice."

1. What are some of the incentives that attract customers into the tiny Bridgehead store?

2. In small groups, brainstorm some other types of co-operatives that could be formed.

Co-operative

Co-operatives are another form of business ownership. The members of a **co-operative** own and control the business and make all business decisions. Regardless of the number of shares the individual member owns, each member has only one vote to cast to determine how the business will function.

Co-operatives can be divided into various types. Many farmers belong to **producer co-operatives**. The member farmers all bring their crops to one central location to sell them. The co-operative is able to monitor the supply of the crop and control its sale and price. Farmers do not compete against each other or undercut each other's prices.

Another type of co-operative is a **consumer co-operative**. Consumers join together in a group to operate a business that provides them with goods and services. The profits of the co-operative are divided among the members in proportion to the volume of business that each member does with the co-operative. This system encourages members to do as much business as possible with the co-operative. A food co-operative is one type of consumer co-operative.

Advantages of a Co-operative

Members have a share in the running of a co-operative. They own and control the business. Each member gets only one vote on issues that affect the operation of the business. This means that no one person or group of people can dominate the co-operative.

Members also benefit because profits are divided so that members who do a high volume of business with the co-op also receive more of the profits.

Co-operatives are able to offer their members favourable prices because goods are bought in large quantities and because of co-operation among producers. They also control the sale and price of goods. Certain types of co-operatives allow members to be more efficient in the operation of their businesses and they prevent unnecessary competition.

Disadvantages of a Co-operative

Most co-operatives have difficulty in raising additional funds when they are needed. Some people are reluctant to invest in a co-operative because they have only the same amount of control over the business as someone who has invested much less.

It can be difficult for decisions to be made concerning co-operatives because of the number of people involved. It is also difficult for an individual to exercise any degree of control over the business.

The commitment of the members may vary. Some members may have more money at stake or take the business more seriously than others. This can cause resentment or hostility between members.

FRANCHISE

Franchising is one of the fastest-growing forms of business ownership. A person who buys a **franchise** is acquiring a licence to manufacture or sell a product or service. The person who purchases the franchise is referred to as the **franchisee**. The seller of the franchise is known as the **franchisor**. Each franchise agreement is slightly different, but generally the agreement permits the franchisee to use the franchisor's name, products, and packaging. The franchisor will usually specify how the franchise is to be operated, what products are to be sold, how the advertising is to be done, and so on.

More than 25 percent of Canadian franchises are in the restaurant sector, and this trend is expected to continue. Experts predict growth in ethnic-food franchises, such as Japanese, Thai, and Middle Eastern, and more outlets serving health foods.

A recent study found that the franchise sector of the economy was outperforming the rest of the economy. For 1992, the study forecast a growth of 12.4 percent for franchising, several times the growth of the economy as a whole.

Advantages of a Franchise

Franchisees buy a business with a proven track record. The franchisor has ironed out any problems and agrees to share expertise with the franchisee. The franchisee does not need to do the research to determine what sort of business will be successful in his or her community.

One specific way in which the franchisor helps the franchisee is in finding a suitable location for the franchise. The franchisor also provides all the packaging, advertising, equipment, and other requirements, including extensive training in the operation of the franchise. Finally, the franchisor usually agrees not to open another operation nearby.

Is this any way to start a business?

Too many people get into their own business with a lot of their hard-earned cash, plenty of good intentions and, quite frankly, a hope and prayer. There's a better way.

By investing in an established, reputable franchise organization you not only get to run your own business but, it's a fact, that you significantly increase your chances for success.

Don't cross your fingers, use them to call the Canadian Franchise Association, a national organization representing the country's best franchise companies and their franchisees. It's a better way.

Before you invest, investigate.

5045 ORBITOR DRIVE, BUILDING 12, UNIT 201, MISSISSAUGA, ONTARIO L4W 4Y4   TEL: (416) 625-2896/1-800-665-4232 FAX: (416) 625-9076

FRANCHISES

Product/Service Category	Sample Franchises
Fast Food	McDonald's, Tim Horton's, A.L. Van Houtte, Harvey's, Druxy's, Pizza Hut, Second Cup, Grandma Lee's, Pizza Pizza, Treats
Auto Repair	Midas, Speedy, Apple Auto Glass, Jiffy Lube, Thruway Muffler, Mister Transmission, Ziebart
Clothing	Athlete's Foot, Benetton, Cotton Ginny, Mark's Work Wearhouse, Tabi, Rodier
Computers and Video	Compucentres, Computerland, Jumbo Video, Captain Video, Radio Shack
Convenience Stores	7-Eleven, Beckers, Red & White

Reproduced by courtesy of Dave Whamond.

Disadvantages of a Franchise

Franchises are expensive to buy. The fees can be as high as $500 000 — a large investment for most people. Furthermore, the franchisee is required to pay an operating fee to the franchisor, which reduces profits.

Owning a franchise is not the same as owning a wholly independent business, and the franchisor may have little say in how the day-to-day operations are run.

POINTS TO REMEMBER

- A sole proprietorship is owned and operated by one person and is the most common form of business ownership.
- Partnerships are formed when two or more people share in the ownership and operation of a business.
- Sole proprietorships and partnerships are subject to unlimited liability.
- Partnerships are relatively easy to form but often dissolve due to disagreements between or among the partners.
- Types of corporations include: private, public, Crown, and non-profit.
- The most important advantage of a corporation is limited liability.
- Members of co-operatives own and control the business, and make all business decisions.
- Franchises are the fastest-growing form of business ownership.

FOCUSING ON BUSINESS

15. What is a *co-operative*? How does a co-operative differ from a corporation?

16. Match the definitions in column 1 with the terms in column 2.

Column 1	Column 2
a. The seller of the franchise	a. Franchisee
b. The buyer of the franchise	b. Franchise agreement
c. The legal document signed by both parties	c. Franchisor

17. The name of a business often indicates how it is organized. With a partner, indicate which form of business ownership would apply to the businesses below.

a. Tajinder's Service Centre

b. Moldaver, Ifejeika and Co.

c. Sears Limited

d. Firestone Company Limited

e. Blitz and Sons

f. Appleton Food Co-op

g. Perkin's Hairstyling

h. Schwartz, Schultz, Shafik and King

EXPLORING BUSINESS

18. With a partner, create a poster to display examples of co-operatives and franchises.

19. Melissa, Vicki, and Mark have graduated from high school and have been friends for a long time. All three have had experience in running small business ventures during the summer and have decided to get together to discuss the possibilities of starting a business.

Over the last two summers, they have each operated a small business selling custom-designed boxer shorts in their schools and neighbourhoods. Their supplier, Kevin Short & Co., provided them with as many boxer shorts as they needed at a wholesale price of $7. The trio now wants to join forces and is considering opening up a retail store and selling shirts, pants, and other forms of casual wear. The dilemma they have is that they do not know which form of business ownership would best suit their needs.

Write a report explaining which form of business ownership you think the three should select and why.

20. Prepare a report outlining the number of businesses that have failed in your province in the last year and the number of jobs that were lost. Also, outline how many new businesses were started in the last year and the number of new jobs that were created. The data can be presented by dividing the businesses into three categories — small, midsize, and large. Use graphs to illustrate your findings.

To gather this information use your resource centre, public library, Statistics Canada, and Chamber of Commerce office.

WORKING WITH MATH

21. Create the table below using a computer spreadsheet program. Calculate the net increase or decrease of businesses for each year given. What conclusions can be drawn from the information?

BUSINESS START-UPS AND EXITS IN CANADA
1979–1989

Year	Start-ups	Exits
1979–80	127 105	92 816
1980–81	134 769	95 996
1981–82	119 126	106 653
1982–83	145 154	192 251
1983–84	138 547	117 371
1984–85	152 213	110 520
1985–86	152 472	122 828
1986–87	161 285	127 085
1987–88	161 931	135 394
1988–89	165 980	140 054

From *Small Business in Canada, 1991: From Best Practice to Competitiveness.*
Source: Industry, Science and Technology Canada. Reproduced with permission of the Minister of Supply and Services Canada, 1993.

22. Create the table on page 71 using a computer spreadsheet program. Calculate the percentage of employment increase or decrease for each industry for the years given.

   a. Which industry experienced the greatest increase?

   b. What do you think the reasons are for this increase?

   c. Provide three examples of the types of businesses in this industry.

EMPLOYMENT BY INDUSTRY
annual averages, selected years, 1949–1989 (in thousands)

Year	Agriculture	Other primary industries	Manufacturing	Construction	Transportation, communication and other utilities	Trade	Finance, insurance and real estate	Service	Public Administration
1949[1]	1077	193	1297	316	416	651	144	822[2]	–
1959	700	197	1496	443	520	947	216	1350[2]	–
1969[3]	516	215	1799	479	689	1278	349	1897	472
1979	484	275	2071	644	903	1808	554	2954	701
1989	428	288	2126	764	961	2186	733	4150	850

[1] Excludes estimates for Newfoundland

[2] Includes public administration

[3] Population aged 15 and over from 1966. Data prior to 1966 are based on population aged 14 and over.

Source: *Canada Year Book*, 1992, p. 156.

KEY TERMS

sole proprietorship	non-profit corporation
liability	articles of incorporation
unlimited liability	limited liability
collateral	co-operative
partnership	producer co-operative
articles of partnership	consumer co-operative
corporation	franchise
private corporation	franchisee
public corporation	franchisor
Crown corporation	

The Global Marketplace

CHAPTER FOCUS

After studying this
chapter you will
be able to:

explain why countries
export and import
goods

•

understand the
importance for
businesses to explore
global markets

•

define the need
for Canada to be
more globally
competitive

•

compare Canadian
businesses that are
becoming more
competitive in the
global market

S CANADIANS, WE ARE FORTUNATE THAT whenever we go shopping we have a wide selection of goods and services from which to choose. If you examine the labels of clothes in the stores, you will notice that they are manufactured in many different countries. Does selling foreign goods in Canada and selling Canadian goods in other countries benefit or harm the Canadian economy? How does this affect the prices consumers pay for goods? In this chapter, we will explore the importance of international trade for Canada. We will examine the Canada–United States Free Trade Agreement and the proposed North American Free Trade Agreement among Canada, the United States, and Mexico.

INTERNATIONAL TRADE

Countries trade with one another out of necessity since no country can produce all the goods it requires. Most countries tend to specialize in producing certain goods based on the availability of resources; for example, Saudi Arabia produces oil and Brazil produces coffee. Countries with limited natural resources develop a particular expertise in other areas; for example, Switzerland has specialized in producing watches and Japan has specialized in manufacturing automobiles and electronics. In turn, this leads to countries wanting to purchase goods from one another. The goods and services bought from foreign countries are called **imports**. The goods and services sold to foreign countries are called **exports.**

International trade is extremely important to Canada's economy. In fact, almost 3 million jobs depend on international trade. Approximately half the goods produced in Canada are exported. For example, coal is exported to Korea and grain is exported to Greece. Canada has nearly 200 international trading partners, but the majority of our trading is done with the United States, Western Europe, and Asia.

Canadian automobile manufacturers use imported parts to produce their vehicles, many of which will in turn be exported.

·················· CANADA'S EXPORTS AND IMPORTS, 1989 ··················

EXPORTS

Energy
Products

Forestry
Products

Industrial
Goods and
Equipment

Machinery
and
Equipment

Automotive
Products

Agriculture
and Fishing
Products

Other

Other
Consumer
Goods

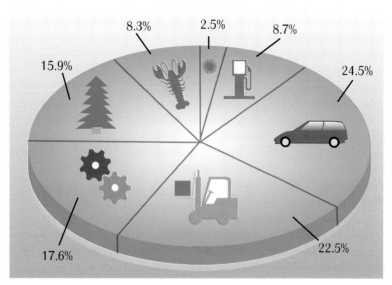

8.3%   2.5%   8.7%

15.9%   24.5%

17.6%   22.5%

IMPORTS

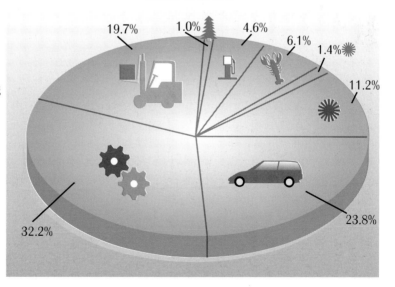

19.7%   1.0%   4.6%   6.1%   1.4%   11.2%

32.2%   23.8%

Source: Statistics Canada

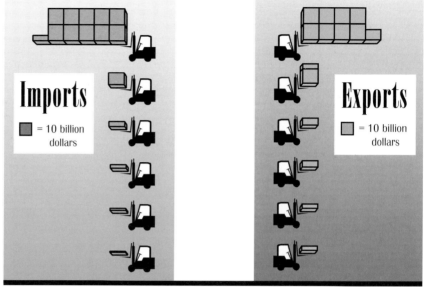

VALUE OF GOODS SHIPPED TO AND FROM CANADA'S MAJOR TRADING PARTNERS, 1991

Source: Statistics Canada

CANADA–UNITED STATES FREE TRADE AGREEMENT

The United States is Canada's largest two-way trading partner. In fact, in 1990, 75 percent of Canada's exports were made to the United States. This is partly due to the **Canada–United States Free Trade Agreement (FTA)** that came into effect January 1, 1989. The Free Trade Agreement created one of the largest free trade areas in the world.

Under the terms of the Free Trade Agreement, all tariffs on the sale of goods between Canada and the United States will be removed by 1999. A **tariff** is a tax placed on imported goods. The tariffs were eliminated on the following goods in 1989: leather, computers, skis, skates, and animal feed. By 1993, tariffs had been eliminated on goods such as furniture, paints, hair dryers, and camera film. By 1998, tariffs will have been eliminated on goods such as appliances, tires, and clothing.

As with all important issues that affect the Canadian economy, not everyone agrees, and the Canada–United States Free Trade Agreement is no exception. Some people believe that the FTA benefits the Canadian economy, while other people think it is doing a great deal of harm. For example, manufacturing companies laid off a large number of workers in the early 1990s. Some people blame the Free Trade Agreement; others claim that the job losses were inevitable as the world economy suffered a general economic downturn.

Supporters of the FTA point out that Canadian producers now have access to larger markets. The population of the United States is ten times the size of Canada's, so Canadian producers have many more people to whom they can sell their products. Second, Canadian consumers are now able to buy cheaper American goods. American products are often cheaper than Canadian products because manufacturing costs tend to be lower in the United States than Canada. Third, people feel that entrepreneurial optimism will increase. Entrepreneurs like a challenge, and selling products to the United States is a new and exciting challenge.

Those people who are opposed to the FTA are concerned that American goods will dominate the Canadian market. As American products increase, Canadian-made products will eventually be eliminated. The increase in American products in Canada will lead to increased Canadian unemployment, and possibly to the closure of Canadian firms. Second, Canadian companies will increasingly be owned by Americans. American companies will buy Canadian companies in order to have better access to the Canadian market. Third, there is fear that there will be a loss of Canadian identity and culture and Canada will become more and more American.

NORTH AMERICAN FREE TRADE AGREEMENT

Canadians have been trading with Mexico for a number of years. For example, in 1905, James Dunn, a Canadian promoter, financed the building of the trolley system in Mexico City. But until 1991, trade with Mexico has been slow in developing. In 1991, Canada exported $543 million in goods and services to Mexico — representing only 1.5 percent of the total Mexican imports — while importing $2.6 billion worth of goods and services from Mexico.

In 1990, Mexico and the United States began discussions of a free trade agreement similar to the Canada–United States Free Trade Agreement. In 1991, Canada joined in these discussions with a view to the possibility of a trilateral agreement (tri- means three), called the **North American Free Trade Agreement (NAFTA)**.

Mexico implemented an economic reform program in 1987, and many analysts now view that country as a market with tremendous growth potential. The population is young and, despite the poverty that covers much of the country, a growing middle class is beginning to demand the goods and services most Canadians take for granted. For example, only one in ten Mexicans has a telephone and just one in eight has a television set, one fifth the rate in Canada. Many view the trade agreement with Mexico as an opportunity to vastly increase Canadian exports as demand for such products grows. As with the Canada–United States Free Trade Agreement, some people believe that NAFTA will benefit the Canadian economy, while others argue against NAFTA.

Those in favour of NAFTA highlight the fact that Canadian producers benefit from the new markets created. Mexico has a young and growing population, and Canadian producers will be able to sell their products in this large market.

Former Prime Minister Brian Mulroney signing the North American Free Trade Agreement on December 17, 1992.

Second, Canadian consumers benefit from cheaper products. Because Mexican labour is cheaper than Canadian labour, Mexican products are less expensive than similar Canadian products. Third, technology-based equipment will enjoy market growth. Canadian manufacturers produce machinery that has more advanced technology than Mexican products, and as Mexico's economy expands, the need for such machinery will increase.

Those against NAFTA are concerned that many Canadian manufacturers will move to Mexico as a result of lower wages and operating costs in Mexico. Second, foreign control of Canadian manufacturing will rise substantially. Canadian companies will be purchased by American and Mexican investors. Third, imports will rise while exports will remain stagnant. Less expensive goods from the United States and Mexico will be imported into Canada.

NO BLUES IN BERRIES

For Oxford Frozen Foods of Oxford, Nova Scotia, blue is the colour of money, as in frozen wild blueberries. In 1992, the privately owned firm harvested 16 million kilograms of wild berries, almost one third of all North American production. As part of its strategy to undercut the competition, Oxford uses a special harvesting machine, which has slashed costs in half. And thanks to the diligent cultivation of foreign markets, Oxford's blueberries now grace dessert trays in Western Europe, Japan, and the United States.

EUROPE

In 1992, two existing trading blocs in Europe joined to form an even larger trading bloc. The European Communities (EC) and the European Free Trade Agreement (EFTA) bloc of nations joined to form a 19-nation trading bloc that allows for the free flow of goods, services, capital, and labour.

Until now, Western Europe, most notably the United Kingdom, Germany, and France, has been the second largest trading partner for Canadian exports. With the dismantling of communism in Eastern Europe and the removal of the Berlin Wall, the potential for European trading is even greater. Canadians will have to become more aggressive when competing internationally. The world is gravitating toward the organization and formation of trading blocs, and Canadians will have to be competitive as part of a new global marketplace.

HAMBURGER DIPLOMACY

For George A. Cohon, president and chief executive officer of McDonald's Restaurants of Canada Limited and vice chairman of Moscow McDonald's, business has always combined the excitement of team sports, the thrill of exploring new ventures, and the challenge of building something new and watching it grow.

As head of McDonald's Restaurants of Canada, he has had the thrill of watching the company grow in Canada from its first store in 1967 to becoming one of the country's largest employers in the food business and the largest single employer of Canada's youth.

"In this increasingly shrinking world of ours, Canadians are also leading the way in opening up new business opportunities beyond our own borders," he says.

Cohon was proud to lead the Canadian team that brought the first McDonald's Restaurant to Russia. This extraordinary venture took nearly 14 years to complete. From the very beginning, the company's efforts were built on a theme of partnership — something that Cohon believes that Canadians have always excelled at in

their personal and business lives.

McDonald's Russian adventure began during the Montreal Olympics in 1976, when Cohon invited a group of Olympic officials from the Soviet Union to one of his restaurants. The delegation fell in

McDonald's in Moscow.

love with the food technology — and the food — and the two countries started talking about a possible joint venture.

The Canadian team spent thousands of hours making presentations to senior trade officials, staff at various ministries, and countless others. Cohon flew the round trip between Moscow and Toronto more than 75 times.

Their biggest break came in 1987, when Mikhail Gorbachev, the last Soviet premier, introduced new laws permitting joint ventures with non-Soviets, unlocking the final door to an exciting new world for businesses in the west. In April 1988, McDonald's Restaurants of Canada signed the largest joint-venture agreement ever made between a food company and the Soviet Union. Less than two years later, through a partner-ship with the Moscow City Council, McDonald's opened a 10 000 m^2 food production and distribution centre and the first McDonald's restaurant in Russia. The restaurant at Pushkin Square in downtown Moscow was, at the time, also the world's largest McDonald's, serving more than 30 000 customers its very first day.

The success of the team's efforts was the result of a lot of hard work on the part of both Russians and Canadians. Before the doors of the first restaurant opened, they had to create many new associations — with Russian suppli-ers, builders, government officials, and with the new Russian managers and crews.

"Throughout the start-up period, there were always people who said it couldn't be done," says Cohon. "But we had two big things going for us. First, we knew what we wanted to do — introduce a food technology into Russia that had proved successful in more than 51 other countries around the world. And second, we had the enthusiasm and energy of the Russian people behind us."

Through it all, the most important lesson they learned — Canadians and Russians alike — was the need to understand the thought processes of each other. For instance, the Canadians learned that the decision-making and approval processes in Russia involved many more people and much more time than in Canada....

The Canadian team was proud to be among the first companies to take part in a major new Russian-Canadian joint venture. Once the trust was established and the language barriers were broken, they found that they had more in com-mon than they had differences.

Summing up, Cohon says, "Time and again, in our experience world-wide at McDonald's, we have found that people from any culture and back-ground working shoulder to shoulder toward common goals can achieve almost anything. That, to me, is the greatest thrill of all in any business."

What do you think are the most difficult obstacles facing a business that wants to expand into another country? Explain.

ASIA–PACIFIC

The Asian Economic Zone represents a market much larger than the European market. The powerhouse of the Asian zone is Japan. Some of the other countries include China, South Korea, Singapore, Malaysia, Thailand, Indonesia, and the Philippines. Although there is no formal agreement among these nations, they are working at co-operation in trade matters.

Taiwan business section. Taiwan is a leading exporter in the Asia-Pacific region.

Canada's trade with the Asian nations accounted for only 11 percent of its total trade, and only 5 percent if Japan is excluded. As trade matters now stand, Canada imports much more from these countries than it exports to them.

It is estimated that by the year 2000, the Asian Pacific region will account for approximately 60 percent of the world's population, 50 percent of global production, and 40 percent of consumption. Canadian producers, who sell 75 percent of their products to the United States, must move outside North America and explore these growing world markets.

FOCUSING ON BUSINESS

1. Why do countries find it necessary to trade with each other?
2. Define *imports* and *exports*.
3. What is the main purpose of the North American Free Trade Agreement?
4. Define a *tariff*.

CANADA'S TRADE WITH MEXICO
(1991)

Top 10 imports from Mexico	Top 10 exports to Mexico
1. Motor vehicles, engines and parts	1. Motor vehicles, engines and parts
2. Computers	2. Newsprint, pulp, and other paper
3. Crude oil	3. Iron and steel
4. Television sets, radios, phonographs	4. Wheat and barley
5. Telecommunications and related equipment	5. Live animals and meat
6. Air-conditioning and refrigeration equipment	6. Telecommunications and related equipment
7. Electric lighting and related equipment	7. Aircraft, engines and parts
8. Fresh fruits and berries	8. Sulphur
9. Fresh vegetables, including tomatoes	9. Refined petroleum products
10. Miscellaneous equipment and tools	10. Asbestos

U.S. EXPORTS SOAR... CANADA'S LAG

EXPORTS TO MEXICO

$billion (Canadian)

From the United States

40				
30				
20				
10				
0				
'82	'84	'86	'88	'90 '91

Year

$billion (Canadian)

From Canada

1.00				
0.75				
0.50				
0.25				
0.00				
'82	'84	'86	'88	'90 '91

Year

Source: *The Globe and Mail*, Sept. 24, 1992

5. Review the information about the Canada–United States Free Trade Agreement. List the one advantage and the one disadvantage that you feel are the most important. Explain your reasoning.

6. How have the changes in Europe created trading opportunities for Canadian companies?

EXPLORING BUSINESS

7. Use different sources of information, such as television news reports, newspapers, and business magazines, to research the status of the North American Free Trade Agreement. Write a newspaper article outlining the advantages and disadvantages of the agreement. What advice would you give the Canadian government concerning the agreement?

8. In small groups, interview a representative of a business that either exports or imports goods. Prepare a list of questions to ask that will provide you with a better understanding of what is involved in exporting or importing. For example, what are the problems? How does a business obtain a licence to export or import goods? What tariffs are paid? What difficulties arise concerning transportation?

9. With a partner, choose a benefit of, or concern about, the Canada–United States Free Trade Agreement. The two of you will take opposing sides. One of you will explain why that part of the FTA benefits Canada and the other will discuss why it hurts Canada. Be prepared to present your debate to the class.

10. Read the following article and answer the questions on page 85.

According to Coca-Cola Ltd. president, Anthony Eames, the real source of competitive advantage in the 1990s and beyond will be superior service. And yet, disturbingly, a survey of 1500 executives found that almost 30 percent believe service quality has declined in North America.

There's no doubt that the need to restructure, to get costs down, to reach out for global markets, has hit home. But when it comes to customer service, we have a long way to go.

Canadians are often too tolerant of poor service. And this tolerance may be undermining our competitive position.

Think about the face we have recently presented to the world. Think how global business must have responded to our postal disruptions.

This may seem like a small item. It's not. In business, poor customer service will ensure a quick exit from the field.

a. Briefly summarize the contents of the article.

b. Think of an occasion when you or someone you know received poor service. How was it handled? Did you return to that business?

c. Assuming the viewpoint of Anthony Eames is correct, what can be done to remedy the situation?

11. At a recent 47-nation conference on providing aid to Russia, Russia's president, Boris Yeltsin, stated that his country would suspend all import tariffs and encourage foreign entrepreneurship. Why would he have said this?

12. Interview a local businessperson to find out his or her opinion of the North American Free Trade Agreement and its effect on Canadian business. Write your findings as a newspaper article.

13. With a partner, prepare a bulletin board display that shows the goods and services that Canadian businesses export to other countries.

14. With a partner, choose a country you are interested in. Research what it is like to do business in that country and compare this with doing business in Canada. Examine factors such as standard of living, weather, politics, education, housing, economy, and any others that affect the way in which business is conducted. Share your findings with the class.

15. In small groups, brainstorm about goods and services that could be exported from Canada to another country. Select the good or service that your group believes has the most potential. Share your idea with the class and explain why your group thinks it represents a good business opportunity.

CAREERS

GLOBAL OPPORTUNITIES

Use newspapers, magazines, television and radio news programs, or any other sources of information available to you, to find out what types of businesses are exporting their products or services to countries outside of Canada. Record information such as:

- why the business expanded globally
- countries in which the business is expanding
- the costs involved
- how long the expansion took
- obstacles encountered
- rewards experienced

Once you have gathered your information, form small groups and compare your findings. Which careers or types of businesses were most frequently involved in global opportunities?

Have you been successful in developing the skill you selected in the Careers activity in Chapter 1? List three examples of how you have used this skill.

1. International trade carried on by the provinces and territories is outlined below. Examine the data and then create an organizer by listing the countries to which Canada exports down the left-hand column. Across the top of your organizer, create and label a vertical column for each province and territory. Then place a check mark in the appropriate columns, indicating that a particular province or territory exports to that particular country.

2. With a partner, select a country and research to find out what goods Canada imports from that country. Create a poster to display your findings.

Province/ Territory	Total Exports	Major Exports	Leading Markets
British Columbia	$17 billion	softwood lumber; wood pulp; paper and paperboard; copper	United States, Japan, United Kingdom, South Korea, Germany
Alberta	$15.9 billion	crude petroleum; natural gas; organic chemicals; wheat	United States, Japan, China, Russia
Saskatchewan	$4.7 billion	wheat; fertilizers; crude petroleum; Canola	United States, Japan, China, Russia
Manitoba	$3.3 billion	wheat; nickel; crude petroleum; office machines and equipment	United States, Japan, China, Russia
Ontario	$74.4 billion	automobiles and trucks; motor vehicle parts and engines; precious metals; office machines and equipment	United States, United Kingdom, Switzerland, Germany, Japan

Reprinted from *Royal Bank Reporter*, Fall 1991, "The Trade Game."
Source: Statistics Canada

3. Form small groups. Each group will be assigned one of the regions listed below. Use your resource centre to prepare a group report outlining the type of products Canada imports to and exports from your assigned region. Share your findings with the class.

United States • Asia-Pacific • Western Europe • Latin America • Africa • Eastern Europe • Middle East

Province/ Territory	Total Exports	Major Exports	Leading Markets
Quebec	$24.8 billion	wood pulp and paper; aluminum; automobiles; telecommunications equipment	United States, United Kingdom, Netherlands, Germany, France
Nova Scotia	$2.3 billion	fish and shellfish; transportation equipment; wood pulp and paper	United States, Japan, United Kingdom, Portugal, Germany
New Brunswick	$3.2 billion	wood pulp and paper; petroleum and coal products; electricity; fish and shellfish	United States, United Kingdom, Japan, Germany
Prince Edward Island	$170 million	vegetables and vegetable preparations; fish and shellfish	United States, Uruguay, Venezuela, France
Newfoundland	$1.9 billion	petroleum and coal products; fish and shellfish; iron ore; newsprint paper	United States, United Kingdom, Japan, Netherlands, Italy
Yukon/Northwest Territories	$534 million	zinc and lead ores, concentrates and scrap	Germany, Japan, South Korea, Belgium

COMPETING IN THE GLOBAL MARKETPLACE

The trading world is changing drastically. As the centres of the world's population shift, and as other regions become more efficient at producing and exporting goods and services, Canada will also have to improve its export record. As the FTA continues to be implemented, and as NAFTA takes effect, Canada will need to look further afield if it wants its economy to continue to grow.

Canada currently relies on 50 leading exporters to generate about 50 percent of its export dollars. The other 50 percent comes from small businesses. We must rely less on a handful of large companies for the bulk of our exports and, instead, develop ways of approaching new markets in order to export to a wider range of countries. Of course there are many Canadian companies who are finding world markets for their products, but we need more of them.

International trade revolves around competition. To compete successfully, Canada must design, produce, and market goods and services in a more attractive manner than our competitive countries. In a study conducted by the International Management Development Institute and the World Economic Forum, Japan is currently considered the most competitive nation. The World Competitive Report ranked 22 countries, as listed on page 89.

The World Competitive Report gives some other interesting statistics that show how Canada performs in the global marketplace. The following five points were highlighted:

- In the category of motivation, Canada was ranked 16 out of 22. The most highly motivated workers were the Japanese and the Austrians.

- Canada is experiencing difficulty in attracting sufficient skilled labour. Canada ranked 14.

COUNTRIES' COMPETITIVENESS RANKS

| Overall | | Country |
'92	'91	
1	1	Japan
2	3	Germany
3	4	Switzerland
4	8	Denmark
5	2	United States
6	7	Netherlands
7	6	Austria
8	12	Sweden
9	13	Ireland
10	9	Finland
11	5	Canada
12	11	Belgium
13	10	Britain
14	15	France
15	18	New Zealand
16	16	Australia
17	14	Norway
18	19	Spain
19	17	Italy
20	21	Portugal
21	20	Turkey
22	22	Greece

Reproduced with permission of *The Globe and Mail.* © 1992.

Source: "World Competitiveness Report"

- The rate of generating new businesses in Canada was very poor. Canada ranked 20. The top-ranking countries were Germany, Portugal, Turkey, and Japan.

- Canada's product quality was poor, ranking 13. Japan, Switzerland, and Germany had the best product ranking.

- Canadian companies did not show a keen willingness to adapt their products for export markets. Canada ranked 15 in this area. Again, the top countries were Japan, Switzerland, and Germany.

What do all these statistics mean? Canada must strive to become more competitive in the global marketplace. It seems obvious that, in order for Canada to compete successfully in the global marketplace, we will have to establish a highly competitive work force. Just as the way of doing business will change in the 1990s, so will jobs. To remain employed, many Canadians will have to upgrade their skills or acquire new ones.

CANADIAN EXPORTS SUCCESS

CHOCOLATE STARS

In Mexico, Saudi Arabia, New Zealand and much of East Asia, candy bar lovers are fighting sweet tooth and nail to get hold of two familiar Canadian brands: William Neilson Ltd.'s Mr. Big and Crispy Crunch. While exports to the United States have proved a hard chew for Neilson's in the mature U.S. chocolate-bar market, demand in the developing world is booming: In 1993, Neilson produced 75 million candy bars for export — 20 percent of the firm's candy bar production. The overseas markets have proved so profitable that Neilson's customers are clamouring for other brands, including Sweet Marie and Malted Milk bars.

BULLISH ON BEEF

Thanks to superior breeding and feeding, Canadian cattle have become the Rolls-Royces of the beef world. And the quality-loving Japanese are beginning to discover this lean and reliable product. The result is that Canadian beef producers and packagers are now supplying some of Japan's finest steakhouses and hotel chains with premium-grade steaks, building a $21-million market in 1992, with plans to increase market share from 1.5 percent to 10 percent by the year 2000. With tariffs against foreign beef coming down, Canadian cattle ranchers expect to parlay their advantages into an even bigger slice of the market.

POINTS TO REMEMBER

- Imports and exports are an essential part of a country's participation in the global marketplace.
- Canada's largest trading partner is the United States, partly due to the Canada–United States Free Trade Agreement; the government is currently exploring a North American Free Trade Agreement that includes Mexico.
- The current changes in Europe, Asia, and other parts of the world have created opportunities for Canadian businesses to do more international trading.
- Canadians will have to spend more time and money doing research and development in order to be competitive in the global marketplace.

FOCUSING ON BUSINESS

16. Do you think that more small businesses should start emphasizing exporting? Why?
17. Why is competition considered important in international trade?
18. Why are the Canadian job market and job skills changing so rapidly?

EXPLORING BUSINESS

19. In small groups, prepare a questionnaire to interview a businessperson. The questionnaire should cover the following topics, in addition to any other topics you would like to ask about.

    - Present economic conditions of the business community
    - Current rate of business bankruptcy and the difficulty being experienced by the particular industry
    - Opinion regarding free trade with the United States and Mexico
    - Impact of the Goods and Services Tax and cross-border shopping on Canadian business
    - Canada's need to expand research and development of new products

    Once the questionnaire has been developed, each member of the group should interview a different person. Write a report summarizing your findings.

20. Read the following quote and write a letter to the editor agreeing or disagreeing with the author's viewpoint. Support your position.

    I have little doubt that Canada will cease to exist as a fully independent country within the next 10 to 20 years.

    This will result not from the constitutional crisis, which has been engineered by politicians for the benefit of political careers, but will be the consequence of Canada's inability to compete in what is rapidly becoming a global economy.

21. Contact your guidance department, resource centre, or nearest Employment and Immigration Canada office and find out which occupations are growing the fastest. Prepare a chart and place it on the bulletin board. Why are these careers growing so rapidly?

22. Read a book or watch a news show about doing business in the global marketplace. Write a report summarizing it.

23. The International Management Institute and the World Economic Forum produced the World Competitive Report. (See page 89.) In this report, five points were highlighted concerning Canada. In small groups, examine each one of the points and make recommendations as to how they can be addressed or improved.

24. It has been estimated that Canadians who cross the border to shop in the United States may be draining up to $500 million in sales from Canadian retail outlets. This will cost the provincial governments a significant amount of money since cross-border shopping causes a loss of provincial sales tax. At the same time, the federal government loses money as a result of the loss of the Goods and Services Tax.

    You have been asked by both levels of government to recommend a solution to the problem. Be certain to consider a solution that will meet the concerns of the governments, the retail stores, and the consumers. Once you have drafted a solution, form small groups and compare and discuss your suggestions. Develop a group response to share with the class.

WORKING WITH MATH

25. The table on the following page shows the total amount of trade Canada had with each region in 1990.

    a. Create the table below using a computer spreadsheet program.

    b. Total the exports and the imports. Which is larger?

c. Calculate as a percentage the imports from each region.

d. Create a bar graph to illustrate the imports from each region.

Region	Exports (millions of dollars)	Imports (millions of dollars)
United States	111 380	87 894
Asia-Pacific	16 235	19 534
Western Europe	14 459	19 626
Latin America & Caribbean	1 321	600
Middle East	1 434	1 157
Africa	1 086	1 125

Source: Statistics Canada

26. In 1970 our exports were $16 820 million. In 1990 they were $76 158 million. Calculate the percentage of increase.

PART 2

The Canadian Economic System

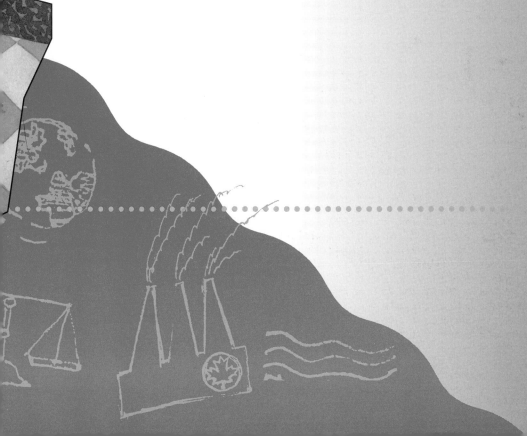

The Canadian Economy

CHAPTER FOCUS

After studying this
chapter you will
be able to:

define five factors
of production

•

define three types
of industries

•

understand the
differences between
free enterprise,
communism, and
modified free enterprise

•

understand the benefits
and limitations of the
three economic systems

EVERY DAY, NEWSPAPERS AND NEWS programs are filled with discussions and reports about the economy. It seems that everyone has an opinion on the economy — but what is the economy, and what is economics?

Canadian consumers can go to stores and buy what they need and want, confident that what they need exists in sufficient quantity and variety to satisfy them. Furthermore, they know that other items can be substituted if they cannot find exactly what they want. How does it happen that the right kinds and amounts of goods and services are available? How does business know what we need and want?

In this chapter, we will investigate the factors of production and their interaction in the free enterprise, communist, and modified free-enterprise systems. Then we will concentrate on Canada's modified free-enterprise economy and examine three types of industries and how they are interrelated.

The first Canadians, both Aboriginal and European, had to provide for themselves all the goods and services they used. As Canada's population grew, it became less and less feasible or practical for people to produce all their own goods and services. They did not possess the range of necessary talents, nor did they have access to the resources that were needed. Businesses arose that were dedicated to producing the many goods and services needed. Today, Canadians work to produce specific goods or services they trade the money they earn for the goods and services produced by the economy.

The decisions on how to use resources must be made carefully so they are not wasted. When business brings human and capital resources together to produce goods and services, it has to be sure it is meeting the needs of consumers. Businesses compete most effectively when they are responsive to consumer needs and wants. Those businesses that do not use resources effectively are not successful.

Canada's **economy**, like all other economies, is made up of the production and use of resources by individuals, businesses, and organizations. **Resources** are the raw materials businesses and individuals use to produce goods and services. **Economics** is the study of these resources and how they are managed. The economy of any country is made up of the resources available. Business and government use these resources to produce goods and services that satisfy the wants and needs of Canadians. Some of these products are also exported to other countries.

In this chapter, we will examine the resources that are needed in the economies of all countries and how these resources are managed under different economic systems.

FACTORS OF PRODUCTION

Canada has an industrial economy. Our wealth as a country is based on the production of goods and services that Canadians use in their daily lives. Goods are items that are produced for sale, such as cars, shoes, electronics equipment, and food. Services do not have a physical form. Instead they are work done by others that we would not be able to do effectively or choose to do on our own. Examples of services are banking, hairdressing, medical care, and car repairs.

All goods and services are produced through a combination of human resources, raw materials, money, and equipment. As we learned in Chapter 1, economists call these the factors of production and have classified them into five groups: land, capital, labour, technology, and entrepreneurship.

Land

Land refers to all natural resources, including minerals and ores, forests, oil, natural gas, property, and water. These resources contribute greatly to the production potential of a nation. Canada has abundant natural resources. Countries that do not have the natural resources they need must buy them from those that do.

Capital

Capital is the machinery and equipment used to produce and distribute goods and services. Capital may be simple tools or complex computers, railroads and highways, buildings, or assembly lines and manufacturing equipment. Money is also referred to as capital because it can be used to buy other forms of capital.

Labour

Labour refers to all the human effort, both mental and physical, that goes into the economy. A construction worker provides labour, as does an engineer or a doctor. The production of goods and services requires a labour force of healthy, educated people.

Technology

Technology is the application of research and knowledge to improve the production of goods and services. Technological advances can improve worker productivity, improve product quality, and lower manufacturing costs. In turn, technological advances can mean lower prices for consumers.

Around the time of the First World War (1914–1918), the assembly line improved the production of cars because they could be made faster and more consistently. Today, computers are being used more and more in the production process to relieve workers of dangerous or repetitive work and to standardize the quality of what is produced. Better productivity and quality, in turn, improve the economy of a country because resources are used more efficiently.

Education is the basis of research and development. The higher the educational level of a population, the more consumer and industrial products are created because more people are employed in research.

Also, there is more formal interest in improving the quality of life, and therefore, a country is better able to raise the standard of living of all who live there.

Entrepreneurship

The entrepreneur brings together the other factors of production through personal effort and financial resources. As we discussed in Chapter 2, this involves taking a great deal of risk. If the business venture is successful, the entrepreneur can receive a significant financial reward and recognition in the community. If the business fails, the entire investment may be lost.

PRODUCING GOODS AND SERVICES

Economists have classified industry into three major categories: primary, secondary, and tertiary.

Primary Industries

Primary industries are those involved in the extraction and processing of basic raw materials. Primary industries include mining, forestry, fishing, farming, and extracting oil or natural gas. Primary industry has always been important for Canada due to Canada's abundance of raw materials. In recent years, however, some of the traditional jobs found in primary industries have been automated and handed over to machinery and computers.

Secondary Industries

Secondary industries take processed raw materials and produce finished goods. The range of secondary industries is wide. Finished goods include grinding wheat into flour and converting oil into gasoline, heating oil, lubricating oil, or naphtha gas. A single product can be used in more than one secondary industry. For example, once wheat is ground into flour (the first secondary industry), it is then combined with salt, yeast, and water to make bread (another secondary industry). If the bread is then used to make bread crumbs, a third secondary industry is involved.

Tertiary Industries

Tertiary industries, also called service industries, provide the many services used by consumers, businesses, and governments. Service businesses are an important part of Canada's economy for several reasons. Consumers are demanding more services than ever, and businesses respond by increasing and improving services. In addition,

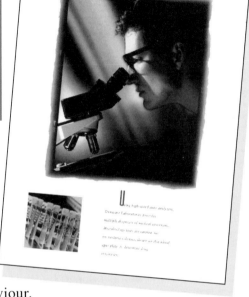

businesses introduce new products in anticipation of what consumers will demand in the future. This is done as the result of market research into trends and consumer behaviour.

Small businesses are likely to be service businesses because they do not require expensive equipment or a large initial investment. As more and more manufacturing becomes automated, workers are turning to the service industries for jobs.

Service businesses are many and varied. Some examples of tertiary industries are trucking, public transit, hotels, restaurants, sports events, law, computer programming, and banking.

ROLE OF FACTORS OF PRODUCTION

All factors of production are present in each category of industries. In primary industries, the land holds the raw materials. In secondary and tertiary industries, the land holds the factories where the goods are produced or the stores where the services are sold.

Capital in the form of money and equipment is needed for all industry, from mining equipment to assembly lines, from a deep fryer in a fast-food outlet to computers in a bank.

THERE'S NO PLACE LIKE HOME

CONNECTING BUSINESS WITH TECHNOLOGY

When Joan Marsh's employer offered her the option to work on contract, she sprang at it. The mortgage specialist at the Canadian Imperial Bank of Commerce in Vancouver was CIBC's top B.C. producer. Self-employment meant she could turn her back on "administrivia" and focus on what she does best: landing new customers for residential mortgages. And she could meet them in her own home and garden.

When Marsh opened Wilson Mandeville Consulting Ltd. two years ago to direct new mortgage clients to the CIBC, she joined the ranks of a new breed of entrepreneur the "home-preneur." A recent study by Ryerson Polytechnical Institute professors Barbara Orser and Mary Foster suggests a surprising number of people work from home. It says more than 2 million Canadian households — nearly a quarter of the total — double as workplaces, for full or part-time business owners (48 percent), for employees who spend the workday home (14 percent), or for employe who bring work home (39 percent). the year 2000, as much as 40 percent the labour force may be working fro home.

Some results surprised even t authors of the study. Although i often considered an urban phenom non, rural residents are more th twice as likely to start

Karen McDermot operates Autoplan Insurance — the home-based insurance business in British Columbia her home on Denman Island.

a home business. And just as many men as women run businesses from the home.

Orser and Foster cite a number of factors fuelling the homepreneur boom. The economy has shifted from natural resources to services, which lend themselves more to home-based work. Today's workers are more educated and mobile. As corporate Canada continues to downsize: jobs are evaporating. Finally, many people with steady jobs are rejecting the 9-to-5 schedule. "The most important reason for the home-based business owner electing self-employment was flexibility," says Orser. "Within corporate Canada, there still is not a lot of work flexibility and autonomy."

Above all, advancing technology is helping home businesses succeed. "Technology is facilitating home work," says Orser. "It's allowing it to happen."

Joan Marsh, for instance, considers a home fax machine "the most wonderful thing invented in the last ten years." She uses hers to send and receive documents to and from the bank and real-estate offices.

To help you stay in touch, some phone companies offer an invisible answering machine. Marketed by Bell Canada as "Call Answer," this voice-mail service takes messages if you're out of the office or on another call. You can retrieve messages from any touch-tone phone by keying in your personal code.

But the centrepiece of most home offices is the personal computer.

With home businesses becoming more sophisticated and more accepted, Joan Marsh finds herself winning on all fronts. She now does less work for more money. And she and her clients enjoy much more freedom. "They can visit me at 7:00 or 21:00," she says. "And I can pop out in to my garden and then come back in and do some more work."

1. How does Joan Marsh use technology to enable her to work at home selling residential mortgages?

2. Describe two kinds of services and support that are being offered by computer companies to attract customers.

3. What are the benefits of working in a home-based business?

All three types of industries require labour. Workers in primary industry may be producing steel, while workers in secondary industry are making cars, and those in tertiary industry are repairing cars.

Every type of industry benefits from technology. Technology has greatly improved the efficiency and safety in mining, a primary industry. Computerization in secondary industries has taken over dangerous and repetitive work, improving the quality of work life. In tertiary industries, many services have been improved with technology. Restaurants and banking have been revolutionized by computer technology.

The final factor of production, entrepreneurship, plays an important role as well. Creativity and risk taking have made Canada a world leader in the production of resources. As well, new secondary industries have been developed by entrepreneurs. One example is the CANADARM (a robotic arm on the Space Shuttle), which was developed for the space industry. Canada excels in the area of information processing, a tertiary industry, and is becoming a strong world competitor.

FOCUSING ON BUSINESS

1. With a partner, create a poster that illustrates the five factors of production.

2. Describe the factor *land* in your own words, and give two examples.

3. What is meant by *capital as a factor of production*? Give three examples of capital.

4. Define *labour as a factor of production*. Give two examples of labour.

5. How is technology a factor of production? Give three examples of technology.

6. Outline the role of the entrepreneur as a factor of production.

7. With a partner, decide which of the following describes a primary, secondary, or tertiary industry.

   a. A company mines potash in Saskatchewan.

   b. A bakery makes muffins.

   c. A steel company takes iron ore and produces cold-rolled steel.

   d. A person starts a business cleaning cars.

   e. A large bank provides account information electronically.

EXPLORING BUSINESS

8. Using the newspaper, select two articles related to each factor of production: land, labour, capital, technology, and entrepreneurship. For each pair of articles, do the following:

   a. Identify which factor of production you are illustrating.

   b. Describe how the article you chose illustrates that factor of production.

9. Working in small groups, each member finds a newspaper article on either a primary, secondary, or tertiary industry, then presents the article to the other members of the group. Describe how the article you chose illustrates that type of industry. When everyone has presented, as a group draw up a list of characteristics of the three types of industries. Make sure you include how each uses the factors of production.

10. With a partner, brainstorm ten capital items that a restaurant, a retail store, and a manufacturer of clothing each would need.

11. A computer business needs someone to work as a computer operator. The person must have skill with word processing, data entry, and data bases, and also be familiar with the products he or she will be using. For someone with five or more years of experience, the business would be willing to pay $30 000 per year, but would hire someone with as few as two years' experience at a lower pay.

    Create the advertisement the company will place in the local paper. Use newspapers to see how job advertisements are written.

12. Form groups of two or three. In your groups, consider starting a business that provides the service of painting houses. Appoint a recorder. Discuss and record the needs of this business, taking into consideration the following requirements: land, labour, capital, technology, and entrepreneurship.

13. In small groups, use newspapers and magazines to prepare a collage for either the factors of production or the categories of industry. Display your collage.

14. What type of industry is dominant in your community? Use the Chamber of Commerce or your local resource centre to find this information. Write a short essay about your findings.

CAREERS

SPORTS AND FITNESS

1. In small groups, brainstorm and list careers in the field of sports and fitness. Your list might include coach, aerobics instructor, equipment supplier, dietitian, physiotherapist, or agent. Which others can you think of?

2. With a partner, select a career that interests you from the list you created in Question 1. Research the career by visiting your resource centre and guidance office, contacting associations and organizations for literature, or interviewing someone in the field you have chosen. If you interview someone, ask if you can videotape the interview to share with the class. Learn about the career by gathering information that includes the following:

   - education required
   - experience required
   - responsibilities
   - salary range
   - skills required
   - any other relevant and interesting information

3. Create a poster to display your career research. Present your findings to the class.

TYPES OF ECONOMIC SYSTEMS

As noted earlier, business and government use the factors of production to produce the goods and services that people need and want. One of the government's roles is to ensure that the country's residents have access to necessary goods and services such as food, clothing, housing, health care, education, and so on. Business helps to produce many of these products and services.

How business and government work together forms a country's **economic system**. In deciding on an economic system, a government and its citizens must consider the following issues:

- Who owns the factors of production?
- Who decides what is produced?
- How are profits and losses distributed?
- Competition
- Benefits
- Limitations

The three types of economic systems we will be looking at are free enterprise, communism, and modified free enterprise. Economic systems are dynamic — they grow and change. The economic system in any country has evolved through history according to changing political and social conditions.

In the discussion of different economic systems that follows, it is important to remember that no country has a completely pure system. All have made modifications because all countries interact with each other and have had to make changes to accommodate global markets.

RIDING THE WAVES

Wheelchair athelete Rick Hansen's Man in Motion tour focused attention on the need to make products, housing, and services more accessible to persons with disabilities. Now Burnaby, B.C. entrepreneur William Asbury aims to make the waterfront more accessible too, with a boat specially designed for paraplegics.

The idea for "Aquacess" evolved after Asbury designed a propeller-driven boat for a friend who had lost his legs. A rehabilitation therapist spotted the vessel and encouraged Asbury to market it as a source of exercise and recreation for persons with disabilities.

The key was to make the boat easy to manoeuvre and sufficiently accessible for individuals with a disability to board without an attendant. Asbury produced a patent-pending design that lets users slide into the cockpit by gripping a grab-bar that submerges the back of the boat. One model works by joystick and electric motor, while another is "rowed" like a rowing machine. Pulling on the "oars" activates propellers that make the Aquacess easier to row than traditional boats.

To propel his $2495 boat to market, Asbury, a former car and raceboat painter, raised $145 000 from family and friends and formed Alternate Mobilization Systems Inc. He unveiled his craft at Independence '92, a Vancouver forum for persons with disabilities. The first Aquacess was christened in January 1993.

Asbury hopes to sell 5000 boats in 1993 to hotels and resorts in Canada and the U.S. Following clinical trials later this year, he hopes to target rehabilitation clinics too.

But Asbury won't stop there. His next project: an all-terrain wheelchair.

Free Enterprise

Under a **free-enterprise system**, all the factors of production are owned by private businesses. The most common example of the free-enterprise system is the economic system of the United States.

Who Owns the Factors of Production?

Private ownership is basic to free enterprise. Businesses own their capital, land, and technology, as well as the right to control by hiring, firing, and directing, the activities of those who supply the labour for business.

Under free enterprise, government cannot force a business to buy or sell any product. Private individuals and consumers also have the right to own property under a free enterprise system. Consumers may own houses, cars, video machines, clothing, investments, and businesses. In order to buy goods and services, consumers must have money themselves, so they earn the necessary money by working for business, for themselves, or for the various branches and levels of government. There are many goods and services available to consumers and their choices of what to buy are limited only by their incomes.

In-line roller skates are a popular consumer item.

Who Decides What Is Produced?

Business owners, in response to consumer demand, determine what is produced under the free enterprise system. Because business owns the means of production, it can produce anything it wants. However, if no consumers are interested in buying a particular good or service, the business will not earn any money. It would have no reason (or ability) to stay in that business. Thus, the buying behaviour of consumers dictates to a large extent what business produces.

But consumers cannot individually make their needs and wants known to every producer. Instead, businesses predict what consumer tastes and preferences will be in the future and use this information to decide which goods and services are likely to be profitable. When these items are offered for sale, consumers show their preferences by how they spend their money.

Competition

New firms enter a market to compete with existing firms because the market is large enough for several companies to make money. The opportunity for businesses to make a profit encourages competition. In order to succeed, businesses must be able to offer consumers an attractive alternative to similar goods or services offered in the marketplace.

When two or more businesses try to sell the same goods or services, the result is **competition**. If Frank wants to buy only one stereo system and he has ten choices of stores all selling stereos, how do the stores try to get Frank's business?

One may offer lower prices while another claims to have higher quality. We generally think of price and quality going together, but this is not always true. Sometimes no difference exists between two products but one has been priced lower to attract customers. A third business may offer better service — for example, an extended warranty or free installation. A fourth may have a location that is more convenient for Frank, while a fifth is open longer hours, and so on. Another way businesses attract customers is through advertising. Consumers need information before they shop, and advertising helps a business communicate to consumers what it has for sale and at what price.

BC Tel demonstrates its understanding of the fiercely competitive environment facing business customers.

How Are Profits and Losses Distributed?

Under a free-enterprise system, all profits and losses belong to the owner(s) of businesses. Because the owners are the ones taking the entrepreneurial risk, they also own the profits earned by the business. Profit is the difference between the money earned from the sale of goods or services and the costs and expenses of producing and selling those goods or services. Profit will be discussed in more detail in Chapter 6.

As well as taking the risks, the owners paid for the factors of production to make the goods and services available. If the product is successful, the business becomes profitable. If not, the business loses money and may eventually go out of business.

Benefits of a Free-Enterprise System

All the decisions about the marketplace are made by business owners and consumers. Business can produce whatever it chooses and whatever consumers want, and it decides how much of each factor of production it will use. A common decision is whether to hire more workers or buy more equipment to run a business. The goal of business is profit, so many decisions are based on how much it will cost to produce the items to be sold.

Consumers benefit by being able to choose among many different brands of products available. Often, other goods can be used as substitutes if one particular item is not available or is too expensive. In theory, workers are free to choose the kind of work they will do and, from their earnings, spend as much as they can afford.

Another advantage is that the competition in a free-enterprise system ensures that resources are used efficiently. Business must use land, labour, capital, and technology efficiently to keep costs as low as possible and make profits as high as possible. This means that new products are constantly being developed, prices are kept down, and high quality is maintained.

Since consumers have many choices of places where they can shop, they will choose the best quality for the lowest price. Business cannot charge whatever it wishes for its products, because the competition will ensure that a lower price is available. Thus, consumers benefit from price competition.

Limitations of a Free-Enterprise System

Under a free-enterprise system, business's only goal is to increase profits. Who, then, is responsible for looking after community interests? For example, who is responsible if a manufacturing process causes pollution, leading to health problems? If there are no laws against child labour, how can children be educated?

"Sorry, sir, but the high-quality items you're used to are no longer made. We can only remind you of them, by charging high prices for the current stuff."

Drawing by Ed Fisher © 1992 The New Yorker Magazine, Inc.

Consumers have freedom of choice in a free-enterprise system. However, what happens if some products are unsafe or of poor quality? Many consumers do not have the information they need to choose wisely. People also tend to believe that a product is good simply because it is sold in the stores. Consumers may find out too late that they have spent their hard-earned money on something of poor quality or, in some cases, they may suffer harm from unsafe products. Businesses will compete to offer the lowest price, but in doing so, they may cut quality to reduce costs.

KELLOGG AND COKE MOVE FAST ON FINAL OUT FOR SERIES PAYOFF

CONNECTING BUSINESS WITH SPORTS

When Blue Jay's pitcher Mike Timlin threw Otis Nixon out at first base to clinch the World Series [for the first time], Canadian baseball fans shouted for joy — and heaved a huge sigh of relief. But marketing executives had no time to celebrate: they were interested in winning a bigger game, the one about to begin on grocery-store shelves.

Although it was almost 1 o'clock Sunday morning, managers at Kellogg Canada Inc. and Coca-Cola Ltd. urgently tried to get in touch with their plant supervisors and packagers.

As the ball reached Joe Carter at first base, Kellogg's production manager received the final go-ahead to start a special product run.

Instantly, the first of 400 000 boxes of Kellogg's Frosted Flakes, featuring Tony the Tiger as a Blue Jay and congratulating the team as World Series champs, started rolling off the line.

A few hours later, the first commemorative cans of Coca-Cola Classic were being filled and sealed at the company's ten bottling plants across Canada.

Coke had already produced more than 5 million "clinch cans" to honour the team's first appearance in the World Series the week before.

When the Jays beat the Braves, Coke issued cans that hailed the Jays as conquering World Series heroes and recorded the score of each of the Series games.

"We were all set for any possibility, winning in five, six or seven games," Coca-Cola brand manager Doug Humfries said. "When the Blue Jays won on Saturday night, all we had to do was a little fine-tuning."

That involved adding an extra game score to the column on the side of the can and shrinking the type size of the scores. That quick reaction was only made possible by more than a month of painstaking preparation.

It helped that each company had secured the position of "official cereal" and "official soft drink," respectively, of major-league baseball. As such, each enjoys the right of first refusal in its product category to conduct a baseball or World Series-oriented promotion.

Kellogg exercised its option and began putting its plans together in early September. First, the concept was cleared through Major Baseball Properties Inc., the New York-based marketing arm for professional baseball.

Once that organization was satisfied that the promotion was consistent with "the image and character of professional baseball," a general package design was drawn up.

But there was a problem. At that point, nobody knew who was going to be in the playoffs or the final.

To cover all the bases, Kellogg approached each division winner immediately after it won the title to get its approval for a promotion if that team advanced to the World Series.

"We guarantee our sponsors that we can make the final decision within ten business days," said the promotions manager for the Blue Jays. "But we know how important a quick turnaround is for them, and we can usually say yes or no in about two days."

Graphic artists went to work imme-diately, putting together packages depicting Tony the Tiger as an Oakland A, a Pittsburgh Pirate, an Atlanta Brave, and a Toronto Blue Jay.

By the time the Jays beat Oakland, Kellogg had two boxes ready, one hailing the Jays as American League Champs, and one celebrating a World Series victory.

Meanwhile, Coke was busy with its own game plan. Work on the original "clinch" can started on October 1, two days before the Jays actually clinched the American League East.

But by October 9, as the Jays' over-powering force kept rolling, Coke decided to take advantage by designing a World Series can as well.

Coke amended the banner on the top of the can to say "World Series Champs" and added a column on the side, which listed the score of each World Series game.

By October 22, the can was ready. When the final out was made, Coke's packager quickly added the game result to the column and the filled cans came off the bottlers' lines within hours.

Why the rush?

Managers for both companies say timing is everything in event-related marketing, as the buying public has a notoriously short attention span — about a month, based on Coca-Cola's experiences.

1. How could each company be ready to go into production before it was known who would even be in the World Series?

2. Why was it important to get these commemorative products?

Communism

Until very recently, communism was the economic system in place in many countries. Some communist countries, such as those in eastern Europe, were highly industrialized, while others, such as Cuba, were less developed. Communism continues to dominate in China, Cuba, North Korea, and Vietnam. All communist countries have followed similar economic principles.

Who Owns the Factors of Production?

Under **communism**, the government owns or controls all the factors of production. In fact, it owns and operates all businesses of any size. Individuals are allowed to own their personal possessions, such as clothing, furniture, and — in some cases — cars, but all houses, factories, offices, farms, and businesses are government-owned. Occasionally, small independent operators are permitted, but they are often very small and are closely watched by government. Government not only decides what jobs are available and who will work where, but also sets wages.

Who Decides What Is Produced?

The goods and services that are available under communism are also determined by the government. Consumer demand has little or no effect on what is supplied, and consumers have little choice of goods and services.

Competition

Under communism, all goods and services are produced and distributed centrally by the government. There is no competition because the factors of production are not controlled by private individuals. Alternative products are not available.

How Are Profits and Losses Distributed?

Since all the factories and equipment is owned by the government, profits and losses belong almost entirely to the government. Prices are set by the government and there is no competition to regulate prices for consumers. When government needs money to provide goods and services for the people, it simply raises prices. Lack of competition also means the consumer has no way to control or influence the price, quality, quantity or style of products available. On the other hand, because it is not necessary for the government to make a profit, prices can be set lower than if individual businesses were trying to earn a return on its investment.

Benefits of Communism

Under communism, all people are guaranteed a basic standard of living. A great deal of importance is given to social services. Health care, education, housing, public transportation, and pensions are provided for everyone. Jobs are guaranteed for all adults.

Theoretically, because government is supposed to act in the best interests of its citizens, decisions are made to benefit the majority of ordinary citizens rather than to satisfy business groups. Energy and capital are not used to create larger profits for a small group. Instead, they are used to make life better for all.

Limitations of Communism

Under communist systems, personal freedom is limited. Farmers may be told what to grow and how much. Factories are told what to produce and in what quantities. Workers have jobs but little freedom to choose the jobs they would like.

In the former Soviet Union, all profits went to the government, who spent a great deal of the money on the military and on the salaries of government officials. The cost of government was high, since a large bureaucracy was needed to control every aspect of economic life, rather than leaving much of it to private businesses and individuals. Little money was used to produce consumer goods, so few products were available. Shortages were common because business had no incentive to produce, leaving consumers with little or no choice about what to buy.

Under communism, workers have little incentive to be productive. The government determines their wages, strikes are often illegal, and it is commonly very difficult to fire anyone. As well, the quality of manufactured products is often low, making exports unattractive to other countries.

Modified Free Enterprise

Canada's economic system is described as **modified free enterprise**. Although the basic elements of free enterprise exist, the government is involved in ensuring the economic welfare of all Canadians. Government may regulate business in a number of ways, such as requiring business to pay a minimum wage or an employees' health tax.

Who Owns the Factors of Production?

In a modified free-enterprise system, businesses, individuals, and governments can own land, buildings, machinery, and investments. As well, governments can enter into joint ventures with private business, as in the Hibernia oil project in Newfoundland. In this way, business and government enter into a partnership to meet a specific need. Government can own property for parks and operate many of the services, such as railroads and postal services, needed by all citizens. It is believed that with such government involvement, ordinary citizens can be protected from business, which seeks only to make a profit.

Who Decides What Is Produced?

The production of goods and services is still driven by consumer demand, but under modified free enterprise, government is involved to make sure that the needs of consumers are met. A privately owned business would not find it profitable to provide postal service or rail access in sparsely populated areas, so the government either requires business to provide these services or provides the services itself. Because governments are not required to make a profit, they are able to provide certain services that businesses cannot.

Competition

Competition is strong in the modified free-enterprise system. However, government sometimes intervenes to control business in the areas of minimum wages, worker benefits, and safety regulations. These controls add to the costs of producing goods and services, but are considered to be in the best interests of individuals living under the system. All businesses within the system must conform to the same regulations, which might put them at a disadvantage when competing with goods and services produced outside the country where these added costs do not exist.

If a private business is the only supplier of a product, the government may set up a business of its own to compete.

In Canada, government regulations prohibit any one company from having a **monopoly**, which means full control of a product or service, with little or no competition. For example, the Canadian Radio-Television and Communications Commission (CRTC) in 1992 decided that Bell Canada had an unfair monopoly on long-distance telephone calls and allowed another company to compete with Bell. Up to this time, Bell's monopoly had been allowed to exist because it was directly regulated by the CRTC. However, the government of the day was petitioned by other telephone companies to change the ruling.

In certain industries, the Canadian government regulates the prices that companies are allowed to charge. Consumer protection laws regulate advertising, packaging, labelling, and credit. Worker safety laws prohibit child labour and ensure that working conditions are safe.

The government recognizes that some laws may inhibit competition but believes that community standards are important.

How Are Profits and Losses Distributed?

Private business earns profits in a modified free-enterprise system, but government applies taxes to those profits. Sales taxes, income taxes, excise taxes, tariffs, and property taxes are examples of taxes the government collects. The result is higher prices for consumers and lower profits for business. The money collected is used to provide social programs, so individuals will benefit who might otherwise suffer hardship. For example, in Canada, health care and education are paid for through both business and consumer taxes. Such taxes are also collected in a free-enterprise economy but are generally lower, since fewer benefits are provided for the people. There is, of course, no true free-enterprise system, as even the United States regulates business to some degree.

············ SOCIAL SECURITY EXPENDITURES BY SELECTED PROGRAMS ············

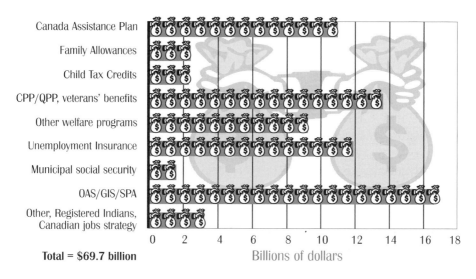

Total = $69.7 billion   Billions of dollars

Source: *Canada Year Book*, 1992, p. 190

Benefits of Modified Free Enterprise

The modified free-enterprise system has the same advantages as free enterprise: freedom of choice, efficiency, new products, and price competition. At the same time, it serves to lessen the limitations of free enterprise by distributing wealth more fairly and protecting consumers. Government intervention is intended to put community standards above the needs of any one industry or business.

Limitations of Modified Free Enterprise

High taxes on business have resulted in higher costs and higher prices to consumers. Some people believe there is a certain loss of freedom whenever there is government regulation. For this reason, some businesses may decide not to locate in a country where industry is regulated. Canada's modified free-enterprise system has affected the Free Trade Agreement with the United States: with our higher costs and prices, there is some doubt about our ability to compete with cheaper American goods.

POINTS TO REMEMBER

- The factors of production refer to the human resources, raw materials, money, and equipment that are used to to produce goods and services.
- The factors of production are classified into the following groups: land, capital, labour, technology, and entrepreneurship.
- Industry can be classified into three major categories: primary, secondary, and tertiary.
- All economic systems must decide (a) who owns the factors of production, (b) who decides what is produced, and (c) how profits and losses are distributed.
- Under a free-enterprise system, private businesses and individuals own the factors of production and profits, and make all decisions about what to produce.
- Under communism, the government owns all the factors of production and profits, and makes all decisions about what to produce.
- Under modified free enterprise, government joins business and individuals in the decision making and ownership so as to distribute goods, services, and profits fairly.

FOCUSING ON BUSINESS

15. What are the three questions you would ask yourself to help differentiate between economic systems?

16. Who owns the factors of production under the economic systems of free enterprise, communism, and modified free enterprise?

17. As a class, brainstorm the benefits of competition under free enterprise and modified free enterprise.

18. Do you agree that modified free enterprise helps to decrease the limitations of free enterprise? Provide examples to back up your ideas and then share them with the class.

19. How are decisions made about what to produce under free enterprise and modified free enterprise?

20. How does modified free enterprise attempt to regulate the amount of profit earned by business?

EXPLORING BUSINESS

21. In your local newspaper or a magazine, find an article that focuses on the regulation or restriction of business by government. Summarize the article and discuss how it demonstrates a modified free-enterprise system.

22. Visit a business in your community and find out:

    a. how the owner got started in the business

    b. the different capital items used in the business

    c. who provides the labour for the business

    d. the government regulations the owner must deal with (for example, minimum wage laws, GST payments, regulations regarding signs)

    Write a newspaper article summarizing your findings.

23. Your friend's parents operate a small retail clothing store in the local mall. They sell the same quality of goods as stores belonging to large chains, but they have difficulty competing because the big stores are so well known. Outline ways they can compete with the big stores and suggest how they should advertise.

24. Pilar operates a restaurant. Costs have been rising on all her supplies and business has not been good lately, but she has a plan. She will start to cut down on the size of portions she serves and raise her prices.

Because she has regular customers, she believes she will make a higher profit this way. Advise Pilar, using what you have learned in this chapter.

25. In small groups, identify five other businesses that could be considered as competition for a movie theatre. Come up with ideas about how the theatre could attract customers. Create a newspaper advertisement that the theatre might run. With the rest of the class, prepare a bulletin-board display of the advertisements.

26. In groups of two or three, visit at least three local stores, a large department store, a smaller specialty chain store, and a small independent store. For five different products — a stereo system, a personal computer, a package of ski equipment, canned spaghetti, and jeans — compare the brand names, prices, quality, service received in the store, and reputation.

    a. Organize your findings in chart form and create a bar graph to compare the different stores on the scales of price, quality, service, and reputation.

    b. Write a short essay of about 300 words listing the places where you would rather shop and explaining why.

WORKING WITH MATH

27. Marc's business earned $5000 last month. His expenses for the month included the following: rent, $800; utilities, $200; telephone, $50; salaries, $2000; and general expenses, $700. What is Marc's profit for the month?

28. Sally bought a CD that cost $20. If provincial sales tax in her province is 8 percent and GST is 7 percent, how much change does she get from $30? In some provinces, the taxes are calculated separately; in others, provincial tax is calculated on the price plus GST combined. Do your calculations based on the system in your province.

29. Study the graph on page 121 and calculate the answers to the following questions.

    a. What has been the change in the percentage of people employed in service industries from 1975 to 1990?

    b. Calculate the percentage of change for each year.

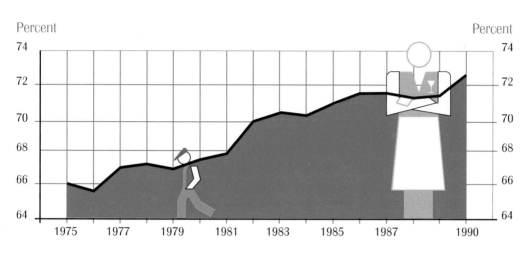

····· EMPLOYMENT IN SERVICE INDUSTRIES AS A PERCENTAGE OF TOTAL EMPLOYMENT ·····

Source: *Canada Year Book*, 1992, p. 417

KEY TERMS

economy

resources

economics

primary industries

secondary industries

tertiary industries

economic system

free-enterprise system

competition

communism

modified free enterprise

monopoly

The Role of Business in the Economy

THE ECONOMY OF CANADA IS MADE UP of the contributions of business, labour, and the government. In a modified free-enterprise system like Canada's, private individuals own property, take the financial and social risks of starting businesses, and keep most of the profits from successful business ventures.

Other private individuals work for businesses, providing the labour and the human resources. They earn money with which to buy the goods and services produced by business.

Governments at all levels participate in the economy. They may regulate business through environmental protection laws or minimum wage laws. Or they may take on the function of business through government-owned enterprises, such as public transportation, public utilities, or Canada Post, that meet specific needs of the population.

In this chapter, we will investigate the role that business plays in the economy, as well as how economic conditions affect the successful operation of business. The chapter includes a discussion of different roles played by profit in the long-term health of the economy. It moves on to a discussion of business cycles and how conditions in the economy, such as inflation, booms, recessions, and depressions, affect the functioning of business.

PROFIT

A business earns a profit when it has money left over after paying all its expenses: wages, the cost of supplies, taxes, and so on. **Profit** is the amount by which the revenue of a business exceeds its expenses. Many Canadians believe that business profits in Canada are high, and, indeed, some corporations are very successful. In many other businesses, however, especially small sole proprietorships and partnerships, profits are modest. Profits are necessary in a modified free-enterprise market economy. They provide the incentive for people to start businesses, and the taxes on these profits contribute in large part to the government programs Canadians enjoy. These reasons for being in business are discussed further below.

Incentive

Businesspeople, especially those who start their own businesses, are taking risks. Often, they have invested their savings in the venture without any guarantee of success. Without the compensation of earning a profit, businesspeople have no reason to invest their money. The potential for profit is the **incentive**, or motivation, which encourages business people to invest.

Return on Investment

People have choices about how to use their money, or capital. Some keep it in the bank, where it earns interest. Others invest in the stock market and earn dividends or capital gains. In order for people to choose to invest in a business, they need the possibility of earning the same **return on investment**, that is, the same amount of money as they would have earned using their money in other ways. Profit is the business investor's return on investment.

Efficiency

There are two factors affecting profit: revenues and expenses. We know that because of competition, prices cannot be raised as much as the owner might like, although prices generally do rise over time as businesses keep pace with one another. The other way to ensure a profit is to make sure that costs and expenses are as low as possible without affecting quality. The more efficient an operation, the more successful it is. Therefore, profit can be used as a measure of the **efficiency** of the management of, or the capacity to control, expenses within a firm. Efficiency can be improved with any combination of updated machinery and techniques, good workers, or good management.

Inconvenience stores

Effectiveness

A business that is not serving consumers will fail very quickly. Successful businesses are those that meet the needs and wants of consumers and that respond to consumer demand. Therefore, profit is also a measure of **effectiveness**, or success, in business and acts as a regulator by making sure that high-quality products are being provided at prices consumers are willing to pay. If the quality of the products drops or the price rises too high, people will no longer buy the products, thereby reducing profit.

Expansion and New Products

Once a business is established, its owners want to ensure that it grows and remains successful. This means updating equipment, finding new processes for manufacturing that are more efficient, and developing new products — in spite of the fact that these improvements are expensive. Since a business will not be competitive in the future if it is not expanding and developing, it needs profits to pay for new development. Thus, some of the profit made by business is used to expand the company, improve techniques, and develop new products. This in turn benefits consumers and employees.

Torpedo Inc. was a bankrupt maker of cribs, wooden furniture and toboggans until it introduced its line of premium-quality toboggans.

Contribution to Society

Business profits contribute to society in a number of ways. First, businesses, which need profits to survive, employ people. Furthermore, one business can support other businesses — its suppliers. This also increases the number of people employed. These employees and workers earn money that they can use to buy goods and services. The more money a society earns, the higher is its standard of living. A society's **standard of living** refers to the number of goods and services enjoyed by the members of that society as a whole.

Businesses in Canada pay between 25 percent and 40 percent of their profits to the government in the form of income tax. They also pay municipal property taxes. Tax money is the revenue of governments. It is used in many ways to improve the quality of life of Canadians. Hospitals, education, roads, and social programs are all funded by personal and business tax money. We will discuss the ways in which the government uses tax money in detail in Chapter 8. Businesses also spend money to support charitable foundations, the arts, and community programs, none of which would be possible if the businesses were not making a profit.

BUSINESS *in action*

FILLING A VACUUM

Five years after arriving in Canada from South Africa in 1971 with $2000, Gillian Smart and then-husband Paul Muser founded a residential construction and painting company in Regina. Business was good, except in winter. To avoid layoffs, Smart answered an ad seeking distributors. She turned down the manufacturer's offer to peddle pay toilets, but saw potential in his other product: central vacuum-cleaning systems.

Smart is still cleaning up. Her company, Beam of Canada Inc. (moved to Oakville, Ont., in 1979) practically created the Canadian market for central vacuums. And this spring, North America's largest central-vac manufacturer opened an office in New York State to begin exploiting the untapped U.S. market.

When Smart got her start, vacuum systems cost $1000 and sold mainly to builders of new, upscale homes. Seeing vast potential in retrofitting older homes, she designed lower-priced products and devised special ducting for existing homes. In 1982, Smart hoped to sell 42 000 vacuum systems within five years. By 1987 Beam had sold more than 300 000.

With sales of $30 million a year – 10 percent from exports – Beam now controls half the Canadian market. Smart says the turning point came with Beam's 1984 decision to make its products itself. "When you manufacture and sell your own products, you're far more in control," she says. "You can make the products you think your customers are looking for. And you're not carrying what everyone else carries."

Beam's biggest challenge came two years ago, after U.S. giant White Consolidated Industries bought Beam Industries Inc. of Iowa, an unrelated company that had supplied parts to Beam of Canada. In February 1990, White served an incredulous Smart with notice of a lawsuit for trademark infringement.

Smart thinks White expected her to crack under the pressure. Instead, she fought in court for 21 months. "Once the fight in you comes out," says Smart, "it's amazing what you can accomplish." She also played it safe, introducing a new vaccum line under the brand name "Smart." Last October the Federal Court of Canada ruled in Beam's favour — but Smart is keeping the new line anyway. "With our heightened efforts to establish the Smart brand name and fight off White's claims," she maintains, "we've actually increased our market share."

Profit Fluctuations

Profits may be higher one year than another for a number of reasons. If a company sells some real estate that has gone up in value, the profits for that year will seem high. Maybe it has just purchased another company that has shown a profit. If a company has recently introduced a successful new product, profits may be high until its competitors catch up or while consumer demand for something new is still high. This is often true of toys and games. Finally, the high profits of one year may be necessary to offset low profits for another year. To get an accurate picture of profits, one would have to follow a company for five or ten years to see its trend in corporate profits.

FOCUSING ON BUSINESS

1. Define *profit*.
2. What is meant when we say that *profit is an incentive to take business risks*?
3. Define *return on investment*. When is profit considered a reasonable return on investment for business owners?
4. What is meant by *profit as a measure of efficiency*?
5. Why is profit necessary for expansion and new product development?
6. Explain the role of profit as a contribution to society.

EXPLORING BUSINESS

7. Use your local newspaper or a magazine to find articles that discuss corporate (business) profits. Find three articles, explain why you chose each, then select one and answer the following:

   a. Briefly outline what the article is saying about profit. It may be about one company or about profits in general.

   b. Comment on whether the author believes profits are too high or not high enough. (A company may be thinking of going out of business because of low profits.)

   c. Identify which of the roles of profit is being discussed in the article.

8. Visit a local business and interview the owner. Try to find out:

   a. whether the profits are higher or lower than last year, and what he or she thinks the trend in the future will be.

   b. whether he or she is pleased with the return on the investment of time and money in the business, and the reason.

   c. what else the owner might do if he or she were not running this business.

9. Arno works for a sporting goods company and earns $35 000 per year. He works 40 hours a week, Monday to Friday. He has an idea for a sports-oriented business of his own that will require an investment of $40 000 in inventory. Arno would like to be self-employed, but he is not sure how to research starting his own business. Arno comes to you for advice since you are a business student. Using your knowledge about profit, prepare a report for Arno outlining the items he will have to consider.

10. Sharma is organizing a T-ball league for the neighbourhood children. The parents are interested, but the project will require money for uniforms, coaching, and refereeing. Sharma agrees to approach local businesses to see if they would be interested in sponsoring a team. Outline what Sharma should say when trying to convince the businesspeople to give money to her organization in order to sponsor a team.

11. In small groups, discuss various answers to the questions below. Appoint a recorder so your ideas will be written down, and a reporter to share your findings with the rest of the class.

   You learned in this chapter that profit or loss is the difference between revenue and expenses. What are the possible sources of revenue for a retail store that offers photographic services? What are the various expenses a store such as this might have?

MEDIA

You will be looking for part-time jobs in the near future and for a full-time job when you graduate. Many of you will attend college or university, and others will enter the work-force after high school. You know you must present yourself well and get the qualifications and experience necessary, but what are employers looking for?

1. With a partner, interview someone working in the field of media. Careers include news reporter, editor, writer, photographer, camera operator, disc jockey, and broad-caster. If you cannot find someone to interview, research the information using a resource centre. Find out the following information:

    *   which personal qualities are important

    *   what level of education is required

    *   importance of related experience

    *   hours of work

    *   opportunities for advancement

2. Create an advertisement for the career you have chosen, incorporating the information from your interview or research.

THE BUSINESS CYCLE

The **business cycle** refers to the fluctuations in the economy. Economies move from prosperity to inflation through recession, some-times into depression, and then to recovery. What all these terms mean and what causes this cycle will be discussed below. First, however, it is important to understand a key economic term: gross domestic product.

Gross domestic product (GDP) is the total value of all goods and services produced in a country over a given period of time, usually one year. The GDP is a measure of all the money contributed to a country's economy from all sources in that country, including foreign investment. It is the most widely used indicator of a country's economic perfor-mance and its position within the business cycle. Canada has one of the highest gross domestic products per person in the world.

Since the level of prosperity of every individual depends on the well-being of the economy as a whole, measures such as the gross domestic product help to define the standard of living for all Canadians. This does not mean that every person has the same amount of money or number of opportunities, but it does mean that as a group we enjoy a certain level of income, goods, and services because of the health of the economy.

THE BUSINESS CYCLE

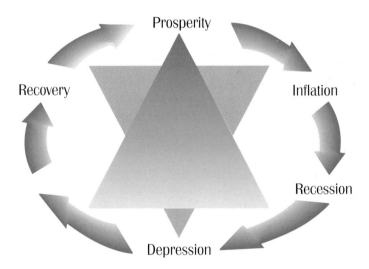

Prosperity

Good economic times are called periods of **prosperity**, or booms. During these periods, the economy is doing well, levels of employment are high, and workers are well paid. Prosperity affects everyone.

As businesses grow and flourish, other companies that supply them also experience prosperity. Businesses spend money on research and development and often expand their facilities to take advantage of the markets that want their goods and services. People start new businesses.

When people have jobs that pay well, they feel secure. They are willing to borrow money to make large purchases, such as houses. They are confident that their incomes will allow them to pay back the loans.

Society as a whole benefits from the demand for consumer goods. The increased amount of tax dollars from successful businesses mean that there is money for social programs, education, health care, and the arts.

THE CHANGING COST OF LIVING

According to the 1918 *Year Book*, a typical Canadian family – father, mother, and three children – needed about $20 a week for such basics as food, lighting, and rent. Of that total, food accounted for about half the expenses. Since then, some prices have gone up 1000 percent. In 1918, for example, a pound of cheese cost about 30 cents. Today, the equivalent (454 g) runs about $4.50. Similarly, a quarter pound (113 g) of coffee that costs about $1 today cost 10 cents back then.

Inflation

Prosperity is a good thing. However, when the economy is booming, prices tend to rise. We discuss supply and demand and how they affect prices in the next chapter, but for now we need to know that businesses are more than willing to supply more and more goods and services during times of prosperity, as long as they can increase their prices. This is not a problem when people are willing to pay the rising prices and they still have extra money to spend. Eventually though, the result is inflation. **Inflation** is an economic situation in which prices are increasing faster than the income of ordinary citizens. The value of money — what goods and services people can afford to buy — declines because wages do not rise as quickly as prices.

Businesses, too, feel the bite of inflation as the costs of their own supplies go up. In order to remain at the same profit level, businesses cannot allow costs to exceed revenues. As prices rise, people demand higher wages. It seems reasonable enough, because the cost of living is rising, but employers cannot afford to pay more if they are to remain profitable or to keep profits at the same levels. The result is that individuals, particularly those with lower incomes, cannot afford to buy the goods and services being offered for sale.

Recession

In a **recession**, the whole economy slows down. It no longer produces as much money as it did during a period of prosperity. A recession occurs for various reasons, usually as a result of a combination of factors. The government may be trying to fight inflation, or there may be a general shift in the economy. Businesses may be feeling under pressure because of increasing wages for their workers. When businesses can no longer afford to pay these higher wages, they reduce hiring and may eventually lay employees off. Individuals, in turn, become reluctant to spend their money freely because they are not sure their jobs are secure and because their incomes no longer keep up with the cost of living. As demand drops, so do prices (although usually not immediately). There is less money generally but those who are spending find their dollars go further.

You can begin to see the downward spiral that is created for the economy. As workers buy less, businesses lose income. Businesses, in turn, lay off more workers, and everyone feels more insecure. Both businesses and individuals pay less income tax because they are earning less income. This happens at the same time as governments need more income because more people need unemployment-insurance benefits and government assistance. The overall standard of living drops during a recession.

Since the end of the Second World War in 1945, there have been nine recessions in Canada. In our recent past, the 1981–1982 recession was followed by a period of economic growth until 1990. Consumer spending weakened in 1990, reflecting increased uncertainty over job prospects and high interest rates. For example, the rapid growth in housing demand came to an end. Labour market conditions also suffered in 1990. The 15-to-24 age group was the hardest hit by the rise in unemployment as firms reduced hiring.

TESTING-TIME

CONNECTING BUSINESS WITH HISTORY & ENGLISH

"In June 1936, when we could see we weren't going to get a crop that year, we gave up our farm south of Shaunavon. We should have left two or three years before, because that country then just wasn't worth farming. If you had no money and no crop and you weren't really farmers anyway, you finally had to get out.

"My husband, Alex, had a 1925 Durant [automobile] that hadn't worked for a couple of years and he towed it into Shaunavon with his team and he told me and the kids to stay put. He'd be back. He took the eldest boy, Dick, along to steer the car and they were gone two days. Then he came back driving the car and no horses. He'd got the car fixed and sold the horses for fifty dollars and paid off a few small bills we had and that was the end of Saskatchewan for us.

"I remember Alex drove into the yard with Dickie about eleven in the morning and nothing would do but that we leave right away. After living in that shack for about seven years, he wanted to leave in an hour or two. He meant it. The man was dead determined. He didn't want to have anything to do with it for another day and night.

"He had made a little trailer and that was hitched behind the car, piled with our things. The washing machine, the sewing machine, blankets, the tent, dishes, clothing, a couple of bedsprings, and I guess that was about it, and the food that Alex had bought in town with the fifty. I think we had about twenty dollars left.

"I asked what about the machinery and the harness and all the tools and the chickens and everything around, and he said to leave it. He'd talked with a man in Shaunavon and he'd come out and take it all away and sell it at an auction. He'd send the money to us at my husband's brother's house. You see, he'd had it all planned. I thought, we'll never see a penny. But, funnily enough, we did. That man sent us about eighty-five dollars a few weeks later. That wouldn't happen today. People were more honest then.

"In about three hours we were gone, and I can't say I looked back with tears in my eyes. That was what the Dirty Thirties did for you. There was no future in those days. Just day to day. You got by, but it wasn't living. No sir, not one bit."

A family during the Depression

1. How did the people in the story make ends meet after leaving their farm in Saskatchewan?

2. How did life in the Dirty Thirties test the survival skills of people? Give examples.

Depression

If a recession is severe or lasts a long time, it may become a depression. During a **depression**, economic activity is extremely low and unemployment is extremely high. So few people are able to buy goods and services that companies cannot stay in business. If an economy is allowed to grow so fast that inflation is steep and people use credit to buy goods and services, depression can be the result.

In a depression, the demand for government services is very high but, because the main source of government revenue is from taxes, social services suffer. The need for welfare and unemployment insurance rises sharply and cuts must be made from other areas such as health care, education, and so on. The quality of people's lives during a depression is often greatly reduced.

During the Great Depression from 1929 to 1939, so many people lost their jobs and so many companies went out of business that there was too little commercial activity to stimulate a recovery until the outbreak of the Second World War in 1939, when military demand stimulated industry to supply the war effort.

During the Depression, prices dropped to almost nothing, but even so, people could not afford to spend their limited money on anything but the most basic necessities. With demand so low, fewer and fewer goods were produced by a shrinking number of companies, which further contributed to the depths of the economy through the thirties.

Recovery

Eventually the business cycle must improve and a **recovery** begins. The fall in national income comes to a stop. There comes a time when individuals must replace clothing and other personal goods, and businesses start to replace worn-out machinery and equipment. After doing without for so long, people are interested again in spending. Businesses begin cautiously to produce a few more goods and services and to hire again. There is a new feeling of optimism and the economy starts to recover, although this is a slow process.

POINTS TO REMEMBER

- Profit is the money a business earns after paying wages, suppliers, taxes, and so on.
- Profits are necessary in a modified free-enterprise system because they provide incentives to businesses, measure a business's efficiency and effectiveness, finance research and development, and contribute to a country's standard of living.
- The business cycle refers to fluctuations in the economy and consists of prosperity, inflation, recession, sometimes depression, and recovery.
- Inflation occurs when prices are increasing faster than the income level of ordinary citizens.

FOCUSING ON BUSINESS

12. What does it mean if a country is experiencing prosperity?
13. What are the characteristics of a boom in the economy?
14. What is inflation?
15. At what point do increasing wages and prices become a problem for the economy?
16. What is a recession? How does a recession occur?
17. What is a depression? Why is it difficult to stimulate a recovery?
18. How does the economy eventually recover from a recession or depression?
19. What is the business cycle?

EXPLORING BUSINESS

20. Referring to the business cycle, describe the economic times in which we are currently living. Using television and radio news and newspapers for information, research the present state of our economy. Collect an article or news item that describes the economy, and answer the following questions:

a. Does the article indicate that we are in times of prosperity, inflation, recession, or recovery?

b. What is the evidence to support your answer to (a) above?

c. How is business behaving as a result of the current economic climate?

d. Write a one-page summary of an article or radio or television news program that dealt with the economy.

21. In small groups, create a questionnaire that you can use to interview people about their views on the economy. Include the questions below and add any other questions you wish to ask. Use the questionnaire to interview a local business person, a relative, or a neighbour. Compare your results with the results of the other members of your group. What conclusions can you draw?

a. Do you believe that today's economic times are those of prosperity, inflation, recession, or recovery?

b. What has been the role of the government in creating the current economic climate?

c. In your opinion, what should governments do to improve the standard of living for ordinary Canadians?

22. The employees of Acme Manufacturing Company are negotiating with the company for this year's contract. The cost of living has risen over the last year. If they are to keep pace with inflation and get a little ahead, the workers will have to receive an additional 8 percent increase in pay. Acme has not had a good year, however. It has lost several important contracts, and the costs of all its supplies and materials have risen sharply with inflation. The company feels that in order to stay in business, it will have to do one of two things: hold wage increases to a minimum or lay workers off. With a partner, role-play the negotiations between the company's and the workers' representatives. If you are the company official, what will you tell the workers? If you are the workers' representative, what will you tell the company's negotiators? With your partner, negotiate until you reach a compromise.

23. You are the owner of a small business. You have been able to maintain a certain level of profit during the last five years. Recently, however, sales have not been good. People in your community seem less willing to spend their money. Rumour has it that one of the local employers may relocate in the United States, putting 400 people out of work. What can you do to help make sales and stay in business?

24. Some people feel that in tough economic times, governments should provide social assistance in the form of welfare or unemployment

insurance to those who are unemployed. Other people feel that simply giving people money will not help. They believe that governments should instead spend money to create jobs or retrain workers who have been laid off. In small groups, discuss these ideas and record your views to share with the class.

25. "The profits of big business are too high. Look at the modest amounts ordinary Canadians earn. Business profits come directly from their pockets. If businesses paid higher taxes, governments could use the extra tax money to fund social programs. Ordinary people make businesses rich but business gives nothing back to these consumers."

In small groups, discuss the ideas presented in this quotation. Which do you agree with? Which do you disagree with? Record your answers to share them with the class.

26. Watch a current-affairs program on television that deals with the economy. It may be a single program or a series. Write a report, of approximately two pages, on the program. Include the following:

a. a brief description of what was said in the program

b. the beliefs about our economy that were presented

c. how the program dealt with the role of governments in improving our economy

d. how the program dealt with the role of consumers in improving our economy

WORKING WITH MATH

27. The Patel family has a combined income of $60 000 per year. The Patels have two children and own a home on which they pay a mortgage that amounts to 20 percent of their income. Their income tax is 25 percent of their income. Food and clothing cost them another 25 percent, and utilities and household expenses come to another 10 percent. They save 10 percent of their income.

a. How much money do the Patels spend per year on each of the expenses outlined above?

b. How much of their yearly income do the Patels have left to spend on other things than those listed above?

c. If the family income was to rise by 10 percent, how much more income tax would they pay?

28. a. Using the information below, create a graph and plot the changes in the gross domestic product for the given years.

Year	Annual Percentage Change in GDP	Year	Annual Percentage Change in GDP	Year	Annual Percentage Change in GDP
1970	2.6	1977	3.6	1984	6.3
1971	5.8	1978	4.6	1985	4.8
1972	5.7	1979	3.9	1986	3.3
1973	7.7	1980	1.5	1987	4.2
1974	4.4	1981	3.7	1988	4.7
1975	2.6	1982	-3.2	1989	2.5
1976	6.2	1983	3.2	1990	0.5

Source: Statistics Canada

   b. Look at the graph of the changes in gross domestic product and answer the following questions:

       i. In which years have the greatest increases occurred?

      ii. In which years have there been the lowest increases or decreases?

     iii. Based on your answers in (i) and (ii), when would you say the business cycle moved from prosperity to recession and then to recovery?

KEY TERMS

profit

incentive

return on investment

efficiency

effectiveness

standard of living

business cycle

gross domestic product (GDP)

prosperity (boom)

inflation

recession

depression

recovery

Demand and Supply

CHAPTER FOCUS

After studying this
chapter you will be
able to:

understand that the
market is made up of
goods and services
provided at a price

•

understand the
relationship between
demand and supply

•

identify the factors that
affect demand

•

identify the factors that
affect supply

•

explain the concept of
elasticity in economics

N THIS CHAPTER, WE WILL INVESTIGATE the factors of demand and supply in the economy. Consumer needs and wants play an important role in the economy. To be successful, businesses must be able to predict what consumers will buy and what price they will be willing to pay for it. In economic terms, businesses are willing to supply what the market demands at a certain price. Demand is affected by the personal incomes of consumers, so conditions in the economy affect both demand and supply. The interrelationship between demand and supply will be examined in this chapter.

WHAT IS A MARKET?

There is a market for any good or service that has a price (clothing, banking services, automobiles, housing) that consumers are willing to pay. A **market** exists wherever buyers and sellers come together, the buyers with money to exchange for the goods or services offered by the sellers. For example, the grocery store is a place where people who are interested in buying food can meet with a business wanting to sell it. The grocery store may be owned by one person or be part of a large chain of stores owned by a corporation. The foods on display have come from many different sources. Each supplier would have difficulty meeting with potential buyers on its own, so the market allows it to display the goods it offers for sale in a known location where buyers will come. The buyers, for their part, have the benefit of seeing a wide variety of foods so they can compare them and decide what they want.

The seller determines the price set for the food, but it is based on the belief that consumers will be willing to pay that price. If the price is too high, people will not buy the goods.

This independent food market offers a selection of fruits and vegetables from around the world.

There are two sides to the operation of a market: demand and supply. The decision to make a good or service available for sale is often made jointly by the consumer and the supplier. For example, pressure from environmentalists and awareness on the part of the public about the importance of protecting the environment have created a demand for more environmentally friendly products.

Demand is very high at low prices, but businesses are unwilling to supply at that level. On the other hand, at higher prices businesses are willing to supply more but consumers are more reluctant to pay. A balance must be reached between consumer demand at a certain price and business's willingness to supply at the same price. This balance is called **equilibrium**.

DEMAND

Demand is the consumer side of the market. **Demand** refers to the relationship between the price of a product and the quantity that the buyer needs or wants. Generally speaking, consumers are willing to buy more

Shoppers carefully examine goods on sale.

of a good or service when the price is low. This is referred to as the **law of demand**. For example, when compact disc players were first introduced into the market, they were fairly expensive and consumer demand was limited. However, as the price of compact disc players decreased, consumer demand increased.

The graph below illustrates the relationship between price and quantity demanded. You might remember when the cinemas decided to lower the price of admission one day a week. How did this decrease in price affect consumer demand? As you can see from the graph, consumer demand increased as the price of show tickets decreased. At a price of $8 a ticket, the quantity demanded is 2000, but at $4 a ticket, the quantity demanded is 3000.

·········· EFFECT ON PRICE OF A CHANGE IN QUANTITY DEMANDED ··········

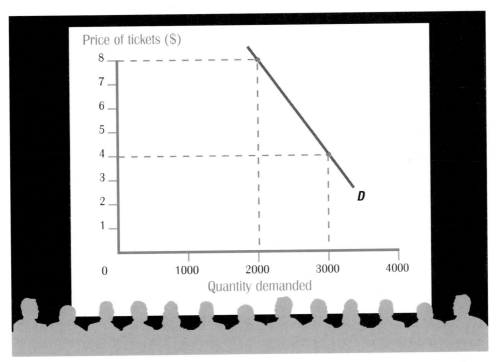

Consumer demand for a good or service can be affected by several factors other than price. These factors include the price of substitute products, the price of complementary products, consumer income, individual tastes and preferences, expectations about future prices, and demography. Each factor and the effect it has on the quantity demanded of a good or service is discussed below.

Price of Substitutes

A good that can easily be replaced by another good is referred to as a **substitute good**; examples are tea for coffee, pop for juice, and margarine for butter. Can you think of other examples of substitute goods? When the price of a good such as coffee increases, consumers will switch to a substitute good, such as tea. The result is an increase in the quantity of tea demanded.

Substitute Goods

Price of Complementary Goods

Two goods that are typically used with one another are referred to as **complementary goods**. Some examples are automobiles and gasoline, rackets and racketballs, shoes and shoelaces, and compact discs and compact disc players. Thus as the price of gasoline increases, the demand for gas-guzzling automobiles decreases. And as the price of compact disc players has decreased, demand for compact discs has increased.

Consumer Income

Generally, the more money consumers have to spend, the higher will be the general demand for goods and services. This is especially true of costly and inessential, or **luxury items**, such as swimming pools or vacations abroad. When incomes decrease, the demand for luxuries declines as well.

Consumers may also buy fewer of certain goods and services when their incomes increase. These goods are referred to as **inferior goods**. For example, if a consumer's income increases, he or she might buy less hamburger and more steak. In this case, hamburger is the inferior good.

Tastes and Preferences

Individual **tastes** and **preferences** — what consumers like or choose — also affect demand. Goods and services that were once popular have been replaced by others. Consumer trends, such as fitness, have influenced the demand for certain goods and services. Concern for the environment has produced a demand for many new products and services while decreasing demand for others.

Advertising has an influence on consumers, which encourages them to spend their money in specific ways. Advertising is aimed primarily at increasing consumer demand for a particular product. If a particular good or service is continually advertised in the media, the purchasing behaviour of individuals will likely be affected.

Governments have recognized the power of advertising to influence tastes and preferences. They have imposed regulations on certain types of advertising, such as advertising aimed at children under the age of 12. The federal government has banned television advertising of tobacco products altogether on the grounds that they harm the health of both users and bystanders.

Complementary Goods

BUSINESS *in action*

THE "ROOT" TO SUCCESS

You might think selling ginseng to China is akin to selling water to Canada, but Langley, B.C., entrepreneur John Latta says nothing could be further from the truth. His company, Chai-Na-Ta Ginseng Products Ltd., has been producing North American ginseng since 1982.

Latta first became interested in the root crop after attending a ginseng auction in Hong Kong in 1978. Stunned to see one wild root auctioned at U.S. $64 000, he says, "something just clicked." Research taught him that North American and Asian ginseng, a root that has been the key to Oriental medicine for more than 2000 years, are two distinct varieties, used for different purposes. Oriental philosophy says that ginseng balances Yin and Yang — the two forces that maintain the body's health. Asian ginseng works to balance the Yang, thought to be the strong hot force, while North American ginseng balances the Yin, the mild cool force.

Learning that North American ginseng is as much in demand in China as the Asian variety, Latta sought advice from growers in Marathon, Wi., the hub of the North American ginseng industry. Latta returned to southern B.C. where he planted two hectares of Canada's first ginseng. Today, Chai-Na-Ta has some 315 hectares of ginseng under cultivation, and 1992 revenues of $7 million.

Although Chai-Na-Ta was launched as a public company, Latta worked solely from his basement and truck, relying on a computer and portable phone, until the company grossed its first million dollars in 1988. Chai-Na-Ta now grows, processes and markets ginseng in capsules, slices and in root form, from seven farm sites in southern B.C. and Ontario, warehouse operations in Langley, a processing facility in China and a marketing company in Hong Kong.

Ginseng is now produced by about 90 growers in B.C., but Latta isn't worried about competition. Chai-Na-Ta's edge is its self-sufficiency in seed, which is hard to come by, and its distribution channels abroad. For Chai-Na-Ta, ginseng is indeed the elixir of life.

Expectations about Future Prices

If people believe the price of something is likely to rise in the near future, they are inclined to purchase it now. Many people purchased a home during the 1980s as rapidly increasing mortgage rates and housing costs drove prices up. Because they had borrowed at a lower rate, they reasoned that their investment would rise in value over time as the cost of borrowing continued to rise. Every time there is news of a price increase in gasoline, people immediately fill up their tanks to avoid paying the new price for as long as possible.

Similarly, when the price of goods or services is dropping, people are likely to put off a major purchase hoping to take advantage of the lower cost in the future. They hope to be able to gauge when the price is as low as it will go.

Demography

The study of the distribution of human populations using statistics is known as **demography**. As the size of the population and the characteristics of buyers change, so does consumer demand. An increase in population creates a greater demand for all goods and services, such as food, housing, clothing, and schools.

·············· CANADIAN POPULATION PROJECTIONS BY AGE GROUP ··············

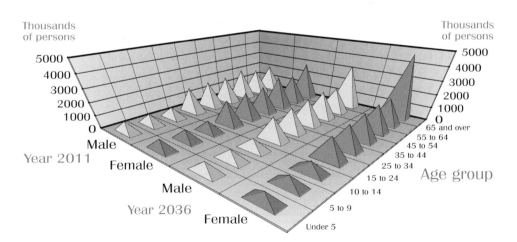

Source: Statistics Canada

CONNECTING BUSINESS WITH ENTREPRENEURSHIP

VAULTING AMBITION

"It's not a glamorous business," says Kaaydah Schatten.... "It's only a profitable business." Schatten, 34, is founder of Ceiling Doctor International Inc., ... a leading industrial ceiling cleaner. She has established 23 cleaning franchises in Canada, 50 in the United States, and has expanded to Japan, Ireland, Germany, Hungary, Mexico, Spain, Republic of Slovakia and Czech Republic. Schatten plans to expand further to include Brazil, the Netherlands, the Pacific Rim, Hong Kong, Indonesia and Korea. And business is still looking up. With her ... globe-girdling expeditions from a condominium on Toronto's lakeshore, Schatten ... is a symbol of achievement in a new field.

But what is more important to her is that she is a Native success — a poor girl from a reserve in Campbell River, B.C., who is now worth upward of $5 million. ... She hopes to inspire other Natives to pursue an entrepreneurial lifestyle. As John Kim Bell, founder and president of the Toronto-based Canadian Native Arts Foundation, puts it: "She is a very successful Native businesswoman and that is unique in our community."

Schatten has always been a go-getter. Born the second of six children ... at seven she was selling eggs to the "rich" of Campbell River, who, she noted, put their money into real estate. When her family moved to Nanaimo, B.C., at 12, she applied for a job in a real estate office. It paid peanuts, but she typed the offers and learned about mortgages. By 17 she was an honours student, working three part-time jobs and heading for success.

Then, in 1972, Schatten was thrown through the windshield of a car in an accident. She lost a hip and a lung and spent a year on her back — thinking. Her insurance compensation amounted to $7000, after legal fees. With this, her first real money, she bought a fourplex, improved it, remortgaged it and bought more property. By the age of 26, she had made her first $5 million on paper. But the federal government cancelled its multiple unit residential building (MURB) subsidy in 1981, and she lost nearly all she'd made....

Her experiences renovating properties led her to ceiling cleaning. Until 1968 there was no efficient way of cleaning acoustic ceiling tiles (which carry a replacement cost of $2 to $3 per 30 cm^2). When dirty, they had to be replaced. But then Clentech Acoustic Clean of Minneapolis invented a chemical method to rejuvenate tiles....

Schatten looked at several cleaning methods (including Acoustic Clean's) and decided they could be improved upon. She spent a year mixing chemicals with the help of a local chemist and searching for a suitable high-pressure pump to spray them in a mist. Then in 1983 she and her companion, Rob Forrest, ... headed for Toronto, where the bulk of the head office ceiling were.

They ... started the first Ceiling Doctor. For the first two years, [Forrest] and Schatten did all the cleaning themselves.

Schatten still owns the original business. When she's not managing her business, Schatten promotes Native rights. She is chair of the Canadian Native Arts Foundation, which provides scholarships, and is active in Native business associations.

1. How did Schatten come to realize that there was a demand for ceiling cleaning services?
2. How has Schatten expanded internationally?

Age also affects demand. Looking at Canada's population by age group over time, we can see that our population as a whole is "aging." People 65 years of age and older have become an increasingly larger proportion of Canada's population. Statistics Canada estimates that 16 percent of the population will be 65 or older by 2011, rising to more than 20 percent by 2013. Due to this trend and the fact that people 65 and over have different needs and wants than other age groups, many businesses are providing goods and services specifically aimed at this increasingly important consumer group.

Businesses also use demographics, or classifications of a population, to make decisions based on factors other than age. An entrepreneur is more likely to establish a farm implements store in rural Saskatchewan than in Regina. There is probably a larger year-round market per capita (per person) for ice cream in southern British Columbia than in the Northwest Territories. Advertising for blue jeans is more likely to be directed at Canadians under 35.

Many businesses are offering goods and services aimed at people 65 years and over.

FOCUSING ON BUSINESS

1. Explain in your own words what is meant by a *market*.

2. What are three consumer buying trends that have developed over the last few years? Think of three services consumers have demanded in response to these trends.

3. What is meant by the term *substitute good*? Suggest substitute goods for potato chips, blue jeans, and domestic cars.

4. What is the law of demand? How is consumer demand determined?

5. Describe a situation in which your choice of goods was affected by price.

6. In each of the following situations, identify which one of the factors affecting demand is being demonstrated: price, price of substitute goods or services, price of complementary goods or services, consumer income, tastes and preferences, expectations about future prices, or demography.

   a. Because of the number of elderly people in your area, you start a business shovelling snow.

   b. While shopping in a store, you notice a new pesticide that is not harmful to plants or animals.

   c. Due to an early frost, oranges from Florida have doubled in price, so you choose grapes from Chile.

   d. You read in the newspaper that resort owners are complaining of a poor season and see that gas prices have risen in your neighbourhood as well.

   e. Shoppers at the local mall are flocking to a store that sells designer clothing because of a half-price sale.

   f. You hear on the radio that the housing market is picking up after the announcement that interest rates will drop.

7. How can businesses use advertising to influence the spending behaviour of consumers?

EXPLORING BUSINESS

8. Using the newspaper, find articles relating to demand events in the economy. Choose one and summarize it briefly. How do you know the article discusses demand? What is the relationship between price and demand in the article?

9. Politicians at all levels of government are continually dealing with issues in the economy. Visit the offices of your member of parlia-

ment or your provincial representative and find out how that level of government is responding to consumer demand for government services such as health care or welfare assistance. Find out how demand has changed recently and how government is responding to this demand.

10. Sarah works as a computer programmer in a medium-sized company. Her husband, Doug, is also employed, and they have two small children. Day-care has always been a hassle for them. Sarah and Doug agree that their quality of life would be much better if one of them could take the children to day-care in their workplace. Sarah decides to find out how many other people at her work are in this position.

    a. How can Sarah and Doug learn whether there is any demand for day-care at their places of employment?

    b. What factors of demand are likely to affect day-care?

    c. Who should supply the day-care?

    d. What benefit is there to the company in providing day-care for its employees?

11. Just after the holiday season, two clerks in a retail store are discussing the amount of high-quality designer clothing that was not sold at the regular price. One wonders if the store did not stock the kinds of clothes that consumers wanted to buy that year. The other points out that, when the clothes went on sale, there was much consumer interest.

    With a partner, role-play the above scenario. Discuss different reasons that consumers did not buy the clothing at regular prices. Use everything you know about demand and prices.

12. Form groups of three or four. For each factor of demand, brainstorm four examples of consumer behaviour in the economy; for example, expectations about future prices — drivers filling up their gas tanks when there are reports about the rise in gas prices.

    Share your findings with the class.

13. Suppose the student council in your school decided to look into holding a dance. They want to be sure before they commit themselves that people will come to the dance.

    In groups of three or four, discuss the following:

    a. How can the student council find out if there is demand for a dance?

    b. How will they decide what music to have? What price to charge?

    c. What should they do to inform the student body of the dance in order to ensure success?

EXPLORING YOUR OPTIONS

Your choice of career is one of the biggest decisions you will make in your life. It should be done with a lot of thought and planning. Although security and income must be considered, it is also very important to enjoy what you are doing, so that you can reach your personal potential by developing and using your skills and abilities. Enjoying a career that fits your interests can mean as much as or more than the money you earn.

1. Visit your school guidance office and arrange to use CHOICES or other available career computer software. These computer programs are designed to help you learn what careers might be suitable for you based on your temperament and ability.

2. Once you have the results from using the career software, choose a career that interests you and research it using your resource centre and guidance office. Prepare a report on the career. The report can be written or presented as a poster.

SUPPLY

If demand is one side, the other side of the market is the supply side. **Supply** refers to the quantity of goods and services that sellers are willing or able to offer consumers. The relationship between the price of a good or service and the quantity offered for sale is called the **law of supply**. From studying the law of supply, we know that as prices rise, the quantity supplied tends to increase. In turn, as prices fall, the quantity supplied typically decreases.

The graph on the next page illustrates the relationship between supply and price. In general, the higher the price a supplier can get from consumers, the more of the product the supplier will make available to the market. Suppose that the prices disc jockeys are able to charge for their services rise from $500 to $800 per evening of five hours. More people will be willing to provide disc jockey services at $800, so the supply of these services will increase.

·················· EFFECT ON SUPPLY OF A CHANGE IN PRICE ··················

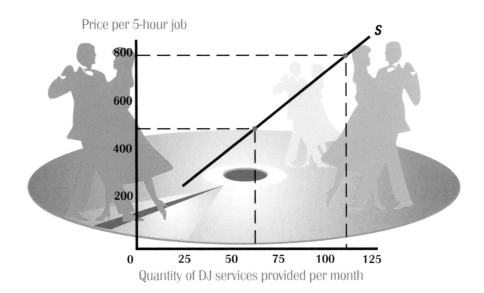

When the price of a good or service is low, the time and cost of bringing that product to market may be too high compared with the price that will be paid for it. In this case, suppliers drop out of the market. In recent years, the cost of wheat farming has become so high relative to the money farmers have been able to make that many farmers have stopped growing wheat and may have stopped farming altogether.

We learned that consumer demand for a good or service can be affected by several factors other than price. The same holds true for supply. The factors affecting supply include production costs, changes in technology, owner's desire, and weather conditions. Each factor and its effect on the quantity supplied are discussed below.

Production Costs

There are many costs associated with supplying a good or service. Some of these are raw materials, rent, wages or labour, interest payments, equipment, and taxes. A change in any of the costs can affect supply. Labour is one of the highest costs a supplier incurs. A wage increase to employees leads to an increase in the cost of supplying the product. In such circumstances, a supplier may be willing to continue supplying the market only if the selling price of the product is increased.

Changes in Technology

Changes in the type and efficiency of machinery available often influence the supply of a good or service. The introduction of computers into the workplace has had a profound effect on every aspect of industry. Word processors and facsimile machines have altered the office completely. Robotics and other computer applications have irreversibly changed production, inventory control, and information systems. An improvement in technology usually causes the cost of producing goods to decrease and producers to increase the quantity supplied. Producers will want to produce more goods because they save money by using the new technology. The saved money leads to higher profits.

Technology has dramatically changed the automotive industry.

Owner's Desire

Many people assume that most goods and services are supplied by people and businesses whose sole aim is to make money. In fact, people start businesses for a variety of reasons. Some want to be their own boss. Others have an innovative idea and want to try it out. Still others want the control and flexibility of being an entrepreneur.

Although all businesses must ultimately make some profit in order to

THE BUSINESS OF BASEBALL

The game of baseball has been played for over a century. During this time, it has undergone many changes, such as the breaking of the colour barrier in 1948 by Jackie Robinson. Other innovations have included night baseball, the lowering of the pitcher's mound, relief pitching, designated hitters, expansion, and domed stadiums. Another kind of change has occurred in the economics of baseball and other major league sports.

The salary structure of major league baseball is a result of several elements. Lucrative television contracts have made baseball as much a business as it is a sport. Free agency has enabled players to share these riches; they can market their services to the highest bidder. Gate receipts are determined in large part by how successful a team is. A winning team brings lots of fans to the ball park to cheer on the stars who have made it possible. The players have reasoned correctly that because they are earning high returns for the team owners, they deserve their "cut" of revenues from the sale of tickets. Court decisions finding owners guilty of collusion (an illegal secret agreement) have further increased salaries. Finally, player agents, paid a percentage of the contracts they negotiate, have pushed player salaries to unusually high levels.

It is, in economic terms, a matter of supply and demand. The leagues keep expanding, boosting the demand for professional quality players. This, and the pressure to hire the very best in order to have a winning team, means that the demand for qualified players is extremely high. The supply of baseball players at this level, however, is low. These factors combine to make seven-figure salaries the equilibrium price for major league baseball players today. If a team is unable or unwilling to pay players these salaries, or if they are unhappy with anything else that may be happening in the organization, they simply go to another team that will meet their demands. After the Toronto Blue Jays won the World Series in 1992, for example, the team virtually disintegrated because many of the key personnel were free agents. Being world champions enabled them to command very high salaries and put them in the driver's seat in contract negotiations. Finally, the playing career of a professional ballplayer is limited. In a field where you are old at 35, supply is even further restricted.

In a sport filled with statistics (ERA, BA, slugging percentage, fielding percentage, RBI, OBA, etc.), salary figures have become unreal. During 1991 the average major league salary skyrocketed by a record 49 percent to $891 188 on opening day,

April 8, 1991 (by contrast, elsewhere in the economy the luckiest workers got raises of 5 percent, while many had to settle for 0 percent!). That's the average! On those opening days, 223 players made in excess of $1 million, 123 players topped $2 million, and 32 players made over $3 million. On opening day of 1990, Robin Yount of the Milwaukee Brewers reached the $3-million mark. All these salaries are annual and often are part of long-term guaranteed contracts that increase over time. Recently, Boston Red Sox pitcher Roger Clemens signed a four-year contract for $21 million, which works out to more than $5.38 million per year. Every time he throws a pitch, he earns $2000! In one year, Clemens will earn more than four times what the average worker will earn in a lifetime. Others are not far behind: Dwight Gooden of the New York Mets, Darryl Strawberry of the Los Angeles Dodgers, José Canseco of the Texas Rangers, Jack Morris of the Toronto Blue Jays, and the list goes on and on. This phenomenon is true not only of baseball. Hockey, football, and basketball players are also winning seven-figure contracts.

1. What do the salaries of baseball players say about our social values and priorities?

2. Explain how supply and demand for top baseball players have led to such huge salaries.

survive, these various reasons for going into business affect supply; for example, although it may be more efficient and profitable for everyone to buy clothes from one central clothing outlet, people will continue to open small, specialized boutiques because they want to sell the clothes they like and to be in charge.

Weather Conditions

Weather conditions are critical to the supply of agricultural goods to the market. Extreme wet or dry conditions may decrease farm output. A decrease in the quantity supplied will result in higher prices. Similarly, if the crop is larger than usual, due perhaps to ideal weather conditions, the farmers may have to reduce their selling price. Weather conditions are, of course, beyond the control of producers.

•••••••••••••••••••••••••••••••• ELASTIC DEMAND ••••••••••••••••••••••••••••••••

ELASTICITY

As we have seen, both supply and demand are affected by price. It is generally true, for example, that the higher the demand, the higher the price consumers are willing to pay and the greater the amount suppliers are willing to provide at that price. Similarly, the quantity demanded of a product increases as the price falls. However, while these relationships hold true, they do not affect all goods at the same rate. Some price changes will affect consumer purchasing behaviour more than others. This is called **elasticity**.

Elasticity of Demand

An **elastic demand** is one in which a small change in the price of goods or services results in a large change in the quantity demanded by consumers. Goods and services that have elastic demand usually include luxuries, such as vacation packages and airline transportation.

Goods or services that can be easily substituted for other goods or services typically have an elastic demand; for example, a slice of pizza from one fast-food outlet can easily be substituted by a hamburger from another outlet. If one holiday package to Jamaica increases in price from $429 to $529, consumers will either buy another package whose price has remained stable, or they will not buy a vacation package at all.

If the quantity demanded of a good or service does not decline to a great degree when the price changes, then it is considered to have **inelastic demand**. Most necessities, such as milk, and other foodstuffs, such as bread and potatoes, have an inelastic demand. If the price of milk increases substantially, the quantity demanded will not be greatly affected since it is considered a necessity by many families. Products with few substitute goods often have inelastic demand. Gasoline is another example of a good with an inelastic demand since it is a product for which there are no substitute goods.

INELASTIC DEMAND

Elasticity of Supply

If a seller can quickly adjust the quantity supplied when the price changes, the good or service has an **elastic supply**; for example, if the price of a manufactured good drops, suppliers are able to cut back their supply to the market until the price increases. In the 1970s, oil from the Middle East could be imported at a price lower than domestic oil, so American producers restricted the amount of oil they produced in order to raise the price. They accomplished this by capping oil wells in Texas to restrict the flow of domestic oil and gasoline. This reduced supply and made gasoline prices rise at the pumps.

If a supplier cannot adjust the supply of the good or service quickly in response to a change in price, then it is considered to have an **inelastic supply**. An example of inelastic supply would be when the price of an agricultural good drops. In this case, suppliers cannot adjust their supply accordingly because of perishability and storage problems.

POINTS TO REMEMBER

- Demand for goods and services is affected by price, substitute products, complementary products, income, preference, expectations about future prices, and demographics.
- Supply of goods and services is affected by price, production costs, changes in technology, owner's desire, and weather conditions.
- A market exists where there is a meeting of buyers and sellers of goods and services who agree through negotiation on the amounts of products that will be sold at a given price.
- Demand and supply for some goods and services is affected more by changes in price than are supply and demand for other goods and services. This is called price elasticity.

FOCUSING ON BUSINESS

14. Define the concept of *supply* in your own words.
15. Explain how demand and supply interact to produce the right amount of goods at the right price.
16. Give five examples of the costs involved in supplying the market with a product or service.
17. For each of the following situations, identify the factor of supply that is being demonstrated: price, production costs, changes in technology,

owner's desire, weather conditions.

a. A store that has been in your neighbourhood for years is going out of business because the competition is charging less than your neighbourhood store can.

b. Electronic calculators are now being given away as gifts; they used to cost hundreds of dollars.

c. A manufacturer warns that increased taxes could result in layoffs.

d. An infestation of insects has destroyed the coffee crop in Colombia.

e. Alan says that he does not care how hard he has to work at his doughnut franchise, it's better than the job he left.

18. Explain in your own words the concept of *elasticity*.

19. In groups of three or four, discuss the answers to these questions. Record your answers, then share them with the class.

For each of the following indicate whether the demand is elastic or inelastic with respect to price and why:

a. steak   c. car repairs
b. school supplies   d. diamond rings

20. In groups of three or four, discuss the answers to these questions. Record your answers, then share them with the class.

For each of the following say whether you think the supply would be elastic or inelastic with respect to price and why:

a. cars   c. natural gas
b. blue jeans   d. pet food

EXPLORING BUSINESS

21. Interview a local retail store owner. Ask him or her the following questions about supply:

a. Who is/are your supplier/s?

b. How many other suppliers are there and how did you choose the one/s you use?

c. How often do you have to order, and when are the goods delivered?

d. Are you able to return goods not sold at the end of a certain time period?

e. How often do the costs of your goods change?

Analyze the information you have gathered. In groups of three or four, compare your findings. Create a chart showing these results and present it to the class.

22. Examine newspapers or magazines for articles about the supply of goods. Select an article and mount it on a sheet of paper. Write a brief comment indicating which factor, or factors, of supply is/are being illustrated and the reasons you chose this factor or factors. As a class, create a bulletin board display of your articles.

23. Filomena and Armand want to go to the baseball game, but when they phone for tickets, they are told that the game is sold out. They decide to go to the stadium anyway, where they see scalpers selling tickets outside the gates at five times the usual cost.

    a. How did the scalpers get the tickets in the first place?

    b. What price did they pay for them?

    c. Explain in terms of demand and supply why the scalpers are now able to charge five times their usual value just before the game begins.

24. You are a summer camp counsellor. It is your job to organize the food for the upcoming barbecue. There will be hamburgers and hot dogs served to the 100 children registered at the camp. With a partner, work out a system to predict the quantities the camp needs to buy in order to satisfy everyone's needs, but not have a lot of leftovers. Share your system with the class. What conclusions can you draw about predicting demand?

25. In Canada today there is said to be a shortage of people to fill some careers, while there is a great deal of competition for other careers. Skilled labour is one area where there is a shortage. Skilled labourers are those trained specifically for a trade such as carpentry, plumbing, die casting, or auto mechanics. In groups of three or four, discuss the following proposals that offer suggestions for dealing with the shortage of skilled labour. Think of both benefits and disadvantages of each proposal. Choose a recorder and a reporter. Report the results of your discussion to the class.

    a. Canada should import skilled workers through immigration.

    b. Canadian schools should direct students into these occupations in order to ensure an adequate supply of skilled labourers.

    c. The government should force unemployed workers into training programs for these occupations.

26. At a factory, the workers are worried that there will be many layoffs in the near future. They have heard that management is considering buy-

ing a computerized production system to replace 50 people currently doing the production job.

Form groups of three or four to discuss this problem and answer the following questions.

a. What factors of supply are affected in this case?

b. What has probably caused the company to consider this change?

c. What options may be open to the workers at this plant if the company goes ahead with the plan?

Choose a recorder and a reporter. Write down the answers you come up with, and report these answers to the class. Individually, write the discussion as a newspaper article.

WORKING WITH MATH

27. Students in the cafeteria were willing to buy a total of 600 hamburgers per week at the price of $2.50. The cafeteria wants to know what will happen to the demand for hamburgers if the price is increased. Through research, the management believes that if the price of hamburgers goes to $3, students will buy 10 percent fewer hamburgers per week. Calculate the revenue from hamburgers at $2.50 and at $3. Should the cafeteria proceed with this price change?

28. Due to price increases from suppliers, a small manufacturer has seen the cost of raw materials go up by 25 percent in the last two years. Costs used to be $100 000 to produce 120 000 units. The selling price of these goods was $3.35 per unit. In addition, there were other expenses that ran consistently at about $100 000 per year. Because the demand for this product is highly elastic and because the competition is aggressive, prices cannot be raised. Calculate the difference in profit in this business before the costs rose and after the costs rose.

KEY TERMS

market	luxury items	law of supply
equilibrium	inferior goods	elasticity
demand	tastes	elastic demand
law of demand	preferences	inelastic demand
substitute good	demography	elastic supply
complementary goods	supply	inelastic supply

PART 3

Government, Labour, and Business

CHAPTER
8

CHAPTER FOCUS

After studying this
chapter you will
be able to:

identify the three levels
of government and
outline the economic
responsibilities of each

•

identify services
provided by different
levels of government

•

describe the different
kinds of taxation as
sources of revenue
for governments at
all levels

•

identify and discuss
governmental issues
arising from taxation
and the provision of
governmental services

Government
in Canada

ANADIANS HAVE ONE OF THE highest standards of living in the world. We have stable governments at all levels — federal, provincial, and municipal. As a result, we enjoy a wide variety of services provided by these governments.

What are some of the services you use every day? When you send or receive mail, you are using the postal service called Canada Post. We have good roads that are ploughed in the winter and maintained in the summer. Flip the switch and the lights come on. These services and many others are provided by governments. The money to pay for them and to pay the salaries of those who work to make sure these services are available comes from taxes on individuals and on businesses.

When businesses decide where to locate, they must consider a number of factors. One factor they consider is which government services are available in their desired location; for example, most businesses, especially manufacturers, need good roads or railways to transport materials. All businesses use public utilities such as water and electricity. It would be inefficient and costly for competing private businesses to provide these services, so they are provided and regulated by the government. In this way, one company provides the service to everyone, and because there is no competition, the cost to individuals is controlled by government.

The availability of good health care and education systems is also important to companies because they need to hire well-educated, healthy employees. Public transit systems help employers by providing employees with a reliable way of getting to work.

In this chapter, we will examine the three levels of government — federal, provincial, municipal — the goods and services they provide, and their sources of revenue. Finally, we will explore issues that concern the public and that we read and hear about daily in the news. These issues include taxation, social assistance, unemployment insurance, welfare, workers' compensation, and pensions.

FEDERAL GOVERNMENT

All governments in Canada are governed by the Canadian Constitution. The constitution was originally set forth in the British North America Act in 1867. In 1982, its name was changed to the **Constitution Act, 1982**. It outlines the responsibilities of each level of government.

Canada Post is a Crown corporation.

The Canadian federal government is located in Canada's capital, Ottawa. It has responsibility for any services that affect the whole nation or that overlap two or more provinces. It is responsible for regulating banking as well as for the military, external affairs, postal services, some taxation, social assistance plans, natural resources, and energy.

These are services most appropriately handled by one elected body — imagine each province providing its own army! In addition, the federal government is in charge of criminal law and all international matters.

Elected representatives do not actually operate government departments but, instead, concern themselves with enacting the laws of our country. Government services provided by full-time government employees are collectively called the **civil service**. These people are not elected, so they continue to work in government jobs even though the governments may change.

As discussed in Chapter 3, the federal government also owns or controls several large businesses known as Crown corporations. Crown corporations provide goods and services that are considered essential for the country as a whole. Canada Post and Via Rail are both Crown corporations.

·········· TOP FEDERAL GOVERNMENT EXPENDITURES, 1990–1991 ··········

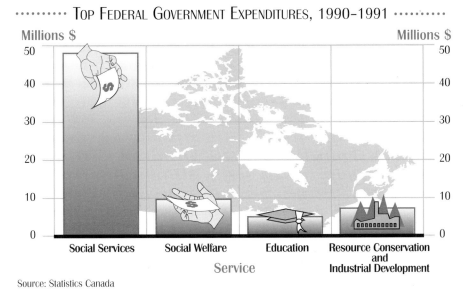

Source: Statistics Canada

PROVINCIAL GOVERNMENT

Health care and education are the two major areas controlled by the provinces. Responsibility for major highways and laws governing municipal affairs are also handled by provincial governments. In addition, provincial governments enact laws concerning provincial matters and collect taxes, such as sales taxes and income taxes, which are used to finance provincial services.

Provincial governments act through their **legislatures**, or places where representatives write laws, which are located in the ten provincial capitals. The Yukon and Northwest Territories have legislative councils but their powers are more limited than provincial legislatures; the federal government is responsible for the administration of these territories.

Canadians enjoy one of the best health-care systems in the world. Each province has its own government-supported health-care plan, but they all provide the same services, such as those of physicians and specialists, for the maintenance of good health and for the diagnosis and treatment of illness and injury. Also included are hospital care and laboratory services ordered by physicians.

The services offered in walk-in clinics are covered by the health-care system.

Some services that provincial plans do not cover may be covered through private health insurance. Examples of such services include semi-private and private hospital rooms, cosmetic surgery, and acupuncture. As yet, no public health-care system covers dental care. However, many Canadians are covered for dental care through private insurance plans subsidized in part or in full by their employers.

All provincial governments tax their residents to pay for their health-care systems. (Taxes will be discussed in more detail later in this chapter.) Some provinces take the money from general revenues. Alberta and British Columbia charge a premium — a small amount per resident to cover health-care costs. Ontario charges a payroll tax to pay for health care; each business must pay to the government an amount based on the money it pays to its employees.

Education accounts for one of the largest provincial expenditures. Policies are made provincially about standard elementary and secondary school programs to ensure that students throughout each province have access to the same standard of education. Provinces also provide much of the money to pay for education in local areas. The rest is provided by local municipalities through property tax.

MUNICIPAL GOVERNMENT

Local political areas such as cities, towns, townships, counties, and districts are called **municipalities**. They are run by elected councillors, aldermen and alderwomen, and education trustees, who make policy decisions about local issues that most affect us every day. They also have the authority to levy property taxes on landowners in order to finance the services that the municipalities provide.

Municipal services include police and fire protection; public transit; garbage collection; the collection and treatment of sewage; snow removal; the provision and upkeep of roads and sidewalks; parks and recreation; and building inspection, zoning, and planning. The appearance and character of each municipality is, in many ways, determined by the decisions made by the municipal government.

···· TOP THREE PROVINCIAL AND TERRITORIAL EXPENDITURES 1990-1991 ····

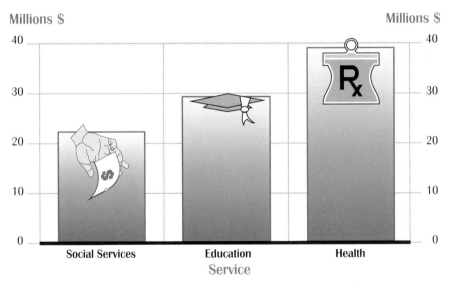

Source: Statistics Canada

SOURCES OF GOVERNMENT REVENUE

All government programs — federal, provincial, and municipal — cost money. The main source of revenue for all levels of government is taxes, which are paid by individuals and businesses. Taxes can take different forms; some of the most common are discussed on the next page.

A municipal worker cleans recycling bins.

Income Tax

Canadians pay a number of different kinds of taxes. Those who are employed pay **income tax** on the amount of money they earn. Income tax is a **progressive tax** because the rate increases as the amount earned increases. Thus, people with lower incomes not only pay less tax, but they also pay a smaller percentage of taxes on their income. Businesses also pay income tax. **Corporate income tax**, the tax paid by a corporation is a **flat-rate tax**. This means that over a certain level of income all corporations pay the same rate of tax. Income taxes are paid to both the provincial and federal governments.

·············· TOP LOCAL GOVERNMENT EXPENDITURES 1989 ··············

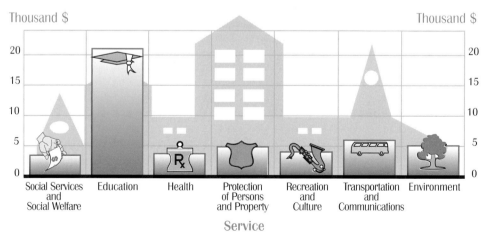

Source: Statistics Canada

BUSINESS WITH COMMUNITY

NEIGHBOURHOOD FOOD CO-OP

Rosemary Dooley, 33, found it degrading to depend on a food bank at the end of every month to feed herself and her two sons. Separated, without child support, and struggling on social assistance, she felt financially trapped. Rent and electricity bills devoured 75 percent of her monthly allowance. The remaining $300 was for food, clothing, and transportation.

"How," she asked three of her single-mother friends, "could we stretch our food dollars?" They decided to pool their food budgets and approach local food wholesalers. With the discounts that come from bulk buying, a family of four could eat for $45 a week, compared with $115 at a supermarket.

Dooley bargained with food wholesalers listed in the Yellow Pages. As coordinator of the newly formed nonprofit Parkhill Food Co-op, she requested food price lists and asked how much they had to buy to get delivery. Then, armed with $180, she ordered a week's food for the four families.

The first shipment arrived in Dooley's living room in November 1990, and the women pitched in to measure, weigh, and reparcel cases and sacks of fresh produce, flour, sugar, grains, frozen foods, and dairy products. Within three months, new co-ops were springing up, and Dooley was placing $7000 in collective monthly orders for 400 families and training nine new coordinators.

The co-op now comprises a dozen families and owns a scale and a meat slicer. Dooley updates price lists on a second-hand computer in her kitchen, distributing copies to members for a cost-covering fee of $1.

"Food isn't an issue any more," says Dooley. Not only are there savings, but better nourishment means better health for both children and adults.

1. What kind of government service is Rosemary Dooley receiving?
2. How has Dooley ended her family's reliance on food banks and helped other families as well?

Property Tax

A major revenue source for municipal governments is taxation of property. People who own property must pay **property tax**. Tenants pay property tax through their rent. In return for property taxes paid, residents receive the benefit of municipal services such as police, fire protection, roads, and education. Utilities such as electricity and water are also provided by the municipality and are usually paid for separately by home owners.

Sales Taxes

In addition to property and income taxes, most Canadians must also pay a retail **sales tax** on most of the goods and some services they buy, from automobiles to haircuts, clothing to entertainment. Sales taxes are provincial taxes, and rates and the goods and services taxed differ from province to province; Alberta levies no retail sales tax.

Goods and Services Tax

The **goods and services tax (GST)** is a federal sales tax. It was introduced on January 1, 1991, as part of a sales tax reform. It replaced an

Canadian citizens opposed the introduction of the goods and services tax.

older tax, called the federal sales tax (FST). The FST was added to the price of Canadian products when they were manufactured. Because consumers did not see the tax added at the check-out counter, they were often unaware that they were paying it. For this reason, it was called a hidden tax.

The GST is similar to the retail sales tax collected by most provinces in that consumers pay it on almost all purchases. It differs from provincial taxes in that it is added to services; for example, lawyers, car mechanics, and accountants, who previously were not required to pay FST, must now charge the GST.

The government refunds —through tax credits— the GST paid by manufacturers and retailers because the GST is a tax on the consumer. The government also gives GST refunds to low-income individuals.

FOCUSING ON BUSINESS

1. With a partner, brainstorm three services provided by each of the federal, provincial, and municipal governments.

2. What benefit is there to making health care a provincial matter rather than a local responsibility?

3. Postal service is a federal jurisdiction in Canada.

   a. Why does the federal government, rather than provincial or local governments, handle postal services?

   b. Should private business be allowed to operate postal services? What would be the advantages and disadvantages of this?

4. Using the information below, create a pie graph to illustrate how municipalities spend the monies received. What are the top four expenditures?

Education	40%	Recreation and culture	6%
Transportation and		Health	5%
communication	11%	General services	5%
Environment	9%	Social services and	
Protection of person		social welfare	4%
and property	8%	Other	5%
Debt charges	7%		

EXPLORING BUSINESS

5. Since 1985, local governments have increased their spending on the environment by 63 percent. With a partner, conduct research to find out what your local government is doing about environmental issues. Share your findings with the class.

6. Obtain copies of a national newspaper and a local newspaper. Read the newspapers and select at least five articles on matters concerning each level of government — federal, provincial, and municipal. Then organize the facts and briefly summarize the issues.

7. Form groups of three or four. Each student must provide his or her findings from question 6 above (the lists of national, provincial, and local issues from the newspapers). In groups, compare your lists. Take each list and put the items into categories given below.

Federal: national unity, the economy, the world

Provincial: health, education, the economy

Municipal: police, social services, quality of life (e.g., parks and recreation, aesthetics, zoning that regulates height of buildings, etc.)

Record your findings and display them in the classroom. Choose one article from each category. Identify the issue and say why this is an issue. What is your opinion regarding this issue?

8. a. With a partner, interview two people in your community: a businessperson and someone who is not in business. Ask them what concerns them most at the federal, provincial, and municipal levels of government. Ask them to rank their concerns in order of importance. Record their answers.

   b. Form groups of three or four pairs. Each pair should provide its findings from the interviews. Compare your results and record them under the following headings:

Federal Issues	– businessperson
	– non-businessperson
Provincial Issues	– businessperson
	– non-businessperson
Municipal Issues	– businessperson
	– non-businessperson

   c. In a class discussion, compare the concerns of the businesspeople and the people not involved in business about each level of government. Do businesspeople have different concerns from those of others?

9. At the time of the provincial election, Lei-Lei says to Karen that she will probably not vote. She goes on to say that she votes only in municipal elections. Her reasoning is that it is really only local issues that affect her directly, so why should she waste her time. "Anyway," she adds, "I don't like any of the candidates in my area."

   As Karen, write an article for the school newspaper responding to Lei-Lei's statement.

10. On a radio talk show, local businesspeople are phoning in to complain that they are required to pay too much income tax, while at the same time they have to pay minimum wages to workers and health-care tax to the provincial government. "After all," says one of them, "it's not as though we get anything out of it." The local member of the provincial legislature is a guest on the show. With a partner, write the responses of both the caller and the guest, then role-play the conversation.

GOVERNMENT PROGRAMS

Few people like to pay taxes. None of us appreciates giving up part of our income. We look at the potholes in the streets and wonder where our property taxes went. We grumble at the check-out counter as sales tax and GST are added to our bill. Why do Canadians pay taxes?

Canadians elect governments to provide services they cannot provide for themselves. Government is "the keeper of the public good." But people do not always realize that deciding to spend in one area means, first, that the money must come from somewhere, and, second, that this money is no longer available to spend on something else.

As part of Canada's mixed economy, all levels of the government provide services to help people who are unemployed, have injured themselves in the workplace, or generally need more help than they are able to provide for themselves. The basic assumption that Canadians make is that all residents of this country have the right to a certain standard of living. It is felt that the price of not having social assistance programs would be destitution, poor quality of life, higher crime rates, and an uncertain future.

Social Assistance

Each province operates its own social assistance program through its tax system and with money that the federal government transfers to the

CAREERS

SUPPLY AND DEMAND FOR JOBS

1. As a class, brainstorm a list of the careers that interest the class. Appoint a recorder to write the list on the board.
2. For each career you listed, refer to the charts above and determine whether related jobs and industries are growing or declining.
3. What are the possible consequences of choosing a career for which there is little demand but a great supply of workers?
4. What can be done for people who are working in declining industries?
5. What can you do now to increase your career opportunities for the future?

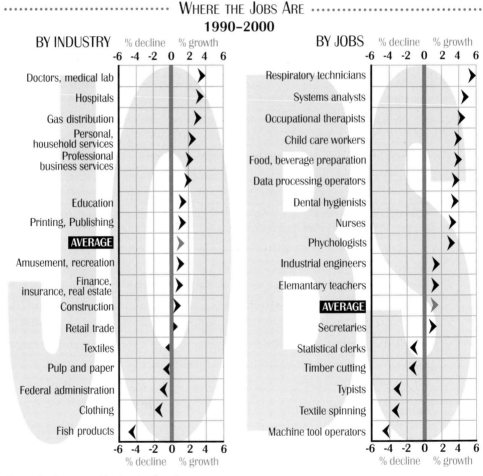

Source: Employment and Immigration Canada

provinces. **Social assistance** is money to cover the cost of food, shelter, fuel, clothing, and other essentials for people who are in need. Services such as job training, counselling, and extended health care may also be covered by social assistance.

Social assistance is paid for by income taxes and sales taxes. Its recipients might be people who are unable to find work and whose unemployment benefits have run out, workers injured on the job, or single parents for whom the cost of day-care is too high. Social assistance ensures that everyone has a minimum standard of living and is sometimes referred to as a "safety net."

Unemployment Insurance

The first **unemployment insurance (UI)** benefits were paid in 1942. Before this, people relied on local charities if they needed help after losing their jobs. Today, every worker must pay unemployment insurance premiums. Employers also pay into the UI fund, a federal program, at a rate 1.4 times that of workers. Any employee who is left jobless after working a specified length of time may collect unemployment insurance to a maximum amount. Unemployment benefits can equal a maximum of 57 percent of a person's wages and may last for one year.

Maternity benefits are also covered by unemployment insurance. Women are entitled to 17 weeks' paid leave after the birth or adoption of a child, and either parent can take an additional 10 weeks of paid parental leave.

Some employees resent the UI deduction from their pay cheques, and businesses find that the payments add to their costs. But, like all insurance plans, people need unemployment insurance when they are unemployed, and no one knows for certain if he or she will ever be out of work.

In poor economic times, there is a sharp increase in the number of people who are unemployed, putting a strain on the fund. But insurance of any kind must be paid out, and Canadians as a society have made the decision that they need this kind of protection.

Welfare

A benefit available to those who cannot work or whose unemployment benefits have run out is called **welfare**. It is funded through a combination of provincial and municipal taxes.

Welfare usually does not pay much, but it is often the only income people have. Some single parents find themselves with no alternative to

UNEMPLOYMENT INSURANCE

In 1914, injured workers, widowed mothers, and the elderly were all granted government aid, but in the midst of the Great Depression, jobless Canadians still had no legislative protection. In 1933, one out of every three Canadian workers was unemployed and had nowhere to turn.

More than 20 percent of the population barely survived on local "relief rations." Some of the country's 2 million unemployed cut wood or broke rocks in local poorhouses for a bag of groceries or bucket of coal; others drained swamps and built roads for 20 cents a day in government work camps.

Until the early 1920s, Canada was still a rural society. The family was the major source of social security. Private charities helped if necessary, but people generally did not look outside their community for aid.

Changes occurred as the Second World War approached. Forty-four percent of the men chosen for selective service were rejected due to poor health, and the government began to accept the unemployed as its general responsibility.

In 1942, the first unemployment insurance benefits were paid; a single person could receive $14.40 per week, and a person with dependents, $18.30. By contrast, in 1989 the average weekly payment was $215.88. Across Canada, these benefits totalled more than $11.5 billion for 1989.

Source: *Canada Year Book*, 1992

welfare because the cost of day-care can be almost as high as the amount of money they could earn in a job.

As with all social welfare programs, welfare costs Canadians in tax money, but the social cost of not helping the jobless is considered to be higher.

Workers' Compensation

Over 1 million Canadians are injured every year in work-related accidents. Many of these injuries are serious enough that the people need time away from work to recover or for a stay in hospital.

Provincial workers' compensation boards pay millions of dollars every year in workers' compensation, a sum paid by the employer to the victims of workplace accidents. This money comes from insurance that the employer pays. In return, the worker gives up the right to sue the employer for negligence. It is another benefit that people often do not appreciate paying for until they need it. Very few workers can afford to be without their pay cheques as they recover from injury. The fact that employers pay higher premiums if their workplaces have a higher number of accidents has also encouraged employers to provide safer working environments.

BUSINESS *in action*

WINNING GOVERNMENT MONEY

With federal and provincial funding programs offering billions of dollars worth of loans, grants and assistance, you might think that all businesses need to do is ask governments for money. But as cash-strapped governments tighten their belts, prying funds loose is becoming harder and harder.

Governments are insisting that entrepreneurs meet tougher standards before getting money, says Eve Giannini, business development and marketing manager in Ernst & Young's entrepreneurial services group in Toronto. The easy-spending attitutdes of the '80s are gone, she says, and governments are now demanding that entrepreneurs undertake a high level of financial commitment themselves before they'll put up public money.

David Rodger, communications director of the Science Council of B.C. in Vancouver, says that when it comes to government money, there are no handouts. "We're looking for an economic payback to the province," he says, "job creation, excellence in science and technology, and innovation."

Governments also look for companies that can best meet their specific criteria, says Giannini. So it's important to eliminate potential hurdles before you apply for assistance. She recommends breaking projects into small parts, identifying specific needs and targeting programs designed to address those needs.

Your plan should also demonstrate that the project won't get off the ground without government funding. In some cases you may be asked to show you've already tried to go the route of private financing.

Pensions

The Canada Pension Plan is available to all Canadians over the age of 65 with the exception of residents of Quebec, who receive money from the Quebec Pension Plan instead. Both employers and employees contribute 2.2 percent of the employees' eligible earnings. The employees' contribution is deducted from his or her pay cheque.

Old Age Security (OAS) is another type of government pension program. However, OAS is based on length of residency in Canada rather than amount contributed. In addition, a person might receive a Guaranteed Income Supplement if he or she receives little or nothing at all above the OAS pension.

There are also private pension plans set up by employers, and registered pension plans that people pay into themselves. To encourage people to buy Registered Retirement Savings Plans (RRSPs), the federal government allows contributions to be deductible for income tax purposes. This encourages Canadians to plan for their own retirements.

All social assistance programs are costly to individual taxpayers, employers, and the government. Naturally, people want to pay as little in tax as possible. However, as a country, we have also decided that we want and need to have these programs in place. There is always discussion about ways to improve these systems so that those who really need it are given help, while not increasing taxes too much.

POINTS TO REMEMBER

- Canadians use many public services that are provided by governments through the use of tax dollars.
- The federal government is responsible for the military, external affairs, postal services, banking, some taxation, social assistance, natural resources, and energy.
- Provincial governments are responsible for health care, education, laws concerning provincial matters, the collection of sales tax, some income tax, local public works such as roads, and the provincial police.
- Municipal governments have jurisdiction over local laws and by-laws, property taxes on businesses and individuals, police and fire protection, public transit, garbage collection, sewage, snow removal, roads, parks and recreation, building inspection, zoning, and planning.
- Sources of governmental revenue are sales tax, goods and services

tax, income tax, unemployment insurance and Canada Pension contributions, transfer payments, licensing, and fines.

- Tax money must be raised to pay for programs such as unemployment insurance, Canada Pension, welfare, and workers' compensation to supplement direct payments by employers and employees.

FOCUSING ON BUSINESS

11. Explain the following taxes:

    a. income tax

    b. property tax

    c. sales tax

    d. goods and services tax

12. What are unemployment insurance benefits? Who is eligible for them?
    Who pays unemployment insurance premiums? What level of govern-
    ment is responsible for unemployment insurance?

13. Why has the federal government decided that it is valuable as a public
    good to pay maternity benefits to Canadian workers?

14. What is welfare? What level of government is responsible for welfare?
    Who is entitled to receive welfare?

15. What is the Canada Pension Plan? Who is eligible to receive it?

EXPLORING BUSINESS

16. On a recent radio talk show, a caller complained that too many people
    were abusing the unemployment insurance system. He laughingly
    referred to it as "working for the government." With a partner, discuss
    and record possible abuses of unemployment insurance. How would
    you decide who "deserved" unemployment benefits? Share your ideas
    with the class.

17. Using the newspaper, find one article on each of the following topics:
    social assistance, unemployment, welfare. Summarize each article.
    Report on one of the articles to the class.

18. Interview two people from your community — a businessperson and a
    non-businessperson. Ask them the following questions about taxation:

    a. Do you agree with the level of benefits received by Canadians
       (unemployment insurance, welfare, pensions, health care)? Why?

b. Do you believe that individual Canadians pay too much, too little, or just the right amount of tax? Why?

c. Do you believe that Canadian businesses pay too much, too little, or just the right amount of tax? Why?

d. How can Canadians continue to receive the necessary amount of social benefits without increasing taxes?

What conclusions can you draw from your interviews? Share your findings with the class.

19. With a partner, debate the following motion:

Only people who have no other source of income should receive Canada Pension.

Consider the following points:

Canada has an aging population. Will there be any money left in the fund when those who are now paying retire?

Should people who have paid into the fund all their working lives receive nothing back for their contributions?

Should taxes be raised to pay for higher Canada Pension costs?

20. Indira works in a retail store. Business has not been good. Hakim, a customer, believes that the goods and services tax (GST) is to blame for the slow sales and complains that the store is making a huge profit because of the GST. "People see that extra 7 percent being added at the cash register and believe that the price of everything has gone up," he says. "Everybody knows that stores are getting rich because they can claim the GST they paid on their purchases." Indira points out that the GST has, in fact, lowered many prices, since it replaced the old federal sales tax. She says, "People weren't aware of the old tax because it was hidden." Take the role of Indira and respond to Hakim about retail prices and GST rebates.

21. A group of doctors and nurses are talking in the hospital where they work about the high cost of health care. One person says that it is wrong to deny anyone proper health care. On the other hand, the cost is getting so high that services are being reduced and beds closed in hospitals that are already crowded. Someone else suggests that if people who use the health-care system were required to pay a small user fee, it would bring money into the system and cut down on unnecessary visits. "It could work," says a third, "but it would have to be done very carefully."

In small groups, brainstorm as many solutions to the health-care funding crisis as you can. Present your solutions to the class.

22. On a recent television talk show, a politician expressed the view that in order to help the economy, the tax system should be reformed. All individuals and corporations should have to pay at least a minimum amount of income tax.

    When questions were taken from the audience, someone suggested that taxes should be paid on all business profits over a certain amount, because businesses have huge profits and consumers have less and less to spend.

    In groups of three or four, discuss the following questions and present your findings to the class.

    a. Should corporations pay a minimum tax? Why or why not?

    b. What problems would business face if all profits over a certain amount were taken as taxes?

    c. Should corporation taxes be assigned for services that benefit business?

    d. Should corporations be forced to provide benefits to employees, which the government currently provides, such as health care?

23. In Canada, businesses pay property tax to municipal governments. This money goes to pay for all local goods and services. Education is the largest single item in both the municipal and provincial budgets. You read an article in which some businesspeople say they resent having to pay for the education system. They feel that as individuals they pay personal taxes and thereby support the education system, but as businesses they don't feel they should have to. "After all," the businesspeople said, "it's not as though companies have children in school!"

    In groups of three or four, discuss the views expressed above. Should corporate property taxes pay for education? What benefit does business obtain from the education system? How else could business and industry contribute to education?

WORKING WITH MATH

24. a. Create the table below using a spreadsheet program. Calculate the average unemployment insurance benefits for the years 1984–1989 paid out for the *regular*, *sickness*, and *parental* categories.

    b. Compare the results from (a) and create a line graph to illustrate how they have changed over this period.

Year and month	Benefits paid (thousand dollars)		
	Regular	Sickness	Parental*
1984	8 825 126	204 559	398 989
1985	8 975 315	220 770	436 376
1986	9 209 882	242 065	476 693
1987	9 076 420	278 693	510 791
1988	9 309 381	325 159	571 384
1989	9 846 725	356 501	637 109

* Parental includes persons receiving maternity, paternity, or adoption benefits.
Source: *Canada Year Book* 1992, p. 164.

25. Yorgos goes to the store and buys the following articles: pants $59.95; shirt $39.95; and two CDs at $14.98 each. Every item is subject to PST of 8 percent and GST of 7 percent. How much change will Harvey get from $160? Use your province's method of calculating the GST.

KEY TERMS

Constitution Act, 1867

civil service

legislature

municipality

income tax

progressive tax

flat rate tax

corporate income tax

property tax

sales tax

goods and services tax (GST)

social assistance

unemployment insurance

welfare

workers' compensation

Labour and Business

CHAPTER FOCUS

After studying this chapter you will be able to:

explain the history of labour unions in Canada

·

describe the negotiating process between unions and management

·

outline the collective bargaining process

·

identify the issues arising in the collective bargaining process

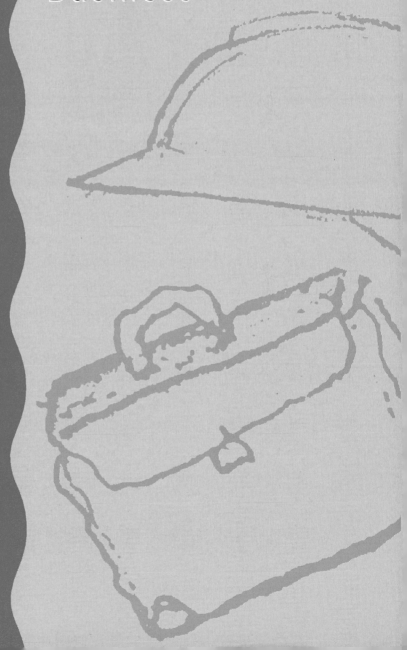

OST PEOPLE IN CANADA HAVE JOBS IN which they are employees of private companies or of the government. They trade their knowledge, skills, and labour for the money they need to live. They must bargain with their employers to get a fair return for the time and dedication they give to them. The employers, in return, receive the profits from selling the goods and services their employees have produced. Some employees join worker associations called unions, or organized labour. In this chapter we will explore the history of unions, how they work, and some of the issues surrounding organized labour.

UNIONS

Workers have found that by banding together they have more power when dealing with their employers. This is called forming a union. A **labour union,** or trade union, is an association of workers who practise a similar trade or who are employed in the same industry and whose purpose is to improve their wages, hours, working conditions, and other matters. Unions negotiate contracts with employers called **collective agreements**. About 30 to 35 percent of working Canadians belong to a union. Non-unionized workers must negotiate as individuals with their employers for raises and benefits. In turn, employers may have policies in place to guide these negotiations.

Why do workers form unions? What is the history of the union movement? These questions are answered below.

Canadian Labour History

Unions have existed in Canada for a long time. Although unions were not legalized in Canada until 1872, the earliest recorded Canadian trade union was a printers' organization formed in 1827 in Quebec City. Other unions followed in Toronto in 1832, and in Hamilton and Montreal in 1833. By 1850 there were approximately 35 unions in British North America. Early unions were local associations made up of groups of skilled workers, such as bakers, carpenters, tailors, and printers. However, by the 1860s and in the following years, more and more Canadian members belonged to unions with their headquarters and most of their membership in another country.

The first association of unions was the formation of the Toronto Trades Assembly in 1871. In 1872, the Toronto Typographical Society, an association of publishing houses, was faced with union demands for a nine-hour working day rather than the usual ten- to twelve-hour day. The publishers rejected the union's demands and the workers went on strike. Many union committee members were arrested since unions were considered to be illegal. The arrests led to wide protests and to a call for political action to legalize unions.

The labour dispute over unions led Sir John A. Macdonald to introduce the Trade Union Act. It also resulted in victories for the nine-hour movements as the Toronto printers won their demands.

Because Canada's early unions were associations of skilled labourers, unskilled labourers had no one to represent them. In fact, the early trade unions, called craft unions, often opposed representing unskilled workers. They wanted to ensure that their members retained special status.

The Knights of Labour formed two assemblies composed entirely of female shoemakers.

In 1881, a United States-based union called the Knights of Labour came to Canada. It wanted to organize all types of skilled and unskilled labourers. Within a decade, there were over 300 local assemblies of the Knights of Labour.

In 1883, unions from across Canada banded together and formed a national labour organization called the Canadian Labour Union. In 1886 it changed its name to the Trades and Labour Congress of Canada (TLC).

In 1902, the TLC expelled all organizations that were not craft unions, including the Knights of Labour. These unions eventually joined with others and in 1927 formed the All-Canadian Congress of Labour (ACCL). In 1940, the ACCL became the Canadian Congress of Labour (CCL).

During the Great Depression, unions met with strong resistance in fighting for better wages and working conditions. However, the union movement made it through the Great Depression and the Second World War. In 1956, the Trades and Labour Congress and the Canadian Congress of Labour joined together to become the Canadian Labour Congress (CLC).

Canadian Labour Unions Today

The rate of growth in labour unions since the 1950s has slowed after the tremendous growth in membership in the first half of the century. Although union membership as a whole is greater, especially with the organization of public-sector workers into such unions as CUPE (Canadian Union of Public Employees) and PSAC (Public Service Alliance of Canada), the percentage of Canadian workers in unions has not risen greatly. There are several reasons why this might be.

Since the 1960s, Canada has shifted from having a manufacturing-based economy to a service-based economy in the 1970s and 1980s,

RIGHT TO STRIKE

Canadians indirectly won the right to strike in 1872 with the passage of the Trade Union Act, which recognized the legality of trade unions. The Act followed the famous Toronto printers' strike of the same year, when more than 100 workers stayed off the job for almost two months, eventually winning better wages and a 54-hour work week. Despite the new Act, however, picketing remained illegal in Canada until 1934.

Canada's most famous strike was the Winnipeg General Strike of 1919 when 22 000 workers from a wide variety of trades, including firefighters and police, walked out mainly for better wages to combat the inflation that followed the First World War. The strike ended violently after a charge on protesters by the North-West Mounted Police left one dead and thirty injured. In the confusion that followed, federal troops occupied the city.

Canada's largest strike occurred in Quebec in 1972, a century after the Toronto printers' strike. The provincial government, hospitals, and schools all faced walkouts by a united group of public-sector unions.

In 1989, more than 2 million person-days were not worked because of major work stoppages, down from nearly 7 million in 1980.

The Winnipeg General Strike of 1919

and more recently to an information-based economy. Traditionally, unions represented factory workers, who have declined in number because of the shift in the economy and the increase in automation. In addition, more women have entered the work force, and although some have become factory workers, most have joined the service sector.

With the organization of public-sector employees, as well as retail and clerical workers and other white-collar workers and professionals, the face of unionism has changed.

Wages, hours, and working conditions were the original issues of unions, and retail and clerical workers still have a long way to go in these areas.

Attempts at organizing groups not traditionally represented by labour, such as retail and clerical workers, as well as bank employees, have met with limited success. Newer unions of this nature have not had the bargaining power of trade unions, and more recently the trend has been for large, traditional unions to organize these groups. This has worked better, since the older unions are backed by the full membership, which collectively does have the necessary leverage with management. Office workers at Inco (International Nickel Company), for example, are organized by the United Steel Workers.

With the introduction of labour legislation, government has co-opted the historical mandate of unions. Some believe that with such things as minimum wages, working conditions, and hours of work now being legislated, unions have out-

The British Columbia Nurses' Union represents its members in negotiations regarding wages, hours, and working conditions.

lived their usefulness. Unions, however, continue to pursue new issues, such as affirmative action, worker benefits, and better job security, especially as computerization of manufacturing and clerical work has resulted in lower demand for labour. Labour legislation is meant to ensure a minimum standard for the workplace. Unions can now turn their attention to other social issues affecting workers.

The Canadian Auto Workers fund a public awareness campaign against family violence.

Economic conditions influence contract negotiations. During times of prosperity, workers receive raises and benefits, but during a recession, workers may be laid off or have their wages frozen. Many companies, both large and small, have financial troubles, and workers are realizing that the trade-off to a large wage settlement may be layoffs or even plant closures.

Union settlements have helped to raise the standard of living of all workers, which in turn have given Canadians more money to spend on the products of business and the economy. However, not everyone believes that unions are beneficial. Although non-unionized workers

·················· UNION MEMBERSHIP IN CANADA, 1971–1990 ··················

Year	Union membership '000	Non-agricultural paid workers '000	Membership as a percentage of civilian labour force	Union membership as a percentage of non-agricultural paid workers
1971	2231	6 880	26.6	32.4
1972	2388	7 052	27.6	33.9
1973	2591	7 327	29.1	35.4
1974	2732	7 769	29.5	35.2
1975	2884	8 102	29.9	35.6
1976	3042	8 238	30.5	36.9
1977	3149	8 400	30.9	37.5
1978	3278	8 538	31.2	38.4
1979*				
1980	3397	8 816	31.2	38.5
1981	3487	9 495	30.1	36.7
1982	3617	9 775	30.4	37.0
1983	3563	9 402	29.9	37.9
1984	3651	9 408	30.2	37.9
1985	3666	9 626	29.8	38.1
1986	3730	9 888	29.8	37.7
1987	3782	10 219	29.7	37.0
1988	3841	10 519	29.5	36.5
1989	3944	10 891	29.7	36.2
1990	4031	11 147	29.9	36.2

* No survey was conducted in 1979.

Source: *Canada Year Book*, 1992, p. 159

have benefited from the actions of unions, many people believe that strike action by unions hurts the economy. Higher costs of labour increase the cost of goods and services generally, and consumers feel

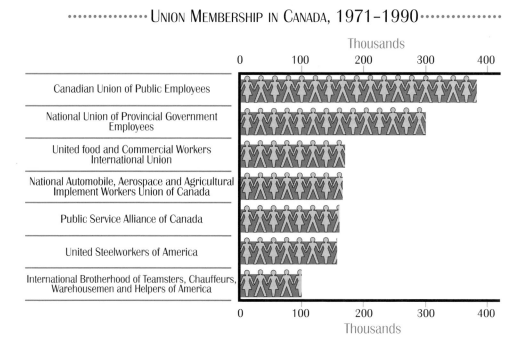

·················· UNION MEMBERSHIP IN CANADA, 1971–1990 ··················

this every time they buy something. In order to afford the wage increases and not raise prices beyond what consumers will pay, business must take less in profits.

Many employers, particularly small-business owners, are against unions. They feel they have taken financial risks and want to be in control of all aspects of their businesses, including how much they can pay for labour.

Perhaps a balanced partnership between labour and management best protects the interests of both. Workers are protected from the arbitrary actions of management, while companies are able to avoid expensive labour disputes. Some companies have discouraged their workers from unionizing by offering wages and benefits comparable to those currently being won in union settlements. In this way, workers do not have to pay membership fees, known as **union dues**, or be subject to the rules and regulations imposed by union executives.

FOCUSING ON BUSINESS

1. Why do people join unions?

2. Explain why workers might be able to negotiate more effectively through a union than they could on their own.

3. What were the members of the first unions most interested in winning from their employers?

4. Why are white-collar workers and professionals now finding that they may want to join a union?

5. Explain why wages and working conditions are no longer the only causes in which unions are involved.

6. How does the economic climate affect union demands and the probability of success?

7. What factors may have contributed to a poor public image of unions?

8. Explain why business owners might not be happy about their workers joining a union, and describe what they may try to do to keep a union out.

EXPLORING BUSINESS

9. a. With a partner, interview two people in your community: a union member and a non-union member. Ask them the following questions and record their answers:

   - Are unions too powerful?

   - Are unions good for the economy?

   - Do companies tell the truth about what they can afford to pay their workers?

   - Do unions hurt the consumer?

   - Do unions do a good job representing their members?

   b. Form groups of three or four pairs. Each pair should provide its findings from the interviews. Make two lists of comments, one from the union members and one from non-union members. (If two or more people gave the same answer, write the comment down only once.)

   Can you reach any conclusions about what union members think as opposed to non-union members? Have one group member record these conclusions on chart paper.

   c. Each group should present its conclusions to the class.

10. You are talking with a friend about the ways in which business and labour can get along better. Your friend suggests that one way to make it easier to deal with unions would be to have a law stating that all workers have to receive the same raise each year no matter what. After all, your friend says, there are minimum wages. Why not have the same raise for everyone too? This would make everyone equal.

    Respond to your friend's idea. How would unions likely receive this suggestion? How would business receive it? Write your answer as if it were a newspaper article.

11. Organize a debate on the pros and cons of unions in today's economy.

- Pro-union argument
- Unions are beneficial to the economy and necessary to the well-being of Canadian workers.
- Anti-union argument
- Unions have served their usefulness and are now hurting the Canadian economy.

Form groups of six. Each group divides into two sides, one to present the pro-union argument and one to present the anti-union argument.

Each side will prepare the arguments supporting its view.

Get together with another group of six. One group will present its arguments and one group will observe. In this way:

   a. The three members of the group presenting the pro-union side put forth their views.

   b. The three members of the group presenting the anti-union side put forth their views.

   c. Each side has a chance to ask questions of the other side.

   d. The group observing the presentation evaluates the debate and declares which side has been more persuasive.

   e. The observing group delivers its debate for the presenting group following the format outlined above.

CAREERS

HOW DO SCHOOL COURSES RELATE TO CAREERS?

Obtain a copy of your school course calendar. Examine the courses offered by each department. Select one course from each department and outline, in a two-page report, how the course is important and what careers you think would require the knowledge and skills taught in the course.

UNION ACTIVITY

Provincial governments are responsible for labour practices in their provinces. It is illegal for businesses to prevent workers from unionizing by threatening them with dismissal. On the other hand, while trying to organize workers, unions are not allowed to interfere with the running of the business. Also, there are regulations in place to ensure that workers who do wish to join a union are represented by the union of their own choosing.

Certification of a Labour Union

Once employees have decided that they want to form a union, they must be **certified**, or accredited, by the government. The union must either have a certain percentage of the employees in a business sign union cards, or hold a vote. Fifty percent of eligible workers must vote in favour of the union for it to be certified.

Once a union is certified by a provincial labour relations board, the employer must negotiate a contract with the union for all the employees represented by the union.

Collective Bargaining

The **bargaining unit** is the smaller branch of each union, which addresses issues in individual factories or regional areas. These units engage in **collective bargaining**, which means that all the union members of the local bargaining unit negotiate as a group with the employer to determine wages, hours, and other conditions of employment. The union appoints a negotiating team that represents its interests, as does the employer. The union presents its demands. The employer also has a

These demonstrators are protesting delays in pay equity negotiations.

proposal of what it is prepared to offer the workers. In a successful bargaining process, an agreement is eventually reached, with each side giving up or modifying some of its demands until both feel they have done the best they can under the economic circumstances.

When the negotiators have reached an agreement that they believe their members might accept — a tentative agreement — the union members vote on it. This approval process is called **ratification**. A tentative agreement may be rejected by the workers if they feel it does not give them the minimum they wanted. The agreement will cover many points. Some of these are wages, overtime, holidays, hours of work, casual labour, benefits, working conditions, and the length of time covered by the contract. For example, workers may be demanding a raise in wages as well as **income protection**, which assures them that their wages will keep up with an increase in inflation or the cost of living. Thus, they might get a 5 percent wage increase with a Cost of Living Allowance (COLA). This means that if the cost of living rises by 6 percent, they will get the 5 percent raise, plus the 1 percent difference so that their wages keep up with the cost of living.

Another important union concern is job security, because, understandably, workers want to know that their jobs are safe. Although companies cannot guarantee that they will not have to lay off workers, they can promise that the people who have the most seniority — those who have worked there the longest — will be the last to be laid off. Similarly, management cannot fire a worker without just cause. In other words, the worker must have committed some offence, such as stealing, or have been incompetent at his or her job in order to be fired.

ICE CREAM PLANT SCOOPS FREE TRADE

A frigid warehouse stacked with Häagen-Dazs may sound like heaven in a sweltering heat wave.

But for the folks at the Ault Foods plant it's also a kind of armory. The luxury ice cream is an important weapon in the battle to keep the Americans from scooping up the dominant share of the domestic market.

Ault Foods has invested $30 million in the past few years to turn the plant into the flagship of their ice cream empire, which has 24 percent of the Canadian market and 46 percent of the Ontario market.

Ault vice-president Larry Morden concedes that free trade is just around the corner in the ice cream business and only the most efficient plant can compete.

"We didn't build a domestic plant here, we built a North American plant," Morden told the minister.

Morden said American plants enjoy a 30 percent lower cost for milk and other raw materials.

Labour costs are also 20 to 30 percent lower. But rather than try to wring out wage concessions, Morden said Ault has tried to work

with the plant's 200 employees and their union in a program called employee-centred management.

Workers meet in small groups to work on methods to improve efficiency and share in bonuses if production targets are met.

But there are some factors which can not be controlled, such as the weather, which can affect sales by 15-20 percent.

"Last year was one of the worst years we ever had. We had just made a tremendous investment in this place and crashed on the weather," said Morden.

Ault Foods Ltd. is on its own this year after formally splitting with it former brewery parent, John Labatt Ltd. With annual sales of $1.2 billion, it has 16 plants in Ontario and Quebec, including in London a milk processing plant which employs about 160 people and a research and development centre which employs 35 scientists and technologists.

Several years ago Ault acquired the rights to produce Häagen-Dazs and Richard D's, two luxury ice cream products. Americans are among the highest per capita consumers of ice cream, especially high-fat products such as Häagen-Dazs.

"We see that gap as a real opportunity for us. But the other side of it is that U.S. manufacturers note the consumption pattern in Canada and see it as an attractive place to market."

Morden said import controls on American milk and dairy products will inevitably disappear, regardless of the outcome of international trade talks now under way, and Ault Foods must work fast to meet the challenge of free trade.

1. In small groups, brainstorm the possible advantages and disadvantages of programs such as Ault's employee-centred management for both union members and management.

2. Using newspapers, business magazines, and news programs, gather information about other business operating programs like Ault's. Describe how these programs have affected the business and union-management relationships.

Grievance Procedures

All contracts contain grievance procedures. **Grievance procedures** outline the steps that both management and the union will follow if a worker has a complaint against management. The complaint is called a **grievance** and usually involves the allegation that management has not lived up to the terms of the contract. Grievance procedures also lay out the steps that management must follow to discipline a worker.

The purpose of grievance procedures is to guarantee that any type of complaint is filed through the proper channels, that work is being done correctly and safely, that small problems do not become big problems, and that workers are not fired without good reason.

Union Shops

If a company, plant, or industry is unionized, it is said to be a **union shop**. This means that in order to work in that industry, a person must agree to join the union within a certain period of time, usually 30 days. Examples of union shops are plumbers' and electricians' unions.

Let's look at how the concept of a union shop affects a unionized construction site. Only members of the construction unions are allowed to work on a unionized construction site. Since union wages are likely to be higher than non-union wages, the costs of construction will be higher. Furthermore, the size of the labour pool is restricted, since although non-union labourers may be available to work, they cannot be hired unless they are willing to join the union.

Conciliation and Mediation

Almost every day in the news, there is a report of a labour dispute of one kind or another. Not all collective bargaining leads uneventfully to an agreement that the union membership accepts.

Union-management negotiations break down when neither side will give in enough to satisfy the other. Each side may feel it would be showing weakness to do so, or they both believe they have already made all the concessions they can.

At this point, the labour laws of the various provinces and federal legislation provide for government assistance. The first step is to appoint a conciliator, a government official who meets with both parties and tries to persuade them to return to the bargaining table. This process is called **conciliation**, and is a requirement that must be fulfilled before a legal strike or lockout can occur. (These terms are discussed in more detail below.)

Conciliators try to get management and the union talking again, but they have no special powers. They cannot order the two sides back to the bargaining table, nor can they force a settlement. If the conciliator succeeds, then a contract is signed. If the talks fail, the union, after a number of specified days called a "cooling-off period," is in a legal strike position and management is in a legal lockout position.

During the cooling-off period, management and the union may use **mediation** to try and settle a dispute. Both the federal and provincial governments employ full-time mediators, but the mediator does not have to be a government employee. Both sides agree on the person who is to act in this role, and the participation of all parties in the mediation process is voluntary. The mediator will exert a lot of pressure on both sides to come to an agreement but, like the conciliator, has no power to enforce a settlement. If the mediator is able to bring the two sides together in an agreement, a contract is signed. If this does not happen, there may be a strike or a lockout.

Conciliation and mediation are often confused because each is a similar process of trying to reach a settlement between management and labour. It is important to remember, however, that conciliation is a legal requirement before unions are allowed to strike or before management is allowed to lock out union members.

Arbitration

In all provinces, the parties may move on to another step. **Arbitration** is a method of settling disputes by an outside third party, called an arbitrator, or before an arbitration board. An arbitration board is made up of three people. One person is selected by each party and the third person is a chairperson mutually agreed upon by both parties. The arbitrator or arbitration board listens to the viewpoints of both the management and the union and then makes a decision that is legally binding.

Arbitration can be either voluntary or compulsory. Voluntary arbitration is usually agreed to by both parties as a means of trying to come to an agreement when conciliation has failed. Under voluntary arbitration, workers choose to exchange the right to strike for binding arbitration of the contract.

Compulsory arbitration as a means of settling disputes is required in a number of areas, for example, where strikes are prohibited. In some provinces hospital workers, police, and firefighters are prohibited by law from striking. Under compulsory arbitration, both parties must accept the recommendations of the arbitrator and there can be no strike or lockout.

Strikes

A **strike** is a union's last resort when negotiations with management break down. Strikes are legal only after a union's contract has expired and a conciliator has tried to resolve the dispute. During a strike, workers withdraw their services: they stop working. The employer will often not be able to provide the goods or services it normally produces. Sometimes, however, the business will try to continue production by having managers fill the jobs of the strikers. If the strike lasts for a long time, the business usually suffers.

The union may not strike until all the members have voted by secret ballot on the decision to strike. A strike vote may be held earlier in the process to see whether, in fact, the union membership is prepared to go on strike. This decision may influence management and the negotiating process.

During a strike, workers do not receive wages, although they do receive a small amount from the union's strike fund, to which they contribute through their union dues.

TYPES OF STRIKES

- **Sit-down strike** – a strike in which employees stop working but stay in their place of employment until an agreement is reached.
- **Hit-and-run strike or rotating strike** – a strike organized in such a way that only some of the employees stop working at any given time, each group taking its turn.
- **Wildcat strike** – an illegal strike not authorized by the union, in which employees walk off the job, thereby violating the collective agreement.
- **Sympathy strike** – a strike by workers not directly involved in a labour dispute, to show support for workers who are involved.
- **Slowdown** – the slowing down of work that occurs when workers put less effort into doing their jobs.
- **Work to rule** – a slowdown caused by employees obeying all laws and rules pertaining to their work.
- **Boycott** – a refusal to buy goods and services from organizations whose employees are on strike (or whose practices are being questioned).
- **General strike** – a strike in which all or most of the workers in a city, province, or country go on strike at the same time.

The effectiveness of a strike depends on how severely it disrupts the normal operations of the company. To make others aware of the strike, workers often **picket** outside the company offices or factory by standing or marching with signs to gain public sympathy, publicize their dispute, and discourage customers from buying the employer's goods or services. Often, other unionized workers will refuse to cross the picket lines in sympathy, causing further disruption of production.

Lockouts

A lockout is a management tool to try to force workers to accept its offer. Like a strike, a lockout is legal only after the union's contract has expired and a conciliator has tried to resolve the dispute. During a **lockout**, management closes the workplace and refuses to let workers in. Workers are not allowed to work. Although lockouts can hurt production, managers try to time them to coincide with a business slowdown or when the business has a stockpile of goods. Lockouts happen far less frequently than strikes.

Although the majority of Canadians are employed by private companies or in the public sector, only about 30 to 35 percent of working Canadians belong to unions. There are differing opinions on the value of unionism to the Canadian economy. Throughout their history, unions have worked to improve wages and working conditions for those they represented. Those not represented by unions have also benefited, since much labour and social legislation resulted from political action by unions.

Originally, unions were created for industrial labourers. More recently, retail and clerical workers, and Canadians in some professions, have joined unions and formed workers' associations. This has allowed them to negotiate contracts with their employers within the bounds of collective bargaining and to enjoy the benefits of group strength.

POINTS TO REMEMBER

- Management/labour history has often involved conflict.
- Organized labour has won many common benefits for all Canadians.
- Many original labour issues are now covered by legislation.
- Management often believes that unions disrupt labour relations that are already good.
- Unions protect workers who might otherwise be treated unfairly by employers.
- Today, unions are turning to social issues and trying to organize retail, clerical, and other white-collar workers and professionals.

FOCUSING ON BUSINESS

12. What is *collective bargaining*?

13. List six items that might be covered in a collective agreement.

14. Explain the difference between a *raise in wages* and *income protection*.

15. What are *grievance procedures*? Why are they necessary?

16. Explain the term *union shop*. How do union shops restrict who can work in the trade?

17. Describe the process of *mediation*. Is it a good idea or not for unions and management to use a mediator? Why?

18. Is a strike an effective weapon against management in a labour dispute? Give reasons for your answer.

19. Is a lockout an effective weapon against the union in a labour dispute? Give reasons for your answer.

EXPLORING BUSINESS

20. Alain and Marc are talking about how they will get to their summer jobs if there is a transit strike. The transit company and its drivers have been negotiating, but it looks as though an agreement will not be reached in time. Alain is worried about getting to work. "It's a long way downtown, too far to ride our bikes," he says. Marc tells him not to worry. "I heard on the news last night that a provincial mediator has been appointed. That means the union will be forced to accept the company's latest offer and there will be no strike." Is he right? Use what you know about collective bargaining to respond to Marc.

21. On a radio talk show, a caller phoning in says that the right to strike should be taken away from all unions. The caller says that strike action by unions has cost the country billions of dollars in lost production and profits. This money was lost as tax revenue for the government and could also have been used to expand business, develop new products, and improve things for all Canadians. Instead it was lost to everyone because a few overpaid, under-worked union people held the country up for ransom.

    Respond to the caller on this talk show.

22. In groups of four or five, discuss whether people employed in essential services (nurses, doctors, firefighters, police) should be allowed to strike. You will need to weigh their rights to the same bargaining processes that all other workers have with the consequences to society if there was an emergency while they were out on strike. Have one member of the group record your findings. Each group will report its findings to the class.

23. In groups of three or four, create a collage of what labour and unions mean to you or to the general public. Collect pictures, headlines, and quotes, and arrange them on Bristol board to make your collage. In a one-page report, explain the theme of your collage and how you incorporated the ideas discussed in this chapter. Be prepared to present your collage to the class.

WORKING WITH MATH

24. Read the information given on page 210 and calculate the following:

    a. the total number of jobs gained during 1990 and 1991

    b. the average number of jobs gained for any industry during 1990 and 1991

THE NEW ECONOMY

NUALA BECK

THE RECESSION'S TOPJOB MAKERS		
Industry		**Job Gain***
1.	Insurance carriers	8153
2.	Accounting firms	7346
3.	Advertising firms	5100
4.	Furniture and appliance stores	4821
5.	Offices of paramedical personnel	1982
6.	Gas distribution	1553
7.	Petroleum drilling	1106
8.	Flour and breakfast cereal products	964
9.	Pipeline transport	933
10.	Tobacconists	916
*Year-end '89 to year-end '91		

Not every Canadian industry cut jobs during the recession. Sixty-seven industries created jobs — and we're talking private sector, not government employment

The top job maker is the insurance industry, which has hired sales and administrative people to handle new products. The industry is also competing aggressively for the retirement savings market.

The hot areas for accounting were receivership and forensic accounting, reflecting the increased focus on bankruptcy and crime.

Advertising seems an unlikely employment source because traditional advertisers have cut budgets. But ads for computers, cellular phones, software, and medical products have proliferated, giving a strong indication that the industry's growth will increasingly come from the new-knowledge economy.

To make the list, industries had to have created employment in each of the last two years, and they had to be in the private sector.

— Nuala Beck & Associates

c. the ratio of petroleum-drilling jobs gained to insurance jobs gained

d. the number of times greater the gain in accounting jobs than pipeline transport jobs

 25. A unionized manufacturer employees 500 people who each earn an average of $11.70 per hour in a 40-hour work week. They have recently settled for a 4 percent raise.

a. What was the total payroll before the raise?

b. How much was the hourly raise for these workers?

c. What is the new total payroll for the company?

d. How much more is labour going to cost the business now?

KEY TERMS

labour union

collective agreement

union dues

certified

bargaining unit

collective bargaining

ratification

income protection

grievance procedures

grievance

union shop

conciliation

mediation

arbitration

strike

picket

lockout

PART 4

The Financial
System
in Canada

Money and Banking

CHAPTER FOCUS

After studying this chapter you will be able to:

describe the barter system and the historical development of currency

•

describe the role of the federal government in regulating financial institutions

•

understand the different types of bank accounts and services that financial institutions offer businesses and individuals

OU HAVE KNOWN THAT MONEY IS important since you were a very young child. You probably received gifts of money from relatives and quickly learned that it could be traded for candy, toys, and other things you wanted. The items people need or want to buy change as they grow older, and money takes on an increasing importance in our lives.

In this chapter, you will learn how money and banking developed from the simple trading of goods and services, and how the federal government regulates banking in Canada through the Bank Act and the Bank of Canada. Finally, you will examine some of the many banking services offered by financial institutions and look at some practical banking matters, such as how to fill out deposit and withdrawal slips at the bank.

HE DEVELOPMENT OF MONEY

Barter

The earliest form of exchange was barter. **Barter** is the trade of one type of good or service for another type of good or service, without using money. Under the barter system, a farmer might trade milk and produce for bread or cloth produced by others in the vicinity. This system works well when the items traded are simple, the distance between the people trading is small, and it is easy to find someone to trade with.

As needs and wants become more varied, it becomes more difficult to trade. The trading can become quite complex. For example, imagine that you need shoes. You find someone willing to trade shoes who needs tools. However, you produce bread. You have to find someone who needs bread and who has tools in order to get the tools to trade for the shoes. In other words, bartering becomes complicated once in-between trades need to be negotiated.

Another disadvantage of bartering is that it is not standardized. How many loaves of bread are equal to one pair of shoes? How many hours of work by a carpenter should be exchanged for milk and vegetables?

What was needed was a **medium of exchange** — in other words, a standard item that people accept in payment of goods and services.

Today, most people in industrialized countries like Canada do not directly produce anything that could be used for exchange. Instead, we exchange our time for money, then use the money to buy what we need and want. Barter is still possible, but usually on a smaller scale. For example, you might want to purchase a second-hand bicycle from your neighbour, but instead of giving money, you exchange baby-sitting services. The idea of money is still there. You and your neighbour must decide how much the bicycle is worth and how much baby-sitting is the equivalent of that price.

Bartering with businesses is also possible, but more complicated. You would have to look for a store willing to trade goods or services for the type of goods or services you have to exchange. In practice, there is limited bartering since business owners need currency to pay their own debts and purchase goods and services. Also, the more expensive the item, the longer the store would have to wait to get the proper exchange of services from you. Imagine trading lawn-mowing services for a new car!

BUSINESS *in action*

BARTER HELPS PAY THE BILLS IN RECESSION-BATTERED '90S

When Brian Hammond recently relocated and expanded his flower shop, not a single loonie changed hands in the renovation process.

In exchange for the signs on his storefront, inside fixtures and plumbing, refrigeration and air-conditioning work done by various companies, he provided silk plants for several offices, the arrangements for numerous social gatherings, including a big birthday party, and countless Valentine bouquets.

Flowers for an upcoming wedding will soon round out the total.

And, inspired by that experience, he has taken to paying as many of his day-to-day operating bills as possible – everything from couriers to printing and advertising costs – by trading his goods and services for those of other frugal-minded entrepreneurs.

In fact, Hammond, who with his wife Johann owns and manages Garrett Florist, carried out some $60 000 worth of transactions in kind in 1992. And he credits bartering with the very survival of his two-year-old business.

Bartering is not a new concept. Indeed, it has been around since time beyond memory, the very foundation of virtually every economic system that has ever evolved. But while it is not novel, it has generally come to be seen as outdated in today's currency-based industrialized societies.

The History of Canada's Currency

Anything people believe is valuable can be used as a medium of exchange. The earliest forms of money included animal skins, beads, shells, stones, jewels, cattle, arrowheads, and tobacco. Small lumps of precious metals, particularly gold and silver, were used as money as early as 5000 B.C.

In North America's early days, aboriginal peoples used **wampum**, small beads or tubes from seashells strung into belts, as a medium of exchange. Although in 1670 it was no longer legal as a medium of exchange, wampum was used until the beginning of the 1800s.

Wampum

Money in the form of coinage and paper currency began to play an important role as a medium of exchange in Canada around 1645. Until this time, there was little need for currency. The currency that did exist came from countries such as France, Portugal, Spain, and England. These currencies became scarce as the demand for money increased with the growth of the French colonies. As a temporary solution to the lack of currency, "playing-card money" was issued in 1685. "Playing-card money" was made by cutting playing cards into quarters and then applying the wax seal of the treasurer and the signature of the governor and intendant. Although the use of "playing-card money" was meant to be a temporary measure, it became an important

Playing-card money

part of French Canada's currency until 1759.

With the growth of business and trade, the need for financial institutions in Canada developed, and banking began to appear around 1792. By the beginning of the nineteenth century, banks in each province could issue their own currency. However, over time it became apparent that a national currency was needed, and in 1870 the government issued its own Dominion of Canada notes in denominations of 25 cents, $1, and $2. Notes in larger denominations were later created.

Paper money has value, like any medium of exchange, only because people accept that it has value. It has no value of its own, except as a piece of paper. Money is worth only what it can buy. Even coins that are sometimes called silver today actually contain no silver.

Purchasing Power of Money

The value of money is in what it will buy. It has a **face value** written on the coin or bill, such as 25 cents, $1, or $10. This face value never changes. However, the amount of money that it takes to purchase goods and services does change over time. **Purchasing power** is the amount of goods or services that money can buy. The $10 bill you have now will buy less than it did 20 years ago and more than it will 20 years from now. A good example of changing purchasing power is movie admission, which usually increases every year. Movies cost more this year than they did last year at this time, partly because the cost of producing movies is always rising. In addition, the cost of running movie theatres increases. It is also possible that some people who might have gone to a movie in the past now wait for it to come out on video or pay television, reducing the size of the audience a theatre can expect.

The change in the purchasing power of the dollar is measured by the **Consumer Price Index (CPI)**. It is compiled monthly from the changes in price of approximately 400 items bought yearly by Canadians and measures the percentage of change in the price of goods and services over a certain period of time. The items that are measured by the Consumer Price Index are meant to represent what the average consumer buys and include such things as housing, entertainment, dry cleaning, haircuts, clothing, and food. Some items are given more weight than others in the calculation of the index; for example, food is weighted more heavily than entertainment. Over the years, some items have been replaced with others as they became more important; for example, more women have joined the work force over the years, so day-care costs have been added to the index. The list of goods and services is updated by Statistics Canada every year.

The Bank Act

The Constitution Act, 1867 gave the federal government the responsibility for regulating banks through the **Bank Act.** The first Bank Act was passed in 1871. It is necessary for government to regulate banking to a certain degree because Canadians rely on banks to look after their money for which they have worked very hard.

The Bank Act, which was last revised in 1980, outlines procedures for opening new banks, the minimum amount of money that is required to open a bank and that banks must keep in reserve, what banks may and may not do, how banks may merge, and the kinds of reports they must make to the Bank of Canada. It allows for the routine inspection of branches and defines two kinds of banks based on ownership: foreign banks and Canadian-owned banks.

Financial institutions in Canada belong to four main groups. The first group, which deals with cash transactions, includes the Bank of Canada, chartered banks, trust and loan companies, and credit unions (called *caisses populaires* in Quebec). The second group is made up of insurance companies and pension funds. The third group consists of investment dealers and brokers, investment fund companies, and small finance and loan companies. The fourth group contains government institutions, such as the Federal Development Bank, that provide financial services to borrowers and lenders.

The Bank of Canada

The **Bank of Canada** was established in 1935 to issue paper currency and, most importantly, to manage Canada's monetary policy. Managing Canada's **monetary policy** involves increasing or decreasing the money supply to influence the economic and financial well-being of the country. As a result, the Bank of Canada has a major role in controlling inflation. Although the Bank of Canada is in the same group as chartered banks, it does not offer banking services to individuals or businesses. You cannot open an account at the Bank of Canada — it is a bank for banks and is often referred to as Canada's central bank.

The Bank of Canada cannot directly control the supply of money, but it does so indirectly through the chartered banks. As mentioned earlier, the Bank Act requires chartered banks to keep a certain amount of their total deposits in reserve. These reserves are held as deposits at the Bank of Canada. Money on deposit in the chartered banks above the level of the minimum reserves is used by the banks to make loans and investments to businesses and individuals. The banks charge interest on the loans and thus earn money for themselves.

The Bank of Canada can transfer money between itself and the chartered banks — via government bonds and other securities — to regulate the amount of money in the system. When the Bank of Canada transfers money to the chartered banks, more money is available for loans. Interest rates go down so people tend to borrow and spend more money. On the other hand, when the Bank of Canada transfers deposits from the chartered banks to itself, this decreases the money supply because chartered banks would have fewer cash reserves. When banks have less money, the interest rates rise and loans are harder to get as banks become more selective about whom they will lend money to. As well, consumers cut back on their borrowing because the cost of doing so increases.

Chartered Banks

The Bank Act regulates the operation of Canada's chartered banks. A **chartered bank** must be Canadian-owned and no one person may own more than a 10 percent share of stock in a chartered bank. These banks are also called Schedule I banks, and their shares are traded on Canadian stock exchanges. The Bank of Nova Scotia, the Toronto-Dominion Bank, the Royal Bank of Canada, the Canadian Imperial

Bank of Commerce, the National Bank of Canada, the Bank of Montreal, and the Canadian Western Bank are all Schedule I banks.

Until 1980, Schedule I banks were the only banks allowed in Canada. But with the revision of the Bank Act in 1980, Schedule II banks were created. These are foreign and Canadian-owned banks that are controlled by only a small number of shareholders and deal mostly with commercial business. Examples of these banks are the State Bank of India and Hongkong Bank of Canada.

Royal Trust, a trust company, offers similar services as the Royal Bank, a chartered bank.

Trust Companies and Mortgage Loan Companies

Trust companies and mortgage loan companies were established under provincial law in the late 1800s and early 1900s. **Trust companies** offer services similar to those of banks. In addition, they operate pension funds and act as transfer agents for company stocks, as trustees for company bond issues, and as administrators for estates and trusts. **Mortgage loan companies** also accept deposits and make loans. Their money is invested in mortgages secured by real estate.

Credit Unions and *Caisses Populaires*

Credit unions, called *caisses populaires* in Quebec, offer services similar to those offered by banks and trust companies. Unlike banks and trust companies, however, they are non-profit organizations. They have owner-members who invest a small amount of money to join. Credit unions are often founded by employee groups, unions, members of a particular religious or ethnic group, or other groups that have a similar bond.

FOCUSING ON BUSINESS

1. Create an organizer outlining the advantages and disadvantages of the barter system.

2. List five things used as early forms of money.

3. Why did paper money come into use in Canada?

4. Explain what is meant by the *purchasing power* of money and why it changes (typically decreases) over time.

5. List five chartered banks.

EXPLORING BUSINESS

6. Your cousin is excited because his parents are buying a new car. "What's so exciting about that?" you ask. He replies, "It's exciting because instead of trading in the old car, they are going to sell it to me. All I have to do is work around the house until it is paid off."

   a. In small groups, brainstorm ways that this family can determine how much the car is worth. Justify each suggestion.

   b. Having decided how much the car is worth, determine how much work around the house will have to be done to pay it off.

7. Explain the role of the Bank of Canada and why individuals cannot have bank accounts in the Bank of Canada.

8. The Consumer Price Index (CPI) was set at 100 in 1986. Since then, prices and wages have generally risen, until in 1991 the CPI reached 125. This means that the cost of living in 1991 was 25 percent higher than it was in 1986. How much more would someone have to pay in 1991 for an assortment of common items that cost $300 in 1986?

9. Using the newspaper, select an article on banks, the purchasing power of money, or the Consumer Price Index. Write a one-page summary of the article in your own words. Create a poster to display your article and summary.

10. Research the price of movie tickets, running shoes, and VCRs now, two years ago, and five years ago.

    a. Create an organizer to record your information.

    b. Create a line graph, where the year is the X axis and the price is the Y axis, to illustrate your information.

    c. In small groups, compare your findings. What were the differences and similarities?

CAREERS

CREATING GOODS AND SERVICES

1. In small groups, brainstorm and list careers that involve the creation of goods or services. Careers include inventor, innovator, chef, industrial designer, carpenter, painter, and landscaper.

2. Select a career that interests you from the list you created in Question 1. Research the career by visiting your resource centre and guidance office, contacting associations and organizations for literature, or interviewing someone in the field you have chosen. If you interview someone, ask if you can videotape the interview to share with the class. Learn about the career by gathering information that includes the following:

   - education required

   - experience required

   - skills required

   - responsibilities

   - salary range

   - any other relevant and interesting information

3. Create a poster to display your career research. Present your findings to the class.

BANKING SERVICES

As well as providing a safe place to keep money, banks offer many services, such as lending money to individuals and businesses. Loans can be used to help finance cars and houses, as well as the launch of small businesses and the activities of large corporations.

Another important financial service is the exchange of currency. If you are travelling out of Canada, you usually need to take with you the currency of the country of your destination. Similarly, if you receive a gift of money in foreign currency or arrive home from a trip with foreign money left over, you need to exchange it for Canadian currency. As an alternative to carrying a large amount of money while travelling, you can buy traveller's cheques from a bank. **Traveller's cheques** can be used like cash and will be replaced if lost or stolen.

Banks and other savings institutions sell and redeem Canada Savings Bonds on behalf of the federal government. Canada Savings Bonds are issued on an annual basis and, although they are issued with a fixed maturity date many years in the future, they can be cashed at any time. People who buy regular interest bonds receive an annual interest payment, and people who buy compound interest bonds do not receive an interest payment until they redeem the bond.

Valuable items, such as jewellery, stock certificates, bonds, insurance policies, wills, deeds, or rare collectibles, can be stored in **safety deposit boxes** at a bank. These locked compartments are located in the bank's vault for security purposes and are rented to individuals and businesses.

Automated transaction machines, or ATMs, provide banking services 24 hours a day. You can deposit cash or cheques, withdraw cash, update your account, pay bills, and transfer money between accounts any time of the day or night, seven days a week, without ever having to actually go into a bank or talk to a teller. Automatic transaction machines can be found in banks, as well as in grocery stores, malls, airports, office buildings, and drive-throughs. Money can also be transferred from one bank to another through electronic networks such as Interac. A customer can go to an automatic transaction machine in a Royal Bank, for example, and access his or her account in a Toronto-Dominion Bank.

Account Procedures

To open a bank account, you must deposit some money; $1 is often sufficient. You need to fill out a **signature card** with your name, address, telephone number, occupation, and signature. Anyone can make deposits to your account, but only you can make withdrawals.

When you have opened an account, you will either be given a **passbook** to be updated during each visit, or you will receive a monthly statement by mail. These items are electronic records of all the transactions that have gone through your account. They include all deposits, withdrawals, transaction fees, any interest earned, and so on.

To make a deposit at the bank, you must fill out a **deposit slip**. You may be depositing cash, cheques, or a combination of both. You may be depositing a cheque from which you would like to keep some cash. All deposit slips require the same information, although they may look slightly different. Note the items in the example on page 226.

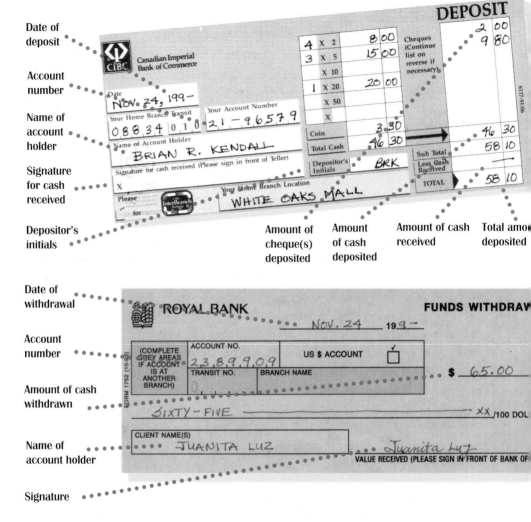

Date of deposit

Account number

Name of account holder

Signature for cash received

Depositor's initials

Amount of cheque(s) deposited

Amount of cash deposited

Amount of cash received

Total amount deposited

Date of withdrawal

Account number

Amount of cash withdrawn

Name of account holder

Signature

You present the deposit slip to the teller along with your passbook and the money is deposited. Your passbook is updated for the deposit (the amount deposited is added to your balance), and the deposit slip is kept for bank records.

When withdrawing money, you follow a similar procedure, except that you fill out a withdrawal slip, as shown above. As with deposits, the teller updates the passbook (this time the amount is deducted) and keeps the withdrawal slip.

Savings Accounts

Many people keep their money in **savings accounts**, and it is easy to see why. You can withdraw your money at any time, but if you keep it in your account, it will earn interest. **Interest** is the amount of money that the bank pays the account holder. Why does money earn interest? The bank uses deposits from customers to lend to other customers. In other words, the depositor lends the bank his or her money and interest is the bank's payment for this loan. Rates of interest vary from bank to bank but, in Canada, the rates are usually similar.

A customer who has a **true savings account** cannot write cheques on it but can withdraw the money at any time. This type of account is intended for people who want to save as much as possible and not withdraw very often. True savings accounts pay the highest rates of interest. Interest is calculated on your minimum monthly balance and is compounded and paid twice a year, at the end of April and at the end of October.

A **daily interest savings account** has a lower rate of interest than a true savings account but the interest is calculated every day, so the customer does not need to worry about minimum balances. **Compound daily interest** is interest that is calculated daily, not only on your balance, but also on any interest that has already been earned. For all savings accounts, there may be a fee for withdrawing money. In some cases, you will be allowed two free withdrawals per month, after which you pay a fee. This differs from bank to bank, so, when opening an account, you should find out the exact fee.

Chequing Accounts

It is not always convenient to withdraw money from the bank every time you need it. Furthermore, it is never wise to carry large amounts of money with you to make purchases. Most people find it necessary to have a chequing account in addition to their savings account.

A **chequing/savings account** is a dual-purpose account that may suit people who want to write only a few cheques and have only one account. A low rate of interest is calculated and paid on the lowest balance for each monthly, biannual, or annual period. There is a service charge for each cheque you write, although some accounts may give you one or two free cheques per month.

Personal chequing accounts are intended only for writing cheques and, for this reason, little to no interest is paid. There will be a fee for each cheque (although your bank may allow one or two free cheques

HOME BANKING BY PHONE

Special telephones will allow Saint John residents to see how their bank balances stack up and conduct other transactions during a test of phones equipped with display screens.

"It's almost like having your personal automated teller at home," says George Coleman, assistant general manager for personal banking at the Toronto-Dominion Bank.

The telephone display screen is an enhanced version of phones that reveal the phone number of incoming callers.

The special telephone — its marketing name is Screen-Talk — features a built-in display screen and several "soft keys" that allow different functions to call up a varity of information.

Two hundred households in the New Brunswick capital have been equipped with the novel phones that also allow an interchange of information between service bureaus and merchants.

Through a series of prerecorded messages, clients can phone the bank and be walked through choices to get at their account balances or do other transactions. Callers can confirm what they've requested by seeing the resulting totals.

The software comes from Phonetix Corp. of Toronto. It's thought the phones of the future will make home banking less confusing and more acceptable.

Merchants are able to send messages, advertise specials and send electronic coupons, while other services such as newspapers or radio stations, for example, could transmit news, weather, sports or 'headline news' reports.

As easy as calling a friend, You can bank by phone.

)'s new
oy-phone service.
you can bank by phone... without all of the
work, running around or waiting in line.
all Bankline and bank by phone.
an pay bills, transfer funds, know your account
ce, or account activity.
convenient, you'll wonder how you ever got along
out it.

1. With a partner, discuss the advantages of Screen-Talk and who might benefit from the service.

2. a. As a class, identify the financial institutions in your community that offer banking services.

   b. In home groups, each member should select one of the financial institutions to research how they are using technology to offer banking services to customers.

   c. Form an expert group of students from other groups who have chosen the same financial institution as you to conduct research with them.

   d. Return to your home group and describe what you learned in your expert group. Compare the different types of services using technology that are offered by each financial institution.

per month), or there may be a flat fee for the privilege of unlimited chequing. People with personal chequing accounts normally keep only enough money in their account to cover any cheques they have written. In some cases, your **cancelled cheques**, or cheques that have been cashed by the person or business you wrote them to, will be mailed to you.

Cathy © Cathy Guisewite. Reprinted with permission of Universal Press Syndicate. All rights reserved.

Current Accounts

Current accounts are for businesses and other organizations, such as a club or the student council. They are strictly chequing accounts that pay no interest. Fees are charged for all cheques and deposits, and a monthly statement is sent so that the organization can check its records against those of the bank.

Cheques

The person or organization to whom you are writing the cheque is called the **payee**. The bank or other financial institution where the account is held is called the **drawee**. Its name is usually printed on the cheque. The person or organization who is writing the cheque and from whose account the money will be taken is the **drawer**. The drawer's name is also often printed on the cheque. The drawer must sign the cheque for it to be negotiable.

The date is extremely important. The day, month, and year must all appear. If the date on the cheque is more than six months previous to the present date, the cheque is said to be **stale-dated** and cannot be cashed. It is wise to cash a cheque as soon as you receive it, so that you have the use of the money as quickly as possible, and so that you do not lose the cheque. In this way, you reduce the possibility of the cheque becoming stale-dated.

Cheques may also be **postdated**. Postdating a cheque means putting a future date on it. This might be an error, but more commonly is done on purpose for one of two reasons. First, you may not be able to deposit money into your account until later in the week, but a store owner allows you to purchase the goods today and give a cheque dated a few days in the future. Second, it is not uncommon to give cheques in advance of the date on which payment is due. For example, a person might pay his or her rent by giving the landlord 12 cheques in January. The landlord will cash one each month, saving the tenant the trouble of having to deliver the cheque each month. In any case, a cheque is not valid (cashable) until the date written on it.

The amount of the cheque must appear in both words and numbers. The entire line on which the amount is written out in words should be filled so that no one can add or change anything. For example, it would be easy to change the amount of a cheque if there was room to write in more words. Thus, nine could easily become nine hundred if a line were not drawn through the remaining space to the right. Naturally, the amount in numbers must match what you wrote, but errors can easily occur. It is important that both amounts match, or the bank will not honour the cheque.

The account number is an important piece of information needed. Printed cheques come with the account number on them already; however, if the number is not printed, you must write it in.

Endorsing Cheques

Before a cheque can be cashed or deposited, it must be **endorsed**. The payee must sign the back of the cheque, as proof that he or she is the person for whom the money is intended. Thus, it is important not to endorse a cheque until you are ready to cash it or deposit it in an account.

Certifying Cheques

The fact that someone has written a cheque is no proof that there is enough money in the account to cash it. The payee may require that the cheque be **certified**. When a cheque is certified, the bank sets the money aside before the cheque is cashed and guarantees the payee that the funds are available. Banks generally charge a fee to certify a cheque.

POINTS TO REMEMBER

- Barter is the exchange of goods or services for other goods and services.
- Early money included animal skins, beads, shells, stones, jewels, arrowheads, tobacco, metals, and playing cards.
- The change in the purchasing power of the dollar is measured by the Consumer Price Index (CPI).
- The federal government regulates banks through the Bank Act.
- The Bank of Canada manages Canada's supply of money indirectly through the chartered banks.
- Financial institutions in Canada include chartered banks, trust companies, mortgage loan companies, and credit unions (*caisses populaires* in Quebec).
- Financial institutions offer a wide variety of services to individuals and businesses.

FOCUSING ON BUSINESS

11. Describe the procedure for opening a bank account.
12. Explain the differences between a daily interest savings account and a true savings account.
13. Explain the differences between personal chequing, chequing/savings, and current accounts.
14. List the items that are necessary on a deposit slip.
15. List the items that are necessary on a withdrawal slip.
16. Describe the components of a cheque.
17. What other bank services are available in addition to being able to make deposits and withdrawals, and write cheques?

EXPLORING BUSINESS

18. Anne is trying to decide which bank account or accounts would best suit her needs. She wants to save as much money as possible, but she also needs to write cheques from time to time. In small groups, discuss what type of bank account(s) would best suit Anne's needs.

19. Sabena notices while doing some personal banking that the bank appears to have made an error in recording her bank balance. An extra zero has been added so that her $200 balance appears as $2000. Sabena is thrilled by this and begins thinking about how she might spend this unexpected fortune. Is Sabena correct in her assumption that the money is hers? Brainstorm the possible consequences to Sabena of spending this money. What should Sabena do?

20. Form small groups and visit a chartered bank, a credit union, and a trust company. Obtain one copy of as many of the following items as you can: deposit slip, withdrawal slip, loan application, personal chequing account statement, and literature and pamphlets describing various banking services offered. Create a bulletin board display of these items, showing the similarities and differences for each of the forms and pamphlets your group obtained.

21. Mr. and Mrs. Mohammed are considering the purchase of a new car. The one they want costs $15 000, and they would have to borrow the money to buy it. This year, the interest rate on new car loans is 10 percent. Their old car would probably last another year but will need repairs. Next year the price of the new car will likely be $15 500, and interest rates are predicted to rise in the near future. However, by then they will have been able to save $2000 as a down payment. With a partner, discuss this situation and advise the Mohammeds on whether to buy the car now or wait until next year.

22. Bill has always kept his valuable stamp collection, insurance policy, and an antique pocket watch at home in his room. However, he is wondering if this is still the best place to store these items. When you suggest a safety deposit box, he replies, "I have a good hiding place; no thief would think to look there. Anyway, safety deposit boxes cost money and I can't afford one." Explain to Bill why he would be better off renting a safety deposit box to store his valuables.

WORKING WITH MATH

23. Use the form provided by your teacher to update the following personal bank record:

Date	Particulars	Cheque	Deposit	Balance
Jan. 2	Balance forward	$627.81		

On January 2, the balance in your chequing/savings account is $627.81. At the end of January, you are updating your personal records and must record the following information in correct date order:

Cheques written:

#42: Rent, January 2: $500

#43: Telephone, January 19: $30

#44: Payment on credit card, January 18: $250

#45: Hydro bill, January 29: $50

Withdrawals:

January 4: cash $50

January 9: cash $75

January 16: cash $180

January 22: cash $62

January 31: cash $120

Deposits:

January 5: pay cheque $450

January 12: pay cheque $422

January 19: pay cheque $396

January 26: pay cheque $479

24. When interest is compounded, the interest is calculated on the balance in an account then added to the total. The next time it is calculated, the new balance is used, so that you get interest on your interest. Thus, if you had $100 in the bank and were earning 5 percent interest per year, at the end of year one you would earn $5.00 ($100 × 0.05) in interest. At the end of year two, you would earn $5.25 ($105 × 0.05) in interest, totalling $110.25.

a. Assume that Penny has $800 in a savings account that pays 6 percent interest per year. Interest is paid at the rate of 3 percent every six months (6 percent in total for the year). Calculate the balance in her account at the end of two years.

b. Now suppose that Penny deposits a total of $200 during each interest period and makes no withdrawals. Calculate the balance in her account at the end of two years.

25. On May 31, a customer presents the bank with a deposit slip for a savings account for a total deposit of $225.63. The last recorded balance in the passbook is $629.80 on May 15. Between May 15 and May 31,

the following cheques had been written: May 19, $139.42; and, May 25, $85.96. Prepare the passbook in correct date order.

26. Prepare deposit slips for the following deposits. Use today's date.

   a. Your personal savings account number is 525-0264. You are depositing your pay cheque of $690.42 for two weeks and a cheque for $27.25. You also wish to get $180 in cash for personal use.

   b. Your personal chequing account number is 6346-854409. You are depositing two cheques, one for $136.50 and one for $63.29, and cash as follows: three $20 bills, one $10 bill, five $5 bills, four $2 bills, and $11.31 in coins.

KEY TERMS

barter	passbook
medium of exchange	deposit slip
wampum	savings account
face value	interest
purchasing power	true savings account
Consumer Price Index (CPI)	daily interest savings account
Bank Act	compound daily interest
Bank of Canada	chequing/savings account
monetary policy	personal chequing account
chartered bank	cancelled cheque
trust company	current account
mortgage loan company	payee
credit union	drawee
caisse populaire	drawer
traveller's cheque	stale-dated
Canada Savings Bond	postdated
safety deposit box	endorsed
automated transaction machine	certified
signature card	

Investing and the Stock Market

CHAPTER FOCUS

After studying this chapter you will be able to:

explain how companies finance new ventures

•

explain the difference between bonds, preferred shares, and common shares

•

describe the conditions that a company must meet before selling shares on an exchange

•

determine how to evaluate stock investments

•

identify where stocks are bought and sold

•

outline the use of stock indices

•

explain newspaper stock quotations and determine their closing prices over a period of time

I N CANADA, BOTH PROPOSED AND existing companies constantly strive to acquire new capital in order to expand or finance new ventures. This financial need of businesses is also true in many other industrial countries of the world. For well-established companies, the raising of new funds is necessary from time to time for the purchase of very expensive items ranging from new machinery to new buildings for plant expansion. For new companies, capital often needs to be raised to cover basic start-up costs and the initial buying of resources.

In this chapter, we will explore how companies raise capital through investors, as well as the benefits and risks of investing from the investors' perspective. In addition, we will examine where stocks are traded and how they are published in the financial section of newspapers.

RAISING CAPITAL

There are two methods to finance new investments for companies: debt financing and equity financing. **Debt financing** involves borrowing money from a bank or other financial institution, or issuing corporate bonds and other securities. No matter what happens to the company in

the future (whether it makes a profit or incurs a loss) it will still owe the money and must pay it back. The second method, **equity financing**, is to raise capital by means of having people invest in the company. This would be accomplished through the issuing of shares.

These methods of raising capital and the varying degrees of risk and liquidity (the measure of how quickly an investor can turn the investment into cash) for the purchaser are discussed on page 240.

STEPS IN BUSINESS EXPANSION

1 ABC Company needs money to expand.

2 The company decides to go public and raise money by selling its shares to investors.

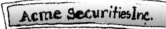

3 The shares are purchased by an investment firm, or group of firms, who then sell them to the public.

4 Through the sale of its shares to investors, ABC Company has raised the money it needs to complete its expansion.

5 The newly-issued publicly-owned shares can now be traded on the stock exchange.

6 ABC shares will be owned by many different investors including individuals, pension funds and institutions. They all participate in our free enterprise system.

Bonds

A **bond** is a certificate issued by a company to an individual or another company acknowledging that it owes a certain amount of money. Selling bonds is similar to borrowing money from a bank, except that, instead of having one loan agreement and one creditor, the company has many loan agreements (the bonds) and many creditors (the bond purchasers).

Bonds are sold by a company to investors for a specific amount of money called the **principal**. The bond will also state the interest that must be paid by the company to the investor and when the interest is payable. Therefore, the investors will receive back their original money as well as a profit, which is the interest. The company has the use of the investors' money until the **maturity date**, the date on which the principal has to be repaid. The company hopes to be able to use the money raised from the bond issued to earn more profit than it has to repay in interest to the investor.

Shares

A **share** is a unit of ownership in a company. The total number of a company's shares offered for sale is called its **stock**. Also, the person who owns shares in a company, the shareholder, may be referred to as an owner of stock. The terms stocks and shares are sometimes used interchangeably.

A company can raise capital by selling shares to the public, but the public needs to be assured that the company is legitimate in its intentions to stay in business and in its attempt to make a profit. In order to accomplish this, the selling and purchasing of shares is usually conducted through a **stock exchange**. This process of buying and selling is regulated by the stock exchange to ensure that it is conducted in a fair manner for both the buyer and the seller. However, before the company can sell its shares to the public, it must first comply with a number of conditions stipulated by the stock exchange.

The stock exchange usually requires the company to issue a **prospectus**. This legal document states: the nature of the company's business; the names of the company officers and directors, as well as the principal shareholders; the amount of money that the company wants to raise; and what the company intends to purchase with the money.

The company must also fulfil the requirements of the stock exchange that pertain to the type of business the company is engaged in. For example, on the Vancouver Stock Exchange, natural resource or mining companies must already have $150 000 of initial capital and must also be willing to raise a minimum of $200 000 by selling shares. Once these and other conditions are met, stockbrokers can sell the company shares through the regulated stock exchange. Stockbrokers receive a commission for their service every time shares are sold or purchased.

Types of Shares

Companies can issue either **preferred shares** or **common shares**. Preferred shares have the advantage of paying out a fixed dividend each year. A **dividend** is a portion of the firm's profits. Holders of common shares receive a dividend only if the company makes a profit and if the company decides to give a dividend to the holders of common shares, whereas dividends *must* be paid to preferred shareholders. Preferred shareholders also have an advantage over common shareholders in the event of the company going bankrupt. If the assets of the bankrupt company are sold, the preferred shareholders will receive their money before the common shareholders. However, common shareholders have the right to attend and vote (one vote for each share owned) at the company's annual general meeting. This is when the board of directors is elected.

FOCUSING ON BUSINESS

1. Explain why a company would want to raise new capital.
2. Define *debt financing* and *equity financing*.
3. What is a *bond*?
4. Describe the features of a bond.
5. Explain the differences between a *preferred share* and a *common share*.

EXPLORING BUSINESS

6. Using the business section of a newspaper, select three articles that discuss company shares or the raising of new capital. Briefly outline what the article says. Comment on whether you believe the company should borrow from the bank or issue preferred or common shares.

7. The Ocean Floor Gold Mining Company wants to raise enough money to buy a state-of-the-art ship that they can use for mining gold from the Pacific Ocean. They know that the ship will cost $4 million to build and equip. If their stock is presently selling for $7.23 per share, how many shares will they have to sell to buy the ship? They also have to pay a 3 percent commission to the stockbroker for selling the shares.

MATHEMATICS

1. In small groups, brainstorm and list careers in the field of mathematics. Your list might include bank teller, loans officer, accountant, stockbroker, computer programmer, architect, statistician.

2. With a partner, select a career that interests you from the list you created in Question 1. Research the career by visiting your resource centre and guidance office, contacting associations and organizations for literature, or interviewing someone in the field you have chosen. If you interview someone, ask if you can videotape the interview to share with the class. Learn about the career by gathering information that includes the following:
    *   education required
    *   experience required
    *   skills required
    *   salary range
    *   any other relevant and interesting information

3. Create a poster to display your career research. Present your findings to the class.

CANADIAN STOCK EXCHANGES

In Canada there are five stock exchanges where stocks are traded daily. The Toronto Stock Exchange (TSE) is Canada's largest and deals in both blue-chip stocks as well as venture capital stocks. **Blue-chip stocks** are usually made up of common shares of well-established com-

A supervisor at the Toronto Stock Exchange signals across the trading floor.

panies. **Venture capital stocks** are stocks of fairly new small to medium-sized companies. The Montreal Exchange (ME) is Canada's oldest exchange, and many of the companies that are listed on the Toronto Stock Exchange are also listed on the Montreal Exchange. The Vancouver Stock Exchange (VSE) specializes in small to medium-sized venture companies. The Alberta Stock Exchange (ASE) is based in Calgary and is mostly a regional exchange for junior oil and gas companies. The Winnipeg Stock Exchange (WSE) is a small exchange that deals mainly with wheat and other agricultural commodities.

Evaluating Stock Investments

Potential investors should always evaluate a stock before considering whether to purchase. Investing in stocks always requires very careful planning. Only a foolish investor makes a purchase because someone gives him or her a "hot tip" on a stock that might increase in value. When evaluating whether you should invest in a stock, you should consider the potential profit and the risk.

When purchasing stock in a company, the investor is taking a chance. This is called the **risk of investment**. The company can be very successful, and the stock can increase and be worth a great deal of money as more people want to buy the stock. On the other hand, the company may prove to be unsuccessful in its business ventures and ultimately go bankrupt. Then the stock would be worth very little or perhaps nothing at all. The investor must estimate how much risk he or she is prepared to accept. It is possible to lose all the money that has been invested. Some companies (blue-chip companies) are well-established with good past performance records. Such companies would have a relatively low risk. Other small and medium-sized companies that are new or have been in business for only a few years (venture companies) might sell stock to try to raise capital for speculative endeavours that may or may not prove to be successful, such as searching for gold on the bottom of the Pacific Ocean. These are higher-risk investments. The lower-risk stocks (blue-chip) are usually more highly priced to begin with and have less potential for spectacular increases in value. The higher-risk stocks (venture stocks, formally called penny stocks) can usually be purchased for less than one dollar per share and have the potential to increase in value substantially if the company's venture is successful.

FOLLOWING STOCK MARKET ACTIVITY

One of the questions most frequently asked by investors is "What is happening in the stock market?" Many financial and market analysts follow the daily activities of the stock market and attempt to forecast what will happen in the future. For the average investor, one of the quickest and easiest ways to see if the general market trend is increasing or decreasing is to look at the stock exchange's share price index.

This index represents a summary of the daily average prices for a range of stocks. Share price indices can be a big help to the investor in that they help to give an overall picture of a stock market trend.

The Vancouver Stock Exchange Composite Index is a measure of the daily average price increase or decrease for the venture stocks of the Vancouver Exchange. The Toronto Stock Exchange Composite Index represents the price movements of the stocks from a select group of 300 companies.

The Dow Jones Averages are among the best known indices in the United States, and are taken from broad categories of stocks traded on the New York Stock Exchange. The most widely followed of these is the Dow Jones Industrial Average (30 leading U. S. manufacturers and distributors). Other Dow Jones Averages include the Utilities Index (15 main utility companies), the Transportation Index (20 leading airline, railroad, and truck companies), and the Composite Index (a combination of the Dow Jones Industrial Average, the Transportation Index, and the Utilities Index).

STOCK MARKET LANGUAGE

When considering whether to invest in a company by purchasing stock, a potential investor is likely to encounter a new set of technical terms that refer to the stock market. A stockbroker will often use these terms instead of giving lengthy explanations to the potential purchaser. This is done in order to save time when discussing whether to purchase or sell a stock. Some of these terms are explained below.

Buy low–sell high The practice of buying a stock when it is inexpensive and selling it when it has risen is price.

Bull market Describes a situation in which most of the prices on the stock market are rising.

Bear market Describes a situation in which most of the prices on the stock market are falling.

Buying on margin The practice of purchasing a stock on credit, the balance being loaned by a broker.

Listed stock The stock of a company that is traded on an exchange.

Unlisted (over-the-counter) stock The stock of a company that is not listed for trading on an exchange but that is still traded (bought and sold) by securities dealers.

Mutual funds An investment instrument through which individuals can direct small amounts of money in order to purchase part of a larger fund that is invested in several different stocks, thus lowering the risk that the investor will lose all of his or her investment.

Bid The highest price that anyone is willing to pay to buy a stock.

Ask The lowest price that anyone will accept to sell a stock.

Board lot A minimum number of trading units that the stock exchange is normally willing to allow for a buying or selling transaction.

Odd lot A number of shares less than a board lot.

Juniors Young companies that do not have an extensive business history on which to evaluate their potential ability for success.

Portfolio The different stocks that an investor has chosen to purchase.

CANADA'S RISKIEST STOCKS

Care to take a walk on the wild side? Consider investing in Canada's riskiest stocks. Recommended by no brokers or fund managers, the portfolio below encompasses 20 companies in *Profit* magazine's 1993 survey of Canada's fastest-growing companies whose shares are publicly traded — and available for purchase by investors with nerves of steel.

Montreal Stocks

TSE COMPLETE STOCK QUOTATIONS

Mutual Funds

Alberta Stocks

Vancouver Stocks

1. Using a computer spreadsheet program, create a spreadsheet to show the name of the company, the 12-month high and low stock price, and the percentage increase in the 12-month high and low stock price.

2. Which company's shares had the highest increase? Which had the lowest increase?

3. Using a newspaper, see if you can determine the prices of these shares today. Which company's shares have increased the most? Which have increased the least? Have any company's shares decreased below the 1993 12-month low stock price?

THE PROFIT 100 PORTFOLIO: 1993

Name	Rank	Exchange*	Stock price Apr. 16, '93	12-month High	12-month Low
Star Data	1	OTC	$0.45	$0.70	$0.05
Softkey Software	2	T, N	8.50	11.50	6.00
ISG Technologies	3	T	17.37	19.37	6.00
Clearly Canadian	6	V, N	9.50	25.00	8.25
National Hav-Info	8	T	0.40	0.60	0.12
Goldcorp	10	T	3.40	3.80	2.30
Liquidation World	12	A	1.07	1.75	0.27
Corel	18	T, N	18.75	24.87	13.50
Barrington	25	T	4.25	4.70	0.80
Chai-Na-Ta	27	T, N	8.25	8.87	4.75
Loewen Group	34	T, N	22.37	23.25	15.75
Dion Entertainment	37	T	6.87	8.25	3.00
Delrina	51	T	8.37	9.50	2.75
Dorel Industries	69	T	12.50	13.00	8.00
Groupe Sani Mobile	72	M	2.50	2.90	2.10
Elan Energy	78	T	17.37	17.37	10.37
MDC Corp.	81	T	1.32	1.90	0.37
Nutrilawn	84	A	0.20	0.24	0.03
InsulPro	94	V	0.28	0.85	0.20
Waterfurnace	95	V	2.25	3.30	1.40

*Exchanges: T-Toronto, M-Montreal, V-Vancouver, A-Alberta Stock Exchange, N-NASDAQ (U.S. unlisted market), OTC-Over the counter

Source: Reprinted from *Profit*, June, 1993

···················· How to Read Newspaper Listings ····················

1. Highest and lowest price paid for the stock to date this year. Venture Mining stock has traded as high as $8.00, and as low as $4.90 during the year. Shares traded under $5.00 are quoted in cents.

2. Abbreviated name of the company issuing the stock. This listing refers to Oil and Gas Exploration Limited's Class 'A' stock.

3. Annual dividend paid by the company. This is a projected annual rate based on dividend payments over the last twelve months.

Year High	Low	Stock	Div.	High	Low	Close	Change	Vol.
$ 17	14\frac{3}{4}$	Acme T. & D	$. 72	16\frac{3}{4}$	16\frac{1}{8}$	16\frac{1}{8}$	-$\frac{5}{8}$	400
29$\frac{3}{8}$	26	Comput Co.	2.28	29$\frac{1}{4}$	29$\frac{1}{4}$	29$\frac{1}{4}$	-$\frac{1}{8}$	100
15	7$\frac{7}{8}$	O & G Expl. A		9	8$\frac{3}{4}$	8$\frac{7}{8}$	-$\frac{1}{8}$	14400
8	490	Ven. Mining		5$\frac{1}{2}$	5$\frac{1}{2}$	5$\frac{1}{2}$	-$\frac{1}{8}$	Z 20
27$\frac{3}{4}$	26$\frac{1}{2}$	Sec. Bank	2.00	27	26$\frac{1}{2}$	27	+$\frac{1}{4}$	19626
345	240	Alpha Oil		280	.70	280	-5	30500
15$\frac{1}{4}$	12$\frac{1}{2}$	Imp Trust	1.20	13$\frac{1}{2}$	12$\frac{1}{4}$	13$\frac{1}{4}$	-$\frac{1}{2}$	64353
5$\frac{1}{4}$	350	West Ont. Mach		400	400	400	+25	205
24$\frac{1}{4}$	15$\frac{1}{2}$	UNITE	.90	21$\frac{3}{4}$	17$\frac{1}{2}$	21$\frac{3}{4}$	+2$\frac{3}{4}$	24780
42$\frac{5}{8}$	39$\frac{1}{8}$	C Fran Ent	2.05	42$\frac{3}{4}$	41$\frac{1}{2}$	42$\frac{5}{8}$	+$\frac{7}{8}$	90874
31	24	Kenora Iron	1.70	27	26$\frac{3}{4}$	27	-$\frac{1}{2}$	908
23$\frac{1}{2}$	19$\frac{1}{4}$	Silv Tel	1.45	22$\frac{1}{4}$	21$\frac{1}{8}$	21$\frac{3}{4}$	+$\frac{1}{4}$	17038
10$\frac{1}{4}$	8$\frac{1}{2}$	Elwood Pkg		9$\frac{1}{2}$	9$\frac{3}{8}$	9$\frac{1}{2}$	-$\frac{1}{8}$	1600
11$\frac{1}{2}$	7$\frac{3}{4}$	Gamma Res		9$\frac{5}{8}$	9$\frac{1}{8}$	9$\frac{3}{8}$	-$\frac{1}{8}$	9724
175	75	SYNBLEND Pr		140	108	130	+8	76200
310	205	IBL Br		275	220	265		27600
150	146$\frac{1}{2}$	Lon Util	3.15	149$\frac{1}{4}$	147$\frac{3}{4}$	149$\frac{1}{4}$	+1$\frac{1}{2}$	344

4. Highest price paid for the stock during this trading session was 16\frac{3}{4}$, and lowest was 16\frac{1}{8}$.

5. Price paid for the last board lot traded was $27.00. This was up 1/4 or 25 cents from the closing price in the previous session.

6. Number of shares traded during the trading session. The symbol z indicates that less than a board lot traded. (A board lot is usually 100 shares)

Reading Newspaper Stock Listings

In the financial section of most city newspapers, you will find the pages that report the daily buying and selling of stocks at various exchanges. Below is a typical newspaper listing of stocks. Some newspapers also report the "most active" stocks and their trading for the day.

On some exchanges, such as the Vancouver Stock Exchange, stocks that trade at prices of over $5 have the cents portion of the stock price quoted as a fraction, for example $5 1/2 represents $5.50. Stocks that have a price of less than $5 have their price expressed in cents, for example 215 represents $2.15. Common fractions are the following:

1/8 = $0.125	3/8 = $0.375	5/8 = $0.625
7/8 = $0.875	1/4 = $0.25	1/2 = $0.50
3/4 = $0.75		

MOST ACTIVE			
INDUSTRIALS			
Bramalea	6 039 000	$\frac{1}{4}$	-.035
Nova Cp Alta	1 703 522	$8\frac{1}{2}$	$-\frac{1}{4}$
Mitel Cp	1 255 034	$11\frac{1}{2}$	$+1\frac{3}{8}$
Int-City Prod	1 064 883	3.35	+.30
Can Pacific	949 891	$20\frac{1}{2}$	$+\frac{1}{4}$
MINES			
Pure Gld Res	1 422 400	.455	+.04
McChip Res	1 242 086	1.35	-.11
Brkwater Res	1 226 300	.115	-.005
TVX Gold	774 550	6.0	$-\frac{1}{4}$
Placer Dome	572 432	$25\frac{7}{8}$	$-\frac{3}{8}$
OILS			
Cdn Nat Res	548 995	20.0	$+\frac{3}{8}$
Cdn 88 Ener	502 600	2.05	-.05
Sask O&G	366 473	$9\frac{7}{8}$	$+\frac{1}{8}$
Cdn Nwscpe Res	327 147	4.40	-.10
Renaiss En	273 718	$31\frac{1}{2}$	$-\frac{1}{8}$
	VOLUME	**VALUE**	
Total	61 243 029	$592.9 mil	

Source: Canadian Press, Sept. 23, 1993

Sometimes an investor follows the daily price quotation in the newspaper and suddenly finds his or her stock is not printed. More often than not, if you cannot find a stock listing, it is because there was no trading in the previous day of trading. In this case, it will be found listed separately in the bid/ask section. There are two less common explanations for this occurrence: either the company has changed its name, or trading of the stock has been halted by the authorities of the exchange. The halting of trading can mean that an announcement will be made about an important issue — for example, the news that an important gold deposit has just been found — that affects the company and that can affect the price of the stock. Normal trading is resumed within 24 hours of such an announcement.

POINTS TO REMEMBER

- A company can finance new investments by borrowing money or issuing bonds, which is called debt financing, or by selling shares, referred to as equity financing.

- A bond is a certificate issued by a company to an individual or another company acknowledging that it owes a certain amount of money.

- A company can issue either preferred shares or common shares. Preferred shareholders are guaranteed dividends and always receive them before common shareholders.

- Stocks are bought and sold through stock exchanges. Canadian stock exchanges include the Toronto Stock Exchange, the Montreal Exchange, the Vancouver Stock Exchange, the Alberta Stock Exchange, and the Winnipeg Stock Exchange.

- Stock investments should be evaluated on potential profit and risk of investment.

FOCUSING ON BUSINESS

8. Define *risk*.

9. Explain the difference between *blue-chip stocks* and *venture stocks*.

10. With a partner, divide the terms listed below and take turns explaining to each other the meaning of each one.

   a. buy low–sell high

   b. bull market

   c. bear market

   d. buying on margin

   e. listed stock

   f. unlisted stock

   g. mutual funds

     h. bid

     i. ask

     j. board lot

     k. odd lot

     l. juniors

     m. portfolio

11. List the five Canadian stock exchanges.

EXPLORING BUSINESS

12. Using newspapers and magazines, select one article on insider trading and one on stock portfolios. Briefly outline the contents of the articles.

13. In a group of three, select a stock that is listed on an exchange. Using your resource centre and contacting a stock brokerage, determine the risk and potential profit of the stock. Does your group think it would be a good investment? Why or why not? Share your findings with the class.

14. Using the newspaper, select a blue-chip company from a stock-exchange listing. Obtain the address of the head office. Write the company a letter requesting a copy of its most recent annual report. Have a partner edit your letter. Revise your letter and then mail it. When you receive the annual report, list the common and preferred stock the company has issued. Does it pay dividends regularly? Would you purchase stocks in the company? Why or why not?

15. With a partner, investigate how computers and other forms of technology are used in stock market activities. Prepare a report outlining your findings and share them with the class.

16. In a small group, form a company and do the following:

     a. Outline all the necessary particulars in the form of a prospectus that you are preparing for the stock exchange.

     b. Decide how many shares you need to sell and the price per share that you need in order to raise the necessary capital to carry out your plan.

     c. Present your prospectus to the class and take a vote to see how many in the class would buy your shares if they had $1000 each.

WORKING WITH MATH

17. Work in groups of three. Each group has $50 000 to spend on shares.

a. Using the newspaper, select at least five but no more than twelve stocks from different companies.

b. Shares must be purchased on specific days as directed by your teacher.

c. You may keep part of your portfolio in stocks and part in cash. The interest paid on the cash balance will be 3 percent annually, calculated on the lowest cash balance for the four-week period.

d. When purchasing stocks, you are required to make your purchases in specific amounts based on the price of shares. If you wish to purchase, for example, a stock whose market selling price is 50 cents, then you must make your purchases in 500-share lots. See the chart below. (When selling your shares, you may sell them in any amounts.)

Price	Board Lot
Under $1	500 shares
Over $1 and under $50	100 shares
Over $50	10 shares

e. Decide how many shares of each stock you want to buy.

f. Calculate the stockbroker fees at 3.3 percent for every buy-and-sell transaction.

g. Design a spreadsheet to keep track of your transactions.

h. Display the results of your profit or loss on a graph.

i. At the end of four weeks, present your results to the class.

KEY TERMS

debt financing

equity financing

bond

principal

maturity date

share

stock

stock exchange

prospectus

preferred shares

common shares

dividend

blue-chip stocks

venture capital stocks

risk of investment

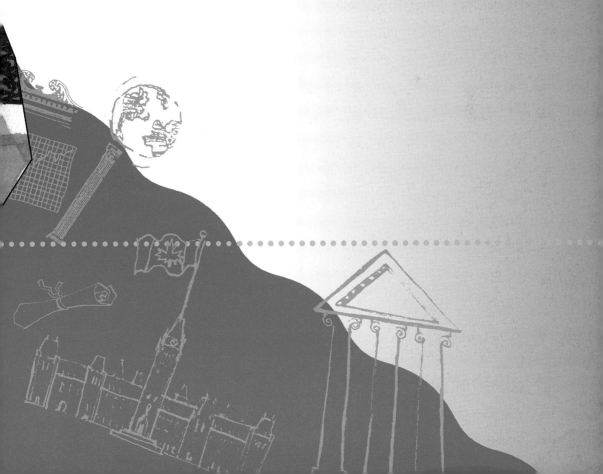

PART 5

The Law
in Canada

The Canadian Legal System

CHAPTER FOCUS

After studying this chapter you will be able to:

distinguish between rules and laws and understand the need for laws

•

explain the roles of common law, precedent, and statute law in our legal system·

•

describe the difference between private law and public law

•

explain the importance of the Canadian Charter of Rights and Freedoms

•

describe our criminal justice system as it applies to adults and young offenders

LAWS ARE NECESSARY TO REGULATE OUR business affairs and ensure that people fulfil their contractual obligations. We also need laws that help to safeguard our private property and even protect our lives. Imagine the chaos if we had no traffic laws.

But our laws have to do more than provide a sense of order. They have to balance the rights of the individual against the rights of society. Thus, the law tries to protect the rights and freedoms of each individual, ensuring that everyone is treated fairly and equally.

Because we live in a democratic country, we all have a part to play in maintaining and improving our legal system, and anyone who feels that a law is unfair has the right — and perhaps the obligation — to try to change that law. In this chapter, we will examine the difference between rules and laws and then briefly explore the origins of Canadian law. We will examine the court system as it applies to adults and young offenders and compare the sentencing options available to judges in the adult system with those available to judges who sentence young offenders.

The Canadian System of Law

Most things we do are governed by rules of some kind. There are rules that govern the games in which you participate, rules concerning the way you behave at school, rules established by your parents, and rules that affect your part-time job. You can probably list many other activities you are involved in that are governed by rules. **Laws** are rules that are enacted by a governing authority and that reflect society's values.

Canadian law is derived from two separate legal traditions: common law and the Napoleonic or French Civil Code. The **common law** system comes from England and is made up of judges' past decisions based on the unwritten but understood laws of the land. These decisions are called **precedents**. The common law system is the root of the law in most of Canada, but in the province of Quebec, the **French Civil Code** governs civil law, which is defined below. It differs from the common law system in that decisions are made based on a comprehensive set of written laws. Precedent is relied on to a much lesser extent.

This ancient tarot card depicts the female figure of Justice. She was not depicted with a blindfold until modern times.

Our laws can be divided into two categories — private law and public law — according to the type of issues being considered. **Civil law**, the more common name for private law, is used primarily to settle disputes between individuals. Civil law deals with business contracts, disputes concerning property, and the rights and obligations of family members. When one person sues another over a private dispute, it is a concern of civil law.

Public law deals with matters that affect society's interests. The most familiar area of public law is criminal law. In Canada, **criminal law** deals with issues in which a wrong has been committed against society. Criminal law is governed by the **Criminal Code**, which lists all the possible offences and sets out the laws that apply to each offence. When someone is found guilty of breaking one of these laws, such as assaulting another person or committing an act of vandalism, he or she is considered to have committed a wrong against society.

One individual cannot sue another individual for a criminal offence, so the state intervenes to prosecute the accused. Because the monarch represents the state, it is said that the Crown is prosecuting the offender. This explains why in a criminal prosecution the case is called, for example, *R. v. Whitehorn*. "R." stands for either *rex* (Latin for king) or *regina* (Latin for queen), "*v.*" stands for *versus* (Latin for against), and Whitehorn is the accused.

Other areas of public law are constitutional law, which deals with the organization of the government, and administrative law, which deals with the responsibilities of governmental officials.

THE ROLE OF THE GOVERNMENT

The government, a body of elected representatives, has the responsibility of enacting laws that will ensure a safe and orderly society. These laws must protect the freedom of individuals from unnecessary restraint and, at the same time, make individuals responsible for respecting the rights of others and the legal system.

As society becomes more complex, laws need to change and new ones have to be created. For example, 20 years ago very few people had computers; today, most businesses and many families own a computer. Laws have been created to control the use of computers to gain access to other people's private information. Another example of new laws being passed in response to new technology are the new laws to control the illegal use and copying of video programs.

Laws passed by governments are called **statutes**. The statutes passed by Parliament are federal statutes and only Parliament can add to or change them. The Criminal Code, for example, is a set of federal statutes. Laws passed by a provincial legislature are provincial statutes. Since roads and education are under the jurisdiction of provincial governments, laws affecting them are examples of provincial statutes. Laws passed by municipal government are called **by-laws** or **ordinances**.

Governments cannot make laws in any area they wish. Certain rules state the kind of laws that governments can create and the level of government that can make the laws concerning particular areas. These rules are contained in the Canadian Constitution. A **constitution** is a document that sets out the legal framework of a country. It defines the nature of the government, the powers of various levels of governments, how government officials are elected, and the rights and responsibilities of the citizens. Our present constitution is called the **Constitution Act, 1982**.

A fundamental part of our Constitution is the **Canadian Charter of Rights and Freedoms**, which limits the power of the government and protects certain rights and freedoms of individuals. The Charter protects the following rights and freedoms:

- **Fundamental Freedoms:** These include the right to freedom of speech, freedom of religion, freedom of the press, and freedom of peaceful assembly and association (the right to belong to groups such as trade unions).

- **Democratic Rights:** These include the right of citizens to vote in elections and to run for public office.

- **Mobility Rights:** These include the right of citizens and permanent residents to travel, to live, or to seek employment anywhere in Canada.

- **Legal Rights:** These include the right to consult a lawyer if you are arrested and to be informed of that right, to stand trial within a reasonable period of time, to be presumed innocent until proven guilty, and to be protected against unreasonable searches, arbitrary imprisonment, and cruel and unusual punishment.

- **Equality Rights:** These include the right to protection against discrimination based on race, national or ethnic origin, colour, religion, sex, age, or mental or physical disability.

- **Language rights:** These include the right of all members of the public to receive services from the federal government in either official language, English or French, and to have children of citizens receive instruction in their first language, English or French.

Although all these rights are very important, they are not absolute. This means they can be limited in order to protect the rights of others. An example of this involves the law concerning roadside spot checks of motor vehicle drivers. The Supreme Court of Canada held that these spot checks were contrary to section 9 of the Charter, which states that "everyone has the right not to be arbitrarily detained or imprisoned." However, the Supreme Court justices went on to say that the spot checks were a reasonable way to reduce death and injury caused by drinking and driving, thus the infringement of the driver's rights was a reasonable one.

R. v. P.R.C. (1993), 8 C.C.C. (3D) 442

The accused, a young offender, was detained for a breathalyzer test. The police initially attempted to contact the offender's mother, but she indicated that she had to remain at her job and said the offender's brother would come to the police station. The offender was told on two occasions that she had the right to counsel, but she declined to exercise that right. However, when she learned that her brother had arrived at the station, she requested an opportunity to speak to him. The police refused to let her do so until the breathalyzer test, which they had already begun, was complete.

The accused claimed that her right to counsel under section 10 (b) of the Canadian Charter of Rights and Freedoms was being infringed and the evidence obtained from the breathalyzer test should not be admitted into court.

Section 10 of the Charter states in part:

Everyone has the right on arrest or detention ...

(b) to retain and instruct counsel without delay and to be informed of that right; ...

1. With a partner, on behalf of the Crown, prepare an argument that would allow the evidence to be admitted.

2. With a partner, prepare an argument to have the evidence excluded.

3. How would you decide the case? Why?

FOCUSING ON BUSINESS

1. Why does our society need laws?
2. What is the difference between *common law* and the *French Civil Code*?
3. Explain the difference between *civil law* and *criminal law*.
4. Define the terms *statute* and *by-law*.
5. What is a *constitution*?
6. What is the main purpose of the Canadian Charter of Rights and Freedoms?
7. List the six kinds of rights and freedoms protected by the Charter.

EXPLORING BUSINESS

8. Obtain two examples of by-laws or ordinances affecting your neighbourhood. These could include examples from your street, park, shopping mall, or any other location you think might have a by-law or ordinance posted. Why do you think these by-laws are important?

9. Using a newspaper, find one article that deals with criminal law and one that deals with civil law. Create an organizer to compare the two cases. What are the cases? How do they differ? How are they similar? How are the police involved? How are the courts involved?

10. In small groups, make a list of all the rules and laws that you come into contact with in a 24-hour period. Divide them into rules and laws. Divide the laws into municipal by-laws, provincial laws, and federal laws. Do you disagree with any of them? Brainstorm ideas on how to become more knowledgeable about Canadian law and how to change laws with which you disagree.

11. *The Canadian Charter of Rights and Freedoms should become the Canadian Charter of Rights and Responsibilities. The responsibilities of all Canadians should be outlined clearly.* In groups of four, debate this idea. First, divide into pairs. Decide which pair should take the Yes side and which should take the No side. If you are on the Yes side, be sure you have thought about which responsibilities should be included in this new Charter.

12. Prepare a scrapbook of at least five news articles that make reference to the Charter. Write a brief summary of each article outlining how the Charter applies. Form small groups and discuss the different issues in your articles. What impact is the Charter having on our way of life? Has the Charter improved our legal system? Explain your views.

CAREERS

LAW

1. In small groups, brainstorm and list careers in the field of law. Your list might include court clerk, court reporter, lawyer, judge, police officer, police-dog handler, and probation officer.

2. With a partner, select a career that interests you from the list you created in Question 1. Research the career by visiting your resource centre and guidance office, contacting associations and organizations for literature, or interviewing someone in the field you have chosen. If you interview someone, ask if you can videotape the interview to share with the class. Learn about the career by gathering information that includes the following:

   - education required
   - experience required
   - skills required
   - responsibilities
   - salary range
   - any other relevant and interesting information

3. Create a poster to display your career research. Present your findings to the class.

THE CRIMINAL JUSTICE SYSTEM

When a crime has been committed, many institutions within the criminal justice system become involved. The government, police, courts, officers of the penal system, and social agencies must co-ordinate their activities to protect the rights of the accused and to represent the interests of society.

The Government
The government, as mentioned earlier, has the responsibility of enacting laws that will ensure a safe and orderly society. These laws must protect individuals from unnecessary restraint and at the same time ensure that we respect the system and the rights of others.

The Police

The police are responsible for enforcing the law and maintaining order in a society. In this role, they investigate a crime if one has been committed.

The police must follow certain procedures after arresting a suspect. The accused person must be told that he or she is under arrest, as well as the nature of the charges. The arresting officer must tell the accused that he or she has the right to consult a lawyer without delay. The accused must be given an opportunity to contact his or her lawyer or be informed of the right to obtain legal aid. An accused who cannot afford a lawyer is entitled to apply for legal aid. An accused who qualifies for **legal aid** can obtain the services of a lawyer who will be paid by the government through the legal aid system. A recipient of legal aid may have to repay the government depending on his or her financial status.

A police officer on duty in Saskatoon.

Once a person is arrested and accused of comitting a crime, he or she has the right to a bail hearing as soon as possible. A **bail hearing** (also known as an interim release) is held to determine if the person arrested should be released or should continue to be held in custody. If the accused is released, he or she might have to provide a certain sum of money, which is known as **bail**, to the court in order to guarantee that he or she will appear for the trial.

The accused has the right to a trial within a reasonable period of time and to be presumed innocent until proven guilty. These rights are guaranteed by the Charter.

The Courts

The function of the courts is to administer the law. The judges must be impartial (must not take sides) and ensure that the accused receives a fair trial. Because the Charter guarantees that the accused is presumed innocent until proven guilty, the Crown has to prove guilt beyond a reasonable doubt. If the person pleads guilty, the Crown reviews the case and the judge sentences the offender.

The system of courts is not identical in all provinces, but it can generally be divided into three levels. At the first level are the Provincial Courts. These courts deal with most criminal cases and also include Small Claims Court, which deals with civil matters. The limit or maximum amount for a lawsuit in Small Claims Court varies from province to province and ranges from $500 to $6000. This first level may also include other special courts.

Some provinces have an intermediate level of courts called County or District Courts. They deal with some of the more serious criminal trials and civil matters whose damages exceed the limit for Small Claims Courts. These courts will also hear appeals from the Provincial Courts. An **appeal** is a request to a higher court to re-examine a case on the grounds that the judge and/or the jury made a wrong decision or that a legal error was made.

The highest level of court in each province is the Superior or Supreme Court of the province. This court is made up of two divisions, a trial court and an appeal court. The trial court hears the most serious criminal trials with a judge and jury, as well as serious civil trials. The Court of Appeal hears appeals from all the lower level courts.

The Supreme Court of Canada is located in Ottawa and is the highest court of all. There are nine justices, or judges, in this court and they hear appeals only from the provincial Courts of Appeal.

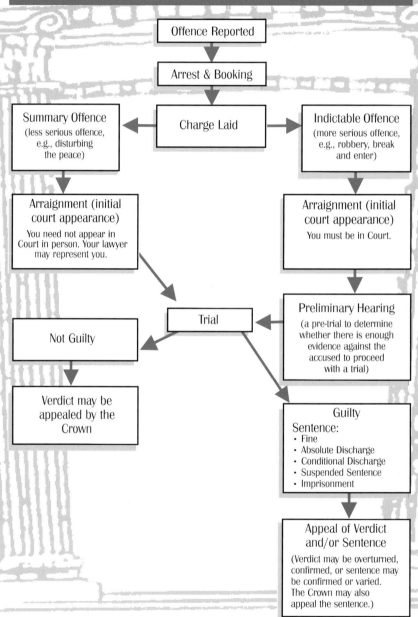

ADULT COURT PROCESS

Offence Reported

↓

Arrest & Booking

↓

Charge Laid

← **Summary Offence**
(less serious offence, e.g., disturbing the peace)

→ **Indictable Offence**
(more serious offence, e.g., robbery, break and enter)

Arraignment (initial court appearance)
You need not appear in Court in person. Your lawyer may represent you.

Arraignment (initial court appearance)
You must be in Court.

↓

Preliminary Hearing
(a pre-trial to determine whether there is enough evidence against the accused to proceed with a trial)

Trial

Not Guilty

↓

Verdict may be appealed by the Crown

Guilty
Sentence:
• Fine
• Absolute Discharge
• Conditional Discharge
• Suspended Sentence
• Imprisonment

↓

Appeal of Verdict and/or Sentence
(Verdict may be overturned, confirmed, or sentence may be confirmed or varied. The Crown may also appeal the sentence.)

Source: Maria G. Franks and Claire McNeil, *Under 19: You and the Law* (Halifax, NS: Public Legal Education Society of Nova Scotia, 1986), p. 19.

SPY-TECH

That stuffed Garfield cat in a corner of the baby's room has a hidden video camera in its button navel. In the hall is a motion-detector alarm and camera system that not only scares off intruders with a loud noise and bright lights, but takes their pictures for posterity, and for the cops.

And what about you? Do you just want a secret hiding place, such as a hollowed-out copy of a biography to tuck away a passport and a few jewels?

But what do you really need, and where can you get it? You can turn to Spy-Tech, Canada's first store wholly dedicated to security and surveillance devices.

The store opened in 1991, when founder/owner Ursula Lebana decided to make a rather extraordinary career switch — from the family furniture business to night-vision video cameras, counterfeit money detectors, and covert metal detectors for dance-club doormen who want to screen out would-be troublemakers.

Indeed, much of her new-found business is in high-end equipment that can be rented out on a weekly basis.

For example, the woman dealing with sexual harassment is a potential customer for an ordinary-looking briefcase that conceals a hidden tape recorder that can be turned on by simply sliding a pen out of one inconspicuous holder and into another. You turn it off by moving the pen back into the original holder.

A standard-looking gym bag hides a portable video camera. A black mesh on the side of the bag is actually optically transparent: the lens can see through it, but you can't see the camera. A hidden button on the side activates the camera, which also records the date and time. And, if you're worried about whether the babysitter is looking after the baby properly, you might want to rent a minia-ture video camera hidden in a teddy bear, plus a time-lapse VCR.

Similarly, a small leather purse holds a microcassette recorder, and a brass fitting near the handle is, in fact, the switch. And there's a splendid umbrella with a microphone fit-ted in its base, and a connection for a voice-activated microcassette recorder in the han-dle. Just leave it in a corner of the office and you can finally become the proverbial fly on the wall.

Mind you, if the latter idea strikes you as a more useful tool for industrial espionage, you might be relieved to know that the antidote is also near at hand. Ms. Lebana subcontracts the services of a real security consultant to sweep your home, office, and car.

If this all sounds like stuff out of a spy movie, it is. Another part of Ms. Lebana's business is renting equipment to local television and movie productions.

Not all of the more than 100 products in Ms. Lebana's store are expensive and exotic. One of her most popular items is the Fox40 whistle.

The Safebook is a real book with its pages hollowed-out and replaced with a plastic com-partment for valuables. For book-free homes, you can buy a Safe Can, an empty can of Campbell's Cream of Asparagus Soup, Ajax Lemon Pledge, STP, or more than 100 others with a screw-on bottom.

Ms. Lebana's favourite gadget is the Silent Policeman Photo Security System. Another Canadian product, it uses motion detectors to pick up any intruder's movement, activat-ing an eardrum-piercing siren and halogen lights. Simultaneously, a camera, locked inside a tamper-proof compartment, takes a time-dated photograph that provides "red-handed" evidence.

Somehow, it doesn't seem very surprising that business has been good; and, indeed, Ms. Lebana says, it started strong and just keeps growing.

Sentencing

When an accused person is found guilty of an offence, the judge has the difficult task of passing sentence. The judge has a number of options and will choose one that is most appropriate for the type of offence committed. In making this choice, he or she will consider the protection of the public, the likelihood of rehabilitation or reform of the offender, and the need for punishment. Options available to a judge when sen-tencing someone include absolute or conditional discharge, probation, suspended sentence, community service orders and fines, and incarcer-ation (imprisonment).

Wizard of Id. Reprinted by permission of Hart and Creators Syndicate, Inc.

Absolute and Conditional Discharges

An absolute or a conditional discharge is usually given to young offenders or to first-time offenders who are convicted of minor offences. A discharge results in the conviction not being registered — in other words, the offender has no criminal record. The difference between the two types of discharges is that an **absolute discharge** carries no conditions and a **conditional discharge** includes any number of conditions that the judge deems appropriate. These could include an order to continue at school, the imposition of a curfew, and so on.

Probation

Probation is an alternative to sending the offender to prison. An offender who is placed on probation is released into the community but will be under the supervision of a probation officer for a specific period of time. As with a conditional discharge, certain restrictions will be included with the probation order.

Suspended Sentence

A **suspended sentence** is one in which the judge has given the offender a jail sentence but, at the same time, has suspended the enforcement of that sentence. Suspended sentences are usually accompanied by probation for a certain period of time. If the offender breaches the probation order or commits another offence, he or she can be sent back to court and the judge can enforce the original sentence.

Community Service Orders and Fines

A **community service order** is a sentence whereby the offender is not placed in an institution but is instead put to work for the community.

A judge may also fine an offender. This type of sentence is usually given for relatively minor offences or when the offender has gained financially from the crime. For example, corporations who break pollution control laws are often fined.

Incarceration

Incarceration means imprisonment. Judges usually consider this form of sentence a last resort. For a sentence of 30 days or less, which is often administered by the local county or municipality, the offender will usually spend the time in a local jail. If the sentence is for less than two years, it will be served in a provincial institution or correctional centre. A person who receives a sentence of two years or more will be sent to a federal penitentiary. In a federal penitentiary, the period of imprisonment can be as long as life.

Social Agencies

There are many agencies that deal with people who come into conflict with the law. Some of these agencies are involved with people after they have had their first appearance in court. The hope is to try and help the person to avoid committing another offence. One such agency, the Elizabeth Fry Society, was created in order to assist female offenders after they have been released from an institution. Many offenders have difficulty re-entering society after release from an institution and need assistance with employment, accommodation, and generally coping with the adjustment back into society.

YOUNG OFFENDERS

The Young Offenders Act became law on April 2, 1984. The Act represented a substantial change in philosophy concerning the treatment of youthful offenders. The **Young Offenders Act** is based on the principle that young people should bear the responsibility for the illegal acts they commit, although they will not be held as accountable as if they were adults. The Act also recognizes that young persons have special needs and require guidance and assistance. Based on these principles, the Young Offenders Act applies only to youths from their twelfth until their eighteenth birthday. Young people over the age of 18 are treated as adults and are dealt with in the adult criminal justice system. Young people under the age of 12 are said to be incapable of committing a criminal offence and are dealt with in the community under the province's child welfare legislation.

Young offenders may be transferred to adult court after appearing in Youth Court.

Although the Young Offenders Act recognizes society's responsibility in pre-venting crime by young people, it also recognizes the need for society to be protected from such illegal behaviour. One way of providing this protection to society is the provision in the Act that a young person 14 years of age or older may be transferred to adult court when the following factors are taken into consideration:

- the seriousness of the offence
- the age, maturity, and previous record of the offender
- the availability of treatment in a correctional facility
- any other factors the court considers relevant

Young people charged with committing a criminal offence are called **young offenders.** Regardless of the seriousness of the offence, they must first appear in **Youth Court**, where they will be tried by a Youth Court judge. If the Crown wishes to apply to have the young offender tried in adult court, the application must be made before the Youth Court judge, who must agree before the case can be transferred.

The Act emphasizes that the young offenders are guaranteed the same rights as adults under the Charter. This means they have the right to be told that they are under arrest, to be informed of the charges, the right to a lawyer or legal aid, the right to be tried within a reasonable time period, the right to reasonable bail, and so on. In addition, the Act protects the identity of young offenders and their families by prohibiting the media from disclosing their names.

BURGLARY OF HOME LAUNCHED HOUSESITTERS FIRM

CONNECTING BUSINESS WITH ENTREPRENEURSHIP

The television was gone. So were the washer, freezer and dryer. Even the dishes and cutlery.

That was when David Ballett decided to go ahead with the idea he'd had since he was a boy.

When he was seven years old, he'd read Forbes and Fortune magazines and dreamed of becoming an entrepreneur.

In his teens, he'd subscribed to *Los Angeles* magazine and had spotted the odd classified ad for a firm offering to look after people's homes while they were away.

Now it was 1976, he was 16, and he and his parents had returned to their home near St. Catharines after a vacation to discover their house had been burgled.

The time was coming, he reasoned, for The Housesitters.

Today, he runs a company by that name out of three two-storey houses on Queen St. E. in Toronto. In 1992, it had sales of $3.6 million, a staff of 42 full-time employees, and more than 1000 "freelancers" across Canada.

He started the business in 1981 while a student at Brock University, running it out of his father's accounting office.

Ads in local newspapers and flyers were financed with the $1500 he had saved as an actor at the Shaw Festival in 1979 and 1980, and as a puppeteer

David Ballet of the Housesitters

at Maple Leaf Village in Niagara Falls, Ont.

Ballett remembers his first customers, the Sieberts, a retired couple.

While they visited Jamaica, he made daily trips to their home, watering their plants, cutting the grass, doing the weeding. Fee: $8 for an hour's visit each day.

"But first, I had to educate people,"

he says. "When people buy a home, how many of them have the locks changed? And people should look for loopholes in the fine print in their insurance policies to see if they're still covered if they're away for 48 hours or more."

(To be successful in the housesitting business, Ballett's firm also walks and feeds pets and even looks after children through its bonded employees.)

He knew he needed a larger market than the Niagara region. Metro [Toronto] beckoned.

By the time he moved to Toronto in 1982, he had four part-time employees in St. Catharines and 50 accounts, with revenue of $2400 in his first year. And $3000 saved.

He lived in and ran his business from a one-room apartment at Yonge and Bloor streets, working as a waiter at a dinner theatre at night, where he made $800 a week in tips.

All his money, after living expenses, went into promoting the business, with friends designing graphics for free — and helping him distribute them on the same terms.

All the time he kept learning from his mistakes.

He spent $600 on an ad in the December-January issue of the O'Keefe Centre's program and didn't get any response.

"I hadn't realized that no one takes them home."

Nor did a half-page ad in the business section of another Toronto daily newspaper result in any business — "and that cost me thousands."

But Ballett did have a sympathetic manager at the dinner theatre, who allowed him to distribute his business card to customers.

By then, he was hiring senior citizens to make his house calls, with charges ranging from $9 an hour to feed pets or water plants, cut grass, or shovel snow, to $22 for an overnight stay.

Ballett's first year in Toronto brought in revenue of $12 000. In 1983, the first year he worked at Housesitters full-time, it rose to $48 000.

Today, Ballett charges $34 a day for a live-in contract or $14 for a daily check. The fee is $75 a day to look after two children.

Since 1985, he's been selling franchises and now has 27 across Canada, with three company-owned operations in Toronto, Montreal, and Belleville.

The next step? Expansion into the United States ....

1. What does David Ballett suggest home buyers should do for security?
2. Based on the demographics for the 1990s, do you think David Ballett's business will continue to be successful? Explain.
3. Survey ten people to find out how many have had their residence broken into. Then, as a class, combine and discuss the survey results.

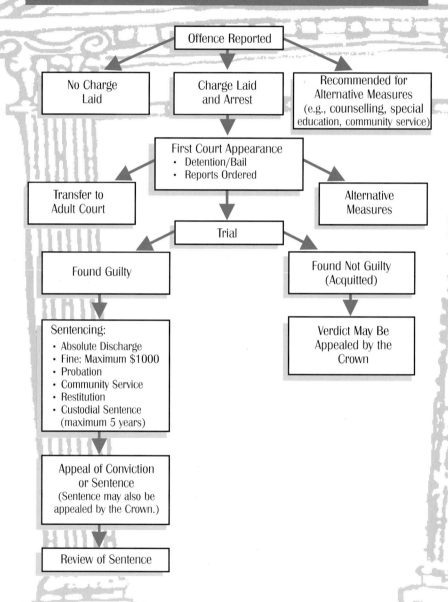

YOUTH COURT PROCESS

Offence Reported

No Charge Laid

Charge Laid and Arrest

Recommended for Alternative Measures (e.g., counselling, special education, community service)

First Court Appearance
- Detention/Bail
- Reports Ordered

Transfer to Adult Court

Alternative Measures

Trial

Found Guilty

Found Not Guilty (Acquitted)

Sentencing:
- Absolute Discharge
- Fine: Maximum $1000
- Probation
- Community Service
- Restitution
- Custodial Sentence (maximum 5 years)

Verdict May Be Appealed by the Crown

Appeal of Conviction or Sentence
(Sentence may also be appealed by the Crown.)

Review of Sentence

Source: Maria G. Franks and Claire McNeil, *Under 19: You and the Law* (Halifax, NS: Public Legal Education Society of Nova Scotia, 1986), p. 17.

Once a young person is found guilty of an offence, the Youth Court must decide on the appropriate sentence, or **disposition**, as it is called in the case of young offenders. A young offender can receive a discharge, which means that no formal conviction is registered, even though there is a finding of guilt. The young offender can be fined up to a maximum of $1000 or placed on probation under the supervision of a probation officer. The young offender may be ordered to do community work or instructed to pay the victim for the damages, which is known as restitution. As a last resort, the young offender may be placed in custody. Until 1992, the maximum term that could be given to a young offender in Youth Court was three years. This was increased to five years in response to public concern over the increase in crime committed by young people.

Records kept by the police, courts, or by any others concerning offences committed by young persons must remain confidential, and their contents may be disclosed only to the young persons, their families, lawyers, and generally to those engaged in the administration of justice. Police records must be destroyed two or five years — depending on the seriousness of the offence — after the sentence has been served.

POINTS TO REMEMBER

- Rules made by the government are referred to as laws.
- Common law originated in England and is based on unwritten but accepted laws. The French Civil Code, used in Quebec, is based on written laws.
- Private (civil) law deals mainly with disputes between individuals. Public law deals with matters that affect society as a whole.
- Statutes are laws passed by federal and provincial governments. By-laws are laws made by municipal governments.
- Canada's Constitution is set forth in the Constitution Act, 1982.
- The Supreme Court of Canada is the highest court in Canada.
- A young person between the ages of 12 and 18 who is charged with committing a criminal offence will appear in Youth Court.

FOCUSING ON BUSINESS

13. Outline the procedure the police must follow when a person is arrested.

14. Explain the purpose of legal aid.

15. What is a *bail hearing*?

16. Explain the purpose of an appeal.

17. What is meant by a *disposition*?

EXPLORING BUSINESS

18. "The Young Offenders Act is too lenient and is doing little to prevent the increase in crime." Write a brief response to this statement. You can either agree or disagree with the statement. Explain your answer.

19. The federal government is conducting a survey in order to assess the public's satisfaction with the Young Offenders Act applying to young people aged 12 to 18. In small groups, discuss the issue and prepare a response outlining your recommendations for the minimum and maximum ages to which the Act should apply. Also, comment on the age at which a young offender should be transferred to adult court. Support your group's position with cases or statistics from newspapers, magazines, or television and radio news programs.

20. In small groups, prepare a questionnaire to interview store owners. You are interested in gathering data on the effects of crime on retail business. Your questions should examine the extent of shoplifting; the age of the offenders; and the effectiveness of the police, the courts, and the criminal justice system in dealing with the problem. Each member of the group should interview two retailers. Share your findings with the class.

21. With a partner, choose one of the following statements and debate it. One of you will agree with it and one of you will disagree.

    "Freedom of speech is the most important freedom and nothing should ever interfere with it."

    "Inmates in a prison should not have the right to vote in an election."

    "The death penalty is the only just punishment for someone convicted of murder."

22. Morley is 17 years old. He has been charged with shoplifting at a store in the local mall. Section 322 of the Criminal Code reads:

322. Everyone commits theft who fraudulently and without colour of right takes, or fraudulently and without colour of right converts to his use or to the use of another person, anything, whether animate or inanimate, with intent, (a) to deprive, temporarily or absolutely, the owner of it, or a person who has a special property or interest in it, of the thing or of his property or interest in it; (b) to pledge it or deposit it as security; (c) to part with it under a condition with respect to its return that the person who parts with it may be unable to perform; or (d) to deal with it in such a manner that it cannot be restored in the condition in which it was at the time it was taken or converted.

Morley cannot afford a lawyer and has a number of questions concerning his defence, the court procedure, and legal aid. He has come to you for assistance. Using your resource centre, prepare a list of the names and addresses of organizations in your community that might be of assistance to Morley.

23. Read the following case:

R. v. Keating (1993), 76 C.C.C. (3d) 570

Mr. Keating was charged with assault and uttering a death threat after an altercation with a youth in a shopping mall owned by Mr. Keating. The youth had come to the shopping mall to purchase something from one of the stores. After making the purchase, he began to skateboard in the mall. There were signs posted in the area prohibiting skateboarding, as this activity had become prevalent and created problems for the tenants and the owner of the mall.

Mr. Keating observed the youth using a planter in the parking-lot area as a skateboard wall. Mr. Keating grabbed the youth by the throat with both hands and shook him. Mr. Keating was angry when he did this and did it without warning. Mr. Keating said, "If I see you around, I'll kill you."

Section 41 (1) of the Criminal Code reads:

41. (1) Everyone who is in peaceable possession of a dwelling-house or real property, and every one lawfully assisting him or acting under his authority, is justified in using force to prevent any person from trespassing on the dwelling-house or real property, or to remove a trespasser therefrom, if he uses no more force than is necessary.

Work in small groups to discuss the case and answer the following questions:

a. Was the youth a trespasser? Explain.

b. Did Mr. Keating use more force than necessary to evict the youth? Why?

c. How would you decide the case? Explain.

WORKING WITH MATH

24. Read the following newspaper article:

Publicize high-risk parolees, 69% say

Canadians overwhelmingly want police to publicize the names of high-risk offenders when they are released from prison.

A new Angus Reid-Southam News poll released recently found that about two out of every three Canadians, or 69 percent, think the practice is a good idea because the public has a right to know when dangerous individuals are freed into their community.

Only 26 percent of those surveyed feel it's a bad idea, because such inmates already have paid their debt to society.

The poll also found massive support for a proposed "stalking" law to protect women from harassment and threats by their ex-husbands and boyfriends.

In recent months, several police forces across the country have announced they will release information, including names, descriptions and in some cases photographs, on parolees labelled as high-risk by prison authorities.

Police and victims' rights groups say the move will allow the public to better protect themselves. But prisoners' rights advocates and defence lawyers have condemned it as a violation of rights that could lead to vigilantism.

The poll also found that more than eight in ten Canadians, or 83 percent, support a new "stalking" law to protect women from harassment and threats by their ex-husbands and boyfriends.

Only 12 percent are against the criminalization of stalking, which is being considered by the federal government.

The telephone survey of 1501 adults, conducted from February 16–22, is considered accurate within 2.5 percentage points, 19 times in 20.

······························ CANADIANS' VIEWS ··························

Do you think it is a good or bad idea to announce publicly when high-risk offenders are being let out of jail on parole?

Province/Territory	Good	Bad	Unsure
Canada	69%	26%	5%
British Columbia	78	14	8
Alberta	82	16	2
Manitoba/Saskatchewan	75	19	6
Ontario	75	21	5
Quebec	51	44	5
Atlantic [provinces]	64	27	9

Do you think stalking (situation where a person persistently bothers or intimidates another person) should be made illegal?

Province/Territory	Yes	No	Unsure
Canada	83%	12%	4%
British Columbia	92	6	2
Alberta	88	8	4
Manitoba/Saskatchewan	85	11	4
Ontario	86	10	4
Quebec	74	21	5
Atlantic [provinces]	81	11	7

Source: Angus Reid poll

As a class, conduct a poll by asking members of the class the two questions at the top of each chart. Record the results on the board under the headings Good, Bad, and Unsure for the first question, and Yes, No, and Unsure for the second question (as in the article). Calculate the percentage of student responses based on these three headings. How do the class results compare with Canadians' views? Create a graph to illustrate your findings.

KEY TERMS

law	Legal Rights
common law	Equality Rights
precedent	language rights
French Civil Code	legal aid
civil law	bail hearing
public law	bail
criminal law	appeal
Criminal Code	absolute discharge
statute	conditional discharge
by-law	probation
ordinance	suspended sentence
constitution	community service order
Constitution Act, 1982	incarceration
Canadian Charter of Rights and Freedoms	Young Offenders Act
Fundamental Freedoms	young offender
Democratic Rights	Youth Court
Mobility Rights	disposition

CHAPTER

13

CHAPTER FOCUS

...er studying this chapter you
will be able to:

distinguish between a
tort and a crime

•

know that not all torts
are intentional

•

explain the importance
tort law in settling disputes
between individuals

Respecting the
Rights of Others

MAGINE THAT YOU ARE A SUCCESSFUL entrepreneur operating an espresso bar. On one particular day, you have repeatedly asked a person in your shop to leave the premises because she is being loud and obnoxious and is disturbing other customers. She refuses to leave. As the owner, do you have the right to remove her from your shop? Or, on another occasion, you pick up a newspaper and read an article profiling you and your shop. Some of the information contained in the article is false and potentially damaging. Do you have the right to sue?

In this chapter, we will explore the area of law that deals with wrongs committed by one person against another and whether they were committed intentionally or unintentionally. In addition, we will examine how the law tries to ensure that every citizen has access to any job, public place, or accommodation and is protected from discrimination in the workplace.

TORT LAW

The area of the law that deals with the compensation of injured parties is called tort law. A **tort** is a civil wrong, as opposed to a criminal wrong. That is, a tort is a wrong committed by one person against another person, rather than against the state or society. Tort law tries to compensate the injured party for damages that were caused intentionally or unintentionally. Tort law can be divided into two categories: intentional torts and unintentional torts.

INTENTIONAL TORTS

Intentional torts are wrongs that are deliberate. As far as intentional torts are concerned, the law applies to three areas:

- intentional interference with a person's property

- intentional interference with a person's reputation

- intentional interference with a person

Someone who believes that a tort has been committed against him or her can sue in civil court. The person who is suing is called the **plaintiff** and the person being sued is called the **defendant**. Both sides present their cases to a judge and sometimes a jury. If the judge agrees that the defendant did commit a tort against the plaintiff, he or she will award **damages** or some other form of **compensation**. Damages are in the form of money. For example, if Vezna lost three days' wages because of an auto accident, the judge could order the defendant to pay Vezna the equivalent of three days' worth of wages. As well, the judge could order payment of extra damages for Vezna's legal fees and to compensate her for any pain and suffering she experienced.

Intentional Interference with a Person's Property

Generally, the owner of property (a house, a car, a store, land, and so on) has the right to decide who is allowed into, or onto, the property. Any unwanted people coming into, or onto, the property are called **trespassers**, and the owner could sue them for the tort of trespass. Under the law, you can use as much force as necessary to remove trespassers from your property. This allows owners of stores and shopping malls to remove trespassers. However, the law does not permit a landowner to set traps for trespassers.

It is possible to interfere with a person's property indirectly, not by interfering with the property itself, but with the owner's rights over the property (say, enjoyment). This tort is referred to as **private nuisance**.

For example, this might occur if a property owner allows a tree to grow to a point where it is hanging over a neighbour's fence. The leaves from the overhanging tree fall into the swimming pool, and the owner is constantly scooping them out. If the neighbour with the tree refuses to correct this situation, the owner of the pool could apply to the courts for an order requiring the tree to be trimmed. In one case, a shopkeeper was awarded damages because the queue awaiting the opening of a theatre habitually blocked the entrance to his store and was found to be a nuisance. There is a related tort called **public nuisance**, which refers to offences that interfere with the rights of the public (for example, pollution). If a limited number of people are affected, there may be compensation requested, but the usual course of action involves the seeking of an injunction that orders the offending party to stop creating the nuisance.

This steel company could be charged with public nuisance if its emissions exceed acceptable limits.

Intentional Interference with a Person's Reputation

Most people feel that their good character and reputation is as valuable as any land or possessions they might own. As a result, the courts will award damages to a person who can prove that his or her reputation or character has been unjustly harmed. This is referred to as the tort of **defamation of character**. There are two types of defamation: **libel**, which means that the defamatory statements were published in some written form; and **slander,** which means that the defamatory statements were spoken. For a defamation to occur, the injured party must be able to show that the statement has either been published or communicated to a third party, that the statement was false, and that it caused the plaintiff harm.

Intentional Interference with a Person

In Chapter 12, we discussed criminal law and how the police and the courts become involved when a crime has been committed. Certain actions may be torts as well as crimes. Suppose Paulo and Jeremy became involved in a scuffle during a basketball game. After the game, Jeremy went to find Paulo to continue the dispute. Paulo was not interested in fighting, but Jeremy was persistent and punched Paulo. Paulo slipped, hit his jaw on the floor and, as a result, broke two front teeth and fractured his jaw.

The police were called and they charged Jeremy with assault. As well, Paulo decided to sue Jeremy in civil court for the wages he lost due to his time off work, for the cost of replacing the two teeth, and for the pain and suffering he experienced as a result of the fractured jaw.

Jeremy's actions resulted in both a crime and a tort. The tort involves two parts. The threat to interfere with a person, or to touch or harm him or her in any way, is called **assault**. The use of force or touching a person without consent is called **battery**.

Jeremy will be prosecuted in a criminal court for the criminal case and will be found guilty or not guilty. Paulo's civil suit will be heard in a civil court, and Jeremy will be found liable or not liable.

Another tort involving interference with a person is false imprisonment. **False imprisonment** occurs if someone's freedom is unnecessarily restrained against his or her will. People are entitled to travel in their

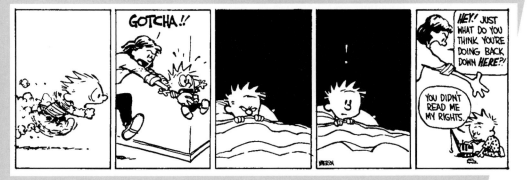

community or in Canada without undue restrictions. If their movements are unjustly restrained, they could sue for false imprisonment.

Security guards in stores must be aware of this right when dealing

VERBATIM REPORTING SERVICES

Anyone who has ever watched a television show or movie about court cases is familiar with the person tip-tapping away at a tiny sort of typewriter while the judge, the witnesses, and the lawyers make their statements. But who could create a business from that seemingly solitary display of high-level typing ability?

Laurie Belsito, that's who. Born in Sault Ste. Marie in 1963 of Italian heritage, she attended a local high school and the Sault College of Applied Arts and Technology, where she studied to be a legal secretary. Then came two years more at George Brown College, studying court reporting. "I could do freelance work, or get hired by the courts," she explains. She chose freelance court reporting.

Then, in 1985, a law was passed and "court reporters were suddenly allowed to open their own businesses." That same year, the entrepreneurial Ms. Belsito received a loan from the Ontario government. Within one year, she had billed close to $50 000; by 1988, she reached $80 000; by 1992, she was up to $250 000; and "I hope we will hit $300 000 to $325 000 very soon. Every year it's gone up!" she proclaims with satisfaction.

The concept for Verbatim Reporting Services ("Freelance Court Reporters") of Sault Ste. Marie is clear: "I have freelance reporters who work for me." Belsito takes "a room rate and a cut of the transcripts." Most of the work involves "examination for discovery," such as collecting evidence, pre-trial work, and so on. Today, five reporters ("including me") and a full-time secretary make up the business.

Apparently, there is only one other firm in the Sault, "so there's very little competition; and they're younger and smaller than me" — an impressive statement from a woman who was 22 when she started her company. Naturally, there are limits in such a field and in such a small city, "but I could get up to a half-million — and it is recession-proof." A growing, stable business, and even regular volunteering for the deaf, using her skills to help others: such is the entrepreneurial, community-minded life of Laurie Belsito.

1. How did the changing of the law create an entrepreneurial opportunity for Laurie Belsito?

2. Why does Laurie Belsito claim the business is recession-proof?

3. With a partner, list ways Laurie Belsito might expand her business.

with suspected shoplifters. Guards must be certain that anyone they have detained has actually stolen the merchandise and not simply forgotten to pay for it. A security guard usually waits until a suspected shoplifter has left the store to be sure that the person cannot claim that he or she was about to pay for the merchandise. If a person is detained and, in fact, has no merchandise or is able to produce a receipt, he or she could sue the security guard and the store for false imprisonment.

FOCUSING ON BUSINESS

1. For each of the following situations, name which right has been interfered with: property, reputation, or personal safety.

   a. A large hole in the road is left unprotected by the city's work crew.

   b. A group of schoolchildren climb over a neighbour's fence on the way to school.

   c. The school newspaper has a cartoon in it that ridicules someone you know.

   d. Your neighbour keeps a large dog as a watchdog. Yesterday, it bit a member of your family.

   e. While in a neighbour's house, your brother falls down some unrepaired stairs and breaks a leg.

2. What is a *tort*? What is *tort law*?

3. Define the tort of *trespass*.

4. Outline the difference between *libel* and *slander*.

5. If a plaintiff is suing for defamation of character, he or she has to prove certain things. List them.

6. What is the difference between *assault* and *battery*?

7. Give an example of the tort of false imprisonment.

EXPLORING BUSINESS

8. Select three newspaper articles that relate to a civil suit involving a tort. State the tort involved, give a summary of the case, and describe the outcome including the amount of the damages. If a decision has not been made, give your opinion as to what you think the decision of the court will be.

9. Your resource centre will have a number of law books that include a chapter or two on tort law. Select one of the books and choose a tort case that is of interest to you. Briefly write down the facts of the case, the tort or torts involved, the decision or outcome of the case, and the reasons for the judgment. Be prepared to share your case with the class.

10. On his way home from school, Godwin crossed over the corner of Moldaver's Nursery. In the process, he stepped into the display flower bed and ruined the owner's prize-winning roses. The owner, Ms. Moldaver, filed a lawsuit against Godwin, stating that the property was fenced off specifically to protect the rose garden.

   a. Which tort would Ms. Moldaver accuse Godwin of committing? Why?

   b. Do you think Ms. Moldaver will win her case? Why or why not?

   c. If Ms. Moldaver wins her case, what compensation should she receive and in what form?

11. Alorn and Hindy went shopping at the local mall. They visited a number of stores and decided to go into the drugstore to purchase a few items. As they left the drugstore, a security guard approached them and asked them to follow him into the security office. Alorn and Hindy asked the security guard to explain the reason for the request. He told them that he saw them taking some articles and placing them in the bag without paying for them. Alorn and Hindy told the security guard that he was making a mistake, but he still insisted that they accompany him. When the contents of their shopping bag were checked, the security guard found that they had paid for all the items. He apologized and told Alorn and Hindy that they were free to go.

   a. Could Alorn and Hindy sue the store and/or the security guard for a tort? Which one? Explain.

   b. What do you think the decision of the court would be? Why?

   c. Assume you found the security guard liable for a tort. How would you decide what damages should be awarded to Alorn and Hindy?

12. Divide the class into seven groups. Each group is secretly assigned one of the following torts:

trespass	assault
nuisance	battery
libel	false imprisonment
slander	

Each group should prepare a role play to illustrate its particular tort. The rest of the class has to identify the plaintiff, the defendant, the tort involved, and provide a definition of the tort.

13. Divide the class into seven groups. Each group selects a different tort from the list in Question 12.

Each group prepares a list of as many circumstances or situations as possible that could result in a civil suit involving its particular tort. For example, the first group will list as many circumstances or situations as it can think of that might lead to a suit involving trespass (for example, walking across another person's property).

Once the lists are complete, each group reads out its examples and asks the class to discuss the potential tort. Are the examples correct? Could you sue for damages? How would you determine the damages?

CAREERS

HEALTH CARE

1. In small groups, brainstorm and list careers in the field of health care. Your list might include: ambulance driver, doctor, nurse, anesthetist, dentist, dental hygienist, naturopath, public health inspector, and medical lab technologist.

2. With a partner, select a career that interests you from the list you created in Question 1. Research the career by visiting your resource centre and guidance office, contacting associations and organizations for literature, or interviewing someone in the field you have chosen. If you interview someone, ask if you can videotape the interview to share with the class. Learn about the career by gathering information that includes the following:
   - education required
   - experience required
   - skills required
   - responsibilities
   - starting salary
   - any other relevant and interesting information

3. Create a poster to display your career research. Present your findings to the class.

UNINTENTIONAL TORTS

By far the most common torts are those that are committed through carelessness. These torts that are committed by accident are called **unintentional torts**. It is possible to sue someone for damages you have suffered even if the person who caused the damages did not intend to do so. One such tort is called negligence. **Negligence** can be defined as a person's careless behaviour that creates an unreasonable risk of causing injury or loss to another person.

It is likely that the driver of one of these vehicles was not acting responsibly and was subsequently charged with negligence.

To determine if someone has been negligent, the courts use the concept of the **reasonable person**. For example, if the case involves a lawsuit against the driver of a motor vehicle, the court will try to determine what a reasonable driver of an automobile would have done in a similar situation. This helps the court decide whether the actions of the defendant were negligent.

The tort of negligence is based on the idea that people have a duty to each other to make certain that their actions are not unreasonable to the point where they have caused damage to someone. This idea applies to businesses as well. A manufacturer has to ensure that the products it makes are safe and not likely to cause injury or harm to the public.

One of the most important uses of tort law is to provide a person who has been injured in a motor vehicle accident with compensation. Drivers of motor vehicles have a duty to drive the vehicle in a reasonable and careful manner; if they do not, they may be found liable. Most provinces will not allow a motor vehicle to be driven unless the owner has some form of insurance, and it is the insurance company that will pay for damages if an accident occurs. For this reason, businesses are usually very careful about whom they hire as drivers and will usually ensure that they have adequate insurance.

A lawsuit that charges a doctor with negligence is called a **malpractice suit**. As well as providing reasonable medical care, doctors and other medical personnel are expected to give patients enough information about their illnesses, treatments, and possible side effects of those treatments to allow the patients to make informed decisions. A doctor who does not read a patient's records and prescribes a drug to which the patient is allergic may be guilty of malpractice.

Generally, the owner of an animal is liable for injury or damage caused by the animal. An owner of a dog may be held liable for an injury caused by the dog if the owner was aware that the dog was dangerous. Owners may also be held liable for the damage caused if they allow their animals to wander onto other people's property. To a certain extent, this applies to businesses that use guard dogs to protect their property. Businesses must post signs warning trespassers about the dogs and fence off the premises to prevent the dogs from getting loose.

Unlike criminal law, tort law considers children responsible for their own actions and, thus, they can sue or be sued. However, because of their age, a lawsuit on behalf of a child must be initiated by an adult who, in legal terms, is referred to as a **next friend**. If a child is sued and found liable, any damages awarded to the plaintiff have to be paid by the child when he or she is older and earning an income.

Under some circumstances, parents may be held responsible for the actions of their children. If the plaintiff can show that the parents were aware of the negligent behaviour of their children and did nothing to prevent it, the parents may be held liable.

EQUAL OPPORTUNITIES

Tort law provides an injured party with access to the courts if the situation needs to be rectified or if the defendant is seeking damages. But what about the person who is fired from a job because of race or religion? Or the person who is denied accommodation because of his or her sex or colour? Or the person who is denied service in a restaurant because of a handicap? These are examples of discriminatory practices that occur quite frequently despite the fact that they are against the law.

To protect all Canadians from unfair treatment or discrimination, the federal and provincial governments have enacted legislation designed to provide equal opportunities in the workplace, in the search

CARR V. GAUTHIER ET AL.
(1992), 97 D.L.R. (4TH) 651

When Mr. Carr, a lawyer, appeared at the scene of an accident where police officers had arrested his son for impaired driving, his son was in the police cruiser. In order to speak to his son, Mr. Carr got into the police cruiser without permission. He was twice asked to leave the cruiser but he refused to do so. He was arrested and charged for obstructing justice.

The police officers were annoyed with Mr. Carr and, when they arrived at the police station, they held Mr. Carr there for some time with his hands tightly cuffed behind his back. The police officer said he could not find the keys to undo the cuffs.

Mr. Carr is suing the police for assault.

1. Which actions of the police might constitute an assault?
2. How would you decide the case? Why?

for accommodation, and in access to public places. These laws prohibit **discrimination**, or the practice of distinguishing among people based on prejudice, on a number of grounds. Each province has provincial legislation prohibiting discrimination. The Ontario Human Rights Code states that every person has a right to freedom from discrimination in the area of:

- services, goods, and facilities (including shops, restaurants, hospitals, schools, insurance)
- occupancy of accommodation (the place where you live, whether rented or owned)
- contracts (oral or written agreements)
- employment (including advertisements, application forms, and job interviews)
- membership in vocational associations and trade unions

It also states that people cannot be discriminated against on the grounds of:

- race
- ancestry
- place of origin
- colour
- ethnic origin
- citizenship
- creed (religion)
- sex (includes pregnancy)
- sexual orientation
- handicap (physical or mental disability)
- age (between 18 and 65 years in employment; 16 and 17 years are included in the occupancy of accommodation; 18 years and over in the other areas)
- marital status (including common-law, divorced, separated)
- family status (being in a parent-child relationship)
- the receipt of public assistance (in accommodation only)
- record of offences (provincial offences, pardoned federal offences) (in employment only)

There are some exceptions in the Code. Also, not all the grounds of discrimination are forbidden in every area.

If anyone feels he or she has been discriminated against on any of the above grounds, he or she should contact the provincial Human Rights Commission, who will hear the complaint and conduct an investigation if necessary. If the injured party can provide evidence of damages, he or she can request compensation. Human rights legislation does not fall under tort law, but does provide a mechanism for the injured party to obtain damages.

POINTS TO REMEMBER

- Tort law enables an injured party to sue for damages that may have been caused intentionally or unintentionally.
- Intentional torts are divided into three types: intentional interference with a person, with his or her property, or with his or her reputation.
- Defamation of character is divided into two types: libel (the written form) and slander (the spoken form).
- Assault, battery, and false imprisonment are all examples of intentional interference with a person.
- Negligence, or unintentional injury, is the most common type of tort. It is used most frequently in motor vehicle accidents.
- The courts will often use the concept of the *reasonable person* when deciding on cases involving negligence.
- Children can sue or be sued in tort law. This is accomplished through an adult called a *next friend*.

FOCUSING ON BUSINESS

14. Define the tort of *negligence*.
15. Explain the importance of the concept of the *reasonable person* in tort law.
16. Define *malpractice* and give an example different from the one found in the text.
17. Explain the law of tort as it applies to children.
18. What is meant by the term *next friend* as used in tort law?

19. Under what circumstances would parents be held liable for the actions of their children?

20. If you believe that you have been discriminated against because of your religion, whom should you contact?

EXPLORING BUSINESS

21. Quite often, people commit torts without even realizing it. Now that you have studied tort law, discuss it with your friends and family. Record three situations in which you or others you have spoken with could have been involved in a lawsuit.

22. Examine newspapers or magazines for the next two weeks. With a partner from your class, select two articles that relate to the tort of negligence. Create a poster using the articles and include a written comment about the case and/or the decision. You might comment on the extent of the injuries, the amount of damages being requested, and so on.

23. Ella Nunes, aged 17, noticed a construction project at the end of the street. Curious to see what was being built, Ella waited until all the workers had gone home and then went to investigate. Because the project was completely fenced in by a two-metre-high barrier, Ella had to climb over it in order to enter the construction site.

    While walking, she tripped over some lumber and broke her ankle. Her parents planned to sue the company for being careless with their materials.

    a. Which tort would Mr. and Mrs. Nunes be suing for?

    b. Does Ella have a chance of winning the suit? Explain.

    c. If the construction company wanted to file a countersuit, what tort would they accuse Ella of committing?

24. Brian Moncik, aged 14, was showing his pellet gun to a neighbourhood friend, Alanna Dennis. He aimed the gun at Alanna's head in jest, and the gun went off, injuring Alanna. She required immediate hospitalization for stitches and nervous shock. Alanna's father filed a lawsuit on Alanna's behalf against Brian's parents. During the trial, evidence indicated that, prior to the accident, other neighbours had complained to Brian's parents about the boy's misuse of the gun. Both a bird and a neighbour's cat had been found dead from pellet wounds earlier in the year.

a. What would be the tort committed in this case?

b. Why was the lawsuit filed against Brian's parents instead of against Brian himself? Explain.

c. What do you think the outcome of the case will be? Explain your answer.

25. Stephan is out walking his dog, Saint. It is 11:00 p.m. and it has been snowing all day. Stephan is passing by Dimitri's house when he slips on the ice in front of Dimitri's driveway. In the excitement, Saint runs off and frightens Mrs. Foley, who is taking her evening walk. Mrs. Foley slips in the snow and injures her hip. Hearing the commotion, Terri goes outside to see what is happening. Stephan is very angry by this time, and an argument arises between Terri and Stephan. Stephan ends up punching Terri in the mouth, resulting in the loss of a tooth. Mr. Kaushaging, a neighbour, rushes out of his house when he sees what is taking place. He runs across Mrs. Topp's lawn and falls into a hole the Topps had started digging for a tree in the spring.

In pairs, answer the following questions:

a. What torts, if any, have been committed in this scenario?

b. If you felt that some torts had been committed, what remedies would you suggest?

26. Can a potential employee be asked the following questions in an employment interview? Explain your answers.

a. What type of accent is that?

b. Will your husband/wife object if you have to work occasional long hours?

c. Do you think you would work effectively with a female supervisor?

d. Which religious holidays will you take off from work?

e. How old are your children?

f. What is your current address and how long have you been there?

g. Do you have any handicap that I should know about?

h. Are you a Canadian citizen?

i. Would you provide a photograph that can be attached to the interview form?

j. Where were you last employed? For how long?

27. Contact your local Human Rights Commission office. Request a summary of the Human Rights Code and prepare a report outlining:

a. the prohibited grounds of discrimination

b. the areas covered by the statute (for example, accommodation, employment, etc.)

c. the procedure to be followed by a person who wishes to file a complaint with the Human Rights Commission

Be prepared to share the report with the class.

28. Mrs. Teno was speaking to her husband on the telephone when her two youngest children asked for money to buy ice cream from a truck. Both children had been instructed many times on the proper and safe way to cross the road and had crossed the street often to buy ice cream. The mother specifically reminded them on that day to watch for cars.

Renata Greco, the driver of the ice-cream truck, was a 19-year-old student who had had little training in the operation of her truck and the selling of her ice cream. Her supervisor, J. B. Zambene, had been concerned more with efficient merchandising than with safety. Renata had been driving south on Academy Drive when she noticed the children waiting on the east side to buy ice cream. She stopped on the west side of Academy Drive, against the curb.

The children had to cross the two northbound lanes, the boulevard, and the two southbound lanes in order to get to the service window of the truck. Renata, while still sitting in the truck, saw a vehicle approaching and warned the children to stop when they were still on the boulevard. After the vehicle had passed, they continued over to the truck. Renata had served four-year-old Diane Teno, the plaintiff, and then served her six-year-old brother.

At this time, a car owned by Wallace Arnold but driven by his father, Brian, was approaching the truck from the north. Had Renata glanced through the large glass windows in the rear of her truck, she would have seen the car. She would have been able to see that the two younger children were in great danger of being struck when they turned to cross the road to go home. As the children crossed the road, Diane Teno was struck and suffered very serious injuries.

Through a next friend, she sued the owner of the ice-cream truck, its driver, and the driver of the car.

a. Draw a diagram of the scene of the accident.

b. Review the case and, in groups of three or four, state whether there was negligence by any or all of the following participants. Give reasons for your answer.

Mrs. Teno   Mr. Zambene
Diane Teno   Brian Arnold
Renata Greco   Wallace Arnold

c. If any of the participants were negligent, what factors would you consider when awarding damages? Explain your reasons.

WORKING WITH MATH

29. Sudeem was seriously hurt in a motor vehicle accident. As a result, he sued the defendant for negligence. Sudeem was off work for three years. At the time of the accident, he was earning $80 000 per annum. He calculated that his raise would have been 10 percent per annum. Sudeem had to pay $4000 in medical bills over and above what was covered by his benefit program. As a result of the accident, Sudeem will always walk with a slight limp, but this will not affect his ability to carry out his duties as a computer operator and programmer. Sudeem wants $25 000 for damages. He has a bill from his lawyer for $8000 and is suing the defendant for legal costs.

a. Calculate the total damages Sudeem is requesting.

b. If you were the judge, what damages would you award Sudeem? Why? Show your calculations.

30. Use the chart "Canadian Criminal Offences" for reference to answer the following questions:

a. Create four bar graphs that compare the number of offences committed by male adults, female adults, male young offenders, and female young offenders for the following crimes:

- total crimes of violence

- total property crimes

- total other crimes

- total drug crimes

In small groups, discuss the statistics on which these graphs are based.

b. Name the two most common Criminal Code offences committed by young offenders. Do these statistics surprise you? Explain.

c. Select any one of the statistics that you find surprising and explain why you find it surprising.

Canadian Criminal Offences

	Number of offences*	Adults Charged		Young Offenders	
		Male	Female	Male	Female
Total Criminal Code Offences	2 888 274	399 841	84 075	115 760	26 180
Total crimes of violence	296 263	110 362	12 984	14 925	3,844
Homicide	766	486	48	35	7
First-degree murder	425	238	17	18	3
Second-degree murder	271	193	26	13	1
Manslaughter	65	55	4	4	2
Infanticide	5	–	1	–	1
Attempted murder	1 039	727	71	60	7
Assault	256 383	99 847	12 103	12 304	3 447
Aggravated sexual assault	463	230	8	22	–
Sexual assault with weapon	985	470	16	63	4
Sexual assault	28 808	9 575	161	1 762	50
Assault, common	166 282	60 230	8 010	6 436	2 481
Assault with weapon or causing bodily harm	38 392	18 535	2 322	2 851	620
Aggravated assault	3 852	2 270	352	286	56
Causing bodily harm	4 061	2 335	249	292	89
Abduction	1 119	178	78	1	2
Robbery	33 045	7 950	647	2 355	337
Total property crimes	1 719 496	158 355	47 673	74 465	17 168
Breaking and entering	432 521	37 654	1 759	25 311	1 769
Theft – motor vehicles	141 512	10 253	630	8 177	777
Theft over $1000	114 938	6 142	1 326	1 807	215
Theft $1000 and under	860 766	60 613	30 077	30 418	12 421
Have stolen goods	33 794	14 621	1 991	6 401	893
Frauds	135 965	29 072	11 890	2 351	1 093
Total other crimes	872 515	131 124	23 418	26 370	5 168
Prostitution	10 591	5 162	5 601	63	404
Gaming and betting	1 382	1 051	154	8	2
Offensive weapons	19 664	7 368	566	1 897	113
Arson	12 506	810	143	530	62
Counterfeiting currency	5 186	350	39	27	6
Disturbing the peace	57 296	7 023	970	940	162
Indecent acts	9 670	2 297	340	123	14
Kidnapping	958	439	27	46	10

(Continued on next page)

	Number of offences*	Adults Charged		Young Offenders	
		Male	Female	Male	Female
Mischief (property damage) over $1000	70 075	3 985	449	1 719	150
Mischief (property damage) $1000 and under	393 743	17 060	1 826	7 110	680
Total drug crimes	59 299	34 764	5 455	2 183	433
Heroin	**1 486**	**768**	**253**	**4**	**2**
Possession	561	321	132	1	–
Trafficking	768	394	109	3	2
Importation	157	53	12	–	–
Cocaine	**15 959**	**9 569**	**1 747**	**248**	**73**
Possession	6 127	4 164	842	98	31
Trafficking	9 532	5 328	877	149	39
Importation	300	77	28	1	3
Cannabis	**33 142**	**21 609**	**2 816**	**1 640**	**306**
Possession	21 835	14 344	1 529	1 183	195
Trafficking	8 473	6 274	965	440	98
Importation	558	167	74	6	12
Cultivation	2 006	824	248	11	1

Source: Statistics Canada

* The number of offences is greater than the number of persons charged because some persons are charged with several offence or with the same offence more than once, and because no charges are laid for some offences.

KEY TERMS

tort	slander
intentional tort	assault
plaintiff	battery
defendant	false imprisonment
damages	unintentional tort
compensation	negligence
trespasser	reasonable person
private nuisance	malpractice suit
public nuisance	next friend
defamation of character	discrimination
libel	

Elements of a Contract

CHAPTER FOCUS

er studying this chapter you
will be able to:

ntify the essential elements
of a binding contract

•

inguish among the different
types of contracts

•

explain the importance
f an employment contract

HEN YOU PLAN YOUR SOCIAL LIFE, you often enter into agreements with friends. As a consumer, you may also enter into a number of agreements with retail stores. Purchasing a set of skis from a store or a hot dog from the cafeteria are agreements. Some of them may be considered contracts. What are the elements of a contract? What makes a contract legally binding? In this chapter, we will examine the elements of a contract and the different types of contracts used in business. We will examine the legal requirements for a valid contract and some of the circumstances that allow a person to not fulfil the terms of a contract.

ELEMENTS OF A CONTRACT

A **contract** is an agreement between two or more parties that is legally enforceable. Five essential elements of a contract must exist for the contract to be legally binding, that is, for the courts to enforce it. These elements are offer and acceptance, competence, consideration, legality, and consent. Each is discussed in more detail below.

Offer and Acceptance

Suppose Ilan advertises in the newspaper that he will pay a reward to whoever returns his lost wallet. Unaware of the offer, Magda finds the wallet and returns it. Ilan does not give Magda the reward. She later learns of the offer and tries to claim the reward. Should she receive it? Why or why not?

Under contract law, Magda would have no claim to the reward. Contract law specifies that, in order to have a contract, there must be an **offer** and the offer must be accepted. In the example above, Magda was not aware of the offer when she returned the wallet. Therefore, there was no **acceptance** of the offer and she cannot claim the reward.

When you enter a store to purchase a magazine, you are offering to purchase the magazine. The storeowner can either accept or reject your offer. Legally, a storeowner has no obligation to sell a product. In practice, however, storeowners are in business to sell their goods and services and will usually not refuse to make the sale.

Suppose you knew that Odette wanted to sell her old computer for $800. You approached Odette and offered her $700. She turned your offer down but stated that she would accept $750. In this case, Odette has made a **counteroffer** that you can either accept or reject.

Competence

Johanna signed an agreement to purchase a used car for $1400. Later, she refused to pay according to the agreement, claiming that she was intoxicated at the time. Can Johanna get out of paying for the car?

Under contract law, an agreement can be binding only if the parties are legally **competent** at the time and thus know what they are doing when they enter into the contract. If Johanna was intoxicated at the time she entered into the contract and the other party was aware of her condition, the court would probably rule that Johanna was not competent at the time she entered into the contract.

These same rules apply to an insane person. The law concerning intoxicated — whether by drugs or alcohol — and insane parties goes on to state that the intoxicated or insane party will be held liable for a contract for **necessaries**, which include food, shelter, and clothing. This means that if an intoxicated or insane person were to enter into a contract for lodging, he or she would be liable to pay for the goods or services.

Under common law, minors have special status regarding contracts. The law states that a person who has not yet reached the age of majority — which is 18 or 19, depending on the province or territory — cannot enter into a binding contract unless it is for necessaries. What is considered a necessary for one person may not be considered a necessary for another, so it is left to the court to decide.

Consideration

Without receiving any benefit, such as a fee, Nadine promised to repair Shiro's roof by a certain day. The repairs were never made and part of the roof collapsed. Has Shiro the right to sue Nadine?

The answer is no. Contract law specifies that, in order to have an enforceable contract, there must be something of value that is exchanged between the two parties. This is known as **consideration**. Since Nadine received nothing in return for the promised repair, the contract is lacking consideration and would not be enforceable.

ELEMENTS OF A CONTRACT

Competence

Acceptance

Legality

Lesley rented rooms in a building owned by Felicia. With Felicia's knowledge, Lesley used the rooms as headquarters for gambling. One month, Lesley did not pay the rent. Can Felicia sue?

In order to have an enforceable contract, the law requires the subject matter of the contract to be legal. A well-known expression states, "You must come to court with clean hands." In other words, the courts will not enforce a contract that involves any illegality. In this case, since Felicia was aware of Lesley's use of the rooms for gambling, the courts will not enforce the contract.

Consent

Aziza is trying to sell a skateboard for $125. Clinton says he will pay $95 for the skateboard and, if Aziza knows what is good for her, she should sell it to him. If Aziza sells the skateboard to Clinton and later changes her mind, the courts will not enforce the contract. Aziza entered into the contract under an implied threat of physical punishment, and both parties to the contract did not *freely* give their **consent**, or agreement. In order for a contract to be enforceable, the parties to the contract must enter into the contract without any form of undue pressure or influence.

Abedis found an old chair in his attic and sold it to a second-hand

dealer for $10. He later learned that the chair was an antique of great value. Abedis demanded that the contract be set aside and the chair returned to him. What is his legal position?

The law does not protect someone from bad judgement or ignorance. The dealer offered and Abedis accepted the $10. Both parties to the contract were competent and consideration was paid. The contract did not involve any illegality, nor was either party under any duress. That is, the dealer did not use improper influence on Abedis to persuade him to sell the chair. In short, both parties freely consented to the terms of the contract, and all the elements of a contract were present. Abedis is stuck with his $10, and the dealer can congratulate herself on having made a good deal.

Social agreements and comments made in jest are not considered contracts. Contract law specifies that the parties to a contract must enter into the contract knowing that they are entering into a legal agreement. Knowing that the contract is a legal agreement means that, if necessary, the courts would enforce it.

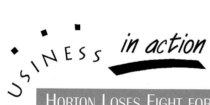

BUSINESS *in action*

HORTON LOSES FIGHT FOR DOUGHNUT CHAIN

Lori Horton has lost her fight to win back the half ownership of the Tim Horton doughnut chain she sold 17 years ago for $1 million.

Horton, 61, the widow of the late hockey star Tim Horton, had claimed in a lengthy series of court hearings that she'd been mentally incompetent at the time of the sale because of drug and alcohol abuse.

She claimed that had she known she didn't have to sell the shares, she wouldn't have, and was trying to recover her half-share of the company or would settle for an additional $10 million.

She also was suing the lawyer she had at the time, alleging that he was negligent and didn't get enough money for her.

Yesterday, in an 84-page judgment, Madam Justice Patricia German of the Ontario Court's general division found that Horton "knew the nature of the financial transaction and that she was not obliged to sell her shares."

Said the judge: "On all of the evidence, the defendants have satisfied me that the transaction was fair, reasonable and honest with respect to Mrs. Horton."

In dismissing the claim, she added, "I am satisfied [that Horton] was mentally competent in 1975 and thereafter...."

FOCUSING ON BUSINESS

1. Explain the meaning of the words *offer* and *acceptance* as they apply to contracts. Give an example to illustrate your answer.

2. What is meant by stating that *the parties to the contract must be competent*?

3. How does contract law apply to minors?

4. Explain how consideration affects contract law. Give an example to support your answer.

5. Explain the meaning of the expression "You must come to court with clean hands." Give an example to illustrate your answer.

6. Why is consent important in contract law?

EXPLORING BUSINESS

7. From the newspaper, select an article that involves a contract law dispute. Write a brief summary of the article outlining the elements of a contract (offer and acceptance, competence, consideration, legality, and consent) as they apply to the dispute.

8. Interview a friend or a member of your family who has had a dispute that involved a contract. Write a report, giving the details of the dispute. Indicate how the dispute related to contract law and which elements of contract law were involved. Outline the decision or how the dispute was finally resolved. Share your findings with the class.

9. Li-Yuan goes to a second-hand store to buy a pair of roller blades. She offers the clerk $45 for a pair that is marked $50. The clerk says no, but, as Li-Yuan is leaving the store, he calls her back and says he will accept the $45. Li-Yuan has changed her mind and does not want the roller blades. Explain contract law to the clerk and state whether Li-Yuan must buy the roller blades.

10. Form small groups. Each group is to design a contract that each person in the group will enter into individually with the teacher. The contract will deal with homework, completed assignments, punctuality, class behaviour, group work, and overall class co-operation and commitment. The contract should cover a three-week period and must be

agreed to and signed by both parties — the teacher and the student. All the elements of a contract must be evident.

11. Form groups of three. For each of the cases below, one student becomes the lawyer for the plaintiff, one student becomes the lawyer for the defendant, and one student assumes the role of the judge. Each lawyer argues the case from his or her position. The judge will then make a decision. Alternate roles for each of the cases.

   a. Brad and Simone are playing basketball. Simone brags, "I can shoot a basket with my eyes shut!" Brad replies, "If you get a basket with your eyes shut, I'll give you my watch!" Simone closes her eyes and shoots the ball, which sails straight through the hoop. Is there a contract?

   b. Vikki sees an advertisement in the newspaper that states that a brand-new chair is selling for $25. Obviously, the advertisement should have stated $250. Can Vikki rush to the store and demand the chair for $25?

   c. Taha offers to sell Sandor his sports-card collection for $700. Sandor states that he will accept the offer if Taha includes the display case and card holders. Is there a binding contract?

CAREERS

TECHNOLOGY

1. You may be planning a career as a musician, editor, artist, architect, interior designer, or accountant. Increasingly, these careers and many others integrate the use of technology. As a class, brainstorm and list careers that use technology and then select six.

2. In home groups, each group member should select one of the six careers to research.

3. Form an expert group of students from other groups who have the same career as you to research, and conduct your research with them. Focus on the formal education needed, what the job is like, and how technology is used.

4. Return to your home group and describe what you learned in your expert group. Prepare a group report on the six careers. The report can be written, illustrated on a poster, or presented as a video or in any other appropriate form.

TYPES OF CONTRACTS

Businesses depend on contracts to function. Contracts ensure that all parties to the contract know what is expected of them and what they can expect to receive in return. Contracts usually involve a payment of money for work done, but companies can also trade goods or services if they choose.

Oral Contracts

You enter into many contracts that are enforceable even though they are unwritten. This type of contract is called an **oral contract**. If you ask a friend to type your essay, promising to pay $3 per page, and your friend agrees, you have entered into an oral contract with your friend. Oral contracts are enforceable in the same way as written contracts. However, if there is a disagreement over the terms of a contract, it is easier to resolve if it is a written contract.

Written Contracts

Written contracts provide protection to all parties concerned — should a dispute arise — since there can be no doubt as to their existence and the terms of the agreement. In fact, the law requires certain contracts to be written contracts. Any contract that cannot be carried out within one year must be in writing. A contract concerning land or real estate must be in writing.

Implied Contracts

Some contracts are neither oral nor written. These are contracts that you might enter into simply by your actions, and are referred to as **implied contracts**. For example, if you raise your hand at an auction, you are implying that you are bidding on an item. If you get into a taxi and ask the driver to take you to a certain location, you are implying that you will pay when you reach your destination. These implied contracts are as enforceable as any other form of contract.

Regardless of the type of contract, all parties to the contract are expected to adhere to the terms of the contract. If one of the parties does not carry out the terms of the contract, it would be considered a **breach of contract**, and the injured party could apply to the courts for a legal remedy. The court could order the delinquent party to adhere to the terms of the contract and/or to pay damages to the injured party.

Business Contracts

Businesses enter into a number of contracts in the course of their every-day operations. A business might sell or buy goods and services on credit using a **credit agreement**. The terms of payment and the rate of interest would be specified in this type of contract. Another business might rent space from a landlord by signing a lease. The **lease** establishes the legal relationship of landlord and tenant by stating the date on which payments are to be made, the amount of rent to be paid, the length of time the lease will be in effect, and so on. A **mortgage**, or an agreement to borrow money to buy property, is a third type of common business contract.

Reprinted by permission of United Features Syndicate

Employment Contracts

The contract between an employee and an employer is a special type of contract. Some terms of an employment contract are negotiated between the employee and the employer, and others are legislated by the government.

HAWES v. SHERWOOD-PARKDALE METRO JUNIOR HOCKEY CLUB INC.
(1992), 88 D.L.R. (4TH) 439

Mr. Hawes was a junior hockey player with the Sherwood-Parkdale Junior Hockey club. He had played three years with the club and was considered a veteran player. In the fall of 1988, Mr. Hawes was having second thoughts about continuing his career in hockey. He was attending university and had good prospects for part-time work, so he gave up hockey.

The team began training in September and by November had played several games and was doing poorly.

The general manager of the team, Mr. Dunn, called Mr. Hawes several times to persuade him to return to hockey. Mr. Hawes finally agreed to play, but requested that the terms for his services be put in writing. Mr. Dunn wrote a memorandum in the following words:

Re: Buck Hawes Nov. 10/88
- Helmet/mask, sweaters, socks, sticks, skates sharpening, equipment repairs, 2 passes
- $2400 for season
- $100 2nd all star
- $150 1st all star
- Release at end of year
- Supply Cooperall Shoulder pads / Elbow pads / Shin pads / Cup
- Win Centennial Cup. Buck will receive any incentives available for play-offs

(Signed) Ralph Dunn G.M.

Between November 10 and December 10, Mr. Hawes attended all the practices and played several games. On December 10, Mr. Hawes was "cut" from the team because the coach felt that he was not playing very effectively.

Mr. Hawes had been paid $400 and is now suing for the balance, $2000, claiming that he had a contract.

1. Examine the wording of the above contract and prepare an argument on behalf of Mr. Hawes.

2. Mr. Dunn claims that all the hockey players were aware that they would be paid about six times per season, in equal instalments. Furthermore, Mr. Dunn claimed that it was the team policy to pay players if they were injured for a short while, but if it was a long-term injury or a dismissal, they would not be paid. How would you decide this case? Why?

An employment contract covers the basic terms of employment: wages, hours of work, benefits, working conditions, a description of duties, and so on. Contracts between employees who are members of a union and their employers — called collective agreements — were discussed in greater detail in Chapter 9. Employment contracts, like other contracts, do not need to be written to be valid. When you agree to baby-sit for neighbours for four hours at $5 per hour, your agreement is a valid contract.

The employer-employee relationship comes from English common law and is called the **master-servant relationship**. *Master* refers to the employer and *servant* refers to the employee (terms commonly used in this sense until the Modern era). This relationship was finally made into law by most provinces in the form of the Master/Servant Act, a statute that specifies many of the terms of the employment contract.

Both provincial and federal governments have passed laws that govern employment contracts. These laws cover minimum wages, hours of work, annual vacations, vacation pay, statutory holidays, child-care leave, and notice of termination. If an employer fires an employee without good reason, or just cause (reason recognized by the law), then the employee can sue the employer for breach of contract. This type of firing is known as **wrongful dismissal**.

Today, the duties of the employer and the employee are governed by many laws. The employer must pay a fair wage in return for the employee's services, must provide the employee with a safe working environment, and cannot discriminate against an employee. The employee has a basic duty to obey all reasonable orders of the employer and to use the property or information of the employer in a careful and reasonable manner.

POINTS TO REMEMBER

- For a contract to be legally binding, an offer must be made and accepted, and consideration must be given.
- All parties to a contract must be competent to enter into the contract.
- A contract is not legally enforceable if the subject matter involves an illegality.
- All parties must freely consent to the contract in order for it to be legally binding.

- Contracts can be oral, written, or implied.
- A contract between an employer and employee is called a master-servant relationship.

FOCUSING ON BUSINESS

12. List the three types of contracts and define each type.
13. What are the benefits and drawbacks of each type of contract in Question 12?
14. Explain the meaning of the term *master-servant relationship*.
15. What aspects of the employment contract does the government legislate?
16. What are the responsibilities of employers under the employment contract? What are those of employees?

EXPLORING BUSINESS

17. Working with a partner, one of you will interview the owner of a business and the other will interview an employee of the same business. Ask each what the responsibilities and duties are of a fair employer. Then ask each what the duties are of a good employee and what expectations employers have of employees. List the answers. Compare your list with your partner's. How similar are the lists? How different? Share your findings with the class.

18. Undertake the necessary research to find the following information:
    a. What is the regular minimum wage?
    b. What is the minimum wage for students?
    c. Which holidays are considered statutory holidays?
    d. Are students entitled to holiday or vacation pay? If so, when would they receive it? How is it calculated?
    e. What is the maximum number of hours a person can work without taking a break?

19. During a two-week period, collect as many examples of contracts as you can. These might include grocery receipts, movie stubs, video rental receipts, and so on. Organize the contracts on sheets of paper and, below each one, state the consideration given by each party.

20. Darren arranged to see a movie with Marjand. At the last minute, Marjand found out that Jen was free and, since he preferred to go with her, decided to do so. Did Darren and Marjand enter into a contract? Explain.

21. Gavin loves sports. As a seventeenth-birthday present to himself, he decided to purchase a set of golf clubs. When Gavin returned home with the clubs, he found that his father had decided to give Gavin his old set. Gavin wants to return the new clubs but is uncertain as to what his legal standing is. Advise Gavin.

22. Form groups of six and role-play the case outlined below. Two students should act as lawyers for the plaintiff, two as lawyers for the defendant, and two as judges.

Orly, a university student, is taking a computer science course next year and decides to purchase a special software program from her friend, Michael. Orly is quite anxious to obtain the program, especially after Michael told her that it was not readily available and that he had paid a very high price for it.

Orly decided to place a deposit of $50 on the program (the price quoted by Michael was $150). The deposit was sent to Michael with the following short note:

Date _____

Michael,
I am enclosing $50 as a deposit on the software. If I find the software is available at a lower price, I will expect a refund as I will not buy the software from you.

Signed _____

Two weeks before the course was scheduled to begin, Orly realized that the same software was available — new — for a price of $75. Orly then demanded a refund from Michael, who refused, stating that a deal is a deal.

Orly was able to produce written evidence of their transaction. This should be used to support the arguments and can be referred to by all the lawyers and the judges.

23. With a partner, select one of the following situations. Each situation can by selected by no more than two pairs. Role-play a scenario based on the situation you select. Be certain to illustrate the elements identified with the situation.

Situation	Elements
Negotiate a price to cut a neighbour's grass	Offer; acceptance; counteroffer
Negotiate a price to shovel snow from a neighbour's driveway	Price is too high; a written contract
Sell a used computer to a friend	Seller will not give a guarantee; consideration
Buy used hockey equipment from a store	Seller's price is too high; acceptance
Buy a compact disc player	Guarantee; implied contract
Buy a bicycle from a stranger	Legality; written contract
Arrange to have a car painted	Guarantee; consideration; counteroffer
Sell a skateboard to a friend	Offer; acceptance; oral contract

24. Select three newspaper articles which deal with contracts that people are in the process of negotiating or that have already been negotiated. Select one of the articles and summarize the contract and any problems that may be involved. Comment on the result if the contract dispute has been resolved or recommend a solution if the contract is still in dispute.

WORKING WITH MATH

25. Use the chart "Number of Police Officers, by Province" for reference to do the following activities:

    a. Calculate the change, as well as the percentage change, in the number of police officers from 1965 to 1991 for the country as a whole, and for each province or territory. Fill in the appropriate columns in the chart.

    b. Create a bar or line graph that compares the number of police officers in each province in 1965 to 1991.

    c. In small groups, discuss possible reasons for the increase in number of police officers over the years in all provinces.

NUMBER OF POLICE OFFICERS, BY PROVINCE

	1965		1975	
	Number of police officers	Population per police officer	Number of police officers	Population per police officer
Canada	32 010	620	50 663	452
Newfoundland	521	940	777	714
Prince Edward Is.	104	1 038	198	596
Nova Scotia	889	848	1 197	690
New Brunswick	582	1 058	1 105	610
Quebec	9 531	602	14 526	428
Ontario	10 773	639	17 439	472
Manitoba	1 184	813	2 036	500
Saskatchewan	1 114	855	1 846	497
Alberta	1 956	744	3 362	540
British Columbia	2 599	711	4 728	520
Yukon	56	268	83	263
Northwest Terr.	128	219	185	229

Source: Statistics Canada

KEY TERMS

contract	written contract
offer	implied contract
acceptance	breach of contract
counteroffer	credit agreement
competent	lease
necessaries	mortgage
consideration	master-servant relationship
consent	wrongful dismissal
oral contract	

1985		1991		1965–1991	1965–1991
Number police officers	Population per police officer	Number police officers	Population per police officer	Change in number of police officers	Percentage change in number of police officers
53 464	477	56 774	475		
927	626	917	626		
180	711	188	693		
1 439	614	1 542	583		
1 175	613	1 298	560		
13 893	476	14 575	470		
18 461	495	21 210	467		
2 086	516	2 193	512		
1 964	519	1 996	499		
4 526	557	4 526	557		
5 784	501	6 149	523		
116	196	117	230		
232	219	238	229		

PART 6

Marketing

CHAPTER
15

CHAPTER FOCUS

After studying this chapter you
will be able to:

explain why marketing is
important to consumers
and businesses

•

describe the functions of
marketing

•

define the four Ps of the
marketing mix: product,
price, place, and promotion

•

explain the importance of
packaging and labelling

•

explain the various channels
of distribution

Functions of
Marketing

 FUNDRAISER TRIES TO SELL YOU A book of coupons as a contribution to charity. You try to convince a friend to go to a show. You may not be aware of it, but both of you are using persuasion to engage in a form of marketing activity.

In this chapter, we will examine the importance of marketing and why a business must be knowledgeable about the marketing environment. We will look at the role played by demographics, the economic environment, competition, social and cultural change, and technology in marketing and business decisions. The need for market research, the selection of the appropriate channel of distribution for the product, the functions of marketing, and the marketing mix will also be explored.

THE IMPORTANCE OF MARKETING

Marketing affects many of your daily activities. Broadly speaking, marketing is made up of all the activities needed to generate an exchange that will satisfy human needs and wants. More specifically speaking, **marketing** involves planning, pricing, promoting, and distributing a product, service, or idea. Every time you purchase an item at a store or watch a television commercial, you are involved in a marketing activity. As you read newspapers, magazines, or listen to the radio, you are being exposed to marketing.

Marketing firms assist businesses in promoting their goods and services.

Learning about marketing will help you become a more informed consumer since you will better understand companies' strategies in promoting their goods and services. In addition, regardless of your career path, it is highly likely that it will contain some aspects of marketing, since you may often have to persuade someone to accept you or your ideas. A teacher needs to devise the most convincing method of presenting a concept. A nurse might need to persuade a patient to do something that the patient really does not want to do.

Marketing activities are crucial to all businesses, no matter what their size is. Production departments organize the manufacturing of products and financial departments manage revenues, but marketing departments must promote the goods or services that generate the revenues. Producing a quality product or coming up with a good idea will not necessarily result in a company's success. Consumers must be convinced that the product fills their needs or wants. The good or service must be brought to the attention of consumers through marketing activities.

SHOESTRING MARKETING

Marketing on a shoestring budget is a lesson that many fast-growth firms learn early. Indeed, 50% of those on Profit magazine's "fastest-growing-companies" list say they spend less than 2% on marketing, proving you don't have to break the bank to spark sales. The success or failure of your marketing plan is not determined by the money you spend, but by how effectively you spend it. A consistent, targeted plan that promotes your company's visibility and follows through by delivering quality will go a long way to attracting and keeping the customers you need....

Industry associations are another source [to] tap to develop contacts and raise profiles. Greg Martin, president of London, Ont. corporate housekeeping firm Martin Building Maintenance [says] industry associations provide an opportunity to mingle with industry peers who may help promote your company in the future through referrals. Plus, he

says, associations allow you to keep up with the latest industry news and trends. Martin is president of the Toronto-based Building Maintenance Contractors Association. "Involvement in industry events adds to our professional image," he says, "and it gets us talked about in the local market."

Generating talk and improving his company's image was also behind Martin's decision to trade employees' $20 cleaning smocks for spiffy $120 uniforms, complete with shoes and ties. When the company landed its first contract to clean and maintain a public mall three years ago, Martin outfitted the cleaners who would work on the premises with new uniforms. In an industry not noted for style, he says, the uniforms garnered a lot of attention. Six months later, Martin's entire staff of 120 were wearing new uniforms, and Martin says the feedback from customers has been extremely positive. "We tried to get away from the traditional image of cleaners," says Martin, "and people notice how

Martin Building Maintenance president Greg Martin with staff

good we look." You can't argue with the results: the company's sales increased to $1.8 million in 1991, up 614% from $252,000 in 1986.

To keep that momentum going, Martin produces a bimonthly newsletter for employees, customers and potential clients. The newsletter tells customers the firm is serious about quality, says Martin. "It looks good, it's professionally done," he says, and it helps convey the company's sense of pride and professionalism.

But Martin warns a polished image is worth nothing if you can't deliver on quality and service. In addition to cleaning staff, Martin employs quality-control managers who visit clients once a month seeking feedback on the company's performance, and making sure the company is meeting its customers' needs.

THE MARKETING ENVIRONMENT

We are living in a world of rapid change. We are constantly being exposed to new technology and new products. These exciting times make marketing activities much more difficult for businesses and provide businesses with great challenges.

Some changes are beyond the control of the business community, yet to compete successfully, businesses must react to constantly changing factors such as demographics, economic conditions, competition, social and cultural change, and technology.

Demographics

Demographics are the characteristics of a population, categorized by age group, sex, income level, and level of education. The statistics make an especially useful tool for businesses that want to target a particular group or market, say, women between 18 and 54 or people over 65.

Canadian demographics change constantly. In the early 1990s, for example, the number of people over the age of 65 surpassed the number of teenagers in the population. This kind of information helps businesses decide on the goods and services they offer, the media they use to advertise products, and even the price of certain products. As the population ages, it is likely that the price of retirement properties will increase, along with the supply of products aimed specifically at people over 65. Advertisers might increasingly employ well-known older people to represent their products.

Business owners and marketers use demographics to help them understand their markets and try to predict the opportunities that might exist. If interpreted correctly, demographics can reduce the risk of business failure.

Economic Environment

As you learned in Chapter 6, the business cycle refers to the changes in the economy as it moves from prosperity to inflation, sometimes into depression, and then to economic recovery. A business must pay careful attention to the current stage of the business cycle and market its goods or services accordingly. During a period of high unemployment in a recession, a business might reduce its advertising and concentrate on emphasizing essential goods and services for the consumer. Price becomes a very important factor during periods of high unemployment. During a time of prosperity, a company might emphasize the luxurious aspect of its goods or services.

Competition

Competition can take many forms. **Direct competition** is the rivalry that exists when two or more businesses produce similar goods or services. For example, Air Canada competes for travellers with British

·················· **DIRECT VERSUS INDIRECT COMPETITION** ··················

Direct Competition   Indirect Competition

Airways, Canadian Airlines International, and virtually every other airline that flies in Canada. In addition, airlines compete with rental car companies and Via Rail, both of which offer an alternative method of travel. This is known as **substitute** or **indirect competition**. When developing a marketing strategy to compete for consumers, a company will want to consider the type of competition with which it is faced.

Social and Cultural Change

As consumers' lifestyles, values, and beliefs change, so do their needs and wants. As a result, they spend their money on different goods and services. A business needs to be aware of these changes and to be flexible in order to survive.

A good example of how changing values can affect buying patterns is the impact of consumers' increased environmental awareness. In the 1970s, consumers wanted convenience and frequently purchased goods in non-reusable containers. However, in the 1990s, consumers want products that are less environmentally harmful with minimal packaging.

As the price of fossil fuels (oil, gas, natural gas) goes up, so too does consumer awareness of energy efficiency. When gasoline prices increased dramatically in the early 1970s, many car drivers switched to smaller, more fuel-efficient cars. In response, automobile manufacturers stopped stressing the luxury of large cars and began to emphasize the affordability and fuel efficiency of smaller cars.

Technology

Technology has had, and will continue to have, a major impact on our lives and on the businesses that supply goods and services for our needs and wants. Many Canadian homes have a microwave oven and a video cassette recorder; 10 years ago, these appliances were not widely used at all. Computers have virtually replaced typewriters in business. Telephone companies use computers to provide customers with such features as voice-activated answering systems.

Technological breakthroughs have a significant effect on marketing. First, they create new industries, which mean new marketing opportunities. Remember, though, that inventing a new product, even one that consumers like, is not enough to ensure success. Both the VHS and Beta systems of VCRs do what consumers want them to do. And yet, in the battle between the two, VHS marketers were able to convince the public that their product was superior. Second, technological changes may alter or even destroy existing businesses. Compact discs have driven vinyl records from the marketplace. Third, new technologies can sometimes stimulate businesses in unrelated fields. For example, a direct relationship has been established between the sales of VCRs and the growth of the snack-food industry.

FOCUSING ON BUSINESS

1. Define *marketing*.
2. a. As a consumer, why is it important for you to study marketing?
   b. Why is marketing important for a business?
3. Define *demographics*.
4. Explain the importance of demographics in marketing.
5. How can the economic environment affect a business's marketing activities?
6. How can competition affect a business's marketing activities?
7. Explain why social and cultural forces have an impact on marketing activities.
8. Describe the impact technology can have on a company's marketing activities.

EXPLORING BUSINESS

9. With a partner, list the marketing activities that you have been involved in during the last 24 hours. Compare your list with the lists of two of your classmates. Which marketing activities were the most common?

10. Create and complete an organizer like the one below. Compare your organizer with a classmate's.

Company (Product)	Direct Competition	Substitute Product as as a Result of Indirect Competition
Roots (sweatshirts)		
McCain (frozen orange juice)		
Nike (athletic footwear)		

CONNECTING BUSINESS WITH ENTREPRENEURS

CASHING IN ON SOCIAL CHANGE

For Margo Oborne, nothing was more frustrating than the search for clothes for her 70-year-old mother. Every time Oborne accompanied her mother to a store, they were greeted by young sales clerks who couldn't be bothered to deal with an elderly invalid. Often, Oborne found she couldn't even get her mother's wheelchair through the store entrance; when it did fit, the entangled clothing racks left no space in which to manoeuvre. And when Oborne found an item of clothing in the correct size, it inevitably fit poorly, taking no account of stooped shoulders, thickened midriffs, or fingers that couldn't fumble with zippers.

So three and a half years ago, Oborne opened Traditions, a store that designs, manufactures and sells clothing exclusively for mature women. And what a market she's tapped! According to Oborne, those aged 50-plus represent 40% of all

Employees Laura, Bobbie, and Willa model Traditionelle de...

Canadian housholds, 55% of discretionary income, and 80% of net worth. Moreover, they're the fastest-growing group in the country, expected to increase at a rate of 55% over the next 20 years, versus the 5% growth expected of those under 50.

Traditions is completely wheel-chair-accessible, with a dressing room large enough to accommodate customer, wheelchair and assistant. And Oborne's staff are what she calls "young seniors," all retirees in their 60s. "They're old enough to appreciate what seniors want, they're very patient and take the time to chat with customers," she says....

The greying of the population is just one of many key trends that have changed the face of Canadian society in the past decade, creating a bounty of new business opportunities for those savvy enough to spot them and turn them to their advantage. Whether it's the swelling number of time-short, dual-career couples, obsession with the environment, or cocooning — staying home to soothe the stresses of balancing career and family — these trends are fuelling new approaches to business and even whole new industries, making winners of the entrepreneurs who act fast enough to seize the opportunities in social change.

What's more, the trends driving business opportunities today are expected to continue for the next two decades.

1. Briefly discuss the social trend that prompted Margo Oborne to open Traditions.

2. List two other social trends that could provide new business opportunities. Be specific and explain your answer.

11. Select a magazine advertisement or television commercial that is marketing an *environmentally friendly* good or service. Be sure to describe the commercial and the good or service advertised. Describe why or how the good or service is environmentally friendly and whether the marketing is effective. Compare your opinions as a class. What seems to be the most effective method of marketing a good or service that claims to cause little or no damage to the environment?

12. New technology can improve our way of life but it can create social and environmental problems. Working in small groups, brainstorm the positive and negative effects of the technologies listed below.

- microwave ovens
- automobiles
- televisions
- robots
- drive-through fast-food restaurants
- automatic teller machines

CAREERS

THE ENVIRONMENT

1. As a class, choose six careers that focus on the environment. Your list might include: environmental officer, environmental chemist, environmental lawyer, environmental reporter, environmental engineer.

2. In home groups, each group member should select one of the six careers to research.

3. Form an expert group of students from other groups who have the same career as you to research, and conduct research with them. Focus on the formal education needed, what the job is like, and how the business relates to the environment.

4. Return to your home group and describe what you learned with your expert group. Prepare a group report on the six careers. The report can be written, presented as a video, illustrated on a poster, or displayed in any other appropriate form.

THE FUNCTIONS OF MARKETING

Marketing has two main functions. First, it helps a business determine its target markets. A **target market** is a group of consumers toward which a business aims its marketing efforts. The members of the targeted group will be similar in some way, such as in age. Every business needs to answer the following questions in order to sell a product, service, or idea:

- Who will buy this product or service (divide possible consumers by sex, age, income level, rural/urban distribution, and so forth)?
- When do they want to buy (season, time of day, time of month)?
- Where do they buy (retail stores, discount stores, mail-order catalogues, region of country)?
- Why do they buy (necessity, luxury, planned purchase, impulse buy)?

To answer these types of questions, businesses frequently undertake marketing research. **Marketing research** is the gathering and analyzing

"I can't figure what went wrong. I made the pitch just the way we discussed, except for that bit at the end—I changed that!"

Hutchings. Reprinted, with permission, from *Marketing Magazine*, August 23/30, 1993.

BODY SHOP: THE STORE AS PACKAGE

"I think what drove our merchandising from the beginning was having no money," says Margot Franssen, president of The Body Shop Canada, a cosmetics retailer whose annual sales at 95 outlets now exceed $75 million.

"We didn't have any money for packaging, so the store had to be package," Franssen says.

She says the stores were made as inviting and appealing as possible through the use of colour, and by arranging products vertically to establish clean lines.

"If you take away the merchandise, you're overwhelmed by all the green in our stores — we use a very deep green base," Franssen says. "I'm 5' 2" and the whole of our merchandising is done on a 5' 2" level. We didn't allow anything to be put behind counters. There had to be testers. Everything had to be clear, legible, and accessible."

Above all, she says the company's merchandising plan is governed by common sense and logic.

"We are not creative for the sake of being creative," Franssen says. "We are creative for the sake of making it easier for the customer."

Q. In what order of importance do you place the following categories: merchandising, trade and supplier relations, product innovation, customer service, advertising, database marketing, and staff relations?

A. Staff relations, customer service, product innovation, merchandising, and trade and supplier relations. We don't do advertising or

database marketing.

Staff will treat your customers like you've treated them, and most retailers don't treat their staff well. If you don't treat your staff well, they'll get you back, subconsciously perhaps, but they'll get you back by treating your customers like dirt.

We really believe that people in retail support, for example, merchandisers and buyers, should not be better compensated than the store manager....

Q. In your opinion, what have been the most startling changes in retail over the past couple of years?

A. The biggest change I've seen is in the attitude of the consumer. Standards have increased tremendously. Customers will simply not accept poor service, they will not accept poor visual merchandise, and they will not accept poor environmental standards or poor corporate culture.

Q. What trends can you see on the horizon that will most affect your business?

A. The trend is servicing baby-boomers that have kids. I'm 40. I have three kids under the age of eight, so I want to go to a store that, one, respects my values and, two, respects my kids....

Q. What qualities does one need to stay ahead of the pack?

A. You have to be daring, you have to be different, and you have to be definite.

We try to be daring. Most people are afraid to make changes. When we put up a poster for Amnesty International, we had mall managers rushing in, telling us to take it down. But it showed people who we were and it really got us far.

We are definitely different. People always ask what the competition is doing, and I say I haven't got a clue what they're doing and I don't care. We do things because we know it's the right thing to do....

1. What does Margot Franssen mean when she says the store had to be the package?

2. Review the first question asked of Margot Franssen and her answer to it. Do you agree with her order of importance of the categories? Explain your reasons.

of data to provide a business with information on consumers' needs and wants. A business that wishes to manufacture a new type of laundry detergent might interview shoppers at a supermarket to determine the brand of laundry detergent they currently buy and why. A beverage company might conduct a taste test to determine consumers' opinions of a new product. Or an advertising agency might phone people randomly to measure the effectiveness of a new television commercial. Regardless of the reason for the research or its form, it has to be carefully planned, administered, and analyzed if the results are to be meaningful.

The second function of marketing is to try to provide consumers with a product they want, when they want it (promotion), where they want it (place), and at a price they can afford and are willing to pay.

THE MARKETING MIX

The components of the **marketing mix** — product, price, place, and promotion — vary for each product. One of the functions of marketing is to help a company design an overall policy to reach the product's target market. This will determine the make-up of the mix and how each component is weighted in the final marketing plan.

Product

The **product** includes not only the good or service itself but also its name, packaging, labelling, guarantees, and so on. Through research and development, many businesses invest a great deal of money developing products that they believe consumers want and will pay for.

Brand Names

A **brand name** is the name that identifies the goods or services of one firm. It can be a word or words, number or numbers, letter or letters, or some combination of these elements. The visual elements of a brand — a logo, symbol, or other such design — are called brand marks. When these brand marks are registered so that no one else can use them, they are called **trademarks**. Apple Computer is a brand name and its trademark is a stylized apple.

It takes many years for a company to establish a brand loyalty. However, once a brand name has consumer loyalty, it can be used for a variety of products. For example, the Ivory name is used for hand soap, laundry soap, and dishwasher soap.

Packaging

Packaging refers to the container or wrapper for a product, the design of the container, and the information printed on the container. The packaging must protect the product while it is on the way to the consumer and often during use by the consumer. A milk carton must not leak, even after the consumer has taken it home.

Second Cup, a retailer of specialty coffee beans and teas, redesigned its packaging. The new design features a more contemporary cup and uses environmentally responsible materials.

The container must attract the attention of consumers. The design of the container and the advertising printed on it can help sell the product. Packaging will often carry slogans, list special features, or provide useful information about the product. "Contains 47 essential nutrients," "Leaves your laundry fluffy and soft," and "Contains no artificial preservatives" are examples of package advertising. In fact, the manufacturer's name alone is an advertisement for the consumer.

Packaging is changing as a response to consumers' demands for less packaging material. More manufacturers are trying to package their products in smaller or reusable containers in response to criticism that packaging contributes to the waste problem. The idea of *reduce, reuse, recycle* is one that will continue to affect packaging in the future.

Labelling

Labelling is the part of packaging that provides the consumer with information. The label can be as simple as the brand name *Chiquita* stamped on a banana or as detailed as the list of ingredients that must appear on all food products. Labels can include information to help the consumer use the product more effectively (cooking instructions, assembly instructions, a picture of the product) and, like packaging, helps to sell the product.

Price

The **price** of a product will, in many cases, be determined by the demand for it. Price will play an important role in how successful the product is. Some businesses price their products low to sell more of them, and others price their products high, knowing that fewer will be sold but that a greater percentage of the selling price will be profit.

A business must always take into account the price that competitors are asking for similar products and how much consumers are willing to pay. Few consumers will pay five dollars for a doughnut, for instance.

Place

Even if consumers are pleased with a new product and its price, its success is uncertain unless it is where consumers can get it when they want it. The manufacturer's choice of channels of distribution is extremely important. A **channel of distribution** is the path a product takes from the manufacturer to the final consumer. The two most common channels of distribution are shown below.

················· **CHANNELS OF DISTRIBUTION** ·······················

Manufacturer

Wholesaler

Retailer

Consumer

Manufacturers make products. They sometimes sell their products to wholesalers and sometimes directly to retailers, depending on the type of product and on the size of the retailer. For example, a cereal maker sells directly to large supermarkets (the retailers), as well as to wholesalers who, in turn, sell the cereal to smaller retailers such as convenience stores.

Wholesalers buy goods or services and sell them to other businesses for resale. Wholesalers usually buy products in large quantities from the manufacturers and sell them in smaller quantities to the retailers. By buying in larger quantities, wholesalers pay less per unit for a product than an individual retailer would who purchases a smaller quantity of the product directly from the manufacturer. In turn, some of the wholesaler's savings are passed on to the retailer.

Retailers sell goods or services directly to consumers. Retailers cover a wide range, from stores such as Eaton's and Canadian Tire to the vendor selling hot dogs from a cart at a baseball game.

The consumer is the end user of the product or service. When you enter a retail store and make a purchase, you are the consumer.

Promotion

Promotion is the component of the marketing mix that informs consumers about a product or service and encourages them to buy it. Promotion is undertaken by five different methods: personal selling, sales promotion, publicity, public relations, and advertising. These methods of promotion are discussed in detail in the next chapter.

POINTS TO REMEMBER

- Marketing involves the planning, pricing, promoting, and distributing of a product, service, or idea.
- Demographics, economic conditions, competition, social and cultural changes, and technology are contributing factors in creating the current marketing environment.
- Determining the target market of a business is one of the most important functions of marketing.
- Product, price, place, and promotion (the four Ps) are the four components of the marketing mix.
- Selecting the most appropriate channel of distribution will ensure that the company's product is located where consumers can purchase it, when they want it.

FOCUSING ON BUSINESS

13. Explain the two main functions of marketing.

14. List the four Ps of the marketing mix.

15. What is meant by *target market*?

16. List two important reasons for doing market research.

17. What is a *brand name*? Give two examples of brand names.

18. Describe some of the functions of packaging and labelling.

19. Define *channel distribution*.

EXPLORING BUSINESS

20. Divide the class into six groups. Each group should select one of the following products: toothpaste, bath soap, toothbrush, laundry detergent, dish soap, or mouthwash.

    As a class, brainstorm a list of questions that can be included in a survey to determine which brand of the above items consumers use the most. Include questions to determine why consumers prefer one brand over others. Each group should then prepare a survey for its product and question at least 15 people of all ages. Prepare a one-page summary of the outcome of the survey, showing the brands available, consumers' choices, and the reasons for their choices. Which was the most popular brand for each product? What were the reasons?

21. Working in pairs, each partner brings two packages to class. One package should illustrate your idea of packaging that is not harmful to the environment. The other package should illustrate what you consider to be packaging that is harmful to the environment. Discuss the reasons for your selections and suggest ways to improve the harmful packaging.

22. Select a product that you think has excessive packaging and/or is not environmentally acceptable. Write a letter to the president of the company expressing your concerns. Be certain to include your name and home address to invite a response. Once you have drafted your letter, have a partner proofread it for organization, grammar, and spelling. Revise your letter if necessary.

23. Form small groups. Each member of the group brings four or five labels from goods used in the kitchen; possible products are jam, peanut butter, or any canned goods. Examine each label from the consumer's point of view. Which of the labels was the most informative? Which was the least informative? Why? How would you make them more informative?

24. Select a product and discuss the channel(s) of distribution for it. If possible, visit a local retail store to assist you with the answer. Prepare a report of your findings. Include the name of the retailer, the product selected, the channel(s) of distribution, and the reasons for using that particular channel.

WORKING WITH MATH

25. Use a computer to create a database with the following information related to the Consumer Price Index (CPI):

CANADIAN CONSUMER PRICE INDEX BY ITEM
1986 = 100

Year	All Items	Food	Housing	Clothing	Trans-portation	Health and personal care	Recreation and education	Tobacco and alcohol
1950	19.0	17.1	19.0	30.3	18.0	15.7	20.7	19.0
1955	21.5	18.7	22.3	32.7	20.2	19.5	24.9	20.0
1960	23.7	20.4	24.2	33.7	24.0	23.8	29.3	21.5
1965	25.7	22.6	25.7	36.9	25.2	27.1	31.3	22.7
1970	31.0	26.9	31.8	43.4	30.0	33.4	38.9	27.3
1975	44.2	44.0	44.3	55.0	40.3	45.4	51.7	34.8
1976	47.5	45.2	49.2	58.1	44.7	49.3	54.8	37.2
1977	51.3	48.9	53.8	62.0	47.8	52.9	57.3	39.9
1978	55.9	56.5	57.9	64.4	50.6	56.7	59.6	43.1
1979	61.0	63.9	61.9	70.3	55.5	61.9	63.7	46.2
1980	67.2	70.8	66.9	78.6	62.6	68.0	69.7	51.4
1981	75.5	78.9	75.3	84.2	74.1	75.4	76.8	58.0
1982	83.7	84.6	84.7	88.9	84.5	83.4	83.4	67.0
1983	88.5	87.7	90.4	92.5	88.7	89.2	88.8	75.5
1984	92.4	92.6	93.8	94.7	92.5	92.7	91.8	81.6
1985	96.0	95.2	97.1	97.3	96.9	95.9	95.6	89.4
1986	100.00	100.00	100.00	100.00	100.00	100.00	100.00	100.00
1987	104.4	104.4	104.4	104.2	103.6	105.0	105.4	106.7
1988	108.6	107.2	108.6	109.6	105.6	109.6	111.3	114.6
1989	114.0	111.1	114.3	114.1	111.1	114.4	116.2	125.2
1990	119.5	115.7	119.5	117.3	117.3	120.0	121.3	136.1
1991	126.2	121.2	124.7	128.4	119.4	128.4	130.2	159.5

This table shows the relative costs, as far back as 1950, of categories of purchases made by Canadian consumers. To compare 1991 costs with those of another year, divide the

1991 index by the index for the year with which you wish to compare it; then multiply that number by your actual cost in the year with which you are making the comparison.

Example: You spent $40 per week on family food purchases in 1960. To calculate what that would be in 1991 dollars, divide the 1991 food index (121.2) by the 1960 food index (20.4). Now multiply the result by $40. The answer, $237.60, is what you would have had to spend in 1991 to buy the same package of groceries that cost $40 in 1960.

Source: Statistics Canada

a. Display and print:

  i. the entire database

  ii. the individual record for the year 1975

  iii. the fields for Food and Clothing

b. Select the record for the year 1990. Calculate the cost in transportation in 1990 dollars if a person spent $5000 on transportation in 1986.

c. If the CPI was 100 in 1986, what was the purchasing power of a family income of $20 000 in 1960?

d. Create a line graph showing the changes in the CPI for the categories of Housing, Health Care, and Recreation/Education for the years 1981 to 1991.

e. Use the information from the graph you created in Step d to discuss how quickly costs have risen in each of these categories.

KEY TERMS

marketing	trademark
direct competition	packaging
substitute/indirect competition	labelling
target market	price
marketing research	channel of distribution
marketing mix	wholesaler
product	retailer
brand name	promotion

CHAPTER FOCUS

r studying this chapter you
will be able to:

plain the advantages and
disadvantages of the five
nods of promotion that make
up the promotional mix

•

in the purpose of advertising

•

scribe the characteristics
of various media

The
Promotional Mix

NCE A BUSINESS HAS DETERMINED ITS target market and taken care of the first three Ps of the marketing mix — product, price, and place — the next step is to address the fourth P — promotion. The business must find a method of making the product or service known to the customer.

In this chapter, we will examine the five methods of promotion that form the promotional mix. These are personal selling, sales promotion, publicity, public relations, and advertising. The purposes of advertising and the advantages and disadvantages of using the various media for advertising will also be discussed.

PERSONAL SELLING

Personal selling is any one-to-one communication of information that tries to persuade a customer to buy a good, service, or idea. The owner of a corner store is using personal selling when he or she asks you if you need any help and then proceeds to sell you something. The sales representative who tries to sell books to your teacher is using personal selling. The representative of a charity who asks you to make a donation is using personal selling. Often an idea is "sold," which may later lead to the purchase of a product. For example, the retailer in a bicycle store may sell the idea of safety on the roads and then sell the cyclist a helmet.

Personal selling has several advantages. First, it is a flexible method of promotion. Sales presentations can be tailored to suit the needs of individual clients. Second, sales efforts are focused on prospective buyers, eliminating unproductive efforts. Third, sales can be finalized immediately while the customer is interested in

The company, Cows, uses personal selling in its store in Charlottetown but sells to the rest of the country by direct mail.

the product. Finally, the personal contact found in this type of selling can help a salesperson develop a long-term relationship with a customer.

However, personal selling also has several disadvantages. First, it is expensive to maintain a qualified sales staff. Studies have shown that the cost of one sales call can be as high as $200. This cost includes such items as salary and travelling expenses. Second, many companies have difficulty finding and keeping qualified, competent sales staff.

These disadvantages have forced some businesses into considering alternatives to personal selling. Some stores and services have moved to self-serve operations such as those found at many gas stations. In return for not receiving personal attention, consumers often pay less for the good or service.

Telemarketing is a popular alternative that uses telephone technology, including facsimile machines, to maintain regular contact with customers. Some companies use computers to take customers' orders and to process them, eliminating the need for order-processing staff.

Another alternative to personal selling is the use of mail order as a method of selling. Some businesses, either by the nature of the business or the type of product being sold, use this form of selling. These businesses do not have retail stores. Potential customers are sent the catalogue, order their goods by mail or phone, and receive the goods by mail.

The AIDA Selling Formula

Many sales training programs teach participants to use the **AIDA** formula. The word is made up of each of the first letters in the four steps of the basic selling approach — attract *attention*, hold *interest*, arouse *desire*, and take *action* to close the sale.

The salesperson's first objective is to attract the consumer's attention. The salesperson must be sensitive to the needs of the consumer and must find some way of arousing his or her interest, perhaps by generating curiosity about the product.

Having gained the consumer's attention, the salesperson must hold the consumer's interest to explain the benefits of the product and create a desire for the product or service.

When the salesperson feels the consumer has an interest in the product, he or she should start to close the sale. Before a sale can be closed, however, the salesperson has to overcome any objections to or concerns about the product or service that the consumer may have.

SALES PROMOTION

Sales promotion covers all the activities designed to stimulate consumers to buy. Discount coupons, rebates, in-store displays, free samples, store demonstrations, and contests are examples of sales promotions.

This Nestlé promotional campaign was held at malls across Canada. The most entertaining performances by shoppers were used in a national television campaign.

Some sales promotions, such as a company representative at a grocery store asking you to taste a new cracker or a free sample of shampoo delivered to your door, are designed to introduce consumers to a new product in the hope that they will buy it. Others, such as the Pepsi Challenge, which is a taste test, are designed to get consumers to switch from a competitor's product to the company's product. Still others, such as in-store displays, try to remind consumers of unfulfilled desires and may introduce a new product or a special price.

PUBLIC RELATIONS AND PUBLICITY

Public relations includes all the activities by which a business tries to maintain its good reputation and promote good will with the public. Public relations does not involve actually selling products. Instead, for example, a business becomes involved in charitable activities or sponsors local (or even national) sports teams. Large companies usually have a public relations department. Smaller companies contract out their public relations activities to a firm specializing in this area.

Publicity, or the act of bringing company activities to the attention of the public, is not controlled or bought by the business and can be either good or bad. A business that is in the news for contributing money to a residence for senior citizens receives positive publicity. A business that is in the news for polluting a town's only source of drinking water receives negative publicity.

MINING FOR MARKETING GOLD

Mark Tewksbury swam the race of his life when he won Olympic gold in Barcelona, Spain. His race to reap sponsorship gold might be just as tough.

Tewksbury, the 24-year-old who electrified Canadians in the 100-metre backstroke, already has four corporate sponsors — and a profile. The latter could help him sign up a couple more sponsors, said the spokesperson for his agent, International Management Group (IMG), Toronto.

"He will be financially secure for years to come," said Blake Corosky, athlete representative, adding that Tewksbury is also an established motivational speaker who makes 50 to 70 motivational speeches a year.

Besides his profile, two other factors could propel Tewksbury to reap rewards in the sponsorship arena, Corosky said. Tewksbury won Canada's first gold in Barcelona, and Corosky said Canada has traditionally done well in Olympic swimming competition, citing 1988 Olympians Alex Baumann and the late Victor Davis.

Nevertheless, signing sponsors "won't be a cakewalk," Corosky said.

"Sports marketing has matured considerably recently, and sponsors now want a worthwhile return from endorsements."

Chris Lang, chairman of Christopher Lang and Associates, Toronto, which claims to be Canada's largest event marketing firm, agrees securing sponsorships could be harder for athletes than beating their competitors in the pool or on the track.

Part of the problem is that Olympic athletes are often "faceless, until they do something," he said. Other key factors include whether an

ow beef helps keep you in the swim of things.

...ears ago, Olympic
Champion Mark
Tewksbury
...stopped eating
red meat.
Soon, he
found that
he was
feeling weak
and tired. But
...orst of all, his
...ce in the pool was
...en his nutritionist
...by eliminating beef
...g out on several important
...r Mark eats beef four or five
...because he knows it's loaded with
...inerals that are essential to his
...nd for a balanced diet.

...ND MINERALS TO HELP
...OUR BEST.
...an, Canadian beef is not only a
...iron, it also provides you with
...of your daily requirement of five
...nts – protein, niacin, zinc,
...d B12. These are essential for
...velopment as well as energy
...nd believe it or not, all this
...up to only 178 calories.

...ITH CANADA'S FAVOURITE
...e to be a gourmet cook to treat
...a good beef meal. From a simple
...rbecue to fun-
...an elaborate
...f, you can

*Olympic Gold Medalist
Mark Tewksbury*

be assured of
success when
you serve
Canada's
favourite main
dish. So
whether
you're a super
athlete or just
someone who
cares about the way
you look and feel, take
a healthy example from Mark.
Make beef an important part of
your balanced diet and you'll
stay right there in the swim of things.

HOW TO COOK UP MARK'S
MANDARIN BEEF STIR FRY:

INSTRUCTIONS: *Marinate beef
in first 4 ingredients. Heat oil in wok
or fry pan. Cook vegetables unseasoned
for 2 min. Move aside. Drain beef,
reserving marinade. Stir fry beef until
lightly browned. Mix in vegetables and
oranges. Add cornstarch to marinade, then
add to wok. Heat to thicken. Serve over rice.
Serves 5.*

For more recipes and nutritional information,
write: Beef Information Centre, 590 Keele St.,
Dept. A, Toronto, Ontario, M6N 3E3.

Beef's got it good.

athlete will continue competing or retire, or whether the sport is expected to drop out of the limelight until the next Olympics.

... One of Tewksbury's sponsors, Investors Group, Winnipeg, quickly jumped on the handshake bandwagon, congratulating him with a half-page ad in the *Globe and Mail* the day following his triumph. Some of his other sponsors — the Calgary-based Beef Information Centre, Bugle Boy jeans, and Speedo Swimwear — are also planning upcoming ad campaigns, said Corosky. (The BIC, for one, ran ads during the Olympic telecast on CTV.)

1. Why does a business sponsor high-profile athletes? Explain your answer.

2. Does an endorsement of a product by a high-profile athlete have any influence on whether you buy the product? Explain why or why not. What products would you be more inclined to buy if they were endorsed by a high-profile athlete?

FOCUSING ON BUSINESS

1. List the five methods of promotion that constitute the promotional mix.
2. Define *personal selling*. What are some of the problems associated with personal selling? How have businesses changed to address these problems?
3. What is *telemarketing*?
4. What does *AIDA* stand for? Describe the steps represented by each letter.
5. Using examples, explain the difference between *public relations* and *publicity*.

EXPLORING BUSINESS

6. Form groups of three. Each member of the group chooses a different one from the following methods: sales promotion, publicity, or public relations. Each member then chooses a different one of the three major media: radio, television, or newspapers. Find at least two examples of your chosen method of promotion in your chosen medium. Evaluate the effectiveness of your examples and share your findings with the class.
7. With a partner, prepare a sales presentation of a CD player to a friend who does not own one. Role-play the sales presentation according to the AIDA formula.
8. Collect examples of sales promotion material that you receive at home over a one-week period. Bring the examples to class. With a partner, evaluate their effectiveness. Would you or your family buy any of the advertised products? Why?

CAREERS

RÉSUMÉS THAT GET RESULTS

Thousands of résumés cross employers' desks every working day. Each has about ten seconds to make an impression. How can you make sure your résumé catches the employers' attention?

Preparing an effective résumé includes these steps:

- Gather your information.
- Choose what is most important to your job objective.
- Select an easy-to-read layout.
- Put together a draft.
- Edit and change your draft until it is as impressive as you can make it.

Step 1

Gather facts about your employment and education history, and identify your skills and accomplishments.

Create a fact sheet of your employment and education, including:

- names, addresses, and telephone numbers of former employers, dates of employment, and names of supervisors
- job titles, job descriptions, a list of your skills, and situations in which you have demonstrated those skills
- names and addresses of educational or training institutions you have attended, the program(s) completed, major areas of study or training, and any awards or recognition received
- volunteer experience, hobbies, other activities, and memberships that illustrate knowledge or experience related to the type of job you are applying for or that show personal initiative (do not list activities that do not reflect initiative or knowledge of the work)
- names, addresses, and telephone numbers of references. Whenever possible, your references should be people who have supervised your work. (These should not be included in the résumé but should be available if a prospective employer asks for them.)

Step 2

Decide on the qualifications you want to emphasize when applying for a job. Your strongest qualifications should be listed first. For example, most experienced workers list work history first, then education and training. However, if you don't have much experience relating to your job objective, you may choose to list education and training first.

Step 3

Choose a format. There are three types of résumé formats.

The *chronological résumé* lists education and work experience in chronological order, beginning with the most recent. The *functional résumé* lists skills without saying where or when you used them. The *combination résumé* lists skills, education, and employment history. Each format has advantages and disadvantages. Purely functional résumés may be appropriate in some circumstances, but studies show most employers like chronological and combination formats best. (A sample chronological résumé is shown below.)

Step 4
Write a first draft.

Step 5
Edit, edit, edit. Then edit some more until you are represented on paper in the best way possible. Use as few words as possible, but make certain the information is clear. Try not to use abbreviations.

1. Prepare a draft copy of your résumé for a prospective employer using either the chronological or combination résumé format.

2. Working in pairs, exchange résumés and provide your partner with constructive suggestions to improve his or her résumé.

3. Revise your résumé and prepare a final draft.

Julianna E. Hobbs
4146 Carey Road
Victoria, British Columbia
V8Z 4J2
Home: (604) 479-9618
Business: (604) 472-8891

Education

1993–present   Camosun College
3100 Foul Bay Road, Victoria, BC V8P 4X8
• Studies in Business Administration

1989–1993   Claremont High School
4980 Wesley Road, Victoria, BC V8Y 1Y9
• Courses in Business, Economics, Computers

Experience

1992–1993   Canadian Imperial Bank of Commerce
4089 Morris Drive, Victoria, BC V8X 1J3
• Clerk: responsibilities included typing and filing

1990–1991   J.E.H. Enterprises
4146 Carey Road, Victoria, BC V8Z 4J2
• Owner of lawn-cutting company: responsibilities included manual labour and operation of busine

Skills
• Working knowledge of word processing and spreadsheet software
• Working knowledge of business operation, including marketing and basic bookkeeping

Activities
• Swimming instructor and lifeguard qualifications

References   Available on request

RÉSUMÉ TIPS

- Keep it simple and clear — one page or two pages at most.
- Emphasize your accomplishments and achievements. Wherever possible, describe how your work benefited your former employers. Avoid using "I" and unnecessary phrases such as "I was responsible for..." or "My duties involved..." Use action words to describe your work: "researched and developed a work plan for" or "supervised a work plan for" or "supervised a team of four."
- Be honest. Don't exaggerate or misrepresent yourself.
- Give yourself credit. List any results or accomplishments that you were responsible for in previous work, whether paid or unpaid.
- Include part-time, summer, and volunteer work.
- Include certificates and special skills or training, such as first aid or having a driver's licence.
- Make sure there are no errors in spelling, grammar, or typing.
- List a telephone number where you can be reached during the day; or list two telephone numbers, one where messages can be left during the day and an evening number.
- Before you prepare the final copy, show your draft to several people for feedback. You need to find out if your résumé gives a clear and appealing picture of your best qualifications.

ADVERTISING

Advertising is any paid non-personal announcement by an identified sponsor to inform a target market about a product, service, idea, or organization. The presentation of the message — the advertisement — can be oral, visual, or a combination of the two.

Advertising has three objectives:

- *Inform* The main purpose of informative advertising is to provide information about the product, its features, how it works, any unique attributes it might have, and how to use it effectively. Informative advertising is often used by advertisers for a new product or to suggest new uses for an existing product. An example of this is the advertisement for Cow Brand baking soda, which suggests that the product can be used to eliminate odours from the refrigerator.

CONNECTING BUSINESS
WITH
ENTREPRENEUR

CLEAR PRODUCTS SEND A MESSAGE

Is the current fascination with clear products as transparent as the emperor's new clothes?

An array of companies are offering everything from cola, dishwashing liquid, and mouthwash to underarm deodorant in a colourless version.

In the business of marketing, the public's perception is what counts, industry experts say.

And the consumer will ultimately be the one to expose which of the many new transparent products offer nothing more than meets the eye.

"Products that are clear as water send a certain signal. It means simple and pure, little is added. This may or may not be true, but the lack of colour symbolizes these values," said Eileen Fischer, a marketing professor at York University.

"In marketing, perception is reality," Fischer said.

The makers of major brands, like Pepsi, Colgate-Palmolive, and Gillette, which put see-through beverages, personal hygiene items, and household cleaners on supermarket shelves, say they didn't set out to make a colourless product for the sake of appearance.

The firms say their aim was to fulfil a variety of consumer demands and, in the end, part of the solution became clear.

"We started with a concept. We wanted to design and formulate a product especially for sensitive skin," said Hugh Ryan,

marketing director of Colgate-Palmolive Canada Inc.

Palmolive Sensitive Skin, a colourless dishwashing liquid, was introduced in Canada in February 1993 and one year earlier in the United States. Its transparency is in vivid contrast to the dark green dishwashing liquid which has carried the Palmolive name for many years. The clear version also sells for 18 percent more than the original.

"We wanted to let people know that the harsher irritants and dyes and the alcohol had been removed from the new product.

"A clear liquid has an appropriate aesthetic value. It's easier for consumers to make the leap of faith that this product is for sensitive skin," Ryan said.

"But we didn't start with the idea of making a clear product and then work backwards from there."

Procter and Gamble Co. introduced Ivory Clear dishwashing liquid in the U.S. in the spring of 1992, and the product is now available in Canada in see-through plastic bottles.

A third smaller company recently introduced yet another clear liquid to get your dishes sparkling.

Fischer, of York University, said it is extremely difficult for a product to distinguish itself when thousands of new and revamped items are vying for consumer attention each year.

"What is really new under the sun? Not much. Clear is a distinguishing feature which helps consumers recognize the product as something new."

But can a cola be clear and still be a cola?

Roger Baranowski of Pepsi-Cola Canada Ltd. says yes.

Unlike clear soft drinks like 7-Up or Sprite, which have a lemon-lime taste, Crystal Pepsi has a cola flavour, but not the heaviness, Baranowski said.

But don't pick up a see-through bottle of Pepsi expecting the familiar taste that captured a "new generation."

"It's not supposed to taste like Pepsi. It's a new soft drink. We're looking for it to take over a new niche within the cola market."

Crystal Pepsi was launched in western Canada in December 1992 and appeared on store shelves across the country and the United States in January 1993.

At around the same time, Coca-Cola Co. began marketing a clear diet cola under the Tab brand name in selected cities. Colourless Pepsi was previously test-marketed in several U.S. cities for about a year.

Baranowski said the cola maker began developing Crystal Pepsi more than two years ago and wasn't just trying to cash in on the current clear-product blitz.

"Some companies are just following what appears to be a trend. We sometimes jump on the bandwagon. But this wasn't one of those times," he said.

The growing popularity of flavoured sparkling bottled waters, like those launched by the Clearly Canadian Beverage Corp., has put a certain amount of pressure on mainstream soft-drink companies, said Ian Osler, a beverage analyst with Sprott Securities Ltd.

Pepsi has the Canadian distribution rights of Clearly Canadian products. But the soft-drink maker wanted to create a cola-based beverage under its brand name aimed at consumers looking for a lighter-tasting drink with fewer calories, Baranowski said.

1. How many "clear" products do you have in your household? Discuss the reasons for purchasing them with your family.

2. If you were to guess what the next "clear" product might be, what would you suggest? Why?

• *Persuade*   Persuasive advertisements try to convince the consumer to purchase one particular company's product or service instead of the competitor's, although the competitor is usually not mentioned. The advertisements for Duracell batteries are examples of these types of advertisements. Persuasive advertising can have an emotional appeal — that is, the advertisement will involve an emotion such as love, pride, or fear. An example of an emotional advertisement is one for chewing gum that appeals to people's feeling that good breath is important and their concern that their breath is bad. Another method of persuasive advertising is the use of testimonials in which a well-known celebrity or a member of an association endorses a product. For example, Silken Laumann, the Canadian Olympic bronze medalist in rowing, endorses Brooks athletic wear. People who buy endorsed products hope that some of the celebrity's success will "rub off" on them.

This Levi's® advertisement reminds customers that the popular clothing manufacturer does not only produce jeans.

• *Remind*   Many advertisements are designed to keep the product or organization visible to the public and could be considered to take a soft approach. This method of advertising is often called institutional advertising; its main purpose is to promote goodwill for the company. Advertisements for charitable organizations, such as Care Canada, are the best examples of reminder advertising.

Once the objectives of the advertising campaign have been established, the type of medium to carry the message is chosen. Should the company use radio, television, newspapers, magazines, billboards, direct mail, or other media? The choice will depend on a number of factors. The advantages and disadvantages of each medium will illustrate how these decisions are made.

MEDIA CHARACTERISTICS

The colour insert offers examples of actual advertisements appearing in newspapers and magazines and on television. Also shown are examples of outdoor advertising and direct mail.

Newspapers

Newspapers provide advertisers with a very timely and flexible medium. Advertisers can select which among the many regional and local newspapers appeal to their target market. Thus, a business that operates only in Vancouver might advertise in the *Vancouver Sun*, whereas a national business would run advertisements in the daily newspapers of all large cities. Newspapers offer advertisers the advantage of responding quickly to local economic and social conditions and allow them to change their advertisements on very short notice. For example, as interest rates change, banks and mortgage loan companies can advertise the new rates to potential customers. The cost of producing a newspaper advertisement is relatively low, but its life is quite short since papers are normally discarded a day or two after they have been read.

Magazines

Magazines offer advertisers a high-quality medium for their advertising. Because many special-interest magazines exist, advertisers can be selective and focus advertisements on target markets. For example, a garden equipment manufacturer would likely advertise in *Canadian*

This advertisement appeared in the *Canadian Rodeo News*.

Gardening rather than in a news magazine such as *Maclean's*. Magazines are usually read in a leisurely fashion, so an advertiser can convey a lengthy or complicated message to the reader. Magazines are usually retained for a longer time than newspapers and are often read by a number of people. Because magazines are published less frequently than newspapers, more time is available for the preparation of the advertisement, but the flexibility associated with newspapers is lost.

HI-TECH AND SPORTS FIND ONE ANOTHER ON CD-ROM

Graphics software developer Corel Corporation of Ottawa has taken the sponsorship plunge with Swimming Canada, and is using the relationship to market products internationally.

Most sponsors devote their efforts to building their ties to domestic consumers, normally their largest target audience. But in Corel's case, international consumers are 95% of its target audience.

Corel, whose president and CEO Michael Cowpland says recently became the world's largest graphics software company (sales last year were $90 million plus), is linking a swimming sponsorship with its just-launched stock-photo collection on CD-ROM disks.

There are several reasons Corel has joined the sports sponsorship team, he says: sport is popular and "motivates excellence"; Canadian athletes have a great track record in swimming and rowing; and sports fits Corel's emphasis on the physical fitness of its employees. "We find it's a good combination, to be high-tech but also heavily involved in sports," says Cowpland.

Corel sells in 60 countries, particularly in the U.K., U.S., Europe and Japan.

Each Corel CD-ROM disk contains 100 stock images, royalty-free and ready for colour separation. In the case of Corel's first sports disk about swimming, Swimming Canada provided the 100 photos used, and receives a 7% royalty for each disk sold (cost: about $60). Corel is marketing the collection to publishers, newsletter editors, pre-press service bureaus, and corporate users around the world.

But the disks also sport another feature: after a short delay, the same images appear, accompanied by sounds or music, on users' computer screens. Cowpland predicts this will be popular, noting only a fraction of computer users are directly involved in publishing. The company plans to produce more than 40 sports-disks, Cowpland says.

Radio

Radio is a popular advertising medium. It is relatively inexpensive and allows advertisers to reach a specific target market because of the range of stations that cater to specific segments of the population. An advertiser can place a message on a station aimed at teenagers, a country-and-western station, or a station that plays classical music. A rock concert would be advertised on a radio station that plays rock music, but a 10 km run to benefit a youth orchestra might be advertised on a classical music station. Radio is a medium that reaches people anywhere, an attractive feature for advertisers. Radios can be portable and people listen to them on the beach or while walking or jogging. As well, most cars have radios and the advertising time during morning and evening rush hours is sought after by advertisers.

Although radio advertising is not expensive, comparatively speaking, advertisers must repeat their message frequently. Many listeners tend to use the radio as background and do not really concentrate on what is being said. People also tend to remember what they see better than what they hear.

Television

Television is the only medium that offers the advertiser a combination of sight, sound, motion, and colour. The people who create advertisements for television can use a wide range of effects to attract the viewer's attention.

As mentioned above, people tend to remember what they see, so many advertisers ensure that their product appears in the commercial. Its method of use or application can be demonstrated, sustaining the viewer's interest. Television also allows the advertiser to select geographic markets. A negative aspect of television for the advertiser is the high cost of producing commercials and advertising, so this medium tends to be used primarily by large corporations.

Direct Mail

Advertising pamphlets, brochures, leaflets, and flyers that are delivered in the mail make up a medium called **direct mail**. Because direct mail can be selective, the advertiser can tailor the advertisement to its target market. A business that buys the subscription list of a fashion magazine to market mail-order clothing knows that the magazine subscribers are more likely to be interested in fashion than people who do not subscribe to fashion magazines. As well, direct mail gives the advertiser a way to distribute samples of their products to potential customers.

However, direct mail can be expensive and is sometimes considered as "junk mail." It is often thrown out without being read. Also, mailing lists can quickly go out of date.

Outdoor Advertising

Billboards, bus-shelter ads, and advertisements on public transit and on the sides of trucks are forms of outdoor advertising. These advertisements tend to be seen by people on the move who are not focusing on the advertisements around them. It is a medium most appropriate for short messages. An advantage is that outdoor advertisements are seen by a large number of consumers, but a drawback is that it is impossible for advertisers to target their market.

POINTS TO REMEMBER

- The promotional mix is made up of personal selling, sales promotion, publicity, public relations, and advertising.

- AIDA stands for attention, interest, desire, and action.

- Advertising is designed to inform, persuade, and remind the target market of the company and its product or service.

- Advertising media include newspapers, magazines, radio, television, direct mail, and outdoor advertising.

FOCUSING ON BUSINESS

9. List the three main objectives of advertising and explain their purpose in your own words.

10. Create a three-column organizer like the one below. Complete the middle and right-hand columns for each type of media.

Media	Advertising Advantages	Advertising Disadvantages
Newspapers		
Magazines		
Radio		
Television		
Direct Mail		
Outdoor Advertising		

EXPLORING BUSINESS

11. With a partner, list the brand names available for one product on the market, perhaps dishwashing liquid or an all-purpose cleaner. What image does each name project? How does the picture and the information on the label emphasize that image?

12. You have been asked to write a slogan for a new brand of laundry detergent called Dash. The manufacturers want to promote the product as being environmentally friendly. Create a slogan and explain why you think it will promote the detergent.

13. a. In small groups, discuss the types of advertisements that would be appropriate for the following sections of a newspaper. Give reasons for your opinion.
    • business
    • sports
    • news
    • lifestyle

    b. Find examples in a newspaper of the following types of advertisements:
    • an ad for a service
    • an ad that connects with social or economic conditions
    • an ad directed at the business community
    • an ad for a consumer product
    • an ad aimed at teenagers
    • an ad for an environmentally friendly product (name the product)

14. Divide the class into two teams. Each team is to select a team name and prepare to play the following game. Each team brings to class a list of at least 15 slogans selected from different media and for different products. Each member of the team should contribute to the list and, as a team, the members select the best 15 slogans to be handed in. Be sure to provide the slogan and the name of the advertiser. For example, "Let Your Fingers Do the Walking" is the slogan, and Yellow Pages is the advertiser. Your teacher will then read out the slogan to the other team, who must figure out the advertiser.

15. Form small groups. Each member of the group should select a different radio station. At home, listen to the radio for at least 30 minutes. Write a report that includes the following: the name of the radio station;

the number of advertisements played in 30-minute time slot; and a list of the products, services, or information advertised.

In your report, answer the following questions: Which advertisements were the most effective? Why? What was the target market for the advertisements?

Compare your findings with those of each member of your group. How does your information compare with that of other groups?

 16. Watch a television program shown during each of the following four time slots. Create and complete an organizer like the one below. Compare your information with a classmate's. Write a brief report outlining how effective the advertisers were in reaching their target markets.

Time Slot	No. of Ads	Product/Service Advertised	Target Market
Sign-on to 12 p.m.			
12 p.m. to 4:30 p.m.			
4:30 p.m. to 7:00 p.m.			
7:00 p.m. to 11:00 p.m.			

17. Select a magazine and analyze its advertising by answering the following questions:

a. What is the name of the magazine?

b. What is the price of the magazine?

c. Where is the magazine published?

d. What do you think the magazine's target market is?

e. List five common types of products advertised in the magazine. Why do you think the advertisers chose to advertise their products or services in this particular magazine? In your opinion, was it a wise choice? Why?

f. Describe the advertising in this magazine with respect to the number of advertisements, size of advertisements, use of colour, and location of the advertisements in the magazine.

g. In your opinion, does the advertising take away from the appeal of the magazine? Why?

h. Which company is advertising on the inside front cover? Inside back cover? Back cover? Do these companies have anything in common? Why do you think these companies advertise in these places in the magazine?

i. Does the magazine contain any unique forms of advertising, such as inserts or pull-out advertisements? Are they effective?

j. Find an advertisement that captures your interest. What made this advertisement so appealing?

k. Examine the first ten pages of the magazine (starting with the inside front cover). How many advertisements appeared? Select another ten pages in the magazine and count the number of advertisements featured. Is there a difference? Why do you think this is the case?

18. Working in small groups, select or design a new product that will provide a unique benefit to consumers. Each group should prepare a written report outlining the following:

- An analysis of the proposed target market. This must include a summary of any marketing research that was done to support your conclusions, including a demographic breakdown of the target market.

- An analysis of any direct or indirect competition against your new product.

- An explanation of the marketing mix as it applies to your product. This will address the four Ps of marketing and should include the packaging and labelling of the product, the price of the product, and the proposed channels of distribution.

Prepare an oral presentation outlining the topics analyzed in the written report. Include in the oral presentation a television or radio commercial that you have prepared for the product.

WORKING WITH MATH

19. Using a spreadsheet software program, create a spreadsheet to present the information on the next page. Then expand the spreadsheet to add the necessary columns, headings, and formulas to calculate and present the dollar amount of 1992 revenue spent on marketing, research and development (R & D), and training. Calculate the 1992 profit or loss as a percentage of the revenue.

············· CANADA'S TOP 10 FASTEST-GROWING COMPANIES IN 1993···············

R A N K	Company, Industry	Revenue	Profit (Loss)	Percent of 1992 revenue spent on		
				Marketing	R&D	Training
1	Star Data Systems Inc. *online information services*	17 078 488	812 173	0.7	5.0	0.5
2	Softkey Sofware Products Inc. *software technology*	61 407 000	10 446 000	14.0	3.0	1.0
3	ISG Technologies Inc. *medical-imaging technology*	15 804 966	(916 534)	32.0	20.0	1.0
4	Columbia Sportwear Canada Inc. *clothing distributor*	13 648 535	85 613	3.0	1.5	0.0
5	Canadian Laser Products Inc. *laser-printer dealer*	7 761 595	43 000	2.0	0.0	0.0
6	Clearly Canadian Beverage Corp. *soft-drink manufacturer and distributor*	175 000 000	16 800 000	3.75	1.0	0.0
7	FirstService Corp. *home maintenance manufacturer*	43 000 000	570 000	7.7	0.0	0.0
8	National Hav-Info Communications Inc. *data communications manufacturer*	10 015 934	(5 083 418)	10.0	7.0	1.0
9	Microforum Manufacturing Inc. *computer accessories manufacturer and distributor*	6 157 012	194 820	1.0	3.0	0.0
10	Goldcorp Inc. *mining*	109 165 000	2 079 000	0.0	0.0	0.0

Source: *Profit*, June 1993

KEY TERMS

personal selling

telemarketing

AIDA

sales promotion

public relations

publicity

advertising

direct mail

PART 7

Accounting

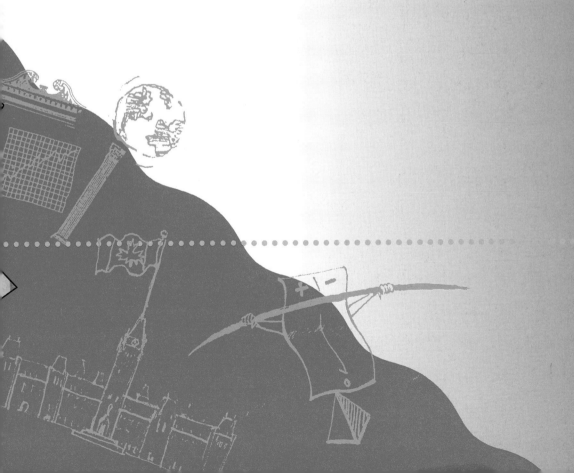

The Balance Sheet

CHAPTER FOCUS

After studying this chapter you will be able to:

identify and describe the basic accounting activities performed in every business

•

identify the various users of financial statements

•

define assets, liabilities, and owner's equity

•

understand the purpose of a balance sheet

•

prepare a balance sheet

USINESS OWNERS AND MANAGERS need financial information to make decisions about their businesses, such as what goods and/or services to sell, what price to charge, and whether they have efficiently used their human, financial, and material resources. Investors need to know whether their investment in a business has earned an adequate return for them. Banks and other lenders must decide whether to lend a company money by assessing the ability of the business to pay back the money it is trying to borrow. Government uses financial information to assess a business for taxes. Where does the financial information for decision making come from?

In this chapter, we will look at accounting. We will discuss financial statements and the uses that owners and managers, investors, banks and other lenders, and government make of the information that those statements contain. We will learn how to prepare a balance sheet to show the financial position of a business. The second financial statement, namely, the income statement, will be discussed in detail in Chapter 18.

FINANCIAL STATEMENTS

In the daily operation of a business, financial events are happening continually. These events involve: buying from suppliers the goods and services to be used in a business or resold to consumers; making cash deposits; and possibly borrowing money from a bank or other financial institution. Every day, the owners make decisions about many aspects of the business.

Accounting is the process of organizing financial information in order to provide the records and statements needed by business decision makers. Accounting involves keeping track of money received from customers and paid to suppliers, salaries and wages, bank loans, mortgages, and purchases of expensive and long-lasting items, such as computer equipment and buildings. The information on which business decisions are made must be accurate. Thus, accounting procedures and standards are vital for every business, from the smallest sole proprietorship to the largest corporation.

Of all the accounting activities, the recording of financial transactions is the most basic and important one. A **transaction** is any financial event that results in a change in a business's financial status. A transaction might involve buying goods that will be resold to customers, having the delivery truck repaired, selling goods or services, borrowing money from a bank, buying a computer, or investing in the business.

Businesses need to record their daily transactions every day to ensure accurate financial records. From time to time, usually monthly or quarterly (every three months), accounting information is gathered into reports called **financial statements**. By law, these statements must be prepared on an annual basis, but interim statements are often prepared for internal use by management. The two types of statements that you will be studying are the balance sheet and the income statement.

A **balance sheet** shows the financial position of a business by reporting its assets (what it owns), its liabilities (what it owes), and the owner's equity (the owner's investment, taking into account accumulated profits and losses).

An **income statement** shows the net income or net loss of a business for a specific period of time by reporting how much revenue was earned and the expenses that were incurred to earn the revenue. Income statements will be discussed in detail in Chapter 18.

Balance sheets and income statements are prepared in a standard format, so that anyone who reads them understands the information given in them in the same way.

Who Uses Financial Statements?

Financial statements prepared by a business are needed by different types of users. The four main users of financial statements are business owners and managers, investors, lenders, and government. Rules have been made concerning the information that must be made available and the information that does not need to be disclosed. Because some users of the company's information are outside of the business and have no way of knowing the details of what happens on a daily basis, there must be some assurance that accounting practices are comparable in all businesses.

"Mr. Killgroe can't be disturbed just now. Faced with mounting fourth quarter losses, he's busy writing a letter to Santa Claus."

Good News, Bad News by Henry Martin. Reprinted by permission: Tribune Media Services.

Business Owners and Managers

Business owners and managers need accurate information to make financial decisions. "Are we charging enough for our goods or services? Are expenses reasonable? Are we spending too much on salaries? Would advertising help boost sales enough to cover the cost of the advertising? Should we change our products; add more; delete one;

start servicing what we sell?" These are a few examples of management decision making, and these decisions are dependent on the reliability of the accounting information generated by the company. By examining the balance sheet and the income statement, management can compare company performance from year to year and see the changes that have occurred as well as any trends that may be developing. For example, if expenses have risen, as usually happens in any economy, but prices have not risen, profits will be lower. A business may be losing money even though it has earned a net profit for a given year, if it earned a lower profit than the previous year. If the profit has not increased from the previous year, the company may be in a downward trend that could prove disastrous. Thus, a mere profit is not enough: it must be a *targeted* profit in order to meet the required returns of investors and management, to ensure future growth, and to cover the amount of profit that could have been earned if the best alternative financial decision had been made.

Investors

If you are thinking of investing money in a business, you must be satisfied that the business is profitable. Investors have to decide whether they should invest in a particular business at all, whether they should invest more in a business in which they are already involved, or whether they should take their money out of a venture (if they have another opportunity or if the business is not doing well). If a business has a large debt, it will not provide as much profit for a return to investors as if it has a small debt. Investors need to know the answers to questions such as: Have the business's debts increased? What was the money spent on? Will this expenditure help the business earn more money in the future? Financial statements provide this information to investors.

Lenders

Banks and other lenders need to know that they will be repaid by a business that owes them money. Financial statements will show a lender if a business is generating enough profit to meet the interest obligations of the debt. Balance sheets show lenders the quality of assets in case they need to claim them to cover the debt.

Government

Much of the financial information prepared by a business is for income

DIRECT MAIL

The Saskatoon *Star-Phoenix* pioneered the "TAGAlong" idea as a way to attract customers who had previously advertised almost exclusively on broadcast media such as television and radio. Small, printed tags were attached by carriers to the elastic band around the rolled-up newspaper. Fast-food retailers used the tags as coupons or promotional announcements, with great success.

Germany

WE BRING CANADA TO *the* REST OF THE WORLD.

Munich and Frankfurt are just two of the 22 international destinations Canadian Airlines
serves. In Europe, we also fly to Paris, Milan, Rome, London and Manchester.

Canadian
Canadian Airlines International

ADVERTISING MEDIA

MAGAZI

Mexico

WE BRING CANADA TO *the* REST OF THE WORLD.

Mexico City is one of five cities we serve in Latin America. We also serve
Sao Paulo, Rio de Janeiro, Buenos Aires and Santiago.

Canadi⬛n
Canadian Airlines International

O *the* REST OF THE WORLD.

Paris from Eastern Canada. It's just one of
ve. In Europe, this includes London, Manchester,
kfurt, Rome and Milan.

nadi⬛n
n Airlines International

In the "We Bring Canada to the Rest of the World" campaign, Canadian Airlines runs a series of full-page ads in a magazine. Readers are challenged to identify the "Canadian" element in the photograph of a foreign location.

1.

2.

3.

There are 1.3 million adults in Greater Vancouver.
You can reach 1.1 million* of them through the two of us.

GET READ. GET RESULTS.
604 732 2478

*NADbank®

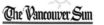 The Vancouver Sun

 **The Province**
THE NEWSPAPER WITH ATTITUDE!

MAGAZINES

ADVERTISING MEDIA

the trail of knowledge...

*T*he challenge to find and produce oil and gas while protecting the environment has taken us down some pretty interesting trails... in the high elevation country of the Rocky Mountains, we spent four years studying the big horn sheep. As well, we are sponsoring an ongoing elk monitoring project in this area.

While most of these studies are related to Shell, we also sponsor research

we believe will bring important information to our industry. From wildlife and vegetation to archaeological and history studies, we support this research to help us better understand and minimize the impact of our operations on the environment.

At Shell, we're on the trail leading to a greater knowledge of our environment – and the ways in which we can protect it.

 Shell *helps!*

When I was growing up, nothing went to waste. But of all the hand-me-downs I got, Dad's were the most fun. I guess Canadian Tire has been a part of my family for a long, long time.

CANADIAN TIRE

There's A Lot More To Canadian Tire For A Lot Less.

OE93-461

This ad originally appeared in a specialty magazine titled *Marketing* targeted to advertisers and advertising agencies. It is an effective method of promoting advertising sales in *The Vancouver Sun* and *The Province* newspapers.

2 Shell recognizes consumers' growing concern with the environment, providing information about the research that it is undertaking to minimize the impact of its operations on the environment.

3 In this advertisement, Canadian Tire appeals to consumers' nostalgia for the past, triggering positive associations with the store.

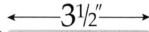

①

1 In this newspaper ad, a
colour photograph of a tropi-
cal vacation scene is used to
arouse readers' curiosity
about the benefits of the
CIBC Aerogold Visa
Aeroplan.

2 The dramatic use of colour in
this full-page newspaper ad
catches readers' attention.
Published in *The Globe and
Mail*, a national newspaper,
this ad is designed to appeal
to interested individuals
across the country.

Visit our Suit Department. Come to the Muse

OUTDOOR AD

1 This eye-catching billboard creates curiosity about the Royal Ontario Museum's collection. An advantage to advertising in such a medium is that it is seen by a high number of individuals.

2 This three-dimensional interior transit card is found inside buses and subway cars. It is very popular with its target audience, teenagers.

3 This transit ad promotes a special service offered by Purolator courier. In summer, Purolator delivers care packages to children's summer camps.

Quick, send him a care package.

He wants to come home early.

Purolator

Is That NB Grown?
Est-ce cultivé au N-B?

4

4 The New Brunswick Grown program is designed to encourage local shoppers to eat homegrown fruits and vegetables. This creative marketing strategy placed the picture of the NB Grown spokesperson peering up at the consumer and asking "Is that NB Grown?" on shopping carts across the province.

See nature's version of
a plunging neckline.

MetroTorontoZoo
WHERE TO GO WHEN NATURE CALLS

OUTDOOR ADS

1 This innovative transit ad uses new technology to play a visual joke. The people riding on the bus become part of the ad—and the joke.

2 Because a billboard such as this one is seen by people on the move, it is a medium most appropriate for short messages. Only a striking image and the simple slogan "Spend Your Energy" are required to remind consumers of the benefits of drinking milk.

SPEND
YOUR
ENERGY

2

Plant your car for a day.

Walk, run, bike, car pool or take transit to work and we'll all breathe a little easier. For more information, call 1-800-End Smog.

LEVER
CORPORATE LEADER OF THE CLEAN AIR COMMUTE

POLLUTION PROBE

3

3 Non-profit organizations also use advertising to promote their messages. Pollution Probe, an environmental agency, produced this poster to encourage people to participate in The Clean Air Commute Day, a day when people were encouraged to leave their cars at home.

POLLUTION PROBE

TELEVISION

1

VIDEO

Two people doing "the wave" at a couch

LOGO: Leon's

SUPER: Wave the payments

SUPER: No down payment.
No monthly payments.

SUPER: No interest. Until
May, 1994.

DISCLAIMER: All applicable taxes payable at time of purchase. Balance due May 15, 1994. O.A.C.

LOGO: Leon's

SUPER: Wave the payments

AUDIO

FANS: (Singing) Nah, nah ...nah, nah, nah, nah ...hey, hey, hey goodbye ...

(THROUGHOUT.)

V.O.: It's Leon's <u>amazing</u> new <u>Wave</u> The Payments Event.
You can get all the <u>quality</u> home furnishings you need <u>today</u> from Leon's <u>huge</u> selection and you don't have to pay til next May.

Everything from wall units to lamps to sofas, <u>and</u> wave goodbye to <u>all</u> the payments. <u>No</u> down payment ... <u>no</u> monthly payments ... <u>no</u> interest til

May ... But you better hurry or you'll miss all the action...

SFX: A BALL BEING HIT AND A CROWD CHEERING.

Snake and Big Danny,
t had become an obsession.

FX THROUGHOUT.
SUPER.

SHOT OF TWO BIKERS,
DRINKING SPRITE.

THEY START TO TAKE OFF THEIR
CLOTHES.

REVEAL BIKERS AT
POOL.

THEY STRIKE A POSE...

AND BEGIN THEIR SYNCHRONIZED
SWIMMING ROUTINE.

the Sprite in you.

● ● ● ● ● ● ● ● ● ● ● ● ● ●

1 Leon's popular television advertising relies on comic characters and humorous scenarios to entertain the viewer.

2 Sight, sound, motion and colour are combined in television advertisements to attract the viewer's attention. This commercial also uses humour to engage the viewer and to ensure that the viewer remembers the product slogan "I like the Sprite in you" – and the product.

1

PACKAGING

2

3

1 A good package design is necessary for the consumer to identify a manufacturer's product from the other items on the shelf. It is often packaging that is responsible for the initial purchase. The elegant packaging of Harden & Huyse chocolates and the wide range of package sizes available encourage consumers to try the product.

2 Every element of an advertisement is carefully designed to create a feeling or mood. This wordmark was created for use in a Shoppers Drug Mart television advertisement.

3 The Clearly Canadian bottle has been carefully designed to differentiate it from other drinks while at the same time make it visually appealing.

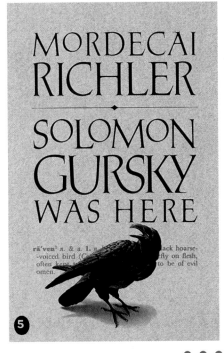

4 This graphic opener is used to introduce concert listings on the MuchMusic network. It is an effective example of how television programming is "packaged" to create a particular mood and to appeal to a specific audience.

5 This intriguing book design helps to persuade the reader to buy the book.

6 The container a product comes in must attract the attention of consumers. This Kellogg's Corn Flakes box, for example, features useful information about the product and special promotional offers to attract consumers.

Boating - be it in yachts, sailboats or sculls - has long been part of life in our harbour cities.

When the great Canadian humorist Stephen Leacock first visited British Columbia, he was asked why he'd never been here before. He replied he'd never come because he didn't realize how wonderful it was. "If I'd known what it was like," he said, "I wouldn't have been content with a mere visit. I'd have been born here."

For your first course, see Vancouver's skyline.

This is the place. So many visitors to British Columbia feel the same way. And it's simple to see why. The fascination may begin with Vancouver but it widens and deepens as they head out.

Along the steep, mountainous coast are snowcapped fjords, long stretches of sandy beach, hidden coves and small seaside villages. Offshore lie dozens of evergreen-forested islands, including Vancouver Island, the pastoral Gulf Islands and the Queen Charlottes, known worldwide for their towering, 600-year-old Douglas fir trees.

The Royal Canadian Mounted Police have played an important role in our history.

TOURISM BRITISH COLUMBIA

ADVERTISING MEDIA

PROMOTION

This promotional brochure, distributed by Tourism British Columbia, features spectacular photographs of the natural scenery of British Columbia. The brochure is one of a number of advertising media used in the campaign to promote travel in the province.

tax purposes. All individuals and businesses, with the exception of non-profit organizations, pay taxes on their earnings. The government needs a business's financial statements to see its earnings, to make sure that all income has been reported, and to make sure that all expenses were allowable. In addition, the financial statements show the government what the business owns and owes, as these items affect the amount of income tax the business pays.

THE BALANCE SHEET

As discussed earlier, a balance sheet is a financial statement reporting assets, liabilities, and the owner's equity in a business on a particular date. It is like a snapshot of a business's financial well-being on the day the statement is prepared. The sections below will explain the meaning of assets, liabilities, and owner's equity and how these amounts can show how a company has performed. Next, we will be preparing a balance sheet for Landscaping Dynamics, which is a typical small business that sells only services. The balance sheet examples throughout this chapter all refer to this service business and its owner, Linda Sutter. In Chapter 18, Landscaping Dynamics will be used to introduce the income statement and will show the relationship between the balance sheet and the income statement.

Assets

You may have heard the word asset used before in a number of ways: "Lesley will be a real asset to the organization" or "Flexibility can be an asset in life." In accounting, an **asset** is anything a business owns that has value. Assets include cash, accounts receivable, supplies, trucks, computers, furniture, land, and buildings. These items are used by a business to make its goods or services available for sale, so they each contribute to earning profits. For example, a truck is used to transport people and tools to a job, or to deliver items sold to customers. Assets, such as cash and accounts receivable, have value because they can be used to buy other assets or services. **Accounts receivable** are the debts owed to a business by customers who have bought on credit; they are classified as an asset since the business can expect to collect cash from the customers in the near future (usually within 30 days).

ON A ROLL FROM ROCK PHOTOS

CONNECTING BUSINESS
WITH
THE ARTS

Back in 1985, a 22-year-old freelance photographer from Toronto was invited to fly out to Vancouver and take some shots of a promising pop singer named Madonna. "I did 15 minutes of work, sent the photos back to the *Toronto Star*, where they loved them, and ran them. Then I shipped them off to my New York agent, who sold them to the *New York Post, People* magazine, and all over Europe. I ended up making $5000 for that tiny bit of work."

Raj Rama, born 30 years ago to parents from India who had migrated to Toronto in the late '50s, took that experience and became his own "New York agent," and the agent for a half-dozen other photographers across Canada as well.

Raj Rama's career, at first, does not seem terribly promising: After graduating from Grade 12 in a Toronto high school, he took photos for the Toronto Sun, then freelanced

Natalie Richard, a MuchMusic VJ, with Bryan Adams

for Maclean's and other magazines. Then, he began taking photos for a popular rock band out of Vancouver called Loverboy, whose opening act was a kid named Bryan Adams. "You take great pictures!" exclaimed the future multi-millionaire singer/ songwriter, and a warm business relationship was born: Rama followed Adams across Canada and the States, taking thousands of photos.

In July, 1988, Rama made his big decision, partly based on the Madonna story, because "I wanted to take a piece of everyone else, instead of everyone taking a piece of me."

And so, armed with his Youth Venture loan, he founded Creative Stock Photography Agency Ltd. Although he doesn't like to talk figures, he admits that by the end of his fifth year in business, "I expect to break a quarter-million." So, when Mutual of Omaha or other major companies need photo shots from across Canada, Raj Rama calls up freelance photographers, who do the shoots. "There's competition, but I go after exclusive niches and companies that others are not tapping into."

Has his youth hurt? "Well," Rama laughs, "they used to ask, 'Who is the kid?' Now they say, 'Sir'!"

Prepare a balance sheet for Creative Stock Photography Agency Ltd. if it has the following accounts at December 31, 19—. You will be able to fill in the amount of capital as you are completing the balance sheet.

Photographic equipment	$20 000
Accounts receivable	1 500
Bank loan	30 000
Photographic supplies	2 000
Accounts payable	4 200
Computer	10 000
Automobile	12 000
Raj Rama, Capital	?
Cash	1 800
Office furniture	3 500
Office supplies	500

Liabilities

Liabilities are the money a business owes to a supplier or lender. The most common liabilities are accounts payable and bank loan payable. **Accounts payable** are debts of a business owed to creditors other than banks for the purchase of goods and services on credit. **Bank loan payable** is simply a loan from a bank. The main difference between accounts payable and bank loan payable is the length of time a business has to pay back the debts. Accounts payable are usually due within 30 days, whereas bank loans can be due in as little as 30 days or as long as five years.

Owner's Equity

The assets of a business are bought with money that is borrowed or is invested in a business by the owner or owners. As the business is operated through the years, all profits are added to, and all losses are subtracted from, the owner's investment. In this way, the owner's equity grows with the successful operation of the business. Therefore, **owner's equity** is the owner's investment plus the total assets minus the total liabilities. If the business were sold, the liabilities would have to be paid and the owner would get what was left.

The Accounting Equation

The **accounting equation** shows the relationship between assets, liabilities, and owner's equity. Assets are shown on the left side of the accounting equation, and liabilities and owner's equity are on the right side. If you know the value of two of the elements, you can figure out the value of the third element. The structure of the balance sheet is based on the following accounting equation.

$$\text{Assets} \quad = \quad \text{Liabilities} \quad + \quad \text{Owner's Equity}$$

Or, in the case of Landscaping Dynamics:

$$\begin{array}{ccc} \text{Assets} & = & \text{Liabilities} & + & \text{Owner's Equity} \\ \$10\,000 & = & \$3000 & + & \$7000 \end{array}$$

FOCUSING ON BUSINESS

1. Identify four different users of financial information.

2. For each of the four users of financial information, explain what they need financial information for and how financial statements are used to satisfy their needs.

3. Why must financial statements be prepared at least once a year by law?

4. Define the term *asset* and give five examples of business assets.

5. Define the term *liabilities* and give three examples of business liabilities.

6. What is *owner's equity*?

7. After a business has operated successfully for five years, would you expect the owner's equity to be higher, lower, or the same as during the first year? Explain.

EXPLORING BUSINESS

8. If assets are $15 000 and liabilities are $3475, what is the owner's equity?

9. If owner's equity is $52 900 and assets are $100 000, what are the liabilities?

10. If liabilities are $33 782 and owner's equity is $17 619, what are the total assets?

11. Identify each of the following as an asset, liability, or owner's equity:

    a. an amount of money owed to the business by a customer

    b. the owner's original investment

    c. office furniture

    d. building and land

    e. bank loan

    f. mortgage on land and building

    g. delivery truck

    h. an amount of money owed by the business to a supplier

    i. supplies used in the business

    j. profits at the end of the accounting period

12. Collect six advertisements related to careers in accounting. Create a poster to display the advertisements and summarize the skills and educational requirements of each.

13. Interview an accountant or a person working in the field of accounting. Find out:
    - why he or she chose a career in accounting
    - the job responsibilities
    - the training or education required
    - if computers are used in the job
    - what he or she likes about his or her career

    Share your findings with the class.

Preparing the Balance Sheet

The balance sheet for Landscaping Dynamics appears below. The following section explains and illustrates step by step how to prepare a balance sheet.

Heading

The balance sheet begins with a three-line heading centred above the body of the statement. The name of the business appears on the first line. The name of the business may or not be the same as that of its owner. The type of statement appears in the second line — in this case, a balance sheet. The date goes on the third line. The heading can be said to contain the who, what, and when of the statement. The balance sheet shows the financial position of the business at a specific time, and for this reason, some accountants will include the words *as at* on the date line. Others will simply write the date — in this case, March 31.

Landscaping Dynamics

Balance Sheet

March 31, 19–

Assets Section

The heading Assets is centred over the assets section of the balance sheet. Assets are listed along the left margin, and the dollar amount of each asset appears on the right. It is important to remember that assets are listed in order of **liquidity**; that is, according to how easily they can be converted into cash. Cash is the first asset recorded and is followed by all other assets. Accounts receivable usually appear right after cash since they are considered to be very liquid. Assets that cannot be converted easily into cash are recorded last.

When a balance sheet is prepared, dollar signs appear in several places. A dollar sign is usually shown with the first amount in any column, with each subtotal in a column, and with the grand total in a column. A single rule is drawn to indicate that a total follows. Grand totals are always double-underlined.

Assets	
Cash	$ 800
Accounts Receivable	1 200
Supplies	1 000
Equipment	3 500
Truck	3 500
Total Assets	$10 000

In our example, Landscaping Dynamics owns several assets. Like all businesses, it has some cash that is used to pay suppliers and for daily operating expenses. The business also has accounts receivable, indicating that it has done work for customers who did not pay cash, but were allowed credit and will pay in the near future. The usual amount of time given for accounts receivable is 30 days. Supplies used in the landscaping business could be anything from garden chemicals and grass seed to the invoices used in the office. As the business grows, Linda Sutter may separate these into office supplies and landscaping supplies. A landscaping business needs a variety of tools and equipment, so the equipment category would include such items as small tools, ladders, and lawnmowers. Finally, the truck would be used to drive to job sites, make deliveries, or visit clients.

Liabilities Section

The liabilities section appears on the right side of the balance sheet and is prepared in the same way as the assets section. The heading Liabilities is centred over the body of this section and the liabilities are listed in the order in which they are to be paid. In other words, liabilities to be paid immediately are listed before those that are due in 30 days.

Liabilities	
Accounts Payable	$ 750
Bank Loan Payable	$2 250
Total Liabilities	$3 000

Accounts payable are amounts that Landscaping Dynamics owes to its suppliers from purchases of goods and services. The bank loan would likely have been negotiated to purchase equipment or the truck that the business owns. Thus, although the equipment and truck are listed as assets, the business does not own them completely until the loan is paid.

Owner's Equity Section

Similarly, the owner's equity section begins with the centred title Owner's Equity and is positioned below the liabilities on the right side of the balance sheet. As shown earlier, the owner's personal investment in the business is listed as L. Sutter, Capital. **Capital** is another word for investment, or an amount of money that is put into a business venture in order to make a profit. If the business were in its first year of operations, the amount in owner's equity would probably be the amount of the owner's original investment. As the business operated through the years, this equity figure would increase with net income and would decrease with net losses. If Landscaping Dynamics has been operating for several years, the $7000 in owner's equity would be Linda Sutter's investment plus or minus the profits or losses.

Owner's Equity	
L. Sutter, Capital	$7 000

The owner's equity always includes the owner's name — in this case L. Sutter, Capital. This shows that regardless of what the business is called, it is the owner who made the original investment and who owns the accumulated profits. If the business is sold or liquidated, the proceeds from the sale will belong to Linda Sutter.

	Total Liabilities and	
Total Assets $10 000	Owner's Equity	$10 000

On a balance sheet, the total assets must be equal to the total liabilities plus the owner's equity. Although there are other formats for preparing a balance sheet, the one we are using presents the information in the format of the accounting equation.

Assets appear on the left and the liabilities and owner's equity appear on the right. This way it can be shown clearly that the total assets equals the total liabilities and owner's equity.

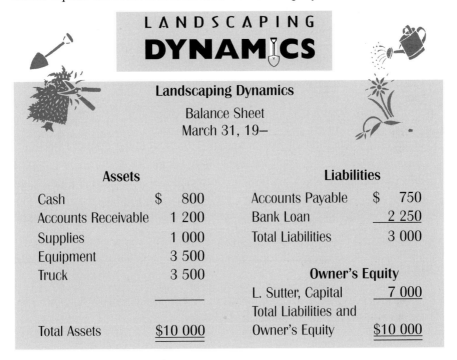

LANDSCAPING DYNAMICS

Landscaping Dynamics
Balance Sheet
March 31, 19–

Assets		Liabilities	
Cash	$ 800	Accounts Payable	$ 750
Accounts Receivable	1 200	Bank Loan	2 250
Supplies	1 000	Total Liabilities	3 000
Equipment	3 500		
Truck	3 500	**Owner's Equity**	
		L. Sutter, Capital	7 000
		Total Liabilities and	
Total Assets	$10 000	Owner's Equity	$10 000

POINTS TO REMEMBER

- Accurate financial information is needed in order to make business decisions.

- Financial statements are used by business owners and managers, investors, lenders, and government.

- A balance sheet is a financial statement reporting assets, liabilities, and owner's equity of a business on a particular date.

- The accounting equation shows the relationship between assets, liabilities, and owner's equity: Assets = Liabilities + Owner's Equity.

Covering Letters

A covering letter is a letter that should accompany your résumé to introduce yourself and to get an interview for a job. A résumé should not be sent without a covering letter.

Covering letters should:

- be no more than one page in length
- be typewritten, concise, free of grammatical and spelling errors, and have a positive tone
- be tailored to each job opportunity, company, or person to whom it is sent
- be organized into three or four paragraphs. In the first paragraph, explain that the purpose of writing is to apply for a job. State the job for which you are applying and how you found out about the position. If the job was advertised in a newspaper, state the newspaper and the date on which it appeared. If you heard about the job from a person, mention his or her name.

In the second (and third) paragraph(s), explain why you are the best person for the job. Briefly show how your skills and experience match those that are required for the job.

In the final paragraph, express thanks to your reader for taking time to consider you for the job and ask for an interview.

Remember to sign your name.

1. Look through the newspaper and choose a job advertisment that appeals to you.
2. Write a covering letter to apply for this job. If possible, use a computer so you can easily revise your letter.
3. In small groups, share your advertisement and covering letter with your group members. Discuss the strengths and weaknesses of each covering letter.

Dear Ms. Wong:

I am writing in response to your advertisement in the Vancouver Province on November 2 for part-time sales staff at the Music Den. The advertisement states that you are looking for conscientious, hard-working individuals with sales experience and good people skills. I believe that I have the characteristics you require and would like to be considered for an interview.

I am a grade 11 student at Maple Ridge Secondary School, where I maintain a B average. My work experience includes one year working at Threads Clothiers on weekends, and three summers as a day camp counsellor at Tall Pines Camp, where I planned and supervised the activities of twenty 8- to 10-year-old children. Both of these jobs gave me the opportunity to communicate, work with people, and solve problems.

I would appreciate an interview at your convenience and look forward to hearing from you. Thank you for taking the time to read my résumé.

Sincerely,

FOCUSING ON BUSINESS

14. a. What is meant by *liquidity* in describing assets?
    b. List the following assets in the order of liquidity: land, accounts receivable, cash, equipment, supplies, building

15. Explain when to use dollar signs on a balance sheet.

16. If the owner of a business purchased a computer for use in handling business finances, how and where should it appear on the balance sheet?

17. Explain how money owed to you can be considered an asset, as in accounts receivable.

18. How does the heading of a balance sheet show the who, what, and when of a business?

19. Why does the owner's equity always belong to the owner personally, even though the business may have a different name?

EXPLORING BUSINESS

20. With a partner, explore careers that involve accounting skills. Select a career that interests you and your partner. Research it further to learn more about the career and how accounting skills are used in it. If your research involves interviewing someone, ask if you can videotape the interview. Prepare a poster to display your research. Share your findings with the class.

21. Calculate your own personal financial position. First, make a list of everything you own and how much it cost when it was bought. In the case of clothing, estimate a value for all your clothes and simply call it Clothing. It will be necessary to make judgements about what you really own. For example, anything that you actually paid for or that was given to you is yours, such as a bicycle, stereo, or ski equipment. You do not own the things in your home that are used by everyone. What about your bedroom furniture? Did you buy it, or do you simply use the furniture bought by your parents? Next, make a list of any debts you may have. It is unlikely that you have credit cards or bank loans, but you may have borrowed money from friends or family. Finally, calculate your financial position using the accounting equation.

For questions 22 to 27, work individually or in pairs to complete the assignments manually and then using a computer spreadsheet.

22. Prepare the balance sheet for Perfect Portraits Photography at September 30, 19—, using the information given: Cash, $1200; Accounts Receivable, $400; Automobile, $13 900; Equipment, $10 000; Accounts Payable, $1150; Bank Loan $7500; A. Koschate, Capital, $16 850.

23. Prepare the balance sheet for Miguel's Muffins at June 30, 19—, from the following information: Cash, $2600; Accounts Receivable, $800; Supplies, $625; Equipment $72 000; Office Equipment, $4225; Accounts Payable, $2200; Bank Loan, $25 000; Mortgage Payable, $40 000; M. De Sousa, Capital, $13 050.

24. Prepare the balance sheet for Redo It, an upholstery company, at May 31, 19—, from the following information: Supplies, $1400; Tools, $3000; Bank Loan, $5000; Accounts Receivable, $1230; G. François, Capital, $85 685; Equipment, $18 000; Truck, $17 250; Land and Building, $105 000; Accounts Payable, $1225; Cash, $9000; Mortgage Payable, $62 970.

25. Prepare the balance sheet for Speedy Delivery Service at April 30, 19—, using the following information: Accounts Receivable, $8025;

Bank Loan, $15 500; Trucks, $60 000; Land, $75 000; Mortgage Payable, $225 000; Accounts Payable, $3750; Supplies, $2900; Cash, $200; Building, $225 000; P. Singh, Capital, $126 875.

26. Prepare the balance sheet for Better Business Consultants at December 31, 19—, from the following information: Bank Loan, $17 000; Supplies, $1200; Office Equipment, $32 000; Accounts Receivable, $2250; Furniture, $9200; Building, $72 350; Accounts Payable, $1030; Mortgage Payable, $100 000; Land, $110 000; Cash, $1800. You will be able to fill in the amount of capital as you are completing the balance sheet.

27. Venture Company, owned by H. Petroff, shows the following information at December 31, 19—.

Cash	$ 1 126.50
Fry Co. (an account receivable)	550.00
Mortgage Payable	85 000.00
Automobiles	29 000.00
Mount Joy (an account receivable)	625.00
Supplies	250.00
General Supply (an account payable)	2 416.95
Land and Building	250 000.00
Bank Loan	26 725.00
Furniture and Equipment	60 540.00
Gagné's Garage (an account payable)	9 765.00
Rama Bros. (an account payable)	4 128.00
Markville Mall (an account receivable)	1 550.00

a. Make a list of the assets and total them.

b. Make a list of the liabilities and total them.

c. Calculate the owner's equity.

d. Prepare the balance sheet for Venture Company.

KEY TERMS

accounting	asset	owner's equity
transaction	accounts receivable	accounting equation
financial statement	liabilities	liquidity
balance sheet	accounts payable	capital
income statement	bank loan payable	

The Income
Statement

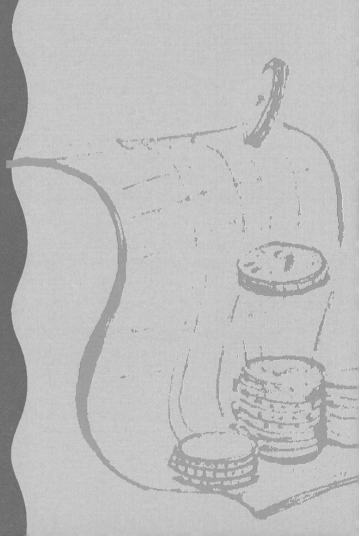

I N CHAPTER 17 WE LEARNED ABOUT the need for accurate accounting information, and also how owners and managers, investors, lenders, and governments use the information on financial statements to make decisions. We have prepared balance sheets and know how to calculate the financial position of a business. This chapter will focus on the second important financial statement, the income statement.

The first type of business we will look at is a service business. Service businesses perform various types of work for customers. Some examples of service businesses are dry cleaners, accounting firms, law firms, photography studios, trucking firms, hair salons, and our example from Chapter 17, landscaping firms. We will continue with Landscaping Dynamics to show how the balance sheet and income statement are related for the same business. Then we will look at how the income statement changes for a business that sells goods or a combination of goods and services.

The Purpose of the Income Statement

The purpose of the income statement is to show the net income or net loss of a business over a period of time. Although a business may wish to produce an income statement more frequently, businesses are required by law to prepare financial statements once a year. Because the balance sheet and income statement show different information, both are needed.

The balance sheet shows the financial position of a business on a given day, typically at the end of the business's fiscal or accounting year. The income statement is the link between the balance sheet prepared at the beginning of the current year and the balance sheet prepared at the end of the current year. Although other financial events occur, it is the money earned from daily operations that increases an owner's original investment. At the end of a year of doing business, an income statement is prepared and the net income or net loss is used to update the amount of owner's equity so that it reflects company performance. How does management determine whether a business has earned a profit?

Businesses generate both revenues and expenses. **Revenue** is the money received from the sale of goods or services. A business may earn revenue by selling goods such as cameras, automobiles, clothing, and furniture, or by selling services such as car repairs, delivery, and decorating.

Expenses are the money a business spends on goods and services that are used to earn revenue. Some examples are rent, wages, advertising, telephone, and insurance.

In the case of Landscaping Dynamics, suppose that the business earns $500 per month for maintaining the grounds of one of its clients. This is not all profit. Landscaping Dynamics had to spend money in order to earn this $500. Some of these expenses would be: the wages of the employees who did the work; the office rent for the business to carry on daily business; the cost of the telephone, hydro, water, and chemicals; and the maintenance costs on the equipment. These expenses must be reflected in any price quote given to a client. Suppose that in order to earn the $500, Landscaping Dynamics had expenses of $400. The **net income**, or profit, for this job would be $100. In order to determine the net income or net loss of a business, it is necessary to subtract total expenses from total revenue.

$$\text{Revenue} - \text{Expenses} = \text{Net Income (or Net Loss)}$$
$$\$500 \quad - \quad \$400 \quad = \quad \$100$$

Preparing an Income Statement for a Service Business

In the previous chapter, we looked at the balance sheet for Landscaping Dynamics. This business must also prepare an income statement to show the operating results for the year that just ended. It is important to know the length of time being used to determine the net income or net loss of a business in order to evaluate company performance. Suppose you were told that a business earned $10 000. Is that good? You do not know unless you know how long it took the business to earn it. Ten thousand dollars earned in one month is certainly different from $10 000 earned over one year. The income statement for Landscaping Dynamics is shown on page 388 and illustrates features of an income statement for a service business.

"... and net profit for the quarter
is — drum roll, please."

Good News, Bad News by Henry Martin. Reprinted by permission: Tribune Media Services.

Landscaping Dynamics
Income Statement
for the year ended March 31, 19–

Revenue		
Landscaping Services	$ 105 000	
Snow Removal Services	75 000	
Total Revenue		$ 180 000
Expenses		
Salaries Expense	102 000	
Advertising Expense	12 000	
Telephone Expense	2 400	
Truck Expense	14 400	
Utilities Expense	2 400	
Maintenance Expense	15 000	
Total Expenses		$ 148 200
Net Income		$ 31 800

Heading

Like the balance sheet, the income statement has a centred three-line heading showing the who, what, and when of the information being reported. The name of the business goes on the first line, the name of the statement goes on the second line, and the date goes on the third line. With an income statement, the business is reporting on financial events that have occurred over a specific accounting period. This is often one year, but it could be any period of time. For example, if management wanted to know how the business is doing on a more frequent basis, an income statement could be prepared monthly. Other common accounting periods for reporting purposes are quarterly (every three months) and semi-annually (every six months). For this reason, the date is written "for the period ended...." In the case of Landscaping Dynamics, the heading looks like this:

Landscaping Dynamics
Income Statement
for the year ended March 31, 19–

Revenue Section

The revenue section of the income statement reports all sources of income generated by operating the business. Other terms used for service revenue are fees and commissions. Landscaping Dynamics generates revenue through landscaping and snow-removal services. During the spring, summer, and fall months, the business maintains lawns and gardens. In order to keep working all year, the business turns to snow removal during the winter months. Therefore, it makes sense to report two different categories of revenue — from landscaping and from snow removal — so that users of the information will know exactly how the revenue breaks down when making decisions about the business. Owners, managers, and investors need to know whether the business is earning as much as possible, because they are the ones getting the benefits of the business. Lenders assess the ability of the business to repay loans on the strength of its earnings, and government will assess the business for taxes based on its income from all sources, so this information must be clear.

To prepare the revenue section, the heading *Revenue* is positioned over the left column, as shown below. Individual sources of revenue are listed and totalled. Notice the proper placement of dollar signs and ruled lines.

Revenue		
Landscaping Services	$105 000	
Snow Removal Services	75 000	
Total Revenue		$180 000

Expenses Section

The expenses section reports all the various costs the business had in order to earn the revenue reported.

Expenses		
Salaries Expense	$102 000	
Advertising Expense	12 000	
Telephone Expense	2 400	
Truck Expense	14 400	
Utilities Expense	2 400	
Maintenance Expense	15 000	
Total Expenses		$148 200

Like revenue, costs are put into categories according to how the money was spent. The purpose of financial statements is to give information; so, while it is possible to have only one account called Expenses with a total of $148 200, this would not give enough information to the users of financial information. Owners, managers, investors, and lenders need to know what the business has spent money on in order to determine how efficient it has been. For example, they would need to compare the cost of, say, advertising or salaries from year to year if they were to assess the profitability of the business over time. When the government assesses a business for income taxes, it needs to know how much was spent in different categories because expenses reduce taxable income (the amount of reported income on which the business is required to pay tax).

Landscaping Dynamics has a number of expenses put into categories that make sense to the management and provide enough information without having too many categories. Without employees, there would be no business, since revenue is produced only when employees perform landscaping or snow-removal services. Advertising is the cost of letting the public know that Landscaping Dynamics is available for business and what its services and prices are. The cost of having a telephone is an important one in any business, important enough in this case to have it in a separate category. Owning a truck means that expenses associated with the truck, such as fuel, repairs, and tires and maintaining landscaping and snow-removal equipment, are vital for the business to keep earning money. Businesses often have another category, called General or Miscellaneous Expense, to which they assign small costs that do not really warrant a category of their own; postage is an example of a general expense. Like the revenue section, individual expenses are listed in the left column, and the total of expenses is put in the right column. Although all these items are expenses, the word *expense* might not be used. Note that dollar signs and ruled lines are used in the same manner as in the revenue section.

Net Income Section

Total expenses are subtracted from total revenues to calculate the net income or net loss of the business for the period being reported. Landscaping Dynamics made a net income for the year, since revenues were greater than expenses. If expenses had been greater than revenues, the business would have had a net loss for the year.

Net Income	$ 31 800

The net income or net loss is used to update the owner's equity with the year's operations. A net income increases equity, while a net loss decreases equity. Net losses are shown in brackets to alert the reader to the situation.

BUSINESS *in action*

THE SUMMER JOB LEADS TO A YEAR-ROUND BUSINESS

When Don Bagozzi graduated from university with a Bachelor of Commerce degree just a few years ago, there weren't many jobs around.

So he took out a Student Venture loan in May of 1990, and started to do lawn and flowerbed maintenance. "I had to make money somehow," he proclaims. "I wasn't too sure how long I'd be in this business, but I quickly discovered that it has unlimited potential. And now that I plan to get into landscaping, there's just no end to it...."

Sales in his first year of work were only about $30 000; second year, maybe $50 000; the 12 months ending June of 1992 found him up to around $100 000; and he hopes to see sales closer to $150 000 in the coming years. All this, thanks to snow plowing in the second year, and some 80 homes, ten townhouses and ten factories to care for (with profits which can run close to 25 percent).

Don Bagozzi already owns three full-sized trucks with plows, two trailers fully equipped with tractors, and other equipment such as snow blowers. But how to differentiate oneself from the many others in the field? "I try to provide good quality and reliable service, with little extras. For instance, I always make sure that flowerbeds are worked around carefully; many miss that." This summer, he is going into landscaping, having "hired a guy from the competition...."

FOCUSING ON BUSINESS

1. Why does the third line of the income statement read "for the period ended ..."?

2. Define each of the following terms:

    a. revenue

    b. expense

    c. net income

    d. net loss

3. Explain why a business needs to prepare both an income statement and a balance sheet.

4. For each of the following service businesses, list two possible sources of revenue.

    a. movie theatre

    b. golf course

    c. garage

    d. photography studio

    e. hair salon

5. For each of the businesses given in Question 4, list five possible expenses.

EXPLORING BUSINESS

For Questions 6 to 10, work individually or in pairs to complete the assignments manually and then using a computer spreadsheet.

6. Copy and complete the following chart:

Time Reported	Revenue	Expenses	Net Income (Net Loss)	Accounting Period
a. year	$40 000	$27 525		
b. October	$117 600		$ 9 381	
c. 3 months		$239 000	($14 000)	
d. semi-annual	$429 000	$335 902		
e. April 1–June 30	$1 125 000	$1 230 000		

7. Prepare an income statement for Beautifully Yours for the month of July, given these amounts: Hairdressing Services, $16 000; Manicure Services, $1600; Wages Expense, $11 500; Advertising Expense, $1000; Telephone Expense, $80; Hydro Expense, $200.

8. Prepare an income statement for Trucks and Trailers for six months ended September 30, using the following information: Delivery Services, $75 000; Trailer Rentals, $35 000; Office Supplies Expense, $9000; Advertising Expense, $5400; Wage Expense, $24 000; Maintenance Expense, $30 000; Gasoline Expense, $5000; Rent Expense, $18 000.

9. Prepare the income statement for The Entertainers Video Rentals at their year end of December 31, using the following information: Salaries Expense, $50 000; Video Rental Revenue, $85 500; Insurance Expense, $2000; Utilities Expense, $3600; Advertising Expense, $12 000; General Expense, $5000.

10. The total revenue for Black Tie Catering for the year was $150 000. The total expenses were $120 000.

   a. Calculate net income or net loss.

   b. What percentage of total revenue is net income?

   c. What percentage of total revenue is total expenses?

Preparing an Income Statement for a Retail Business

In the first section we learned about the income statement for a service business. Now we look at the income statement for a retail business. A retail business is: one that sells goods, such as sporting goods, groceries, cars, or hardware; or one that sells a combination of goods and services, such as a photographer who also sells frames and albums, or an appliance store that also repairs appliances. The income statement for Vince's Variety Store is shown on page 394; it illustrates features of an income statement for a retail business.

Retail businesses must first purchase the goods they sell, called **inventory**, then price them to cover their costs and earn a profit. Buying inventory for resale adds a section to the income statement, called the **cost of goods sold**, a separate category of information related to the cost of making goods available to consumers. How does a retail business decide if it has made a profit?

Suppose a stereo shop sells a VCR for $750; the store had to spend $300 to buy the VCR from the manufacturer or wholesaler. In addition, there were other expenses associated with the sale, such as the employees' salaries, rent on the store, insurance, and utilities, that amounted to another $200. A retail business must first subtract the costs of the goods sold from the selling price to calculate the **gross profit** on the sale.

Vince's Variety Store
Income Statement
three months ended June 30, 19–

Revenue

Grocery Sales	$ 60 000	
Confectionery Sales	20 000	
Magazine and Newspaper Sales	10 000	
Net Sales		$ 90 000

Cost of Goods Sold

Groceries	35 000	
Confectionery	10 000	
Magazines and Newspapers	7 000	
Cost of Goods Sold		52 000
Gross Profit		38 000

Operating Expenses

Rent Expense	12 000	
Utilities Expense	4 000	
Insurance Expense	1 000	
Car Expense	5 000	
Miscellaneous Expense	3 500	
Total Operating Expenses		25 500
Net Income		$ 12 500

$$\text{Sales} - \text{Cost of Goods Sold} = \text{Gross Profit}$$
$$\$750 - \$300 = \$450$$

Next, in order to find the net income on the sale, the expenses must be subtracted from the gross profit to get the net income.

$$\text{Gross Profit} - \text{Expenses} = \text{Net Income}$$
$$\$450 - \$200 = \$250$$

Heading

The heading of an income statement for a retail business is identical to that for a service business; the name of the business is on the first line, the name of the statement is on the second line, and the accounting period is on the third line.

Vince's Variety Store

Income Statement

for three months ended June 30, 19–

Revenue Section

The revenue section contains revenue from all sources, as it did in the service business; however, retail businesses usually call their income sales, since they are selling goods.

Revenue		
Grocery Sales	$ 60 000	
Confectionery Sales	20 000	
Magazine and Newspaper Sales	10 000	
Net Sales		$ 90 000

Vince's Variety Store has three sources of revenue, since it sells three different categories of goods: groceries, confectionery, and magazines and newspapers. The store could combine all these and simply call the result sales, but breaking them down gives more information for making business decisions.

Cost of Goods Sold Section

The cost of goods sold section shows the costs to Vince's Variety Store of purchasing the goods they sell.

Cost of Goods Sold		
Groceries	$ 35 000	
Confectionery	10 000	
Magazines and Newspapers	7 000	
Cost of Goods Sold		$52 000

Since the revenue was broken down into categories, the cost of goods sold is broken into the same categories so it can be easily compared with the sales. This way it is also possible to analyze the amount of profit that each category of goods generates. The cost of goods sold is directly linked to individual units of product sold. Goods are priced individually too, so it is easy to know the gross profit for any item in the store.

Gross Profit Section

Total revenue, which is termed net sales, minus cost of goods sold equals gross profit. Gross profit shows the amount of money available to cover daily operating expenses. By calculating the amount of profit coming directly from units of product sold, the business knows how much each category of goods contributes to paying the other costs of doing business.

Net Sales	$ 90 000
Cost of Goods Sold	52 000
Gross Profit	$ 38 000

Operating Expenses Section

The operating expenses section shows the daily operating expenses of the store. As with the service business, expenses for a retail business are broken into categories that make sense to the owner of the business. Expenses cannot be directly linked to individual units of product sold; they are daily operating costs, such as the rent, that for the most part would have to be paid regardless of whether any goods were actually sold or not.

Operating Expenses		
Rent Expense	$ 12 000	
Utilities Expense	4 000	
Insurance Expense	1 000	
Car Expense	5 000	
Miscellaneous Expense	3 500	
Total Operating Expenses		$ 25 500

BERRY FARMERS

Eldon Neufeld was a city boy, he says, the son of a Saskatoon taxi driver. But like Oliver Douglas, the main character in the 1960s television sitcom "Green Acres," he had a hankering for farm living. In 1982, he turned his back on his career as a home builder and invested $300 000 in a 16 ha farm southwest of the city. "I went from driving a Mercedes to a $1000 Toyota," says Neufeld, now 38.

He and his 37-year-old wife, Delphine, also set themselves a daunting task: taming the Saskatoon berry, which grows wild on bushes but is notoriously difficult to farm. Now, their Riverbend Plantation employs 30 people and sells berry jams, preserves, Belgian waffles, soup and sausages, as well as the berries themselves. In the spring of 1993, the Neufelds opened a display of local artifacts, including rare types of patented barbed wire. "It's like Knott's Berry Farm," says Eldon, "but I don't have a big amusement park — yet."

Prepare the income statement for Berry Farmers Ltd. for the month of August 19— if the business has the following revenues and expenses:

Sales	$225 000	Cost of goods sold	$156 000
Restaurant revenue	165 000	Cleaning expense	4 000
Wages expense	50 000	Advertising expense	1 000
Maintenance expense	800	Miscellaneous expense	750
Farm supplies expense	6 000	Utilities expense	1 500
Kitchen supplies expense	40 000		

COMPLETING A JOB APPLICATION FORM

A job application form is a request for employment. It does not guarantee you a job, but it provides the employer with information about you that is related to the kind of job for which you are applying. Because hiring decisions should be based on your ability to do the job, federal and provincial human rights legislation has made it illegal to discriminate on the basis of race, ancestry, place of origin, colour, citizenship, gender, sexual orientation, criminal record, marital status, and disabilities, unless it can be proven that they are somehow related to the job. In some cases, for example, it may be true that physical strength is required to do the kind of heavy lifting that is involved in, say, the moving business.

1. Visit three local employers and obtain a job application form from each. Complete the forms, keeping in mind the following advice.

   • Read the form before filling it out.

   • Follow the instructions carefully. Some applications ask you to print or use ink. Other sections say "For office use only." You will have to determine whether you are to write on, above, or below the lines given. Employers look to see that you can follow simple instructions.

   • Be neat and accurate. Use correct grammar, spelling, and punctuation.

   • Focus your responses on the requirements of the employer.

   • If a question does not apply to you, fill the space with a short dash, or print N/A, meaning *not applicable*. If you leave it blank, the employer may think that you did not see it or that you chose not to fill it in.

2. Create a poster to display your completed applications.

3. Create an organizer comparing the questions on the application forms that are similar and the questions that are different.

4. Review the application forms to see if they contain questions requesting information that would not be necessary in order to do the job and make a note of any that do. Why do you think these questions were included?

APPLICATION FOR EMPLOYMENT

PERSONAL INFORMATION

Surname	Given names	Social Insurance Number

No. and street	City/Town	Province	Postal code

Home telephone number	Languages you speak/read/write
Business telephone number	English ☐ French ☐ Others (specify) ☐

Are you willing to relocate? Yes ☐ No☐	Position or type of work sought	Do you have a Driver's Licence? Yes ☐ No ☐

EDUCATION

School	Name and Address	Course of study	Years attended From To	Circle last year completed	Did you graduate?	List diploma or degree
Postsecondary				1 2 3 4/5	Yes ☐ No ☐	
Secondary				1 2 3 4/5	Yes ☐ No ☐	
Other (specify)				1 2 3 4/5	Yes ☐ No ☐	

EMPLOYMENT EXPERIENCE

Most recent employer/ Name and address	Name of supervisor	Position/Title held	Dates of employment From To
	Reason for leaving		Final salary
	Duties/Responsibilities		

Employer/Name and address	Name of supervisor	Position/Title held	Dates of employment From To
	Reason for leaving		Final salary
	Duties/Responsibilities		

Employer/Name and address	Name of supervisor	Position/Title held	Dates of employment From To
	Reason for leaving		Final salary
	Duties/Responsibilities		

For employment references may we contact your present employer? Yes ☐ No ☐   Former employers? Yes ☐ No ☐

OTHER REFERENCES

Name and occupation	Address	Phone number

List hobbies, skills and other experiences you feel are of value.
_____
_____

The facts set forth in my application are true and complete. I understand that if employed any false statement on this application may be considered sufficient cause for dismissal.

Signature of applicant _____

Date _____

Net Income Section

The final section shows the net income or net loss for the accounting period.

Gross Profit	38 000
Total Operating Expenses	25 500
Net Income	$ 12 500

The net income is the actual profit of the business and is calculated by subtracting total expenses from gross profit. It is compared to the net incomes for previous years to determine trends and make decisions about the future.

POINTS TO REMEMBER

- An income statement is prepared to determine how a business has performed for a specific period of time by showing the net income or net loss.

- For a service business, Revenue – Expenses = Net Income.

- When preparing an income statement for a retail business, the cost of goods sold must be included. Sales – Cost of Goods Sold = Gross Profit.

- Gross Profit – Expenses = Net Income

FOCUSING ON BUSINESS

11. Explain how a *retail business* differs from a *service business*. In small groups, brainstorm to compile a list of the retail and service businesses in your community.

12. What is the name given to the goods purchased and waiting to be sold in a store?

13. Explain what is meant by the *cost of goods sold*.

14. Would the cost of transporting goods to your store be classified as part of the cost of goods sold or of the expenses? Explain.

15. What information is provided by the gross profit section?

16. For each of the businesses given below, list one source of service revenue and one source of sales revenue.

   a. hair salon

   b. video store

   c. paint and wallpaper store

EXPLORING BUSINESS

17. In small groups, research the uses of technology in accounting. Your research can involve using books and business magazines, conducting interviews, and visiting computer stores. Share your findings with the class.

18. Decide whether each of the following is revenue, an expense, or cost of goods sold.

   a. fees earned

   b. purchases of inventory

   c. wages

   d. commissions earned

   e. advertising

For questions 19 to 23, work individually or with a partner to complete the assignments manually and by using a computer spreadsheet.

19. Copy and complete the chart given below:

	Revenue	Cost of Goods Sold	Gross Profit	Expenses	Net Income (Net Loss)
a.	$100 000	$40 000		$50 000	
b.		$35 000	$72 000	$49 000	
c.	$37 000		$22 000		($5 000)
d.		$47 000		$25 000	$12 000
e.	$228 500		$113 225	$116 780	

20. Prepare an income statement for Classy Clothiers for the month of November, using the following information: Sales, $62 000; Cost of Goods Sold, $39 500; Advertising Expense, $2000; Rent Expense, $3000; Salaries Expense, $10 000; Hydro Expense, $125.

21. Prepare an income statement for The Village Pharmacy for the quarter ended September 30 using this information: Dispensing Fees, $20 000; Cost of Goods Sold, $45 329; Miscellaneous Expense, $ 4000; Sales Expense, $85 119; Advertising Expense, $ 3000; Rent Expense, $6000; Maintenance Expense, $ 3500; Utilities Expense, $775; Telephone Expense, $240.

22. Prepare the income statement for Wilderness Adventures at their year end of December 31 using the following information: Salaries Expense, $12 375; Truck Expense, $1500; Rent Expense, $7700; Telephone Expense, $300; Advertising Expense, $2000; Rental Revenue, $25 289; Supplies Expense, $30 000; Equipment Sales, $35 791, Cost of Goods Sold, $23 476; Insurance Expense, $2200.

23. Prepare an income statement for Hobbies and Crafts for the year ended April 30, 19—, using the following information: Sales of Games, $96 453.18; Advertising Expense, $5000; Cost of Games, $48 712.34; Wages Expense, $32 000; Sales of Crafts $52 345.87; Cost of Crafts, $29 167.98; Repairs Expense, $12 000; Sales of Books, $33 540; Cost of Books, $18 943.56; General Expense, $1326.87.

24. Prepare an income statement for Blockbuster Sales for the year ended December 31, 19—, from the information given below:

Cash	$ 25 000
Accounts Receivable	65 000
Cost of Goods Sold	126 000
Rent Expense	24 000
Accounts Payable	25 000
Sales	205 000
Service Revenue	76 000
B. Block, Capital	289 000
Office Equipment	65 345
Delivery Expense	32 000
Truck	18 500
Utilities Expense	9 000
Bank Loan	30 000

KEY TERMS

revenue

expense

net income

inventory

cost of goods sold

gross profit

PART 8

Consumerism

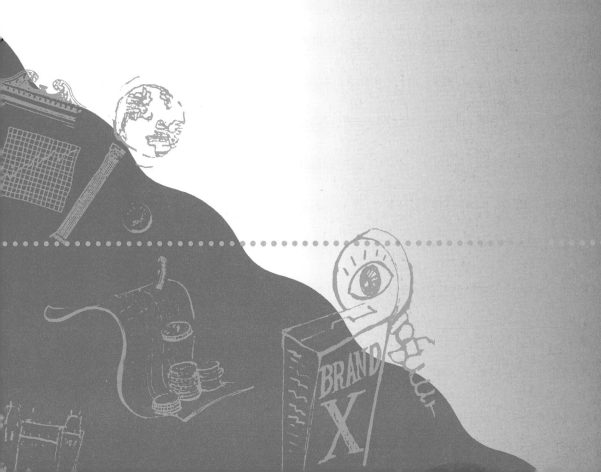

The Wise Consumer

E ARE ALL CONSUMERS, FROM THE youngest among us to the oldest. At different stages in our lives, we buy different things. Parents of young children will buy diapers, infant car seats, and toys. Teenagers tend to buy clothing, compact discs, and concert tickets. Adults are more likely than teenagers to buy furniture, houses, and insurance policies.

The marketplace offers a wide variety of goods, all competing for consumer dollars. Our spending level depends on the amount of money we earn, but the availability of credit allows us to buy goods and services now and pay for them later. A wise consumer uses credit cautiously. How can you become a wise consumer?

In this chapter, we will explore what makes us buy certain goods and services, and we will present a process for spending wisely. How can we prepare a budget to ensure that we have the money we need to purchase what we want? What is the role of savings? We each have our own combination of needs and wants. The key is to balance them with our financial resources in order to have satisfying lives.

WHY SPEND WISELY?

People work hard for their money. Most people need to budget their money carefully. They have to think of the future and make sure that they buy only what they really need and want. You may have $20 in your pocket, but this does not mean you can spend it immediately on anything you want. That money may be meant for school supplies, to pay for a field trip, to buy a birthday present, or to save. Every time you spend money on one thing, you have given up your option to use it for some other purpose. Consumer spending choices must be made every day. As you earn more money, and with the availability of credit, it is easy to increase your spending, but you must make spending decisions carefully.

In addition to being able to afford a purchase, being a wise consumer means getting the best value for your money and analyzing your needs and wants to ensure your satisfaction with the choices you make. Determine your needs ahead of time, then shop for quality and price. That green sweater may look great, but if it does not go with anything you own, it may not be a wise choice.

···· TOP TEN PERSONAL EXPENDITURES ON CONSUMER GOODS AND SERVICES ·····

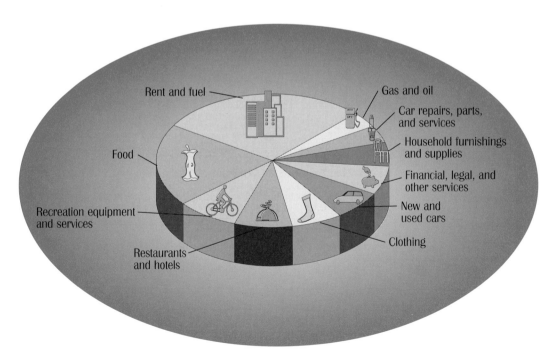

Wise consuming means balancing the need to spend your money carefully with the amount of time and energy it takes to make a purchase. Time, like money, is a resource, and people today have many demands on their time. You, for instance, have school, homework, family obligations, and perhaps a part-time job. Spending several hours travelling to save $1 on a tube of styling gel is probably not a wise use of your time. Spending several hours travelling to save $200 on a compact disc player, on the other hand, probably is.

Factors Affecting Purchasing Decisions

We spend money for a variety of reasons. Some purchasing decisions are based on our needs and wants, while others are external, such as advertising and sales promotion.

Human Needs and Wants

All of us have needs and wants. As you learned in Chapter 1, needs are essentials such as food, shelter, and clothing. Yet if people bought only what they needed, the professional sports, entertainment, and luxury-car markets would all disappear. Wants are as important in consumer spending as needs. How do needs and wants affect buying behaviour?

People of all ages often want to buy the same things owned by people they associate with. This desire to be like those in your group, and therefore to be accepted by them, is known as **peer pressure**. Teenagers might want certain brands of running shoes, while adults spend extra money on specific models of watches or brands of bottled water.

The expression "keeping up with the Joneses" comes from the tendency of friends, family, and neighbours to buy the same things in a competition for material possessions. If our neighbour has a new car, we want to be seen with the latest model car too, even if we cannot afford it. Buying bigger and more expensive items in order to show them off is called **conspicuous consumption**.

Impulse buying, or making purchases you had not planned to make, is another factor in consumer spending behaviour. Almost everyone has had the experience of, for example, going to the grocery store for milk and coming home with cheese, crackers, and a litre of gourmet ice cream. Impulse buys almost always satisfy a want rather than a need.

All these types of buying behaviour (buying because of peer pressure, conspicuous consumption, and impulse buying) can get consumers into financial trouble. None is based on consumers carefully evaluating their needs or whether they can afford something.

PREFACE TO *THE CANADIAN GREEN CONSUMER GUIDE*

By now, most people know we're in danger.

We've heard about the thinning ozone layer, the greenhouse effect, acid rain, the destruction of the world's forests, arable lands, and drinkable water. The danger we're in is enormous: if we don't do something about it, its results could be as devastating as those of a world-wide nuclear catastrophe. We have finally realized that we cannot continue to dump toxic chemicals and garbage into the water, air, and earth of this planet without eventually killing both it and ourselves — because everything we eat, drink, and grow has its ultimate source in the natural world.

However, most people don't know what to do. In the face of such an enormous global problem, they feel helpless. But although the problem is global, the solutions must be local. Unless we begin somewhere, we will never begin at all. An absence of small beginnings will spell the end.

During the depression and the war, conservation was a way of life. It wasn't called that. It was called saving, or salvaging, or rationing. People saved things and reused them because materials were expensive or scarce. They saved string, rubber bands, bacon fat, newspaper, tin cans and glass bottles, old clothes. They made new things out of old things; they darned socks, turned shirt collars. They grew Victory Gardens. "Waste not, want not" was their motto.

Then came the end of the war, a new affluence, and the Disposable Society. We were encouraged to spend and waste; it was supposed to be good for the economy. Throwing things out became a luxury. We indulged.

We can no longer afford our wasteful habits. It's Back to the Basics, time for a return to the Three Rs: *Reduce. Reuse. Recycle. Refuse*, too, to buy polluting products, and *rethink* your behaviour. For instance, use less energy: cut your overhead and increase profits, and stave off a tax hike. Dry your clothes on a rack: humidify your home and lower your hydro bill. Leave excess packaging at the store: let *them* dispose of it. Manufacturers will get the message pretty quick, not just from you but from disgruntled retailers. Start a compost heap. Vote for politicians with the best environmental platforms. Choose non-disposables: razors with real blades instead of the plastic chuck-it-out kind, fountain pens rather than toss-outs. Shop for organic veggies; do it using a shopping basket so you won't have to cart home all those annoying plastic bags that pile up under the sink. Lobby for country-of-origin labels on all food, so you know you aren't eating destroyed Amazonian rainforest with every hamburger bite.

Pollution control, like charity, must begin at home. It's true that industries are major polluters, but industries, in the final analysis, are market- and therefore consumer-driven. If enough of us refuse to buy polluting products, the manufacturers will go out of business. Even a small percentage swing in buying patterns can mean the difference between profit and loss.

This is wartime. Right now we're losing; but it's a war we can still win, with some good luck, a lot of good will, and a great many intelligent choices. This book is a guide to some of those choices. Although they are about familiar, harmless-looking, everyday objects, they are, in the final analysis, life-or-death choices.

And the choice is yours.

Margaret Atwood
Toronto
July 1989

1. In small groups, brainstorm ideas to add to Margaret Atwood's list of ways to reduce, reuse, and recycle.

2. Write an article for *The Canadian Green Consumer Guide* about how reducing, reusing, and recycling not only saves our natural resources, but also helps us to spend money wisely.

Advertising and Sales Promotion

Advertising is an external factor in consumer spending. Most people believe that they are not affected by advertising, yet anyone who works in retail selling or marketing will tell you that advertising does work and affects consumer spending. Most advertising is created to attract consumers' attention to the product being advertised, but occasionally consumers feel manipulated into buying something they do not really need. The packaging — how the product is wrapped and presented — can attract consumer attention, perhaps because of the distinctive design or because of the information it provides.

Sales promotions, in-store price reductions, two-for-one offers, money-off coupons, and so on, also influence consumers' behaviour, particularly with impulse buys. Most of us cannot resist a sale.

Brand names, which can be a name, term, logo, or design, are used by manufacturers to identify particular products, and often influence consumers to buy. Consumers often believe that certain brand names stand for consistent quality and are often loyal to goods they buy all the time, despite the choices that may be available in the marketplace, and sometimes despite the fact that the preferred product is more expensive.

BUSINESS *in action*

A SWEET NICHE ON THE PRAIRIES

With a bit of prodding, Anthony Hardenne finally concedes that, yes, he was a "party animal" in high school. But not at university. Oh, no, he worked hard that first year of a liberal arts program at the University of Saskatchewan. Trouble was, his marks were still dreadful. "I was just a poor student," Hardenne recalls. "It wasn't for me." He quit in 1983 and never returned.

Not a very promising start. But Hardenne has proved luckier than most. He had big dreams and a father with deep pockets and a ready ear for business. Long an amateur gourmet, Hardenne fancied opening up a small specialty food company in his home town, Saskatoon. Father Jean, though, had a related but better idea: Why not produce handmade Belgian chocolates? The elder Hardenne, who immigrated to Canada from Belgium, never joined the trade himself, but he still had lots of friends in that business back in Europe.

Dad convinced son, then brought in Belgian chocolate expert Phillip Wyckhuyse in 1984 as a partner in the venture, which they dubbed Harden & Huyse Ltd. in phonetically easy deference to their respective surnames. Armed with $30 000 in start-up capital and new equipment from Europe, the partners opened a shop in Saskatoon and garnered $65 000 in sales the first year. The Hardennes later bought out Wychkhuyse's stake in the company, but they kept the original name and business has been sweet ever since. This year, Harden & Huyse expects revenue of almost $750 000, about 80 percent of that derived from just three holidays: Christmas, Easter, and Valentine's Day.

Belgian-style chocolates have long ranked among the world's best, and in aspiring to that lofty mantle, Harden & Huyse, like its peers, hasn't skimped on raw materials. It still imports chocolate from Belgium, fruit purée and nougat from France, marzipan from Germany, liqueur from Italy, and caramel from Switzerland. The resulting handmade chocolate assortments are priced from $3 for two morsels to $30 for a box of 32, all produced in Saskatoon and sold in two company-owned outlets in that city, plus one in each of Regina and Winnipeg, and elsewhere through wholesalers.

Saskatoon might seem an unlikely home for fine chocolates, but the Prairies have become a fertile ground for such ventures. The 10-year-old Chocolaterie Bernard Callebaut, for instance, has grown beyond its Calgary base to boast 16 stores in Western Canada, and the upstart Casteleyn family of Brandon, Manitoba, is trying to fill the same mold. But Harden & Huyse, which generates 90 percent of its sales in Canada, is hoping to build up a much bigger international presence. Anthony Hardenne, the firm's 27-year-old president, is fresh from trade junkets to Tokyo and Washington, and the company recently spent $150 000 redesigning its packaging, so that any assortment of different-size boxes can be fit snugly into a single-size shipping container for export.

Comparison Shopping

Shopping around for just the right product at just the right price is called **comparison shopping**. Most people agree that some serious thought must go into the purchase of expensive items, such as a home, car, vacation, or major appliance. These purchases involve large commitments of money and sometimes even borrowing. Unlike something that costs much less, you cannot replace such major items quickly if you decide they are not what you want after all. Wishing you had chosen a different shirt is not the same thing as wishing you had chosen another summer vacation. One way to avoid expensive mistakes is to do comparison shopping and use a decision matrix. A **decision matrix** is a chart that helps you organize the information you gather as you do your comparison shopping. If you purchase a stereo, you must first identify your criteria in order of importance. Your list is neither better nor worse than another person's list. Suppose you identify these items in order and you have narrowed the choice down to four stereos. Set up the criteria and the choices as shown in the decision matrix below.

Criteria	Stereo A	Stereo B	Stereo C	Stereo D
• Less than $2000	$1800	$4000	$1000	$1500
• Good sound quality	very good	excellent	fair	good
• CD player	included	included	not included	not included
• Warranty	3 years	5 years	1 year	3 years
• Graphic equalizer	yes	yes	no	yes

Next, you complete the decision matrix with the information found while you were comparison shopping. Then review the choices to determine which would best satisfy the criteria you have identified for the purchase, and you can make your decision. In this example, Stereo A appears to be the best choice as it has the best combination of features at the price you can afford to pay. Although Stereo B is clearly a superior model, it has a price much higher than you can afford, and price is identified as the first criterion. Stereos C and D are within your price range but do not measure up in the other categories.

The main advantage of comparison shopping is the knowledge that you have the best deal to meet the criteria that will satisfy your need or want. Carefully thinking out your criteria before going out to look reduces impulse buying.

What could possibly be the disadvantage of comparison shopping? Generally, consumers should comparison shop. However, sometimes you miss a good deal because the item is sold while you are shopping around. Carrying comparison shopping to extremes may mean driving many kilometres to save ten cents on a can of food, while spending several dollars' worth of gasoline and hours of your time. Finally, there is some fun in occasional impulse buying. Allow yourself to be impulsive sometimes on less important expenditures, such as going to a movie, and be careful when making more important purchases.

FOCUSING ON BUSINESS

1. List three reasons why you should spend money wisely.
2. How do advertising and sales promotions influence consumer purchases?
3. Think of a situation in which you bought something and were not satisfied once you got it home. Why did this happen? What did you do about it?
4. Is something a good value just because it is on sale? Explain.
5. What is *conspicuous consumption*?
6. Explain why people sometimes feel the need to "keep up with the Joneses."
7. Evaluate this statement. "Impulse buying is always wrong. Every purchase should be carefully researched."
8. What are the advantages and disadvantages of comparison shopping?

EXPLORING BUSINESS

9. "Time is a valuable resource, and wise a consumer must take time into account."

   With a partner, brainstorm as many situations as you can in which time is a factor in purchasing decisions.

10. You are a writer for a consumer magazine. Write an article that gives consumers tips on spending their money wisely.

11. Choose a product that you might be interested in purchasing: stereo, compact-disc player, bicycle, etc. Visit four different stores that sell the item and compare the stores using the following criteria: price,

brand name, quality/performance, assistance from store employees, warranty, and other factors. Use a spreadsheet software program to create an organizer to record your information. Then write a brief report recommending which store you would buy from and why.

12. Describe to a partner your most recent experience of impulse buying. What were the factors that influenced your impulse buy?

13. Gary wants a leather jacket. It seems that all the really popular people have them, and Gary thinks that if he buys one he might become part of that group at school. He withdraws money from the bank and buys a leather jacket for $500. He cannot wait for Monday to wear the jacket and goes around telling everyone how much it cost.

   a. From what you learned in this chapter, what factor or factors have influenced Gary in this purchase?

   b. Do you think Gary will become more popular, now that he has a leather jacket? Why?

   c. Was this a wise purchase? Why?

   d. What problems might arise from Gary's actions?

14. Using newspapers and magazines, select two advertisements that aim products at teenagers. How do these advertisements influence teenagers' purchasing decisions? In small groups, share your ideas.

15. In small groups, prepare a decision matrix for a family vacation. Decide on ten criteria that would be important to a family of two adults and two children, aged twelve and eight. Next, brainstorm and collect information on five possible vacations that would be of interest to this family. Create a decision matrix by discussing whether each vacation would satisfy the criteria you have chosen. Make a recommendation based on the results of the decision matrix. If possible, use a spreadsheet software program to create your decision matrix. Present your findings to the class.

16. Consumer goods and services are designed for people of all ages and interests. As you know, people have different buying patterns at different times in their lives. In small groups, complete an organizer like the one below by discussing the purchasing goals of people in each of the age categories and their reasons for buying. Then imagine you are in that stage of your life and think of five purchases you might make. Present your findings to the class. Give reasons for the choices that your group has made.

Age	Purchasing Goals	Reasons	Items
under 6			
6–10			
11–14			
15–19			
20–30			
31–45			
46–65			
over 65			

THE INTERVIEW

You have responded to an advertisement, sent a résumé and covering letter, completed a job application, and now you are going to an interview. The interview is the final hurdle in your job search. The factual information you provided about yourself got you this far, but the employer will decide on the basis of the interview whether to offer you the job, so you must prepare. Here are some tips about preparing for interviews.

- Know as much as possible about the business or organization before you go. You can easily find out what it sells, the kinds of customers it attracts, and the prices it charges. Your research may also uncover other useful information — the company sponsors children's sports teams, or it is environmentally responsible, for example.

- Prepare a short summary of your career goals, skills, experience, education, and strengths to present at the interview. Gear this as much as possible to the research you have done about the employer, so that you will appear to be a suitable candidate.

- Find out well in advance where and when the interview is, how to get there, and how long it will take by the route you have chosen. Build in some extra time for delays and to avoid rushing in at the last minute. This will be a signal to the employer that you may have trouble getting there on time after you are hired.

- Take your résumé with you. Even if you have already sent a résumé or filled out an application, the interviewer may not have it handy, or there may be more than one person interviewing. It will say clearly that you are prepared.

- Dress appropriately. Very casual clothes are not appropriate. Be neat and clean in your appearance. If you are not sure what to wear, ask someone whose judgement you value.

1. Working in groups of four, each group should choose a different job from the following list.

   - day-camp counsellor
   - retail sales position
   - server in a fast-food outlet
   - self-serve gas bar attendant
   - cartoon character at an amusement park

2. Split the group into two pairs. One pair prepares the research done by a candidate prior to going for an interview. Discuss what you know about the job. Research information you may not know, such as the usual rate of pay for that job or the expected qualifications. Prepare a list of questions a candidate might ask an interviewer about this job. Predict the kinds of questions an interviewer might ask, and prepare responses to those questions.

   The second pair prepares the questions that might be asked by an interviewer for the job. Some frequently asked questions are:

   - Tell me a little bit about yourself.
   - Why do you want this job?
   - What qualifications and qualities do you possess that you feel make you the right person for this job?
   - If you have held other jobs, how did you get along with your former co-workers?
   - If you have held other jobs, why did you leave?
   - What is your greatest strength?
   - What is your greatest weakness?

   Brainstorm questions that a candidate may ask about your company, and formulate answers to those questions. Be able to describe your organization and the duties of the job.

   Take turns interviewing one another for the job in front of the class.

PERSONAL FINANCE

Making a Budget

"I don't know where my money goes" is a familiar complaint. Many people have trouble keeping track of their spending or knowing when they can or cannot afford a particular item. Is affording something as simple as having the money in your pocket, or can you have $20, yet not be able to afford a $20 purchase? To answer these questions, we need to learn about budgeting. A **budget** is an estimate, often calculated on an annual basis, of money available to be spent. Budgets are prepared and used by businesses and individuals to help plan spending. Let's look at personal budgets.

The first step in budgeting is knowing how much money you have to spend. For most people, this is determined by the money they earn after taxes have been deducted.

Suppose that Pat Ellis takes home $1000 every two weeks. She wants to prepare a budget to help her manage her earnings. She takes the second step in making a budget, which is to identify the regular payments that have to be made from the money available. Pat pays rent of $800 per month, makes a car payment of $300 per month, pays approximately $25 per month for the telephone, makes Visa payments of approximately $100 per month, buys gasoline for the car at $25 per week, and buys food, for which she spends approximately $40 per week. Note that some amounts are approximate: Pat's monthly phone bill is sometimes more than $25 a month, sometimes less, but $25 is the average, so this is the figure she should use.

PAT'S REGULAR MONTHLY COSTS	
Rent	$ 800
Car payment	300
Telephone	25
Visa payment	100
Gasoline	100
Food	160
Total	$1485

The third step is to determine how much money is left over for anything else you might want to buy. There are many possibilities, of course, but some typical expenditures for Pat are clothing, entertainment, and savings. Calculate the amount left over by subtracting the monthly regular costs from the total available for the month. In Pat's case, she is left with $2000 – $1485, or $515.

Now that you know how much money is available after regular expenses, the fourth step is a decision on what you want to use it for. Pat must make some lifestyle decisions in order to best spend the money available to her. Clothing is a necessity, but how much clothing? At what price? What about other things? Suppose Pat has decided to save as much money as possible. She wants to take a vacation, and she also knows that emergencies can occur: her car or her computer could break down and need maintenance. Pat hopes to be able to save $150 per month. This leaves her $365 ($515 – $150) for clothes and entertainment. Will she spend exactly this amount every month? No, but it gives her an idea of the amount of money she has to work with. She may decide to save more in order to take a holiday. Pat decides that her weekly budget for entertainment is $25. At $100 per month, this leaves her with $265 to spend on clothing and other items.

The fifth step is to draw up your final budget. The monthly budget for Pat Ellis will look like this:

Monthly Income	$ 2 000
Expenses	
Rent	$ 800
Car payment	300
Telephone	25
Visa payment	100
Gasoline	100
Food	160
Savings	150
Entertainment	100
Clothing	265
Total Expenses	**$ 2 000**

You may or may not agree with the way Pat spends her money, but it is her decision, based on her needs and wants. Some expenses, such as rent and car payments, are fixed for long periods of time; however, it is important to remember that other expenses are approximate. Pat may not spend exactly $100 on gasoline every month. Some months, she will drive more than others. Some months, she will not be able to save money; other months, she will spend less and save more. The importance of the personal budget is to provide the individual with spending guidelines that he or she has carefully and realistically determined.

Let's go back to an earlier question: is affording something as simple as having the money in your pocket, or can you have $20 yet not be able to afford a $20 purchase? You can afford something when spending the money will not leave you short of something else you need, or cause you to not stick to the budget you have set for yourself. Your budget should be reviewed from time to time, at least once a year. Pat may exceed her budget for clothing one month and make up for it by not buying anything the next month but, by the end of the year, she should be within her own guidelines. Finally, when Pat's finances change, such as if she gets a raise, so should her budget. Will she save more or spend more? This is her decision.

Overspending

People overspend from time to time, and usually it does not have a serious effect on their budget. A fancy restaurant meal one night means you will eat more simply the rest of the week. These are decisions that people face every day. You may decide that the old roof will have to last one more year so you can take a Caribbean vacation. Consistently overspending, though, can be a serious problem. What if that old roof starts to leak and needs repairs that cost $1000? Making up for a lack of savings by overusing a credit card or running all your credit cards up to their

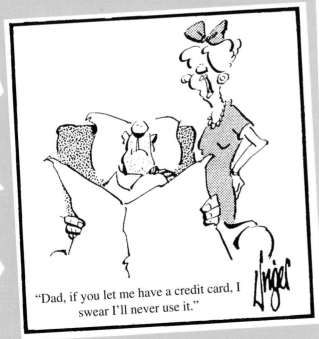

"Dad, if you let me have a credit card, I swear I'll never use it."

maximum balances is a recipe for trouble. People can get themselves into great difficulty by not controlling their spending habits.

POINTS TO REMEMBER

- People need to spend wisely in order to conserve money, time, and energy and to be satisfied with their purchases.
- Purchasing decisions are affected by both internal and external factors: human needs and wants, advertising, consumer health and safety, conspicuous consumption, impulse buying, packaging, peer pressure, and sales promotions.
- Comparison shopping for expensive or durable items will help consumers get the best value for their money.
- Using a decision matrix can help consumers make wise decisions when comparison shopping.
- A personal budget should reflect your needs and wants, as well as ensuring that all your expenditures are covered.
- A budget should be reviewed and updated from time to time, or whenever there has been a financial change in your life.

FOCUSING ON BUSINESS

17. Summarize the steps in making a personal budget.
18. Are savings a required part of someone's personal budget? Explain your answer.
19. If many of the figures on a budget are approximate, and some expenditures may not even occur in a given month, why should they appear on the budget?
20. List three ways in which a person's financial situation might change, thus requiring a change in his or her personal budget.
21. Evaluate this statement: "You cannot predict emergencies. Therefore, they should not be part of a personal budget."
22. Why should a personal budget be reviewed at least once a year?
23. If your financial situation has not changed in several years, is it still valuable to review your personal budget each year? Explain your answer.

EXPLORING BUSINESS

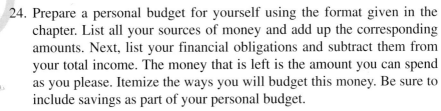

24. Prepare a personal budget for yourself using the format given in the chapter. List all your sources of money and add up the corresponding amounts. Next, list your financial obligations and subtract them from your total income. The money that is left is the amount you can spend as you please. Itemize the ways you will budget this money. Be sure to include savings as part of your personal budget.

25. In pairs, find a magazine or newspaper article on family budgeting. Discuss what the article is saying about setting goals, savings, and borrowing and credit. Summarize your findings in a brief report.

26. Pablo has just got his first full-time job, in which he will be earning $24 000 per year. He is excited as he tells his friend Ahmed about it. "Just think, Ahmed, that's $2000 a month. First, I'm going to buy a sports car, then I start looking for an apartment. Of course, I'll need furniture...."

    "Hold everything," Ahmed interrupts. "I think there are a few things you haven't considered."

    Take the role of Ahmed. Use what you know about budgeting to advise Pablo about his plan.

27. Rina has been working for six months. She wants to keep track of her money and has asked Adèle to help her with a personal budget. While talking about financial decision making, Adèle mentions savings. Rina says that savings should not properly be part of a budget because they are not a monthly obligation, such as rent. Rina has obtained a copy of a standard budget and savings are not listed.

    a. Should Rina include savings as part of her personal budget? Explain your answer.

    b. Is Rina correct when she says that savings do not belong on a budget because they are not included on the standard form that she has? Explain your answer.

    c. Take the role of Adèle and explain to Rina why she might want to include savings as part of a monthly personal budget.

28. Refer to the example of Pat Ellis given in the chapter. Suppose that Pat marries Hervé, who earns $30 000 per year.

    a. In small groups, brainstorm (i) the items that might be part of the new family budget Pat and her husband make, and (ii) the possible decisions they might make regarding housing, transportation, entertainment, and vacations.

b. Prepare a budget for Pat and Hervé based on the results of your group discussion.

29. In small groups, prepare a budget for a family of five with two working parents, one who earns $40 000 per year, and one who earns $28 000 per year (assume these figures are after tax and all deductions). There are three children, ages twelve, eight, and five. The couple is buying a house. The mortgage payments are $1200 per month. They have a monthly car payment of $300 and are paying back a bank loan at $450 per month. Prepare a monthly budget following the format given in the chapter. You will need to research the following other costs:

- weekly food bill for a family of five
- approximate telephone bill if they have basic service and make five long-distance calls per month
- gasoline and routine maintenance for a four-year-old car driven 30 km per day
- approximate clothing costs for a family of five
- approximate entertainment costs for a family of five in these circumstances
- savings goal for this family

Add a report, in which you explain how you arrived at the figures you did and what are the sources of your research material.

WORKING WITH MATH

30. Linda earns $42 000 per year. The total deductions from her weekly pay cheque are 25 percent for income tax and $45 for all other deductions.

a. What are Linda's total weekly deductions?

b. What is Linda's weekly take-home pay?

c. If Linda's rent is $800 per month, and her car payment is $425 per month, how much money will she have left for all other expenditures?

31. Branko's credit card statement contains the following information:

Balance owing from last month	$500
Payments made this month	$180
New charges this month	$250
Monthly service charge	2%

   a. Calculate the amount of the service charge on the unpaid balance.

   b. Calculate the amount that Branko owes this month if the service charge is only on the unpaid balance, not on new charges.

   c. If Branko plans to leave an unpaid balance of $200 for next month, how much should he pay this month?

KEY TERMS

peer pressure	comparison shopping
conspicuous consumption	decision matrix
impulse buying	budget

Consumer Credit and Protection

CHAPTER FOCUS

After studying this chapter you will be able to:

understand the advantages and disadvantages of consumer credit

•

know the types of consumer credit

•

understand how to apply for credit

•

know how to establish and maintain a good credit rating

•

explain the role of a credit bureau

•

understand how governments and private agencies provide consumer protection

P EOPLE ROUTINELY BORROW MONEY TO buy expensive items such as homes and cars. Being able to borrow money for such items can raise people's standard of living. When consumer spending is high, a country's standard of living improves as well. Most people, for example, could not buy a new car or a home if they had to wait until they had saved the entire amount rather than being able to purchase on credit.

In this chapter, we will be examining consumer credit. Consumer credit has important advantages, but it must be used wisely to avoid serious consequences for the borrower. In addition, we will be looking at consumer protection. We have already discussed the need for careful purchasing, but some consumer problems are matters for the legal system. Finally, we will explore how to make complaints work for you when all avenues for consumer satisfaction have failed.

CREDIT AND ITS USES

Credit is trust in a person's — or a company's — ability and intention to pay at a later date for goods and services purchased in the present. The terms of short-term borrowing are usually from 30 days to one year. If you buy a pair of jeans or pay for the services of a dentist on credit, you will be obligated to pay this debt within a specified period of time. Typically, the lender will set up monthly payments, so that even though the entire sum is not due in 30 days, some minimum amount is. One advantage of consumer credit is that money is available for emergencies. If your refrigerator breaks down and you do not have cash, you will be able to replace it as long as you have a credit card.

Consumer credit also helps an individual's cash flow. It may not be convenient to wait until your next payday to make a purchase. Consumer credit can tide you over until you get paid, but you should pay the balance of your credit card when the bill comes in. In fact, some credit-card companies require users to pay the full amount due when the bill is received.

A third advantage of consumer borrowing is leveraging, or borrowing to make purchases you cannot afford, given your own financial resources. Consumers can buy such things as furniture, insurance, restaurant meals, and clothing immediately, without having to wait until they have earned the money.

Cathy © Cathy Guisewite. Reprinted by permission of Universal Press Syndicate. All rights reserved.

Drawbacks of Credit

Using consumer credit can have disadvantages. First, borrowing is very expensive since interest is charged on unpaid amounts. Second, a person's cash flow is affected by having to make monthly payments. Paying off loans and credit cards becomes a monthly obligation that takes money you might use for something else. A third disadvantage is that many people who believe they will be able to handle consumer credit often turn out to have little willpower when it comes to spending. They are, in fact, spending money they do not have. They do not pay off the entire balance of their credit cards. Instead, they make minimum monthly payments, then pay interest on the remaining amount, and their balance increases by the amount of the interest charge. They are unable to participate in any kind of savings program and may end up having no money for emergencies because they have spent to the limit of the credit allowed on their credit cards. Finally, easy access to credit may mean that people make hasty purchases or buy things they do not really need. Impulse buying is increased with consumer credit.

TYPES OF CONSUMER CREDIT

Credit Cards and Charge Accounts

Many different credit cards are available. A **credit card** allows its holder to charge goods and services to his or her account on the understanding that he or she will pay the amount when the bill arrives from the credit card company. Large organizations such as Visa, MasterCard, and American Express issue credit cards, as do gasoline companies and retail stores. Some credit card companies charge yearly fees; some offer rebates if you spend over a certain amount. They all charge interest on the unpaid balance and, even though the figure may not sound like much, it works out to a considerable sum of money per year. All credit card companies are in the business of lending money for profit, and the more their customers spend, the more money the companies make by charging interest.

A **charge account** is similar to a credit card, but is given by an individual business to a particular customer for the customer's use at that business only. The business does not issue a card; instead, there is an agreement that the customer can charge purchases. Someone doing home renovations, for example, might maintain a charge account at a builders' supply store. The interest rates on charge accounts are similar to those on credit cards.

BUSINESS *in action*

CREDIT CARD COSTS

An estimated 46 million credit cards were in circulation in Canada in 1991, or 2.3 cards for every Canadian over the age of 18. Of those, more than 24 million were MasterCard or Visa, 24 million were cards issued by large department stores, and 3 million were

gasoline cards. Other cards, such as American Express and enRoute, and cards issued by small financial institutions and retail stores constituted the remainder.

The total number of Visa and MasterCards more than doubled from 1981 to 1991 – from 12 million to 24.3 million. MasterCard and Visa credit cards were used for more than 617 million transactions in 1991, 2.5 times the 1981 level. The volume of sales in 1991 was $40 billion, compared to $11 billion in 1981.

From 1986 to 1991, the number of merchant outlets in Canada accepting Visa or MasterCard increased by 50 percent to more than 857 000. The average sale per transaction charged to Visa and MasterCard increased from just under $42 in 1981 to almost $67 in 1991.

For the approximately 50 percent of credit card users who do not avoid interest charges by paying off their credit card balances each month, these cards are a relatively expensive form of credit. That's because the rate of interest is considerably higher than what's charged for other types of consumer loans.

Conditional Sales Contract

A **conditional sales contract** is a legal, binding, written sales agreement between a buyer and a seller. The buyer is purchasing an expensive item on credit. The contract includes the cost and description of the item, any down payment, and the credit terms (interest rate, monthly payment, due date). If the customer is going to be making regular payments on the purchase, an **instalment contract** will be written that sets out all the interest to be paid until the end of the term with the principal. This total will be divided into equal payments according to the agreement (24 monthly payments if the term is two years).

Loans

An alternative to a credit card is a loan. Choosing the right kind of loan for your situation is important. A **demand loan** is negotiated with a bank or finance company rather than with a retailer, as a conditional sales contract is. If the borrower misses a payment for any reason, the lender has the right to demand full payment of the entire loan immediately. Demand loans are typically short-term loans. The borrower must pay interest monthly on the unpaid balance; payment can be monthly or in a lump sum.

Even when you buy real estate, you are involved with consumer credit. The collateral for a first mortgage is the real property itself. Rates for first mortgages are lower than those for other loans because they are for longer terms. Second or third mortgages are demand loans with much higher rates of interest.

It is also possible to obtain a mortgage for items other than real estate. In the case of a **chattel mortgage**, the collateral for the loan is personal property, such as furniture. If the borrower fails to make payments, the bank or finance company can seize the asset.

Applying for Credit

How do you get credit? Stores and lending institutions follow a procedure that has three steps. The first step is to complete an application for credit by providing personal and financial information, such as name, address, occupation, employer, income, assets, other debts and the amounts of their payments, and any other information that might affect the decision to extend credit to the person. If the applicant is requesting credit for a specific item, this will also be part of the information asked. The more money a person wants to borrow, the more detailed the infor-

CONNECTING BUSIN
WITH
THE ARTS & TE

A Hit Show for Teens on Managing Money

A commercial-free show with an off-beat mascot, produced in Halifax, that beats out other CBC prime time shows in an off-prime time. In a pig's eye, you say?

It's *Street Cents*, a show with a slick, hip format designed to help teens become street-smart consumers.

The program was conceived and developed by John Nowlan, its executive producer, who knew first-hand the pressures his own teens faced from their peers and mass advertising, and wanted to create an adolescent version of the successful CBC show, *Marketplace*.

Youngsters today have a lot of money but little guidance about how to spend it, Nowlan says. "That's what we figure our role is — to wisen them up a bit."

Set in a warehouse, the primary cast is a gang of four — two men and two women. Benita Ha has the untraditional job of mechanic and Jonathan Torrens has been known to take on the nurturing task of babysitting. Brian Heighton — who plays the sleazy businessman Ken Pompadour — represents all the negative aspects of consumerism.

Defying the adage "never work with kids or animals," the group shares the stage with Moui, a Vietnamese pot-bellied pig. The show began with a good-natured pig named Penny, who outgrew the part. It

Street Cents' cast. Clockwise from the left: B Ha, Brian Heighton, Jonathan Torrens, and Dirksen with Moui.

was followed by Nickel, a miniature pig from Quebec with a bad disposition and worse bathroom habits. Moui, which is Vietnamese for dime, has all the desirable qualities of his predecessors.

The show is interactive television at its best. Kids are encouraged to phone-in their beefs by dialing 1-800-565-BEEF. Letters read on the show net a T-shirt for the authors. Features called *Streeters* and *Street Census* criss-cross the country, questioning and polling teens. Bubble gum is test marketed by a group in Ontario. A girl in British Columbia tries out rainwear. A group in Newfoundland finds the best bubble bath. Not surprisingly, they find the best product is often not the most expensive or the "name" brand. Really bogus products are deemed "fit for the pit" and dropped into a smouldering hole in the ground.

In the process, a number of teens are gaining on-air television experience. "Part of our mandate is to develop good young performers and presenters," Nowlan says.

For "journalistic integrity," Nowlan wanted the show to be commercial-free. This would also make it more accessible for use in schools. A pilot was produced with funding from the Government of Nova Scotia. This in turn helped generate more funding from 32 sponsors from across Canada, mainly government agencies, "none of whom sell to kids."

Studio facilities and staff are provided by CBC Halifax. Nowlan, among others, wanted Halifax to become a major network centre in Canada. So the studio that brought us *Don Messer's Jubilee* and Anne Murray song-and-seascape specials now produces a show that is nationwide in format with a core of east-coast talent, except for its Gemini Award-winning writers, who are from Vancouver. A teen panel makes sure the writers use teen language and are up to date on teen fads.

The formula appears to be working. *Street Cents* draws about 425 000 viewers and has a "reach" (those who watch any part of the show) of one million. On occasion it has beat out such CBC prime time shows as *Kids in the Hall* and *Adrienne Clarkson Presents*.

Approaches have been made to PBS and The Learning Network for broadcast in the United States, either intact or with inserts produced by American field teams. Nowlan has also looked into markets for the show in Europe and Asia. As well, there is also some interest in a French language version of the show, he said.

1. What other forms of media might be an effective way of communicating consumer information and money management skills to teens. Why would they be effective?

2. If you were responsible for the next episode of *Street Cents* what would you like it to cover in regards to managing money? Share your idea with a partner.

mation will be required.

Next, the lender investigates the applicant to ensure that the information given was correct and complete. The lender might contact the employer to verify the information about work history and income, and to get an idea of whether the job is a steady one. If this is a first-time credit application, the lender may contact a credit bureau to obtain information about the applicant's credit record. Information about length of residence and the location of the person's home, bank account balances, and assets listed as potential collateral may also be investigated. These checks take some time, especially if the applicant has no credit history.

Finally, the application is evaluated by the lender. This may be the actual store or place of business, a bank, or a credit card company if the person is applying for a credit card.

Establishing a Credit Rating

It is important to establish a credit rating. A **credit rating** is an integral part of a person's or a company's reputation and measures their ability and intention to pay back their debts. An individual who applies for a credit card and carefully uses it for smaller purchases, will find it easier to obtain other more important loans later on. Credit applications are evaluated on three criteria, often called the three Cs of credit. They are:

- character
- capacity
- capital

Character refers to an individual's personal reliability. It is important that the applicant has lived at his or her current address for a while. Although people do move, a history of many previous moves might indicate unreliability. An active bank account is an indication of the steady, controlled use of money.

Capacity refers to the applicant's ability to repay the loan. Good intentions are not enough. The lender must have assurance that the applicant's present job and income level are likely to last into the future. His or her expenses are also a factor. Household bills, food, car payments, mortgages, rent, and other debts will all be competing with the new loan for the individual's income. If the amount left over after present financial obligations are met seems too low to cover the new debt, the lender will reject the application.

Capital in this case refers to the applicant's financial worth. The lender is looking for assets of value that the applicant can pledge as collateral. These assets might include homes, cars, furniture, appliances, savings, investments, and insurance policies. If the borrower cannot repay the loan, the lender may claim and sell the assets that the borrower has offered as collateral.

It is important for both women and men, single or married, to establish a credit rating. Historically, married women in Canada did not have credit ratings of their own. Instead, they shared their husband's ratings. In the event that the marriage ended, either through divorce or death, a wife could discover that she had no credit history and no way to obtain credit. Today, all married women should establish separate credit ratings from their husbands, so that if the marriage ends they will be able to carry on financially without hardship. Even nowadays, women often find it more difficult to obtain credit than men do.

Keeping a Good Credit Rating

Keeping a good credit rating, once one has been established, is vital. Failing to make regular payments or defaulting altogether damages a person's credit rating. His or her next loan application may be rejected. It is particularly distressing if someone cannot get a mortgage because he or she has handled credit cards badly.

Borrowers who are unable to make a payment for any reason should contact the lender and explain the circumstances. After all, the lender's

TIPS FOR KEEPING A GOOD CREDIT RATING

- Don't sign a credit contract until you have read it and understood it. If you don't understand it, ask questions until you are satisfied.
- Never sign a blank sheet. Your signature is your promise to pay, and a contract is a legal document. Know its implications.
- Always pay your bills promptly; you have an obligation to pay. If you find yourself in temporary financial difficulties and you can't meet the payment date, let the company know before the due date; credit grantors are helpful in arranging payments.
- Try to pay off any debt quickly. Avoid prolonged "low monthly payments."
- Deal with known, respected, and established companies.
- Make sure you understand the total cost of your purchase. Add up those monthly charges.

greatest risk lies in not being paid back. The payment period may be extended or delayed, or a new agreement with more favourable terms might be possible. Being clear and honest with lenders is the best way to protect a credit rating.

CREDIT BUREAUS

A **credit bureau**, sometimes called a credit reporting agency, is a profit-making service that provides information about your credit record to retailers and other businesses that grant credit. The service it provides is to save lenders the trouble, time, and expense of searching out financial information themselves for each credit applicant. Lenders pay the credit bureau to become members and pay additional fees every time they use the service. The lender can contact the credit bureau and not only verify the information that is on the application form, but ask for any other pertinent information that may be in the person's file. For example, if you have ever been rejected for a loan or credit card, it will be on file with the credit bureau.

What if the information at the credit bureau is incorrect? Mistakes can be made, and circumstances can change. You have the right to view your file with the credit bureau and update or amend it. Periodically checking it is a good idea. Having a loan application rejected is not the time to discover a mistake at the credit bureau!

Consequences of Not Paying

What happens when borrowers do not pay their debts? If you have pledged an asset as collateral and do not keep up your payments, the lender can seize the asset. This is called **repossession**.

People in very serious financial trouble may have to declare **bankruptcy**. This means they file a letter with a court stating that they cannot meet their debts. However,

"You can't plead insanity."

people who declare bankruptcy cannot simply walk away from their debts. They may have to sell off assets — cars, houses, furniture, and other possessions — to pay what they can.

Creditors can legally seize, or **garnishee**, a percentage of a borrower's salary or wages until a debt is paid, leaving the borrower with less money overall. Failure to pay the rent can result in the **eviction**, or legal expulsion, of the tenants, who may then find it quite difficult to find other rental accommodations.

Finally, creditors can sue debtors in small claims court for what is legally called **action on a debt**. This action could result in wages being garnisheed or in the forced sale of assets. Clearly, the best way to avoid this or any other consequence of non-payment of debt is to take on only the amount of debt you can pay back, and to always be conscientious about keeping up payments.

FOCUSING ON BUSINESS

1. With a partner, discuss the advantages and disadvantages of credit.
2. Describe briefly these forms of consumer credit: credit cards, charge accounts, conditional sales contracts, instalment contracts, demand loans, mortgages on real estate, and chattel mortgages.
3. For each situation given below, identify the source of consumer credit:
   a. Sharma negotiates a new car loan at the bank. The loan is secured by the car.
   b. The local hardware store has always given Peck Painters in-store credit because of the great amount of business they do there.
   c. Friendly Finance is the company that Fine's Furniture deals with when it provides credit for its customers.
   d. Borrowers' Haven Finance Company informs John that if he misses a payment, the loan is immediately due and payable.
   e. Bill and Sally have their home financed through Canada Trust.
4. Explain why it is important to establish a good credit rating early in life and then maintain it.
5. Describe four items on a credit application and how they are used to evaluate the application.
6. What are the three Cs of credit and how do they help lenders make their decisions?

7. How does a credit bureau operate? What can you do if you are concerned about your credit bureau file?

8. List four consequences of non-payment of a debt. Describe a situation in which each might occur.

EXPLORING BUSINESS

9. Examine the following credit card statement:

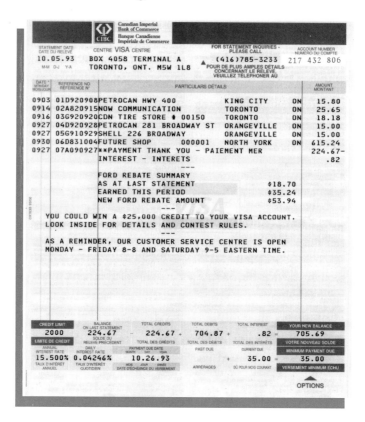

a. How much is the total for the new purchases?

b. How much has been received in payments?

c. What is the statement date?

d. What is the payment date?

e. How much interest has been charged?

f. What is the rate of interest charged?

10. Laurent and Charles are shopping. Laurent has chosen the items he wants and is at the cashier. When the total is rung up, he hands over his Visa card. The clerk calls in the request and informs Laurent that his Visa card is at the limit. Laurent then hands the clerk his MasterCard, and the same thing happens. Finally, Laurent asks if he can write a cheque. The clerk calls the manager, who refuses to take Laurent's cheque. Laurent is furious. As he stomps out, he tells Charles that he will never shop there again; he has lots of money in his chequing account and the manager has embarrassed him.

   a. Why does the manager refuse to take Laurent's cheque?

   b. Do you agree with the manager? What would you tell Laurent?

   c. Is the manager responsible for Laurent's embarrassment? Explain.

11. Promila is furnishing her first apartment. She picks out some furniture she likes and the total comes to $2400. The salesperson asks if she would like to finance her purchase over 24 months. Promila agrees, thinking that she can afford $100 a month. She is astonished to learn that she will actually be paying $128 a month. "There must be some mistake," she says. "I can't afford that!"

   a. Explain to Promila why the monthly payments are not just the sale price divided by the number of months.

   b. What other options does Promila have?

12. In small groups, role-play a situation about buying an expensive item (furniture, stereo, vacation) and having to finance it. Discuss the various sources of credit and their advantages and disadvantages. Present your performance to the class.

13. Arrange to have the manager of the local credit bureau visit your classroom. As a class, interview the manager. Be sure to include the following questions:

   • What is the role of the credit bureau?

   • What types of businesses are members?

   • Can private individuals pay the fee and become members? Why or why not?

   • What records are kept? How are they kept? How has computerization made the credit bureau's job easier?

   • How does the credit bureau get its information?

   • How do the members get the information they need?

   • How is the credit bureau financed?

14. Desmond has seen several of his friends get into financial trouble. One had his car repossessed, while others spend much of their income paying off loans and other debts. Desmond makes up his mind that this will not happen to him. His solution is to pay cash for everything. He says, "If I do not have any credit cards or loans, when I am ready it will be easy to apply for a loan."

   a. What is right about Desmond's evaluation?

   b. What is wrong about Desmond's evaluation?

   c. Suggest a course of action for Desmond regarding credit.

15. Rivka is applying for a loan. In addition to the personal information consisting of name and address, the application asks that any other debts and expenses she might have be declared. Rivka lists two of her five credit cards and the bank loan for her car. She omits the instalment loan for her furniture. She reasons that all these debts might hurt her chances of getting another loan. The other three credit cards are for smaller stores, and the instalment loan was negotiated in another city before she moved here.

   a. Is Rivka correct in assuming that her other debts will hurt her chances of getting this latest loan?

   b. What do you think of her reasoning about the items she chose to omit?

   c. Is her credit history available? How?

   d. Which will hurt her chances of obtaining a loan more: admitting to all her debts, or trying to hide some of them? Explain your answer.

16. In small groups, role-play a situation about a couple or an individual applying for credit. Include the application, the evaluation, and the interview with the credit manager. Review the information contained in this chapter.

CAREERS

FOLLOWING UP THE INTERVIEW

After a job interview, the next step is the follow-up. Immediately after the interview, it is important to write a **follow-up letter** (thank-you letter) and send it by the next day. Take this opportunity to thank the interviewer for the time taken to consider you for the position. Then highlight your skills and abilities that relate to the job. As you did when composing a résumé and covering letter, it is easy to edit and revise your follow-up letter if you are using a computer. Remember, your letter should be free of grammar and spelling errors. (Refer to the sample below for proper formatting of a follow-up letter.)

1. Using the newspaper, select a job that interests you. Assume that you have just come from the job interview. Write a follow-up letter.

2. Working in pairs, edit your partner's letter. Revise your letter.

Dear Ms. Warrick:

I would like to thank you for the time you spent with me during my visit to MultiMedia Inc. yesterday. I enjoyed learning about your organization and the exciting opportunities available.

As I expressed during the interview, my past sales experience has taught me how to work independently and effectively organize a work schedule. I hope I will have the opportunity to use these skills to fulfil the needs of MultiMedia Inc.

Thank you again for your time and attention. I look forward to hearing from you soon.

Sincerely,

CONSUMER PROTECTION

Caveat emptor, which means *let the buyer beware* in Latin, is a basic idea in consumerism. There is no substitute for consumers realistically evaluating their needs, wants, and resources and then actively searching for the best ways to satisfy them. However, no matter how careful an individual is, things sometimes go wrong. It is not always possible to research every aspect of every purchase, and consumers do not always know their rights. When unscrupulous business practices and outright fraud are added to this situation, the need for consumer protection is obvious. Instead of *caveat emptor*, it is possible to protect your rights. The situation then becomes *caveat venditor*, meaning *let the seller beware* in Latin. Making sure that the buying and selling of goods and services is fair and that consumers are protected is a responsibility and concern of both federal and provincial governments and private agencies.

Federal Legislation

At the federal level, the agency that primarily oversees consumer protection is **Consumer and Corporate Affairs Canada**. It was established in 1967 to represent consumer interests and to regulate business. Regional offices across Canada handle consumer complaints and help consumers in the marketplace.

Consumer and Corporate Affairs Canada also tests products used by young children, such as car seats, toys, and cribs, and establishes safety standards. Baby toys, for example, cannot have small parts that a baby could remove and swallow. A product that does not meet the agency's standards is removed from retail stores.

Competition Act

The **Competition Act** is a federal law governing advertising and business practices. Anyone who violates this law will be prosecuted in criminal court. A conviction will result in a fine or imprisonment. The Act allows the government to investigate and prosecute companies that lessen competition by restraining trade. A large part of the Competition Act is concerned with mergers and acquisitions, but it is also devoted to controlling unfair business practices that eventually hurt consumers. The Act also makes a number of pricing practices illegal.

False and Misleading Advertising

Advertising is legal, but advertisements have to be truthful. Consumers can have difficulty detecting advertising that is deceitful. A good rule to remember is that, if something sounds too good to be true, it probably is. It is **false advertising** to say a product will do something when it will not. Unfortunately, false advertising is not usually clear-cut. A store that advertises that its purses are all leather might be selling purses made of a synthetic which looks so much like leather that the ordinary observer cannot tell the difference and would be unlikely to complain.

Misleading advertising is even trickier than false advertising. Misleading advertising distorts the truth about the goods being offered so that consumers are led to believe one thing through wording or promises, but something else turns out to be true. For example, a sale is advertised in which an item is being sold at 70 percent off the regular price, but when you get to the store, the item is sold out. In fact, only a few of these items were available and were quickly sold. It is also misleading advertising to announce a 20-percent-off sale when all the prices in the store had been raised by 20 percent earlier. Obviously, there is no sale — the goods are being offered at their regular price.

Bait-and-Switch Selling

Bait-and-switch selling is an illegal sales technique. A store will advertise a special — for example, a certain model of stereo at a bargain price — but does not have a reasonable quantity available for sale. When you get to the store, you discover that the model is sold out, but other, more expensive models are available. You were lured into the store under false pretences. The retailer hopes that once you are there, you will buy one of the more expensive stereos.

Pyramid Selling

Pyramid selling is an illegal distribution and sales scheme. One person enlists another person to sell something, usually directly to consumers. The first person then receives a commission from the second person's sale. Although this sounds straightforward, imagine this scheme with 20 or 30 levels. Each level is entitled to a commission from each sale made by each person lower down on the ladder. At the top, a few people earn money doing nothing, while at the bottom, the sales representatives who are actually doing the selling must give the majority of their income away in commissions. To pay all the commissions, the price charged to consumers is inflated. In theory, anyone can enlist others to sell the product and thus earn commissions, but in practice only a few people at the top make money.

Illegal Pricing Practices

Price fixing is an agreement between or among businesses to charge the same price for similar products rather than competing on price. The result is that consumers do not have alternatives based on price.

Price discrimination is the practice of selling goods more cheaply to one person or company than to another. This manipulates the marketplace and forces some businesses out, while others become more powerful, thus lessening competition and consumer choice.

Using **predatory pricing**, a business charges very low prices in order to reduce competition. Although consumers may initially benefit from such a price war, eventually, with competition reduced, the prices go back up and the natural checks and balances of competition are gone.

Under **price misrepresentation**, a business is not truthful about its selling prices; for instance, it may raise prices and then have a sale. Consumers should be able to clearly identify the best prices in the marketplace.

The last unfair pricing practice is **resale price maintenance**, a practice by which a manufacturer sets the price at which wholesalers and retailers must sell the product, and threatens to cut off the supply of goods if they do not comply.

All these practices limit competition and prevent consumers from being able to buy the best quality of goods at the lowest price.

Hazardous Products Act

The **Hazardous Products Act** was passed in 1969 to ensure consumer safety after numerous incidents of injuries to children occurred from dangerous products and toys. The Act is concerned with the labelling, advertising, and sale of hazardous products. It prohibits the manufacture and sale of very dangerous products and regulates the sale of products that can harm us. Products such as cleansers, bleaches, and polishes may be hazardous to both children and adults and must be labelled with warnings, depending on the type of product and its danger. A set of universal warning symbols has been created and the appropriate symbol must appear with the written warning to inform consumers of the danger. The product label must also contain first aid information. The labels are intended as a warning only. It is the user's responsibility to use the product as directed and keep it out of the reach of children.

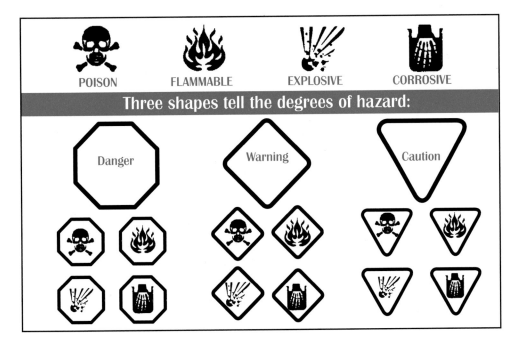

Textile Labelling Act

With the development of synthetic fibres came the need for more information. Natural fibres — cotton, silk, wool, and linen — require certain types of care. Synthetics such as nylon, acrylic, polyester, and rayon need different care. The **Textile Labelling Act** requires that the following information be put on labels of all clothing, household textiles, and fabric sold by the piece:

• the types of fibres contained in the fabric by generic name, such as cotton, nylon, and rayon

• the amount of each fibre present in a quantity of 5 percent or more. For example, if a fabric consists of 50 percent cotton and 50 percent linen, the label must say so

• the identity of the dealer by name and address or identification number

	Stop	Be careful	Go ahead
Washing	Do not wash	Hand wash in lukewarm water. Machine wash in lukewarm water at a gentle setting – reduced agitation. Machine wash in warm water at a gentle setting – reduced agitation	Machine wash in warm water at a normal setting 50°C. Machine wash in hot water at a normal setting 70°C
Chlorine Bleaching	Do not use chlorine bleach	Use chlorine bleach as directed	
Drying		Dry flat. Tumble dry at low temperature	Tumble dry at medium to high temperature. Hang to dry. Drip dry
Ironing	Do not iron	Iron at low setting 110°. Iron at medium setting 150°	Iron at high setting 200°
Dry Cleaning	Do not dry clean	Dry clean – tumble dry at low temperature	Dry clean

Consumer Packaging and Labelling Act

The **Consumer Packaging and Labelling Act** establishes guidelines for the packaging and labelling of all consumer products sold in Canada. Labels must contain the following information:

- all ingredients listed in descending order by proportion or as a percentage on food products

- information in both French and English
- net amount in metric units
- the name and address of the company responsible for the product in case consumers have any questions, complaints, or comments about the product
- a *best before* date on most perishable foods, except fresh fruit and vegetables

Packaging can be misleading. The Packaging and Labelling Act prohibits the packaging of a small article in a large box in order to make the consumer believe that the package contains a greater amount than it does. Some package sizes have been standardized to avoid confusion.

Food and Drugs Act

The **Food and Drugs Act** regulates harmful products that could cause injury or illness if not used properly or if swallowed. The Act also regulates matters such as packaging and advertising of food and drug products.

Products such as children's toys decorated with lead paint, which are considered to pose an unacceptable hazard to consumers, are banned.

Provincial Legislation

Every province has passed a **Consumer Protection Act**. Consumers who sign a contract to make a purchase on credit must be told the total credit charges in dollars and cents, as well as the true rate of interest, so that they can compare these charges when shopping for credit or loans.

Door-to-door sellers must be licensed. This protects buyers from fraudulent selling and misleading sales. Of course, it is up to the consumer to ask to see the licence. The Acts provide for a **cooling-off period** in door-to-door sales; during this time, consumers may cancel the contract in writing. The law does not apply to sales made in the seller's place of business, because the buyer always has the option of leaving. The length of the cooling-off period ranges from two days in Ontario to ten days in Newfoundland. In other provinces, the periods are four, five, or seven days.

All provinces have a **Trade Practices** or **Business Practices Act**, which outlines unfair or misleading business practices, such as saying that service or repairs are needed when they are not, saying that a product has a specific use when it does not, using a celebrity to endorse a product if he or she does not, in fact, use it, and misrepresenting the price at which a product is sold. If a consumer can prove that a contract involves an unfair practice, he or she has the right to cancel the contract. These Acts also set a method for consumers to claim compensation if they have been subjected to an unfair business practice.

Better Business Bureau

Consumer laws protect not only consumers, but also reputable businesspeople, from those who deal dishonestly. The **Better Business Bureau** is a non-profit agency of member companies that have paid membership fees. Its goals are to inform consumers, to protect purchasing power, and to encourage honest business dealings. Consumers have some assurance that a member of the Better Business Bureau is likely to be a safe company with which to do business.

Complaint Procedures

Even though you are trying as hard as possible to be an informed consumer, you sometimes buy something that needs to be returned. Customer complaints, as identified by the Ministry of Consumer and Commercial Relations, most often involve:

- wrong information about a product or service
- poor or incorrect advice from advertising, the salesperson, or both
- faulty goods
- inability to get spare parts, fix product faults, or get after-sales service
- the salesperson not listening politely or not giving clear details about a situation
- prices that differ from those advertised, quoted, or agreed upon
- failure on the part of the seller to contact the customer if there is a change in a situation; for example, if repairs cost more than estimated or delivery of needed parts is delayed
- products that do not meet customer's expectations

Remember always to keep bills and receipts as evidence of your purchase. Sellers are not required by law to take purchases back, although it is generally in their best interest to have a returns policy. You do have to be able to prove you bought it from the company you are returning it to. Sometimes sale merchandise cannot be returned, and you are informed of this at the time of the sale. The receipt will be stamped "Final sale," and you know that you are buying at your own risk.

Some complaint procedures are listed below.

- Take the item back to the seller.
- Telephone the seller to explain the problem.
- Write a letter of complaint to the seller.
- If the complaint is about an unfair business practice, contact the agency of the provincial or federal government in your area.

Reputable businesses value their customers and are happy to correct mistakes that have occurred. Return the goods to the store. The salesperson who sold them to you may remember the sale, but may not have the authority to refund your money. You might have your purchase replaced or get a cash refund, credit toward another purchase, or credit to your account.

If a verbal complaint is unsuccessful, consider a written complaint. A written complaint should include your name, address, and telephone number. Provide details of the sale, name of the product, date of sale, and price. Describe the problem and explain what you have done so far to solve it. Keep your tone polite. Rudeness or insults will not help you get satisfaction. Be sure to attach copies of receipts or other supporting documents. Keep the originals for your own records. Finally, suggest what you would like to see happen to satisfy you. Keep a copy of the letter and send the original by courier or registered mail, so that there is a record of it having been sent and received. If you do not receive a reply, contact one of the consumer protection agencies. Small claims court is another course of action, although it is generally a last resort.

POINTS TO REMEMBER

- Consumer credit is short-term borrowing that allows people to extend their financial resources, but credit costs money through interest payments and must be carefully managed.
- It is important to establish and keep a good credit rating.
- Credit applications require information relevant in evaluating your character, capacity to repay, and capital available.
- Individuals have the right to view and amend credit bureau information.
- Results of non-payment of debts might be difficulty in getting credit, bankruptcy, wages being garnisheed, repossession of goods, eviction, and legal action.
- Federal and provincial legislation protects consumers from unfair and misleading business practices, including false and misleading advertising, bait-and-switch techniques, and pyramid selling.
- Consumer complaints can be made in person, by phone, or by mail.

FOCUSING ON BUSINESS

17. Explain the terms *caveat emptor* and *caveat venditor*. Why does consumer-protection legislation not replace wise consumer practices?

18. Identify the unfair business practice in each of the following situations:

    a. Alain receives an advertising flyer that offers leather boots at 70 percent off the regular price. When he gets to the store, there is only one pair, in a small size.

    b. Gina reads an advertisement for a ten-carat gold chain. The price is only $10, so she sends away for it. When she later receives the chain, she realizes it is definitely not gold.

   c. Paul travels across town to a sale featuring 30- to 50- percent price reductions on stereo equipment. When he gets to the store, he is told that there was only one model on sale and that was sold a day ago.

   d. Marie is invited to a house party where she is told about a line of products that she can sell from her home. All she has to do to become a distributor is to convince others to sell for her, and she can collect commissions from their sales.

19. Name the federal government agency that regulates consumer protection, and describe its function.

20. Explain five unfair business practices that are controlled by the Competition Act.

21. Describe how a reduction in competition hurts consumers.

22. How does the Hazardous Products Act protect consumers?

23. How does the Textile and Labelling Act protect consumers?

24. Why is there a need for packaging and labelling regulations for food?

25. Outline the steps in making a consumer complaint.

EXPLORING BUSINESS

26. Obtain and read a copy of Canadian Consumer or Consumer Reports. Both are consumer-oriented magazines that rate products and services by testing them. Choose a product of interest to you and summarize the product testing that was conducted. Include information about:

   a. the types of product and brand names tested

   b. what kind of testing was done

   c. the results by brand names, listing in order the best and worst buys

   d. the relationship, if any, between price and quality

   e. the relationship, if any, between the most popular brand and testing results

   f. whether your perception of this product has changed as a result of the tests

   What conclusions can you draw about the relationship between price and quality?

27. Dana returns to the store where she purchased an article a week ago. She does not have her bill any more, but she has managed to find a bag from that store to return it in. She finds the clerk who made the sale and angrily tells her that the item is no good and that she demands a

cash refund. The clerk replies that it looks like sale merchandise and that there is a policy of no cash refunds. By the time Dana speaks to the manager, she is very angry.

a. Evaluate Dana's actions in this case.

b. Is Dana justified in yelling at the sales clerk? Why or why not?

c. How would you handle this situation if you were the store manager?

28. Frank is using a chemical to remove paint from a piece of furniture. He reads the directions on the can and learns that the product is both corrosive and flammable. Further instructions say to use the product only in a well-ventilated area and wear gloves. Frank is anxious to get on with the job and ignores these instructions. "They are just for people who don't know what they're doing," he reasons. "Besides, I don't have time for all that stuff."

a. Do you agree with Frank's analysis? Why?

b. What can happen if Frank uses this product in an unventilated room?

c. What can happen if he uses it without gloves?

d. If Frank is injured because he used the product incorrectly, will he be successful if he sues the store where he bought it?

29. Form small groups, and choose one of the following situations:

• a door-to-door seller pressuring a homeowner to sign a contract for expensive home improvements

• a consumer returning merchandise to a store

• a consumer who is a victim of misleading advertising

Prepare and present a small play depicting the situation you chose.

30. In groups of two or three, prepare a collage or bulletin board display on the theme of consumer protection. Collect materials from magazines, newspapers, and Consumer and Corporate Affairs Canada. Present your collage to the class, explaining why you chose the items you did.

WORKING WITH MATH

31. At a car dealership you see the following chart of terms posted:

DRIVE AWAY THE CAR OF YOUR CHOICE
EASY PAYMENT TERMS

Price of Car	MONTHLY PAYMENT 12 months	MONTHLY PAYMENT 24 months	MONTHLY PAYMENT 36 months
$ 9 200	$ 828	$ 445	$ 317
12 000	1 080	580	425
17 000	1 535	830	600
18 500	1 680	910	653

a. What are the total payments on each of the cars for 12, 24, and 36 months?

b. How much interest is paid on the cars for 12, 24, and 36 months?

c. What general statement can you make about the term or length of a loan and the amount of interest you pay?

32. Using the information in the previous question, prepare a bar graph showing the four cars and the monthly payments for 12, 24, and 36 months.

KEY TERMS

credit

credit card

charge account

conditional sales contract

instalment contract

demand loan

chattel mortgage

credit rating

character

capacity

capital

credit bureau

repossession

bankruptcy

garnishee

eviction

action on a debt

caveat emptor

caveat venditor

Consumer and Corporate
   Affairs Canada

Competition Act

false advertising

misleading advertising

bait-and-switch selling

pyramid selling

price fixing

price discrimination

predatory pricing

price misrepresentation

resale price maintenance

Hazardous Products Act

Textile Labelling Act

Consumer Packaging and
   Labelling Act

Food and Drugs Act

Consumer Protection Act

cooling-off period

Trade Practices/Business
   Practices Act

Better Business Bureau

ACKNOWLEDGEMENTS

Text Credits

Pages 10 and 11 "Breakfast for hungry students" by Stephen Kimber. From *Chatelaine*, December 1992; *page 20* "What things do I do well?" from *Do you know what I've always wanted to be? Your Future is Your Call*, Government of Canada, Minister of State for Youth. Reproduced with the permission of Employment and Immigration Canada and Supply and Services Canada, 1993; *page 23* "The daughter of invention" by Adam Dooley. Dooley is a freelance writer in London, Ont.; *page 25* "Bowling for dollars" by Richard Spence. Reprinted courtesy of *Profit*, the Magazine for Canadian Entrepreneurs; *page 27* "Question 25." by Adam Mayers. Reprinted with permission - The Toronto Star Syndicate; *pages 34 and 35* "Preserve our trees, no flyers please" by Jake MacDonald. From *enRoute* magazine, September, 1992; *pages 39 and 40* "What do I like to do?" from *Do you know what I've always wanted to be? Your Future is Your Call*, Government of Canada, Minister of State for Youth. Reproduced with the permission of Employment and Immigration Canada and Supply and Services Canada, 1993; *page 41* Adapted from "Climbing the walls" by Debra Black. From *enRoute* magazine, December 1992; *pages 42 and 43* "Can't you hear the whistle blowing?" by Cathy Hilborn, *Profit*, September 1992; *page 57* "Very special effects" by Daniel Kucharsky, *Profit*, March 1992; *pages 58 and 59* "Smart Card Shuffle" by Daniel Stoffman, *Report on Business Magazine*, March 1993; *pages 62 and 63* "Bridgehead gifts a way of giving twice" by Daniel Girard. Reprinted with permission - The Toronto Star Syndicate; *page 79* "No blues in berries," *page 90* "Chocolate stars" and "Bullish on beef" copyright 1993 Jared Mitchell. Originally published in Report on Business Magazine, April 1993; *pages 80 and 81* "Hamburger Diplomacy" reprinted courtesy of McDonald's; *page 84* "Quote from Anthony Eames" from *The Globe and Mail*, January 24, 1992; *page 92* "Quote from David Dennis" from *The Globe and Mail*, April 6, 1992; *pages 102 and 103* "There's no place like home" by Cathy Hilborn, *Profit*, December 1992; *page 107* "Riding the waves" from an article in *Profit* by freelance writer Diane Luckow; *pages 112 and 113* "Kellogg and Coke move fast on final out for series payoff" by Bob Papoe. Reprinted with permission - The Toronto Star Syndicate; *page 127* "Filling a vacuum" by Cathy Hilborn, *Profit*, September 1992; *page 132* "The changing cost of living" from *Canada Year Book 1992,* p. 476. Reproduced by authority of the Minister responsible for Statistics Canada 1993; *pages 134 and 135* "Testing-time" from *Next Year Country* by Barry Broadfoot. Used by permission of the Canadian Publishers, McClelland & Stewart, Toronto; *page 148* "The root to success" by Jennifer Myers. Reprinted with permission from *Profit*, the Magazine for Canadian Entrepreneurs; *pages 150 and 151* "Vaulting Ambition" by Gordon Donaldson, *Canadian Business*, January 1989; *pages 158 and 159* "The business of baseball" reprinted with the permission of CBC International Sales, Educational Sales Division; *page 175* "Neighbourhood food co-op" by Martha Tancock, *Chatelaine*, March 1992; *page 182* "Unemployment insurance" from *Canada Year Book 1992*, p. 152. Reproduced by authority of the Minister responsible for Statistics Canada 1993; *page 183* Adaptation of "Winning government money" by Johanna Powell. Article appeared in *Profit*, December 1992; *page 193* "Right to strike" from *Canada Year Book 1992*, p. 151. Reproduced by authority of the Minister responsible for

Statistics Canada 1993; *pages 202 and 203* "Ice cream plant scoops free trade" reproduced with permission of *The London Free Press* from an article by Hank Daniszewski; *page 210* "The recession's top jobmakers." Appeared in *The Globe and Mail*, July 21, 1992; *page 217* "Barter helps pay the bills in recession-battered '90s" by Barbara Aarsteinsen. Reprinted with permission - The Toronto Star Syndicate; *page 228* "Home banking by phone" reprinted courtesy of Credit Union Way. Adapted from an article originally in *The Globe and Mail*; page 239 "Steps in Business Expansion" adapted from "You can participate in business expansion". Courtesy of The Toronto Stock Exchange; *page 246* "Canada's riskiest stocks" from *Profit,* June 1993; *pages 248, 249* Courtesy of The Toronto Stock Exchange; *pages 266 and 274* Reprinted with permission of the Public Legal Education Society of Nova Scotia; *pages 267 and 268* "Spy-tech" by Gerald Levitch. Appeared in *The Globe and Mail*, March 20, 1993; *pages 272 and 273* "Burglary of home launched housesitters firm" by John Picton. Reprinted with permission - The Toronto Star Syndicate; *page 278* "Publicize high-risk parolees, 69% say" by Stephen Bindman, Southam News; *page 286* "Verbatim reporting services" reprinted from *30 Under 30: Building Ontario Businesses with Youth Venture Loans*, published by the Ministry of Economic Development and Trade. For more information call (416) 326-5820; *page 293* "Ontario human rights code" excerpted from *Human Rights in Ontario* (ISBN 0-7729-7633-3). Reproduced with permission from the Queen's Printer for Ontario; *pages 306 and 307* "Horton loses fight for doughnut chain" by John Picton. Reprinted with permission - The Toronto Star Syndicate; *pages 323 and 324* "Shoestring marketing" by Jennifer Myers. Reprinted with permission from *Profit*, the Magazine for Canadian Entrepreneurs, June 1992; *page 328* "Cashing in on social change" by Marlene Cartash. Reprinted from *Profit*, September 1992; *pages 332 and 333* "Body Shop: the store as package" reprinted by permission of Brunico Publishing Inc © 1992; *pages 346 and 347* "Mining for marketing gold" by Ken Riddell. Reprinted courtesy of *Marketing Magazine*; *pages 348 - 351* "Résumés that get results" from *New Brunswick Prospects: A Guide to Education, Training and Employment*, produced by the New Brunswick Career Information Partnership in cooperation with the Canadian Career Information Partnership; *pages 352 and 353* "Clear products send a message" by Maureen Murray. Reprinted with permission - The Toronto Star Syndicate; *page 357* "Hi-tech and sports find one another on CD-Rom" by Ken Riddell. Reprinted by permission of *Marketing Magazine*; *pages 372 and 391* "On a roll from rock photos" and "The summer job leads to a year-round business" reprinted from *30 Under 30: Building Ontario Businesses with Youth Venture Loans*, published by the Ministry of Economic Development and Trade. For more information call (416) 326-5820; *page 397* "Berry farmers" reprinted from *Maclean's Magazine*, Maclean Hunter Ltd., July 5, 1993, page 50; *pages 410 and 411* "Preface to *The Canadian Green Consumer Guide*" by Margaret Atwood. From *The Canadian Green Consumer Guide* by Pollution Probe. Used by permission of the Canadian Publishers, McClelland & Stewart, Toronto; *pages 412 and 413* "Entrepreneurs - Harden and Huyse chocolates" by Kenneth Kidd. *Report on Business Magazine*, June 12-19, 1993; *page 430* "Credit card costs" from *The 1993 Canadian Global Almanac: A book of facts*. Source: Consumer and Corporate Affairs Canada; *pages 432 and 433* "A hit show for teens on managing money" by Marion Gill. *Broadcast Week*, June 12-19, 1993; *page 435* "Tips for keeping a good credit rating" from *The facts about credit and you* (REV 02/92-25M, ISBN 0-7729-8748-3). Reproduced with permission from the Queen's Printer for Ontario.

Readers wishing further information on data provided through the cooperation of Statistics Canada may obtain copies of related publications by mail from:
Publication Sales, Statistics Canada, Ottawa, Ontario, Canada K1A 0T6, by calling 1-613-951-7277 or toll-free 1-800-267-6677. Readers may also facsimile their order by dialing 1-613-951-1584.

Photo and Illustration Credits

Page 7 Vancouver Sun Photo/ Mark Van Manen Photographer; *page 10* Blaine Fisher; *page 23* Doug Forster Photography; *page 25* Lorella Zanetti; *page 34 and 35* Courtesy of Desert Rose Productions; *page 37* Alex Meyboom; *page 41* Vivian Gast Photographer; *page 42* The Globe and Mail/ Fred Lum; *page 52* Susie King; *page 58* Tony Foushe; *page 62* Courtesy of Bridgehead, Inc.; *page 66* Courtesy of the Canadian Franchise Association; *page 74 The Globe and Mail/* Bryce Duffy; *page 78* Canapress Photo Service/ Fred Chartrand; *page 80* Canapress Photo Service; *page 82* R. Ian Lloyd/ First Light; *page 90* (*top*) Chocolate bars by B. Klassen, (*bottom*) Drawing of cow by Anne Matthews; *page 100* (*top*) Courtesy of Fishery Products International, (*bottom*) Courtesy of TransCanada Pipelines Ltd.; *page 101* Courtesy of Dynacare Health Group Inc.; *page 102 Vancouver Sun* Photo/ Peter Battistoni Photographer; *page 108* Jan Becker; *page 109* Courtesy of BC Tel. Photo: R. Gordon Garrison/ McKim Baker Lovick/ BBDO; *page 112 The Toronto Star/* Mike Slaughter; *page 126* Dan Paul; *page 127* Eden Robbins; *page 135* Glenbow Archives, Calgary (ND-3-6742); *pages 143, 144, 152* Jan Becker; *pages 146 and 147* Randy Rozema; *page 148* Reprinted with permission of Chai-Na-Ta Ginseng Products Ltd.; *page 150* Courtesy of The Ceiling Doctor; *page 157 The Globe and Mail/* Bryce Duffy; *page 158* Courtesy of Opeechee Co; *pages 170, 172, 174* Jan Becker; *page 175* Alex Meyboom; *page 176* Canapress Photo Service/ Anand Maharaj; *page 192* National Archives of Canada/ PA-115431; *page 193* National Archives of Canada/ C-037329; *page 194* Canapress Photo Service/ W. Leidenfrost; *page 195* Courtesy of Canadian Auto Workers Union; *page 201 Kitchener-Waterloo Record*; *page 202* Courtesy of Ault Foods; *page 217 The Toronto Star/* A. Dunlop; *pages 218 and 219* National Currency Collection, Bank of Canada. Photography: James Zagon, Ottawa; *page 222 The Globe and Mail/* Roger Hallett; *page 226* (*top*) Reprinted courtesy of Canadian Imperial Bank of Commerce, (*bottom*) Reprinted courtesy of Royal Bank of Canada; *page 229* Courtesy of Toronto Dominion Bank; *page 238* Nicholas Vitacco; *page 243* Canapress Photo Service/ Blaise Edwards; *page 258* Courtesy of the Royal Ontario Museum, Toronto, Canada; *page 264* Courtesy of Saskatoon Police Service Identification Section; *page 267 The Globe and Mail/* Stephen Quinlan; *page 272 The Toronto Star/* Dick Loek; *page 284* Courtesy of Ministry of Environment and Energy; *page 290* Metropolitan Toronto Police; *page 322* Courtesy of Cundari Group Ltd. Design, Michael Lang. Copy, Rob Worling. Photography, Detlef Schnepel; *page 323* Mark Mainguy; *page 328* Courtesy of Traditions; *page 332* Courtesy of The Body Shop; *page 335* Second Cup Coffee Co's Coffee Packaging; *page 343* Courtesy of COWS Ltd; *page 345* Courtesy of Nestlé Canada Inc.; *pages 346 and 347* Courtesy of the Beef Information Centre; *page 352 The Toronto Star/* Keith Beatty; *page 354* Courtesy of Levi Strauss & Co Canada Inc. Photographer: George Simhoni; *page 356* Reprinted from *Canadian Rodeo News*; *page 357* Courtesy of Swimming/Natation Canada. Photographer: Marco Chiesa. Swimmer: Michelle Pilling, Canada; *page 372* Courtesy of Raj Rama; *page 397* Courtesy of Riverbend Plantation/Saskatoon Berry Farms Ltd., Saskatoon, Sask.; *page 413* Courtesy of Harden and Huyse Ltd.; *page 430* Reprinted courtesy of Royal Bank of Canada; *page 432* Courtesy of CBC Television. Photo: John Sherlock; *pages 445, 446 and 447* Consumer and Corporate Affairs Canada. All other illustrations by Sharon Matthews, Matthews Communications Design.

Colour Photo Credits

Saskatoon Star-Phoenix 'TAGAlong', Supplied by *The Star Phoenix*; Canadian Airlines advertisement, Courtesy of Canadian Airlines International and Chiat/Day Inc. Advertising; Nadbank advertisement, Courtesy: *The Vancouver Sun*, Creative: Timm Williams Design, Verkvil Communications; Shell advertisement, Courtesy: Shell Canada Limited; Canadian Tire advertisement, We would like to thank Canadian Tire for the use of this image; CIBC Aerogold Visa Aeroplan advertisement, This reproduction is authorized by Air Canada and the Canadian Imperial Bank of Commerce. Aeroplan is a registered trademark of Air Canada. Aerogold is a trademark of Air Canada. CIBC is an authorized licensee of the Marks. CIBC, Air Canada, Licensees of the VISA Mark; Phantom of the Opera advertisement, Appears courtesy of Live Entertainment of Canada Inc. Concept/Art Direction: Echo Advertising, Toronto. The Mask design and Mask and Rose design are trademarks of The Really Useful Group PLC © 1986; ROM billboard, Courtesy of the Royal Ontario Museum. Advertising Agency: Geoffrey B. Roche and Partners; Trident transit ad, Courtesy of Warner-Lambert Co. and Backer Spielvogel Bates Advertising; Purolator transit ad, Courtesy of Purolator Courier. Advertising Agency: Scali, McCabe, Sloves (Canada) Ltd. Photographer: Kimberly Guy Fairbank; New Brunswick Grown shopping cart ad, Reprinted courtesy of the New Brunswick Department of Agriculture (N.B. Grown Program) and the Saint John office of Corporate Communications Limited; Metro Toronto Zoo trans ad, Courtesy of Metro Toronto Zoo and Chiat/Day Inc.; Pollution Probe poster, Reprinted with permission from Pollution Probe, Toronto, 1993; Milk Marketing billboard, Courtesy of Milk Marketing Board. Advertising Agency: McKim Baker Lovick BBDO; Sprite television commercial, Reprinted courtesy of Coca-Cola Ltd. Advertising Agency: McCann-Erickson Advertising; Leon's television commercial, Reprinted courtesy Leon's Furniture Advertising agency: Doner Schur Peppler Advertising; Clearly Canadian advertisement, Courtesy of Clearly Canadian Beverage Corporation; MuchMusic graphic opener, Courtesy of MuchMusic, Harden & Huyse packaging, Courtesy of Harden & Huyse Ltd., Intel packaging, Courtesy of Intel Corporation; *Solomon Gursky Was Here* book jacket, Produced for Penguin Books Canada Ltd., Design by David Wyman, Illustration by Gerard Gauci; Kellogg's Corn Flakes box, Reprinted with permission of/Registered Trademark of Kellogg Canada Inc.; Celebrate wordmark, Courtesy of Paul Sych; Tourism B.C. brochure, Courtesy of the Province of British Columbia, Advertising Agency: McKim Advertising.

GLOSSARY

absolute discharge The release of an offender without conviction or conditions.

acceptance Approval.

accounting equation The relation between assets, liabilities, and owner's equity whereby if you know the value of two, you can figure out the value of the third.

accounting The procedure of recording, sorting, and analyzing, and preparing records of economic data related to business transactions.

accounts payable The money a business owes to creditors other than banks.

accounts receivable The money owed to a business by customers that have bought on credit.

action on a debt The legal term for a suit filed in a small claims court by a creditor against a debtor.

advertising Any paid public notice about a product, idea, or organization presented visually or orally.

AIDA The initials of the four steps of the basic selling approach: attract *attention*, hold *interest*, arouse *desire*, and take *action* to close the sale.

appeal A request to have a case heard again by a higher court or judge.

aptitude A natural talent.

arbitration A method of settling disputes by the decision of a third party.

articles of incorporation A document that brings a corporation into existence, which contains the names of the corporation and incorporators, and any restrictions on the allowed business activity that the corporation may conduct.

articles of partnership Also called *partnership agreement.* A written contract, signed by business partners, stipulating the terms of the partnership, to be upheld in court in the event of any future disputes.

assault The act of striking a person, or threatening by act or gesture.

assets The valuables that a person or a company owns.

automated transaction machine Computerized machines that provide banking services 24 hours a day.

bail hearing Also known as *interim release.* A hearing held to determine if a person arrested should be released on bail or held in custody.

bail The sum of money necessary to set a person free from arrest until he or she is due to appear in court for trial.

bait-and-switch selling An illegal sales practice that consists in advertising a product that is not available and offering the consumer a more expensive alternative.

balance sheet   A report on the assets, liabilities, equity, and accumulated profits and losses of a business on a specific date.

Bank Act   A document giving the federal government the responsibility for regulating banks to protect the money of depositors.

Bank of Canada   A national bank established in 1935 to issue currency and manage Canada's monetary policy.

bank loan payable   A loan from a bank.

bankruptcy   The state of a person or business declared by a law court to be unable to pay his, her, or its debts and whose property is distributed among his, her, or its creditors.

bargaining unit   The smaller branch of a union, which addresses issues in individual factories or regional areas.

barter   A type of trade that consists of exchanging one type of goods or services for another without using money.

battery   An assault causing bodily harm.

Better Business Bureau   A non-profit organization of member companies that provides information to consumers on buying wisely from, and avoiding cheating by, businesses.

blue-chip stocks   The common stocks of well-established companies.

bond   A certificate of debt issued by a company promising to pay it back by a certain date.

brainstorming   The discussion of sudden ideas to solve a problem.

brand name   The name that identifies the goods or services of a business.

breach of contract   A violation of the terms or conditions of a contract.

budget   An estimate of money available and money to be spent.

business   The production and sale of goods or services.

business cycle   The fluctuations in the economy, from prosperity to inflation through recession or depression, to recovery.

by-law   Also called *ordinance*. A local law made by a city for the control of its own affairs.

caisse populaire   A credit union in Quebec or other francophone areas of Canada.

Canada Pension Plan   A pension plan available to all Canadians over the age of 65, based on the amount contributed when the person worked.

Canada Savings Bond   A bond issued by the Canadian federal government at a guaranteed rate of return in order to raise money for its endeavours.

Canada–United States Free Trade Agreement (FTA)   Commercial agreement under whose terms all tariffs on the sale of goods between Canada and the United States will be removed gradually by 1999.

Canadian Charter of Rights and Freedoms   The part of the Canadian constitution that limits the power of the government by protecting the individual.

cancelled cheque   A cheque that has been cashed.

capacity   The ability of a credit applicant to repay a loan.

capital   Also called *investment*. (1) Money that is put into a business venture in order to make a profit. (2) The machinery and equipment needed to produce goods and services. Example: a typewriter. (3) A credit applicant's financial worth.

caveat emptor   Latin expression meaning literally *let the buyer beware*, or you buy at your own risk.

caveat venditor   Latin expression meaning literally *let the seller beware,* or you sell at your own risk.

certified   (1) Guaranteed, as with a cheque for which sufficient funds have been set aside by the drawee from the drawer's account. (2) Accredited (as by the government).

channel of distribution   The path that a product takes from the manufacturer to the consumer.

character   The qualities of stability and morality that indicate a person's reliability to pay back a loan.

charge account   An arrangement between a business and a customer to purchase goods or services on credit at that business.

chartered bank   Also called *Schedule I bank.* Any of the seven privately owned banks chartered by Parliament and working under the provisions of the Bank Act with an extensive network of branches.

chattel mortgage   A type of loan in which personal goods are pledged as security for the payment of a debt.

chequing/savings account   An account for people who want to write a few cheques and receive interest on their savings without having a separate chequing account.

civil law   Also called *private law.* The body of law that regulates and protects non-criminal private rights and is controlled by civil courts.

civil service   A government service provided by full-time employees.

co-operative   A form of corporation in which the members of the co-operative own and control the business, and make all the decisions. Example: a farmer's co-operative.

collateral   The security offered by the borrower against a loan, such as property pledged as guarantee for repayment.

collective agreement   An employment contract drawn up by a bargaining committee and authorized by a labour union to act for its members.

collective bargaining   The act of negotiating by the members of a local bargaining unit, as a group, with the employer to determine conditions of employment, such as wages, hours, etc.

commitment   A pledge or promise.

common law   The body of law based on custom dating from the ancient unwritten laws of England, and recognized by the courts.

common shares   A type of stock which carries voting privileges, without any priority in the payment of dividends.

communism   An economic system in which the government owns or controls all the factors of production.

community service order   A command to perform a specified number of hours of work for the community or a charity.

comparison shopping   A comparison of the price and quality of a product in different businesses before purchasing it in order to obtain the lowest price for the highest quality.

compensation   Something given to a victim as a satisfactory return for a loss or injury.

competent   The state of being capable of good judgment when entering into a contract.

competition   The result of two or more companies trying to sell the same goods or services.

Competition Act   A federal law that governs advertisement and business practices.

complementary goods   Two goods that are typically used with one another. Example: car and fuel.

compound daily interest   The interest calculated on the principal plus the unpaid interest accumulated.

conciliation   An effort made by a government official (the *conciliator*) to resolve the differences between a union and its management before a legal strike can occur.

conditional discharge   The release of an offender with no conviction, but with one or more conditions, e.g. a curfew, set by the judge.

conditional sales contract   A legal, binding, written sales agreement between a buyer and a seller, which sets out the conditions for payment on credit.

consent   Acceptance or agreement.

consideration   Valuables exchanged by the parties entering into a contract, which induce them to be bound.

conspicuous consumption   The purchase of goods or services for the purpose of showing off.

constitution   The set of principles and rules according to which a nation is governed.

Constitution Act, 1867   The document which outlines the responsibilities of each level of the Canadian government.

Constitution Act, 1982   The constitution of Canada since 1982.

consumer   A person or business that consumes goods or uses services.

Consumer and Corporate Affairs Canada   The federal agency that oversees the protection of the consumer.

Consumer Packaging and Labelling Act   A law that sets guidelines for the packaging and labelling of all consumer products sold in Canada.

Consumer Price Index (CPI)   A measure of the changes in the purchasing power of the dollar over a period of time, usually one month.

Consumer Protection Act   A law that ensures that a consumer is informed of the total credit charges and the rate of interest when making a purchase.

consumer co-operative   A co-operative owned and operated by the consumers, which provides them with goods or services.

consumer goods   Products that individual people buy from the producer.

contract   An agreement that is enforceable by law.

cooling-off period   A time (ranging from two to ten days) during which a consumer may cancel in writing a contract made on a door-to-door sale.

corporate income tax   The flat-rate income tax paid by corporations.

corporation   A business owned by its owners, the shareholders, and legally existing independently of them.

cost of goods sold   The total cost of a product or service to a business before it is sold, and necessary to calculate the profit.

counter offer   An offer made after an initial offer has been turned down.

credit agreement   A contract specifying the terms of payment after the merchandise or service is received.

credit bureau   Also called *credit reporting agency.* A business that collects information on the credit ratings of individuals or companies and offers this information as a service to subscribers.

credit card   An identification card that entitles its holder to charge the cost of goods or services.

credit   The trust in a person's ability and intention to pay later for goods or services purchased now.

credit rating   The financial standing or reputation of a person or company.

credit union   A co-operative non-profit association similar to a bank, which makes loans to its members at a low rate of interest.

Criminal Code   The collection of laws and rules dealing with crime.

criminal law   The part of public law that deals with wrongful acts against an individual or against society.

Crown corporation   A public corporation owned by federal, provincial, or municipal governments and whose function is to provide a special service to the public.

current account   A chequing account for businesses and other organizations.

daily interest savings account   A savings account on which the interest is calculated every 24 hours.

damages   A sum of money awarded by the courts to a victim as compensation.

debt financing   A method of obtaining capital to invest in a company through borrowing from a bank or financial institution.

decision matrix   A plan to organize information prior to comparison shopping, comprising a list of criteria and products in the form of a table that makes comparison easy to visualize.

defamation of character   A tort in which a statement harms a person's reputation or esteem.

defendant   The person who is being sued in civil proceedings.

demand loan   A loan, negotiated with a financial institution, in which the lender can demand full payment at any time if the borrower misses a partial payment.

demand   The relationship between the price of a product and the amount that the buyer is willing to pay.

Democratic Rights   The part of the Canadian Charter of Rights and Freedoms that deals with a citizen's right to vote and to run for public office.

demography   The study of human population (births, deaths, age, density, etc.) and its distribution using statistical methods.

deposit slip   The slip that is filled out when depositing money into an account.

depression   An extended period during which economic activity is extremely low and unemployment is extremely high.

determination   The firmness of mind with which a commitment is carried out.

direct competition   The rivalry that exists between businesses that are trying to sell similar goods or services.

direct mail   Advertising delivered directly to the consumer by mail.

discrimination   The act or practice of making or showing a difference based on prejudice. Example: not giving a woman a job for which she is qualified because she might become pregnant.

disposition   A Youth Court sentence.

dividend   A share in the profit of a company, payable to the owners of the company (the shareholders).

drawee   The bank or institution where the drawer's account is held.

drawer   The person or organization from whose account the amount of the cheque is withdrawn.

economic system   The combined work of businesses and government.

economics   The study of resources and how they are managed.

economy   A system of managing the production, distribution, and consumption of goods.

effectiveness   A measure of the success of a business.

efficiency   A measure of the capacity to manage and control expenses in a business.

elastic demand   A demand for a good or service that varies greatly when the price changes.

elastic supply   The supply of a good or service that can be increased or decreased quickly when the price changes.

elasticity   The varying effect of price changes of goods or services on consumer behaviour when purchasing them.

endorsed   Signed on the back, as with a cheque before it can be cashed by the payee.

entrepreneur   A person who recognizes an opportunity and assumes risk to undertake a business venture.

Equality Rights   The part of the Canadian Charter of Rights and Freedoms that deals with a citizen's right to be protected from discrimination based upon race, religion, skin colour, sex, age, or disability.

equilibrium   The balance reached between the willingness of a consumer to pay a given price and the willingness of a business to supply at that price.

equity financing A method of obtaining capital to invest in a company through selling shares to investors.

ethics The standards of conduct in a given society.

eviction The legal expulsion from rented premises due to failure to pay the rent.

expenditure See *expense.*

expense Also called *expenditure.* The money a business spends on goods and services.

exports Goods and services sold to foreign countries.

face value The value stated on (the face of) a bond, cheque, coin, or bill.

factors of production The elements that make production possible: land, capital, labour, technology, and entrepreneurship.

false advertisement Advertising claiming that a product or service has or does something that it does not.

false imprisonment The act of limiting or taking away a person's freedom unnecessarily and against his or her will.

Federal Sales Tax (FST) A tax formerly charged by the federal government on goods as they were manufactured (as opposed to when they were sold).

finance The management of money.

financial statement A periodic record of business transactions.

flat-rate tax A fixed-rate tax (as opposed to a progressive tax), for example, 10 percent of the income.

Food and Drugs Act A law regulating products that can be harmful if not used according to directions or if swallowed.

franchise A licence to manufacture or sell a product or service.

franchisee The person who purchases a franchise.

franchisor The person who sells a franchise.

free enterprise A system under which all the factors of production are owned and managed by private businesses, which own their own land and capital, and manage their employees with little or no government interference. Example: the system in the United States.

French Civil Code The French body of law, based largely on a set of written laws.

Fundamental Freedoms The part of the Canadian Charter of Rights and Freedoms that deals with the individual's freedom of speech, religion, expression, and association.

garnishee To withhold, as with the wages of a debtor in order to pay a creditor.

globalization The operation of foreign businesses in a country.

good An item that can be possessed and used. Example: a loaf of bread.

goods and services tax (GST) A federal tax added to the value of goods and services at the moment of purchase.

grievance A complaint.

grievance procedures An outline of the steps that both management and union will follow when a worker has a complaint against the management.

gross domestic product (GDP)   The total value of all goods and services produced in a country over a given period of time, usually one year.

gross profit   The money made on the sale of a product, after subtracting the cost.

Guaranteed Income Supplement

Hazardous Products Act   A law ensuring consumer safety from dangerous products by forcing the manufacturers to label and use other forms of information to warn the consumer of any products that may be hazardous.

human resources   The people in a business: employees, managers, and owners.

implied contract   A contract that begins with an action. Example: signalling to a waiter to order food in a restaurant.

imports   Goods and services bought from foreign countries.

impulse buying   The purchase of goods or services without thinking about it beforehand.

incarceration   Imprisonment.

incentive   A motivating potential for profit.

income protection   An increase in wages to match the raise in the cost of living.

income statement   A report showing the net income or net loss of a business for a specific period of time.

income tax   The tax paid on money that is earned.

industrial consumer   The consumer of industrial goods: a business.

industrial goods   Products that businesses purchase from producers.

inelastic demand   A demand for a good or service that does not vary greatly when the price changes.

inelastic supply   The supply of a good or service that cannot be increased or decreased quickly when the price changes.

inferior goods   Goods of lesser quality, which consumers with low income can afford.

inflation   An economic situation in which prices increase faster than income.

initiative   The ability to take action without being prompted by others.

innovator   A person who creates a new or improved way of doing something.

instalment contract   A written agreement stating that the interest will be paid in equal payments throughout a set period of time.

intentional tort   A tort committed by intention rather than through carelessness.

interdependence   The reliance and need of each other (mutual dependence).

interest   The money paid for the use of money borrowed, loaned, or invested; usually in the form of a percentage.

interim release   See *bail hearing*.

inventor   A person who discovers a new product or service.

inventory   A detailed list of articles with their estimated value, which the retailer has for sale.

investment   See *capital*.

labelling The part of the packaging that provides the consumer with information about the product. Examples: brand name, list of ingredients.

labour Also called *work.* The human element of production — whether mental or physical.

labour union Also called *trade union.* An association of workers for the purpose of dealing collectively with their employers.

land The natural resources used to produce goods and services. Example: a mine.

language rights The two parts of the Canadian Charter of Rights and Freedoms that deal with the individual's right to receive service from the federal government in either official language, English or French, and a citizen's right to have his or her children receive instruction in their first language, English or French.

law A set of rules recognized by a community as binding on its members.

law of demand The rule whereby consumers are able or willing to buy more of a good or service when the price is low, thereby driving prices down (or to buy less of a good or service when the price is high, thereby driving prices up).

law of supply The relationship between the price of a good or service and its quantity offered for sale.

lease A contract that establishes the legal relationship between a landlord and tenant.

legal aid A form of support given by the government to individuals who cannot afford to pay for a lawyer's services.

Legal Rights The part of the Canadian Charter of Rights and Freedoms that deals with the individual's right to consult a lawyer when arrested and to be informed of that right, to stand trial within a reasonable period of time, to be presumed innocent until proven guilty, and to be protected against unreasonable searches, arbitrary imprisonment, or cruel and unusual punishment.

legislature The location where representatives of the people make laws for a country or province. Also, the body of representatives who make these laws.

liabilities The money a business owes to suppliers or lenders.

liability What is owed to creditors.

libel A written or otherwise permanent form of defamatory statement.

limited liability The liability limited to business assets — as opposed to personal assets — in case of bankruptcy.

liquidity A measure of the capacity of an asset to be converted into cash.

lockout The closure of a workplace by the management to force the employees to agree to terms.

luxury items Goods that are costly and not indispensable for life.

malpractice suit A lawsuit in which a doctor is accused of negligent or unprofessional treatment of a patient.

management The organization and planning of business activities.

manufacturer A business that produces goods.

market (1) A consumer or consumers willing to pay for a good or service. (2) A place where a buyer and a seller come together to exchange goods or services for pay. Example: a flea market. The act of a buyer and seller coming together for the purpose of buying and selling goods or services.

marketing The process of planning and implementing a strategy for the promotion, sale, and distribution of goods or services.

marketing mix The four components of marketing: product, price, place, and promotion.

marketing research The gathering and analyzing of data to provide a business with information on consumer needs and wants.

master-servant relationship The common-law term for the employer-employee relationship.

maturity date The date on which a bond plus interest is paid to the investor.

mediation A friendly intervention by an appointed person to bring about a agreement between management and a union.

medium of exchange A third item through which two other items can be exchanged. Examples: money, food, metal.

misleading advertising Deceptive advertising that does not make false claims outright.

Mobility Rights The part of the Canadian Charter of Rights and Freedoms that deals with a citizen's or a permanent resident's right to travel, set-

tle, or work anywhere in Canada.

modified free enterprise A system that is largely free enterprise, but where the government is involved to ensure the economic welfare of the people. Example: the system of Canada.

monetary policy The policy of increasing or decreasing the supply of money to influence the economy of the country.

monopoly The complete control of a commodity or service, with little or no competition.

mortgage A loan of money to buy property, in which the property, usually land, guarantees the payment of the debt.

mortgage loan company A bank or a trust company that takes money in deposit and makes loans based on real-estate investments.

municipality A local political area no larger than a city: district, county, township, town, city.

necessaries Goods and services that are suitable to a person's circumstances and necessary at the time of purchase (as opposed to luxuries).

needs The lack of useful or desired essential goods or services.

negligence Careless behaviour that results in damage or injury.

net income Profit.

next friend A person who can initiate a lawsuit in behalf of a child.

non-profit corporation A corporation whose main purpose is not profit-making but, for example, fundraising or conducting research.

North American Free Trade Agreement (NAFTA) Commercial agreement similar to the Canada–United States Free Trade Agreement that includes the third country in North America: Mexico.

offer An expression of willingness to pay.

Old Age Security (OAS) A pension plan available to Canadians over the age of 65, based on the length of residency in Canada.

oral contract An unwritten contract (as opposed to a written contract).

ordinance See *by-law.*

owner's equity The difference between total assets and total liabilities, a company's net worth.

packaging The container or wrapper of a product.

partnership A form of business organization in which two or more people jointly share the ownership and operation of the business.

passbook A bankbook in which a record of the account holder's transactions is kept, usually issued for savings accounts.

payee The person or organization to whom a cheque is written.

peer pressure The pressure put upon an individual to do certain things that will make the individual behave like others in a group.

persistence Perseverance: refusal to be discouraged even in the face of difficulty or obstacles.

personal chequing account An account for the sole purpose of writing cheques, on which no interest is paid.

personal selling The one-to-one communication between individuals for the purpose of selling a good or service.

picket To be stationed beside or near a place of work where there is a strike.

plaintiff The person who is suing in civil proceedings.

postdated Not yet valid, as with a cheque dated anytime after the present date.

precedent A case or judicial decision that serves as a guide for future similar situations.

predatory pricing Extremely low pricing to reduce or eliminate competition.

preference The act of favouring one good or service over another.

preferred shares A type of stock that gives the investor guaranteed priority over common stock in the rate and payment of dividends.

price discrimination The practice of selling goods or services more cheaply to one person or company than to another.

price fixing An agreement between or among businesses to charge the same price for similar products rather than competing on price.

price The cost of a good or service expressed in money.

price misrepresentation The practice of giving the wrong idea of price in order to deceive.

primary industries The industries involved in the extraction and processing of basic raw materials.

principal The sum of money that has been borrowed (as opposed to the interest on it).

private corporation A corporation with a maximum of 50 shareholders and whose shares are not offered to the general public.

private law See *civil law.*

private nuisance A civil wrong caused by interfering with an owner's use and enjoyment of his/her property. Example: letting a tree overhang a neighbour's property.

probation The practice of letting a convicted offender, especially a first-time or a young offender, go free under the supervision of an officer.

problem The difference between the present situation and the desired one.

problem solving Finding the answer to a problem.

producer A business that makes goods or provides services.

producer co-operative A co-operative in which the members monitor the supply of the product, its sale and price.

product A good or service that is sold.

production The process of converting the resources of a business into goods and services.

profit The amount of capital by which the revenue of a business exceeds its expenses.

progressive tax The income tax whose rate increases gradually as the amount of earned income increases (as opposed to *flat-rate tax*).

promotion The part of marketing that advertises a product to enhance its sale.

property tax A tax paid on property. Example: tax paid on rented apartment.

prospectus A legal document describing and advertising the business.

prosperity Also called *boom.* A period during which the economy does well, with low levels of unemployment and good pay for workers.

public corporation A corporation with an unlimited number of shareholders and whose shares are offered to the general public.

public law The body of law that regulates and protects a society's interests such as crime.

public nuisance An act or omission which interferes with the public interest. Example: pollution.

public relations The activities that promote a company's reputation and good will among consumers.

publicity The action of bringing something to the attention of the consumer.

purchasing power The amount of goods or services that a given amount of money can buy.

pyramid selling The illegal practice of enlisting successive levels of people to receive a commission from the same sale.

ratification The formal approval of an agreement.

reasonable person   A person who is fair and moderate by using reason.

recession   A period during which economic activity is slow and unemployment is high.

recovery   A period during which economic activity increases after a recession or depression.

Registered Retirement Savings Plan (RRSP)   A private pension plan in which the individual can deduct contributions from his or her income taxes.

repossession   The act of seizing an asset offered as collateral when the borrower fails to pay a debt.

resale price maintenance   A practice by which a manufacturer sets the price at which wholesalers and retailers must sell a product with the purpose of reducing competition.

resources   Raw materials.

retailer   A person or business that sells goods or services in small amounts directly to the consumer.

return on investment   The profit made on an investment.

revenue   The money received from the sale of goods or services.

risk   The chance of loss or bad consequences.

risk of investment   The chance of loss or bad consequences when making an investment.

safety deposit box   A box in the vault of a bank, for the storage of valuables such as original documents, bonds, jewellery, etc.

sales promotion   An activity or activities designed to stimulate consumers to buy goods and services.

sales tax   A tax paid on retail sales.

savings account   An account in a bank, trust company, or credit union on which interest is paid.

Schedule I bank   See *chartered bank.*

secondary industries   The industries that produce finished goods from processed raw materials. Examples: bakeries, clothing industry.

self-confidence   The belief and trust in oneself.

service   A helpful act (work) in exchange for pay. Example: hairdressing.

share   A unit of ownership in a company.

signature card   A card that is signed when opening up a bank account, to identify the signature of the account holder when making withdrawals.

slander   A spoken defamatory statement.

social assistance   A form of basic help to citizens, which covers the cost of essentials such as food, shelter, and clothing.

sole proprietorship   A business that is owned and operated by one person.

stale-dated   No longer valid, as with a cheque dated six months or longer before the present date.

standard of living   The number of goods and services enjoyed by the members of a society as a whole.

statute   A law enacted by a legislative body.

stock exchange   The place where stocks and bonds are bought and sold.

stock   The total amount of shares offered for sale by a company. This term is also used to describe part ownership in a company.

strike   The general quitting of work in order to force an employer to agree to the employees' demands for higher wages, improved benefits, and the like.

substitute good   A good that can easily be replaced by another, especially when the price goes up. Example: margarine.

substitute/indirect competition   The rivalry that exists between businesses that offer alternative products or services.

supplier   A business that supplies the consumer with goods or services.

supply   The quantity of goods and services that sellers are willing or able to offer consumers.

suspended sentence   A court's decision to postpone sentencing for a certain period of time, during which the offender is put on probation.

target market   A group of consumers toward which a business aims its marketing efforts.

tariff   A tax placed on imported goods.

taste   The sense of perceiving a good or service as desirable.

technology   The application of scientific research and knowledge to the production and distribution of goods and services. Example: fax machine.

telemarketing   Marketing that uses telephone technology to contact customers or potential customers.

tertiary industries   Also called *service industries*. Industries that provide services. Examples: banking, mass transit.

Textile Labelling Act   A law requiring information on the type and amount of fibre present and the identity of the dealer to be printed on the labels of all clothing and textiles.

tort   A civil wrong (as opposed to a criminal wrong) for which the courts will award the victim compensation for loss or damage.

Trade Practices/Business Practices Act   A law that outlines unfair or misleading business practices such as lying or misrepresenting a product.

trade union   See *labour union*.

trademark   A mark, symbol, or picture that identifies a product as being produced by a particular company, and that is protected by law. Abbreviated: TM.

transaction   A financial event in which money changes hands. Example: buying, selling, borrowing, transferring.

traveller's cheque   A cheque that can be used as cash and easily replaced if lost or stolen.

trespasser   A person who enters another person's property without permission.

true savings account   A savings account that does not provide cheque-writing privileges.

trust company   A company formed by a group of individuals or companies controlling stock of the constituent companies in order to simplify management and defeat competition.

ultimate consumer   The consumer who purchases a good directly for personal use.

unemployment insurance (UI)   The benefits paid by the government to people who have lost their jobs.

unintentional tort   A tort caused by careless conduct or negligence.

union   See *trade union*.

union dues   The membership dues paid by union members to favour their cause.

union shop   A company, plant, or industry that is unionized.

unlimited liability   The responsibility of a sole proprietor to pay all the debts of a business from his or her personal assets if necessary.

venture capital stocks   Formerly called *penny stocks*. The high-risk stocks of fairly new small to medium-sized companies.

wampum   The seashell beads strung in belts and sashes, formerly used by aboriginal peoples as money.

wants   Goods or services that people enjoy having but are not indispensable.

welfare   A benefit to someone who is unable to work.

wholesaler   A person or business that buys goods or services in large amounts and resells them to other persons or businesses in smaller quantities; these buyers resell to the consumer.

worker's compensation   Money paid to workers who have suffered an accident at the workplace.

written contract   A contract that is put on paper and signed (as opposed to an oral contract).

wrongful dismissal   The dismissal of an employee for reasons other than those recognized by the law.

yield   The potential profit or capital gain that an investor can be expected to receive from a particular stock.

young offender   An offender aged 12 to 18.

Young Offenders Act   A law, passed in 1984, that gives young offenders more responsibility than they previously had, without treating them like adults.

Youth Court   A court where young offenders are tried (as opposed to an adult court).

INDEX